THE AMERICAN EXPERIMENT

THE AMERICAN EXPERIMENT

DIALOGUES ON A DREAM

DAVID M. RUBENSTEIN

THORNDIKE PRESS
A part of Gale, a Cengage Company

**LIBRARY OF CONGRESS CIP DATA ON FILE.
CATALOGUING IN PUBLICATION FOR THIS BOOK
IS AVAILABLE FROM THE LIBRARY OF CONGRESS.**

ISBN-13: 978-1-4328-9352-1 (hardcover alk. paper)

Published in 2021 by arrangement with Simon & Schuster, Inc.

Printed in Mexico
Print Number: 01   Print Year: 2022

*To the public servants who
protect our democracy*

"We the People of the United States, in Order to form a more perfect Union, establish Justice, insure domestic Tranquility, provide for the common defence, promote the general Welfare, and secure the Blessings of Liberty to ourselves and our Posterity, do ordain and establish this Constitution for the United States of America."

— Preamble to the
United States Constitution,
1787

CONTENTS

INTRODUCTION

The story is too wonderful not to be apocryphal: as Benjamin Franklin is leaving Independence Hall in Philadelphia at the conclusion of the Constitutional Convention, he is supposedly met by a woman — reputed to be Elizabeth Willing Powel, a prominent Philadelphia socialite — who asks him what type of government the delegates have given the country, a republic or a monarchy. Franklin's simple response: "A republic, if you can keep it."

For the ensuing 230-plus years, the American people, through extraordinary and at times existential challenges, have kept the republic. Creating such a form of government from scratch was an unprecedented, bold experiment in self-government — the American Experiment.

Without doubt, all fifty-five delegates to the Constitutional Convention would be shocked that the compromises they cobbled together from May to September of 1787 (even with some subsequent twenty-seven constitutional amendments) have survived this long.

How did this experiment endure over centuries against all odds? Beyond the constitutional amendments, what legal, social, economic, political, and religious factors came together to ensure the republic's survival? In my view, the republic persisted and grew into the most powerful nation on earth as a result of a unique combination of factors that came together in a serendipitous way.

I analogize this to our planet: had the mass that became Earth been much closer to or farther away from the sun, life as we know it almost certainly would not have evolved. That advanced forms of life occurred here required an unbelievable set of factors to coalesce in a unique way.

Similarly, had some of the factors that combined to create the United States not been present to the right degree at the right time, the country as we know it would not have been formed, survived, or evolved to its current state.

These factors — our genes — created a country unlike any other. There are many who believe that this unique set of genes has created the world's best country, and that there is therefore a corresponding obligation to spread those genes around the world. Whether or not one holds that view, there is no doubt that America's genes, as they developed, matured, interacted, and co-alesced, sustained the experiment that the Constitution's framers created.

But that experiment was not and is not without its challenges. The Civil War was the most existential challenge to the republic's future. Because of their commitment to slavery, the Confederate states seceded from the United States, precipitating a four-year war in which about 2.5 percent of the American population died in combat or from its aftereffects. And even after the Union won and slavery was ended, life for freed slaves and their descendants produced at least another century of second-if not third-class citizenship.

Though perhaps less existential, other significant challenges have shaped the country's forward path: Reconstruction and its Jim Crow aftermath, women's suffrage, the Great Depression, World War II, the civil rights movement, the Vietnam War, Watergate, the 9/11 attacks, the Iraq war, the fight for women's equality beyond the vote, the struggle for gay rights, and the Black Lives Matter movement, among other major social, political, and economic challenges.

The American Experiment is clearly still ongoing. That was evident from two new challenges to this experiment in 2020 — challenges that could not have been anticipated even a year earlier. The first was the COVID-19 pandemic, which had killed more than 600,000 Americans as of June 2021. The pandemic changed the way the country lived, worked, learned, and survived to a greater extent than any other single occurrence in American history since World War II.

COVID forced Americans to adapt to a remote work life, to worry constantly about their health and mortality, to develop a vaccine in record time, and to vaccinate a record number of Americans — all while dealing with the effects of a recession and enormous loss of jobs, productivity, and, of course, human lives.

All of those COVID consequences tested the country's resolve and resilience. Of course, COVID-19 was not a uniquely American phenomenon. But it affected the United States in a unique way. The U.S. president, Donald J. Trump, openly defied the scientific and health-care communities, and both minimized and politicized COVID's impact. And, perhaps as a consequence, the country suffered disproportionately — with 4 percent of the world's population, the U.S. had incurred 16 percent of the world's COVID deaths as of June 2021.

The second major challenge the U.S. faced in 2020–21 was the reaction by President Trump to his election loss to former vice president Joseph R. Biden Jr. The result was a two-and-a-half-month stress test of democracy — really unlike anything the country had experienced since the outbreak of the Civil War.

From the day after the election until the day(s) — January 6–7, 2021 — that Congress finally certified the Electoral College victory of Joe Biden and Kamala Harris, President Trump and a large number of his allies worked hard to convince his supporters that the election was fraudulently stolen from him. Whether President Trump really believed the election was "stolen" (there being no real documented evidence of systemic election fraud), it is clear that a great many of his supporters did hold that belief — perhaps fueled by the president's daily statements to this effect. A May 2021 poll showed that more than 60 percent of Republican voters believed the election was "stolen" from President Trump.

After the election, President Trump and his supporters filed sixty-five lawsuits to overturn part or all of the election process. But essentially all of these suits were dismissed for lack of proof or standing.

The courts' consistent refusal to accept the meritless election fraud claims from President Trump and his advocates demonstrated the strength and independence of the judiciary — at all levels. (The Supreme Court rejected the claims that reached it, without any comment on the merits.)

The election administrators responsible for counting the votes in each state also demonstrated a commitment to a nonpartisan, democratic-values-must-prevail approach. Even the Republican administrators, often at great personal and political risk, consistently refused to succumb to entreaties from President Trump to overturn their states' results.

The country's political leaders were more of a mixed bag. It is not surprising that Democrats refused to accept the claim of election fraud. What is surprising is that so many Republican officials were willing to accept the fraud charges when there was no visible evidence at all for such claims. (None who supported those claims apparently felt that their own elections, held at the same time, were invalidated by any fraud.)

In the House of Representatives, 139 Republicans were willing to lend their support to an effort to overturn the Electoral College vote; and there were eight senators who supported that effort (led initially by Senator Josh Hawley, who was then joined by Senator Ted Cruz, both highly educated and trained lawyers). But before the vote could occur in either house, hundreds of protesters — "insurrectionists" who were Donald Trump supporters — overcame the small Capitol Police contingent and invaded the Capitol — the first such unfriendly invasion since the British burned it in 1814. Five individuals died as a result of the invasion, and many more were injured. Subsequently, hundreds of these insurrectionists were charged with various crimes.

The invasion shocked the members of Congress, who could have been injured, if not killed — but they were able to escape (in many cases just barely) to secure locations. The invasion also shocked the whole country, and indeed the rest of the world, a global television audience watching disbelievingly in real time. This was the kind of invasion one might heretofore expect in a volatile third-world country but not in the mighty United States, the symbol of Western democracy.

But it did occur in the U.S., and no doubt left an unforgettable, jaw-dropping impression on all who saw or heard about it. Just as Americans remember precisely where they were when President Kennedy was assassinated or when the events of 9/11 occurred, they will forever remember where they were on January 6.

Had Congress not been invaded by protesters, the effort to overturn the Electoral College vote would still almost certainly have failed, though the debate would have taken longer. But the incursion made the members rush to vote on the certification that night (and into the early hours of the next morning), and they returned to the House and Senate together to do so. And in doing so, the Congress showed that the democracy and the country's core values — its genes —

prevailed, but with a scar that damaged America's self-image and the image of the country abroad.

But could the result have been different? Suppose Vice President Mike Pence had followed President Trump's strong request that Pence not certify the results. Suppose, as a consequence, the election was determined by a vote by state delegations in the House of Representatives, where the Republicans had a majority of state delegations. Or suppose the military had decided to support President Trump's claims, following a declaration of military law. Fortunately, none of those unprecedented possibilities occurred — this time.

Who deserves the real credit for ensuring that the 2020 presidential election process — and America's genes — worked in the end? Foremost in my view is the judiciary: the federal and state judiciary, which made clear that the election fraud claims were in essence the only fraud involved in those cases. And they did so promptly, clearly, and decisively. Had they acted otherwise, there would no doubt have been more fuel in the arsenal of those seeking to overturn the election's rightful winner. While the legal decisions did not by themselves end the efforts of those seeking to overturn the election, they thwarted the momentum of those efforts, leaving only a limited number of political allies and mob violence to try to destroy the democratic outcome.

In the end, U.S. genes relating to democracy and the rule of law proved too strong to overcome, thankfully. But the country did receive an unwanted wake-up call. A large number of Americans recognized that the country's historic core values are simply not shared by all Americans, or at least not to the extent presupposed. And thus many Americans recognized that more work must be done to heal the divisions in the country, if we are to ensure that our effort to build a "more perfect union" can once again be a beacon for democracies around the world.

Despite the challenges from the pandemic and the contested election, the country survived, though not without real adverse impact on our healthcare, economic, and political-legal systems: more than 600 thousand Americans lost their lives in less than eighteen months, a recession took hold, unemployment increased significantly, the Capitol was invaded, the president was impeached, and America emerged with less confidence in its government.

But in the end, science was heeded, the pandemic receded (due in part to vaccines and the coordinated vaccination program immediately put in place by President Biden), the economy recovered, the rule of law prevailed, and American democracy pro-

21

ceeded, though not without difficulty and angst. That said, while our nation's economy, health-care system, and democracy endured, the impact of these events is likely to be felt for decades, if not longer.

This survival occurred, in my view, because America's genes ultimately came together and enabled the country to overcome these existential challenges.

But what about the next time a similar crisis occurs? Will the experiment in democracy be able to withstand challenges — internal or from abroad?

It is to be hoped that the answer is yes, for America's genes are too strong, too embedded, too resilient. But we cannot relax, or let down our guard. And we cannot allow our genes to wither by a lack of knowledge about them, or a failure to appreciate what they have represented for the country and will likely represent in the future.

What are these genes that I am talking about?

Like the human body, America has an extraordinary number of genes — qualities that bring us together and have made the whole American Experiment work. In this book, though, I want to focus on just those genes I consider the most essential — the ones that truly have been indispensable to our coalescing to produce and sustain America.

22

1. **Democracy.** The Constitution's drafters provided the country with a republic, or a form of representative democracy. The idea that a democratic government is the most desirable form seems ingrained in the American psyche and soul. The Founding Fathers abhorred a dynastic form of government. They wanted no King George or equivalent.

   That said, they lacked complete trust in their fellow citizens, thinking they might not be fully qualified or informed to vote directly for a president (thus they gave us the Electoral College) or for senators (the state legislatures had that power until the Seventeenth Amendment granted it to the citizens). While the key to a representative democracy is majority rule, and that still does not fully exist in this country (consider the Electoral College or the Senate's filibuster rules), the concept is built into America that democracy — the majority rules — is a preferred form of government.

2. **Voting.** Democracy is meaningful only if citizens have the right to vote and if that vote can have an impact.

The United States has clearly struggled with this issue throughout its history — not allowing African Americans to vote (by law before the Fifteenth Amendment and by practice through the ensuing Jim Crow period), nor permitting women to vote (until the Nineteenth Amendment). Even today, efforts are regularly made in some jurisdictions to suppress minority voter turnout, by making voting a complicated, time-consuming, and somewhat arduous and painful process, thereby discouraging some citizens from voting. Those efforts accelerated in many states following the 2020 election, initially most visibly in Georgia and Florida.

The right to vote has been hotly contested over the centuries, and even now, precisely because most Americans believe that voting can change governments (and their lives). A large percentage of Americans regard the right to vote as sacred and will travel long distances and wait for hours to vote, if necessary. That was evident in the 2020 presidential election, some voters in certain states waited a dozen hours or more in line to exercise their right to vote.

To be sure, Americans who are of voting age historically vote in smaller percentages than citizens in other Western democracies. Turnout of voting-age Americans for the 2020 U.S. presidential election did rise to 62 percent; the previous five presidential elections saw only about 55 percent. In other Western democracies, such as Denmark and Sweden, turnout has averaged over 80 percent historically. And, of course, voter turnout in nonpresidential elections in the U.S. is often dramatically lower.

There is no compelling or acceptable explanation for the lower voting patterns in the U.S., other than perhaps an assumption by many nonvoters that their fellow citizens will vote in ways that produce sufficiently acceptable results, obviating the need to vote oneself. Of course, there are always some citizens who feel their vote will not make a difference — i.e., a Democratic voter in a heavily Republican state or a Republican voter in a heavily Democratic state.

But the seemingly low turnout should not be seen as evidence that Americans generally feel voting is an unimportant feature of the country's values.

3. **Equality.** The Founding Fathers certainly recognized the hypocrisy of talking about the virtues of equality when the country had nearly a half million slaves with no prospect of their ever achieving equality. But those at the Constitutional Convention decided that the political exigencies of getting a constitution in place required allowing the southern states, at a minimum, to maintain slavery. And the idea that women should be guaranteed any rights at all was not even discussed. Protections for other disenfranchised groups or minorities were also not on the Founding Fathers' agenda, the soaring language of the Declaration of Independence notwithstanding.

While the U.S. still struggles with the concept of achieving equality for all citizens, and true equality is still not a near-term reality, there is a general view within the country today that equality of opportunity and rights, for all citizens, is an important part of what America is supposed to be all about. There will still be challenges to reaching this goal for all Americans (and I doubt we will really get there in my life-time).

That said, recent decades in the U.S. have seen widespread efforts to facilitate opportunities for those segments of society not truly treated as equal in the past — including gays, individuals with physical and mental disabilities, religious and ethnic minorities, immigrants, and former felony convicts, among other groups. The goal of producing greater equality has not been without controversy, but generally there has been a view recently that the concept of equal rights and opportunities cannot be overlooked in the future if the words of the Declaration of Independence are to have real meaning.

4. **Freedom of Speech.** There are many freedoms that seem essential to Americans, but perhaps none is more fundamental than the freedom of speech. It is not a surprise, therefore, that it is included in the First Amendment to the Constitution.

There have been long and heated struggles about what can in fact be said or published within the Constitution's meaning. But the courts in this country have generally given a wide swath to the First Amendment and have typically prohibited only speech that might clearly endanger the country's security, or the safety of individuals or the public.

It should be noted that an important element of this freedom is the right — if not obligation — of citizens to participate in their governmental process by questioning government and inquiring about its actions.

5. **Freedom of Religion.** Also in the First Amendment is the freedom of religion. Those early settlers who arrived from Europe were often seeking religious freedom, and the concern that a government might restrict or favor a certain type of religion has been a worry of Americans throughout our history.

The country has endured religious discrimination throughout large parts of its history, and those issues still exist in some areas. But there is no doubt that under the laws in this country, and with the overwhelming support of the American people, the free exercise of one's religion (or nonreligion) is an essential American gene, one repeatedly upheld by the courts.

6. **The Rule of Law.** There are few

countries that place such a high value on the rule of law, as opposed to political whim or bias, as does the United States. Where else do federal officeholders swear an allegiance to a 230-year-old Constitution? Where else are the rulings of the highest court in the land widely accepted as the law, even when a decision is five-to-four?

What accounts for this reverence for the law and the general obedience to it? There are no doubt many answers, but my view is that the courts — especially the federal courts — are seen as honest and populated by talented individuals, focused on fairness and obedience to the law.

While legislative leaders, in federal or state governments, are clearly not held in the same high regard, the American system of government places high value on the binding outcome of the legislative process. The absence of the rule of law in many other countries has solidified the view that, while the courts and legislatures in the U.S. are far from perfect in their decision-making, the stability brought about by an adherence to their decisions makes the rule of law an indispensable American gene.

This was evident in the Trump election challenge — the courts invariably held against the Trump advocates' position, and that was almost universally accepted as the law of the land. Similarly, the law was followed in the way the Electoral College votes were counted. Congress's decision in counting the election votes was accepted as the final and binding decision on the election's outcome.

7. **Separation of Powers.** The drafters of the Constitution feared giving too much power to one person or to one part of the government that they were creating. So they developed the concept of separation of powers, or checks and balances. No branch would have too much power, and the power of one part of government could be checked by another part of government. The idea was a bit novel at the time.

The original concept gave the most important powers — the power of the purse and the power to wage war — to the legislative branch. This branch, the Congress, may have been initially viewed as first among equals — it was, after all, described in

Article One of the Constitution.

In time, the executive branch, led by the president, has developed far more power than anyone ever anticipated at the Constitutional Convention. That has been true of the judicial branch as well, with its power, first announced by the Supreme Court in 1803 in *Marbury v. Madison,* to declare laws unconstitutional. While the three branches may operate somewhat differently than initially conceived, the separation of powers concept has certainly taken hold, and the belief in a system where power is divided is clearly an important American gene.

8. **Civilian Control of the Military; Peaceful Transfer of Power.** The Constitution made the president commander in chief, establishing the concept that the military would be subject to civilian control. That choice reflected the concern about a powerful military ultimately controlling the government, as had frequently happened in Europe. With the military subject to civilian control, the prospect of a military coup was greatly diminished. As a result, there was an expectation of a peaceful transfer of power, unlikely to be

31

disrupted by military interference.

This concept has worked well over the centuries. There have been no military coups in the U.S., and power has been transferred peacefully after elections — a gene thought to be indispensable to the country's stability and achievements.

This was quite evident in the aftermath of the 2020 election, when the U.S. military leadership made clear that it had no role to play in the election outcome — no martial law and no politicization of the military.

9. **Capitalism and Entrepreneurship.** The word *capitalism* does not appear in the Declaration of Independence or in the Constitution. But from the early days of the republic, the economic construct of capitalism took hold and became a gene in the growth and strength of the American economy. Socialism and communism never had a serious chance of dislodging capitalism in this country, though obviously that was not true around much of the rest of the world.

There are many variants of capitalism, but in the U.S. there has been a strong reliance on an entrepreneurial-led capitalism. New companies are started by creative and enterprising individuals, grow into large companies fueling economic and employment growth, and are displaced over time by even newer ventures more attuned to changing technologies and needs. And while government regulates these companies in the public interest, it does not own or control them or attempt to do so.

It is evident that the considerable wealth created by these types of free-market capitalist activities may make some individuals very affluent, and at times may also produce undesirable levels of income inequality. But just as clearly, the businesses created by this system create jobs and grow the economy to the country's overall benefit. Of course, other countries have a capitalist tradition, and an entrepreneurial bent. But no other country seems to have a gene favoring entrepreneurial activity — and capitalism — to the same degree as does the United States.

10. **Immigration.** To a greater extent than with any other country, the United States is widely seen as having been built by immigrants. In the nation's early days, everyone and anyone was welcome, though those

who came from abroad were primarily from western Europe. When immigrants began arriving from other parts of the world in the late nineteenth century, concerns arose about the reduced homogeneity of the population, and immigration constraints were imposed after World War I.

That changed in the 1960s, and immigrants from around the world, particularly those with desired skills, were more regularly welcomed, and the country was again seen as one that recognized the value of immigration. While there was an interruption in that perspective from 2016 to 2020, and there remain real concerns about rampant illegal immigration at our southern border, today the country is generally again seen as having an immigration gene, welcoming those who enter legally (i.e., meet our immigration law requirements) and who work to improve the country with their skills, hard work, and knowledge.

11. **Diversity.** At the country's inception, its population was largely western European colonists, Native Americans, and enslaved Africans. Those in control of the country

favored Western Europeans for virtually all of society's benefits, believing that they had the greatest intellectual capabilities and moral strengths.

Over several centuries, though, as the U.S. population dramatically changed in composition — by 2045, the country will no longer be majority non-Hispanic white — diversity has increasingly come to be seen as a strength of the country. There is thus a push in all parts of American society to encourage and take advantage of the country's increasing diversity. Stated differently, there is now a relatively new gene in America — the realization that diversity brings clear strengths that are desirable, and thus is to be encouraged and pursued if America is to remain a vibrant force in the world.

12. **Culture.** Every country has a distinctive culture — a set of beliefs, customs, practices, and aspirations that unite the country's population and tend to provide a common purpose. The U.S. is no different, though American culture has perhaps evolved more over the years than the cultures of much older countries with less diverse population growth.

In the country's early years, its

culture was seen by those in Europe as not being particularly refined, impressive, or attractive. That changed in the late 1800s, as the U.S. put the Civil War behind it, expanded, grew in wealth and population, and managed to create new ways of expressing its values and thoughts in the performing arts, the visual arts, literature, architecture, education, athletics, and philanthropy. What could be more distinctly American than jazz, Hollywood movies, Broadway musicals, abstract art, baseball, Thanksgiving dinners, and Fourth of July celebrations?

In so many cultural areas, the United States has become a global leader over the past hundred years or so, and the result is that its culture is increasingly viewed with envy in many parts of the world.

To be sure, there is not one American culture. America has the highest immigrant population of any country and thus has too diverse a population for there to be a single culture whose parts are shared by everyone. But if there is a shared element to America's culture, it is increasingly the view that the country should allow individuals to pursue their talents and ambitions, largely unfettered by central control or government interference, with merit and skill prevailing to the greatest extent possible. That is America's real culture gene.

13. **The American Dream.** In every country, there are stories of individuals who started life with modest resources or social status but somehow rose to positions of great influence, wealth, social standing, and leadership. In the United States, unlike in some other countries, this upward trajectory seems to be a central tenet of what is most encouraged and admired — using skill, talent, and hard work to rise to the top from the bottom.

This phenomenon has been labeled the American Dream. Earlier it might have been called a Horatio Alger story, after the author who wrote numerous stories of young boys (and one girl) who overcame hardships to rise to the top of their area of activity.

This type of occurrence is still very much admired in the United States, and can well be said to be a key gene within the country. That said, it is increasingly recognized that the

American Dream is not as readily attainable by those who face overwhelming discriminatory barriers (because of race, religion, gender, sexual preference, or ethnicity) or cultural roadblocks (due to language challenges or educational backgrounds). Ironically, this recognition has actually increased the praise for those who are able to succeed despite these odds.

Added together, these thirteen genes have produced a wide range of events in the course of this country's history; they have enabled the American Experiment to blossom, far more than the founders even imagined possible. I recognize, though, that my views on what qualities make America so distinctive may not be held by other observers or other Americans. So I thought that I could perhaps get a better, fuller snapshot of what others think through a public opinion survey.

Toward that end, I asked the Harris Poll organization to do a representative survey of Americans about what they think makes America distinctive. The poll of 2,000 Americans was conducted shortly before the 2020 elections. The full results appear in Appendix II of this book.

Interestingly, the most distinctive quality was viewed as the freedom of speech, with 64 percent of the respondents citing that freedom. Only one other quality polled above 50 percent — the opportunity to vote in free and fair elections, cited by 51 percent. A large percentage of those surveyed cared so much about a number of the freedoms they cherish that they indicated a willingness to risk their lives to protect them, with freedom of speech again polling at the top. Younger Americans tended to value these distinctive qualities to a lesser extent than older Americans. And younger Americans tended to be less concerned that everyone view America as the "best" country.

As to what those surveyed would most like to see America change to improve the country, the support for any given action was not overwhelming — but the two actions most cited were ending systemic racism and providing accessible, affordable health care for everyone.

This concern about racism is also reflected in the survey respondents' view that the country is still significantly affected by its having sanctioned slavery. And, while the Founding Fathers did sanction slavery, there is a widely held view that the founders' ideas (or at least rhetoric) about equality and freedom may not be as valued by today's leaders.

Despite the concerns, Americans greatly value living in the U.S., and by overwhelming numbers do not want to leave for another country. As to the future, despite the stresses of the pandemic, economic decline, and racial confrontations, a majority of Americans still feel the country's best days are ahead of it, and still expect to achieve the American Dream — good signs overall.

In two previous books, *The American Story* and *How to Lead,* I tried to cover subjects relating to American history and leadership by editing and providing my perspective on interviews that I held, respectively, with well-known historians and then with leaders from many walks of life.

So I thought, perhaps tempting fate, that I would use the same approach in *The American Experiment,* a book about how a certain unique combination of qualities produced, over two centuries, a distinctive country — the United States of America. Here I have combined interviews I have conducted in recent years with both well-known historians and well-known leaders, each knowledgeable about, or the embodiment of, some of these singular American traits. As with the previous two books, the conversations have been edited for length and consistency, and updated as needed, in consultation with the interviewees.

I have tried, through these interviews and some of my own perspectives, to show how various qualities possessed by Americans — essentially our genes — have produced a series of events, over the country's history, which enabled the Constitutional Convention's initial experiment in representative democracy to evolve into a country that, in the ensuing two-plus centuries, became — and remains — the world's economic, political, military, scientific/technological, and entrepreneurial leader.

The genes that coalesced into the American Experiment at times worked well together, and at other times produced unfortunate outcomes. In my view, an understanding of America today really requires an understanding of the genes that produced the American Experiment. Such an understanding can better help Americans now and in the future make this experiment work better for all Americans, and thereby produce a country which actually achieves the goals that the Founding Fathers' uplifting language set for the nation.

In short, this American Experiment, while imperfect and evolving, has produced a country generally pleasing to a large part of the American population. But this experiment is not so pleasing as to keep Americans from recognizing that, while this unique country is still the envy of many in the world, the United States has still failed to live up to all of its founding ideals. And the country's

41

shortcomings are increasingly apparent. This experiment is certainly better today than some might have thought would be the case at the country's founding, but with much progress still to be made in many areas. And there is no guarantee, if Americans ignore or minimize the genes that produced the country's strengths over the past two centuries, that continued global leadership of the United States is inevitable.

My hope is that some who read the interviews in this book will be inspired to help lead the way to our continued progress and thereby avoid the historical fate of other countries that also at times were once the envy of the world.

David M. Rubenstein, June 2021

■ ■ ■ ■

1
Promise and Principle

■ ■ ■ ■

"We hold these truths to be self-evident, that all men are created equal, that they are endowed by their Creator with certain unalienable rights, that among these are Life, Liberty, and the Pursuit of Happiness. That to secure these rights, Governments are instituted among Men, deriving their just powers from the consent of the governed."
— Preamble to the Declaration of Independence, July 4, 1776

Jill Lepore
on 400 Years of American History

David Woods Kemper '41 Professor of American History and Affiliate Professor of Law, Harvard University; author of *These Truths: A History of the United States* and 13 other books; Staff Writer for the *New Yorker*

"It is our obligation as historians and as citizens to think about the relationship between the past and the present and to reckon with whether the nation has lived up to the promise of the Declaration of Independence."

From the beginning, America was an ideal — a new land, with fresh opportunities for those adventuresome enough to pursue them, in the belief that in so doing they could create a new, better life for themselves and their families.

As America grew from outposts and thriving colonies into the United States of

47

America, those responsible for creating a new country and government idealized their invention: their government would provide liberties, freedoms, equality with a benevolence that other governments had never explicitly provided.

These would be guaranteed (albeit only for white males) in founding documents that would take on the character of religious icons — i.e., the Constitution was deserving of faith and allegiance, rather than any leader or group of leaders.

Over the centuries, this experiment in democratic self-governance evolved, as social mores, legal principles, economic realities, foreign challenges, and cultural perspectives changed, though not always for the country's betterment.

Capturing in an understandable way how this governing experiment occurred over the centuries has always been a challenge for observers of America. Doing so in a way that really captures the perspectives of those who were not the powerful and traditional leaders of American society has truly eluded a great many historians. But not Jill Lepore.

Her epic history of the United States, *These Truths,* provides a look at the country from the sixteenth to the twenty-first centuries, in a novel-like writing style that focuses on those whose voices have not always been reflected in comprehensive books about the nation.

That should probably not be a surprise, for Jill Lepore is not only an endowed professor of American history at Harvard University but the author of more than a dozen critically acclaimed books and a regular and much-read contributor to the *New Yorker* on the subjects of history, law, and public policy.

With *These Truths,* Jill Lepore also essentially became the first woman to write a comprehensive history of the U.S. — hard to believe, but that is the case. Not surprisingly, she was able to bring a different perspective on some of the most important issues faced by women in our country's history, such as the right to own property, to vote, to hold office, to be paid fairly, to overcome career challenges, to confront sexual harassment and violence, and, in general, to have equal protection and opportunities.

In recounting the entire history of the United States, Jill Lepore has taken the American experiment — with all of its ideals, challenges, successes, and failures — and provided an overview of so many of the American genes that have given us America in 2021.

I interviewed Jill Lepore at the New-York Historical Society on October 7, 2019. On reflection, my only regret about the interview was that Professor Lepore had not written the U.S. history textbooks I read in high school or college. I know that her doing so would have assured I actually wanted to finish the whole book.

DAVID M. RUBENSTEIN (DR): For most people, writing a nine-hundred-page book on American history would take a lifetime. Did you ever regret doing it while you were working through it?

JILL LEPORE (JL): It was really fun to write, actually. That's embarrassing to say. I feel bad when people have writer's block, because I have a problem — I write too much.

I decided to write the book because I've been teaching this material for decades now — for maybe thirty years — and over the years I've been asked, here and there, would I write a single volume on the American Revolution? I've always thought textbook writing would be depressing. It doesn't really come alive on the page.

I was asked, one more time, to write a single-volume, single-narrator history of the United States as a textbook. As an American political historian, I thought, "I should take up this invitation to do this work of public service." I thought the nation needed an accessible, new history that took into account the incredible revolution in scholarship over the last half century.

DR: You begin your book with a discussion

about the "discovery" of this country by early settlers, and you talk about Christopher Columbus. He has been vilified by some people in recent years. Do you think vilifying him was appropriate?

JL: I think we should spend some time collectively rejecting the either/or there. I understand we're inclined to ask, "Is he a villain or is he a hero?"

Teachers and textbook writers understand that the story of the United States begins tens of thousands of years ago, with migrations of people we would now call Indigenous Americans, and that this story is vitally important to who we are today. The story of European conquest is a story of tremendous violence, of religious violence, of a legal regime that is in many ways with us and still bears a lot of scrutiny.

That said, it was an interesting and puzzling question for me: Where to start a history of the United States? The easiest, straightforward way is "I'm going to start with the Declaration of Independence." That's when the United States begins.

But that doesn't really offer an explanation for a country wrestling with these problems. How is it that we are descended both from European colonizers and from Indigenous peoples and from Africans kidnapped from their homes and brought as forced laborers?

51

To be a nation, we have to all accept that we're descended from all these people.

DR: You point out in your book that when Columbus arrived, he didn't actually hit North America, he hit some islands in the Caribbean, and that there were ten or twenty million people living on the continent. Is that right?

JL: Yes. There were many more tens of millions than that. The European invasion of the Americas was a genocide. A lot of those deaths were caused by disease. The acts of violence, the forced enslavement of Indigenous peoples, the attempt to erase the sophistication and diversity of Native cultures: all this is a legacy whose agony we bear with us still.

The reason I begin with Columbus and 1492 and then move backward to Indigenous life earlier was that I decided to tell the story in large part about how our political arrangements are the product of our technologies of communication as much as our ideas.

It was extremely significant that Columbus could write in his diary and tell the queen and king of Spain he took possession of these lands, and decided that these people have no language, because he didn't understand it. The technology of writing is hugely important in that historical moment, and we can see the power dynamics differently if we pay attention to technology.

DR: When I was in grade school, I remember people saying that Columbus went to discover a new route to the East, but it wasn't clear that the world was round and he was maybe risking falling off the globe.
That wasn't the case. He was just looking for a cheaper way to get to Asia?

JL: Yes. But he was also a former slave trader and, in effect, a crusader. He wasn't only a seeker of knowledge.

DR: I like to cite him as the first private equity investor, because he had a deal with Queen Isabella. He got 5 percent of the gold and 10 percent of the profits, but there was no gold and no profits, so in the end he didn't really make any money out of it. But it's called the United States of America. Why didn't Columbus get billing rights?

JL: Let me just take seriously your private equity argument. There is a really important interpretation to offer with regard to the European conquest of the Americas, which is that it makes possible the emergence of capitalism, because of the vast wealth that Europeans extract from the natural resources and from the forced labor of Native peoples and Africans and bring to Europe. That consolidates wealth in a way that makes possible the emergence of capitalism. Setting aside how we want to think about Columbus, on a much larger scale of economic history, it is a really important development.

The naming largely has to do with Amerigo Vespucci, who wrote a book called *Mundus Novus (The New World),* after his voyage to what came to be called Brazil. When a German mapmaker named Martin Waldseemüller went to make a map in 1507, he didn't know anything really about Columbus, but he had read Vespucci's book, which had been widely translated. On the map, as an honor to Vespucci, he called this blob of land "America."

DR: The original sin of this country was slavery. The English people who came over to colonize weren't slave owners at the time. How did slavery get started in this country?

JL: Many of the English, in fact, were slave owners. They didn't bring enslaved people with them to New England, but many of them had already made voyages to or had family that had made voyages to the Caribbean and had slave plantations in places like Barbados and Jamaica.

The Atlantic trade in slaves dates to the middle of the fifteenth century and had its origins in Portugal and Spain engaging in raids of people along the West African coast. That happened before Columbus made his voyage. It's one of these terrible accidents of history that this new trade in people from West Africa was just beginning to churn when Portugal and Spain began founding colonies in the New World.

DR: I thought originally it was indentured servants who were the precursors of slaves here and who could, after a couple of years, become free.

JL: The first Portuguese slave-trading voyages begin in the 1440s, buying people and selling people as chattel. That is the case throughout South America, throughout the Caribbean, it's the case in early Virginia, and it is also the case in New England.

Well into the eighteenth century, a lot of white people are indentured servants. They're not free either. The conflation of "if you're black, you're enslaved, and if you're white, you're free" begins to emerge by the end of the seventeenth century.

DR: We ultimately had thirteen colonies. After the French and Indian War, the British said, "You need to pay for some of the protection we've given you," and they began to impose taxes. That didn't work out to the satisfaction of colonial leaders. Do you think that the British could have prevented a revolution from occurring?

JL: A, they did prevent one, and B, there were two. A complicated answer. We now think about how there were thirteen colonies, but really there were twenty-six, because there were the thirteen colonies in the Caribbean, which nobody really distinguished in any meaningful way. From the vantage of London, those are the colonies — all of them.

The Caribbean colonies are the ones England really wanted to keep. Those colonies, which were just brutal death camps for Africans, were the sugar plantations. That was where England was making the most money off its colonies.

The English colonists in the thirteen mainland colonies, when they were protesting first the sugar tax and the stamp tax and then later the taxes in the 1770s, kept trying to recruit the colonial assemblies in Barbados and Jamaica. They're like, "We're sending a petition to Parliament complaining about this tax. Are you with us?"

In the Caribbean, these slave-owning plantation owners would say, "We are outnumbered by our enslaved property thirty to one here. So you guys go off and rebel, but we actually need the British army." During the war, Britain essentially made a choice to give

56

up on the northern colonies, because why keep these sad colonies when all the riches are in the Caribbean?

DR: George Washington was seen as the general who won the war for us. Even if he hadn't been such a good general, would the British eventually have said, "Good-bye, we really don't get that much out of the North American colonies"?

JL: Counterfactuals are hard to give a compelling answer to. But I do want to say something about the other revolution, the one the northern colonies lost, which was the revolution of enslaved people who fought on the side of the British during the American Revolution because the British promised them their freedom.

The American victory was an incredible tragedy for enslaved people who were seeking their freedom. Britain had abolished slavery, and they had every reason to expect that the colonies would abolish slavery if they had not become independent.

DR: By the time of the Revolutionary War, there were about 450,000 enslaved Blacks in the United States, and about two million white Americans.

At the beginning of the Revolution, during the Second Continental Congress, a commit-

57

tee was formed to write an explanation of why they would break away from England if they voted to do so. The Declaration of Independence was written largely by Thomas Jefferson. The title of your book relates to the Declaration. Can you explain the title and the inconsistency between "these truths" and the reality?

JL: We all know that Jefferson is famous for "We hold these truths to be self-evident, that all men are created equal and endowed by their Creator with certain inalienable Rights, and among these are Life, Liberty, and the pursuit of Happiness."

I take the Declaration of Independence very, very seriously as a founding document for this nation. I take very seriously the idea that a nation is the only creation of human civilization that has been able to guarantee rights.

I chose *These Truths* as the title for my book because of something I don't think we reckon with fully as citizens — certainly not as often or as deeply as we need to: that an obligation of being a citizen in a democracy is the act of inquiry. Jefferson also says in the Declaration of Independence, "Let [these] facts be submitted to a candid world."

The document is essentially a product of the Enlightenment and its passion for empirical observation and research and experiment.

The nation is an experiment, and this is the statement of our obligation to participate in the experiment and to be keen observers of the results.

But it is also an experiment that has been fraught from the start, from long before the start. Even where Jefferson got those ideas is quite fraught. And it is our obligation as historians and as citizens to think about the relationship between the past and the present and to reckon with whether the nation has lived up to the promise of the Declaration of Independence.

DR: When Jefferson wrote the Declaration, the most important part was not the preamble, it was the sins of King George and so forth. Why is the preamble now perhaps the most famous sentence in the English language? It became the creed of our country, though the country didn't live up to the creed.

JL: There's a piece of the story that is really important to remember, which is that when Jefferson talked about equality, that all men are created equal, he was talking in a very narrow political sense about the political equality of propertied, educated men. Why that preamble has become ubiquitous and why it is cherished is not because of what Jefferson meant when he wrote it, but because of the work that Black abolitionists did in the 1820s and 1830s to reinterpret those words.

Go from 1776 to the fiftieth anniversary of the Declaration of Independence. A lot of things happen as part of that celebration. Among other things that happen to be going on in the 1820s is an evangelical religious revival. Many Americans are born again, including many free Blacks in the North. The attraction of evangelical Christianity for them is the spiritual call of equality. Male or female, Black or white, we are all equal before God.

A lot of preaching Black abolitionists in the North reinterpret the equality of the Declaration of Independence as a universal equality of all people. "We hold these truths to be self-evident, that all men are created equal" — well, then, we can't have slavery. And it becomes the manifesto for the abolitionist movement. That's the Declaration of Independence we cherish.

DR: When Abraham Lincoln gave his Gettysburg Address, he was referring to the preamble, and he was in effect saying that all white and all Black people should be equal. Is that right?

JL: Right. That's what people know about the famous Lincoln-Douglas debates in 1858, when they're both running for a Senate seat in Illinois. Stephen Douglas says, "The Declaration of Independence was never meant to include Black people." Lincoln says, "No, show me where in these documents it says this is a white man's government."

Lincoln has largely gotten that argument from Frederick Douglass, the great abolitionist who had been born into slavery and escaped. Douglass had been part of that movement to reinterpret the Declaration of Independence.

And Lincoln constitutionalizes that. That's what the struggle of the Civil War is over. But it becomes the new constitutional truth of the nation.

DR: Reconstruction, which was largely a disaster in the 1870s and '80s, led to Jim Crow laws, the Ku Klux Klan, and so forth. Do you think any of that could have been prevented if Lincoln had survived?

JL: The Compromise of 1877 [which resolved the 1876 presidential election by having federal soldiers leave the southern states] is what people generally refer to when they say Reconstruction failed. Well before that, during Andrew Johnson's besmirched presidency, the Confederacy is allowed to win the peace. That appeasement of the Confederate South is the single worst thing that happened in American history, in my view.

61

DR: Why did America become so economically powerful in the latter part of the nineteenth century?

JL: There's a fairly vigorous debate among historians about that. I would point to the obvious things. Our natural resources are peerless. Also, bankruptcy protection was huge in the nineteenth century. Until bankruptcy reform in the 1840s, only Wall Street brokers can declare bankruptcy. Ordinary businesspeople can't. But we democratize bankruptcy protection, because Americans decide risk is good, and if you want to encourage risk, you have to be willing to give people a clean slate. That's part of a democratic sensibility too.

So the economic risk-taking in which Americans engage in the nineteenth century, American businessmen in particular, makes the United States economy leapfrog past others for a time.

DR: Woodrow Wilson is reelected president in 1916, and we go into World War I. Was it inevitable that the United States would fight in the war? Was it inevitable that we didn't join the League of Nations afterward?

JL: I don't believe in historical inevitability. Everything is contingent. Everything could have gone differently. I tend to not be very excited about presidential biography because it has a political consequence, which is to inflate our impression of the power of the presidency. The influence of the executive office is out of whack with our constitutional system.

But in the case of the League of Nations, it really did come down to what Wilson did — how he handled going to Paris, how he became very sick with the Spanish flu there; then later how he had a stroke and then lied to his cabinet that he had suffered a stroke. There are a lot of weird, freaky accidents of history around Wilson and the League of Nations.

DR: One of the accidents of history, you could argue, is that Franklin Delano Roosevelt became president of the United States. Even though he had come down with polio, he managed to keep that from being largely known, and was elected for four terms. Do you think FDR was the transformational U.S. president of the twentieth century?

JL: I think the most transformational movement of the twentieth century was the constitutionalization of the New Deal. Therefore, Roosevelt would be high on my list of important presidents. When I think about Roosevelt's presidency, I am attracted to explanations that have less to do with him than with

63

how Americans came to accept the idea of the New Deal and its social welfare state — a set of arrangements that many Americans had been hostile to before. People didn't know objectively how bad his polio was, but they knew he was a person who understood suffering. And that allowed for a kind of leadership that you don't see very often on the national stage.

DR: Why don't we discuss some of the modern-era presidents and the social effects of their leadership? Take President John F. Kennedy. He only served about a thousand days in office. Do you think he has left a legacy we still have?

JL: Everybody leaves a legacy. The most significant moment in Kennedy's presidency was the Cuban Missile Crisis. He gets credit for saving the world from nuclear war. How many people can you say that about?

DR: A good point.

JL: Some years ago I took two of my kids to the Kennedy Library and Museum [in Boston]. I remember going into the room that was about John Kennedy's relationship with Bobby Kennedy, his attorney general. And you know what's going to happen to both of them.

I remember afterward having lunch with my sons and saying, "What do you make of that story? Does it make you want to go into public service?"

They said exactly the opposite. What it communicated to them was that there's no winning. There's no making the world better by running for office. This is a deeply cynical thing to say, but I think President Kennedy, who was cherished as an idealist at the time and in the immediate aftermath of his death, actually is a kind of buoy in the water signaling the end of idealism.

DR: Many people would say that, post–World War II, the best foreign policy decision the United States has made was probably the Marshall Plan. The worst foreign policy decisions, some would say, were Vietnam and the invasion of Iraq. How do you compare the impact on society, and on our standing in the world, of Vietnam and of Iraq?

JL: Eisenhower famously said that he feared for the nation when someone who had not seen combat occupied the office. Our worst military decisions have been made by people who never saw military service. The turn to an all-volunteer military is a good part of what is responsible for the forever wars of the end of the twentieth century. A legacy of Vietnam was the end of the draft, but the end of the draft worsened American foreign policy.

DR: In the book, you spend a fair amount of time on women who were not prominently mentioned in the textbooks I read. One has gotten a lot of attention in recent years. Her name was Phyllis Schlafly. Why were you so fascinated by her?

JL: Let me back up a little to the broader question of including women. Women and people of color have been political actors all throughout American history. They were ignored and stripped out of other people's histories. We forget how bamboozled we are by so much bad history that circulates in our world.

I went to a kindergarten class a few years ago that was studying the American Revolution. Each kid had to choose a person and then write a little biography and make a costume and a poster.

I asked, "Who are you studying?"

"Benjamin Franklin," "George Washington," "Alexander Hamilton," "John Paul Jones," "Patrick Henry."

"Are any of you studying women?"

They looked at me, and they're all like, "Ooh, cooties, no." I said, "Why not?" And this little girl raised her hand and she said, "Because there were no women then."

She was smart as a whip. This was just what

she had observed from what she was learning and from the posters in her classroom. We don't reckon with the cost of using books where the women have been taken out.

So back to Phyllis Schlafly. She is a hugely important driving force in the realignment of the party system in the middle decades of the twentieth century, the most important kind of field general of the conservative movement.

She has been doubly ignored, because — to be frank about it — most academic historical scholarship is written by people with a liberal bent who historically have done a poor job including conservative thinkers and figures. And the history that's written by conservatives generally is written by men who don't think women have a lot of political power, or should. So liberal academics ignore her and conservative academics ignore her.

DR: You point out in your book that the Equal Rights Amendment was actually passing legislatures unanimously until Schlafly began the effort to stop it in the '70s. You think it would have been ratified but for her?

JL: But for her and the army that she put together. One of the things that's important about Schlafly is she begins being a major political figure in the 1950s as the head of the Republican Federation of Women's Clubs, and she inaugurates what I call a new political style in American politics. It becomes a partisan style, the female moral crusade, an adaptation of something between McCarthyism and Goldwaterism. She's behind the nomination of Barry Goldwater, the conservative who wins the Republican nomination in 1964.

Then she gets pushed out of the Republican Party in the late '60s, when they're like, "We need to steer back toward moderates like Richard Nixon." She reinvents herself as a moral crusader arguing against the ERA, which becomes a signature issue for the Republican Party, even though the ERA was introduced in Congress in 1923 and Republicans had supported it, had it in their platform, since 1940. The Republicans had always been in support of the ERA until Schlafly said, "This is how we will reimagine the party."

DR: Planned Parenthood, which today is synonymous in some people's minds with support for abortion rights, was a Republican organization, more or less. That shifted. How did that shift come about?

JL: Planned Parenthood's history is long and tangled, but it is very much bound up in that party realignment in the '60s and '70s. Going into the 1960s, its message is that the way to consolidate the American middle class is for people to choose the family size that they want.

It's not a hyperpartisan organization, but it is predominantly a Republican organization. George H. W. Bush famously supported contraception. Nixon was even what we would now call pro-choice for quite some time.

DR: George Herbert Walker Bush was so much in support of Planned Parenthood that he had a nickname in the House of Representatives. What was that nickname?

JL: "Rubbers."

DR: When our country was started, women who were married did not have the right to own property. They couldn't vote. They weren't allowed to be officeholders. It's hard to believe today, but many leading so-called feminists then opposed the right to vote for women. Eleanor Roosevelt, for a while, was initially against the right to vote. Why were so many women not in favor of the right to vote?

JL: One of the reasons that women didn't get the right to vote for a long time is that men feared women would vote as a bloc. But it turns out women don't vote as a bloc at all, and the parties have to vie for them. That's why issues involving women and family and children tend to be hyperpoliticized, because in the beginning of the twentieth century, it was a struggle for those new voters.

The main thing that women fought for in the nineteenth century was not the right for women to vote, it was the end of slavery. It was part of a Christian evangelical movement. Women were disproportionately church members, and it was a moral reform movement. They also fought for temperance.

They thought they were fighting for an end to forms of tyranny, especially household tyranny, and those things included women not having the right to own property and not having the right to vote. The narrowing of the struggle for women's rights to the right to vote was actually pretty problematic for the larger movement.

In the early 1970s, after women lost the ERA, the women's rights movement got narrowed to a fight for the right to abortion. All the other things that women had been fighting for became secondary to that, which was a disaster, in my view, for feminism.

DR: How do you think technology is changing the American character, if at all?

JL: This is why I start with Columbus writing in his log. Our technologies of communication shape our political order all the time. For instance, I have made the argument that the realignment of the party system, which has happened several times in American history, has always coincided with a technological innovation.

So the invention of the penny press in the 1820s and 1830s makes possible the democratization of American politics and the rise of Andrew Jackson and the founding of the Democratic Party. The radio makes possible the New Deal. Television makes possible the emergence of the modern conservative movement. So we can think about the effects of cable television, talk radio, and the Internet, kind of all at once, starting in the 1980s.

It's easy to get distracted by the period from the founding of Facebook and social media to the present, just in the last decade or so, but talk radio, cable news, and the Internet and social media are all one big glommed-together disequilibrium machine, politically.

DR: Some professional historians would say you can't be a real historian if you're writing about something that happened within the last ten or fifteen or twenty years. Let's have fun and talk about the impact on American history of the Obama and Trump administrations.

JL: When I did my big outline for the book, I planned to end on Barack Obama's inauguration, because it's a great ending, and also because historians are quite reticent to write about the recent past. Then, after Trump's election, I decided I needed to go forward to that, because it's such a significant political moment.

Weirdly — and this will seem to undermine the importance of Obama's eight years in office — the most important legacy of Obama's presidency was his election itself. The triumph over centuries of racial prejudice and division, that this nation could elect a person of color president, was an incredible moment that completely shakes up the whole historical narrative.

DR: What about the Trump administration?

JL: Hard to say. Also hard to say in a fully broad-minded and nonpartisan way. What we would say, looking back fifty years from now, has to do with where this goes. At the moment, it does seem to be that the legacy of this administration and this cultural moment is our contemporary epistemological crisis — that it is very difficult for people to know how to know things. "You're biased, I don't believe you, you're lying." Our larger structures of epistemological authority are in crisis.

DR: Why do you think it is that people are not focused on history anymore — so much so that, for example, two-thirds of Americans cannot name the three branches of the federal government?

JL: Those findings — like that people can't identify the three branches of government — have been remarkably consistent since they were first empirically tested, beginning in 1948. But with regard to our general failure to want to think historically or to study the past in a meaningful way, we live largely in a world where there's a crisis of other forms of knowledge. We don't read poems to know things. I think we should. We think the only way you can know something now is with data, and the bigger the data, the better.

The purpose of the computer, working with that kind of data, is to make predictions about the future. Which is to say, all we seem to want to know is about the future and not about the past.

DANIELLE S. ALLEN
ON THE DECLARATION OF
INDEPENDENCE

James Bryant Conant University Professor,
Harvard University; author of *Our
Declaration: A Reading of the Declaration
of Independence in Defense of Equality*
and other books

"It's important to recognize that the compromises and structure of the Constitution were already in play at the moment of the Declaration."

The Declaration of Independence was adopted by the Second Continental Congress on July 4, 1776, and its text was sent to each of the colonies, to George Washington to read to his troops, and to King George III.

And the Declaration served its purpose: letting the world know that the offenses of King George III against the colonies were so intolerable that only one remedy — independence — was an appropriate and justified outcome.

At that time, relatively little attention was

given to the Declaration's preamble. Subsequently, well after the Revolutionary War, the preamble became the best-remembered part of the Declaration, for it was seen as containing the founding creed of the U.S. It became, as well, the founding creed of other countries and of disenfranchised parts of our society and other societies:

> We hold these truths to be self-evident, that all men are created equal, that they are endowed by their Creator with certain unalienable Rights, that among these are Life, Liberty, and the pursuit of Happiness. . . .

That sentence, drafted by Thomas Jefferson, with some editing by John Adams and Benjamin Franklin, had its obvious flaws. It clearly excluded all women and the country's half a million slaves from the "self-evident" right of equality. But the preamble eventually helped unleash the desire for equality among all Americans.

To be sure, in the effort by so many Americans to achieve equality, there have been many violent and bloody struggles since 1776. And they continue today in a number of areas. Whether the goal of achieving equality would even exist in America if the Declaration had been drafted differently is unknowable. But it does seem that the "equality" concept is more ingrained in Americans than in the people of most other countries.

In recent years, there has been a revival of interest in what Jefferson and the Second Continental Congress actually meant by the precisely chosen words that were included in the Declaration. One of the leading scholars behind this revival has been Danielle Allen, a professor at Harvard and the author of *Our Declaration: A Reading of the Declaration of Independence in Defense of Equality.* Professor Allen, who has also held senior positions at the University of Chicago and the Institute for Advanced Study, has helped to reignite scholarly interest in what Jefferson really intended with his magical — and inspiring — words about equality. I interviewed her on November 12, 2019, at the Library of Congress as part of the Congressional Dialogues series.

DAVID M. RUBENSTEIN (DR): The Declaration of Independence is important in our history, but it's not a legal document. It's not the Constitution. Why should anybody care today about what the Declaration says?

DANIELLE S. ALLEN (DA): I'm going to give you the case for why the Declaration is indeed a legal document. In order to do that, however, I have to remind you of what is in the second sentence:

That to secure these rights, governments are instituted among men, deriving their just powers from the consent of the governed, that whenever any form of government becomes destructive of these ends, it is the Right of the People to alter or to abolish it, and to institute a new government, laying its foundation on such principles and organizing its power in such form, as to them shall seem most likely to effect their safety and happiness.

The last clause is the most important part because it lays out the responsibilities of citizens — to make a judgment about how your government is doing, and then, if necessary, to alter it by doing two things: laying the foundation on principle, and organizing the powers of government to deliver on those principles.

Now, this was not just airy-fairy fancy language. It was a to-do list. When we come to the Constitutional Convention in 1787, there was one supremely important individual whom people don't pay enough attention to anymore — not James Madison, but James Wilson.

Wilson, who was from Pennsylvania, signed the Declaration and the Constitution. He was one of the only people who really thought about the relationship between them. Wilson made the case that the new constitution they had just signed rested on the basis of the Declaration of Independence. He quoted the sentence I just recited to you and said, "On this basis, everything we have erected stands."

DR: It doesn't say "The Declaration of Independence" in the document. Why did they call it that?

DA: Independence was voted on July 2, 1776, and the text of the Declaration on July 4, 1776. But somebody was already in the business of sneaking out copies. They had leaks in the Continental Congress. The result of that was an early newspaper printing and also the first book publication of the Declaration in July 1776. In that book publication, the header along the top of the page says "Declaration of Independence."

DR: So it wasn't Thomas Jefferson?

DA: Just a printer.

DR: When the colonies were set up, the British didn't tax them at first. When did the British say, "We're going to impose taxes on you," and why was that such a shock?

DA: By the middle of the 1760s, the British government had gotten itself embroiled in the French and Indian War on this continent and the Seven Years' War in Europe. They were in debt. What do you do when you're in debt? You extract taxes. And so in 1764 the British introduced the Sugar Act, and it goes from there.

DR: The Americans said, "Wait a second. We haven't had taxes before, and what about the principle of no taxation without representation?" What did the British say about that?

DA: James Otis, another neglected name, in 1764 wrote a pamphlet defending the rights of the British citizens of the colonies. He is the one who gets the credit for the "no taxation without representation" line. The issue wasn't just taxation. That was certainly a key issue, but it was also that Britain was changing how they were handling judicial cases. There was a general sense of an incipient breakdown of the rule of law.

DR: When did the first British troops come over to enforce the taxation?

DA: British troops were consistently in the colonies. They had been there for the French and Indian War. The Stamp Act of 1765 was the act where Britain required that you had to pay for every piece of paper, whether it was used for a legal document or a newspaper or whatever else. This is the first point of real uprising. There's even some skirmishing with the British troops.

It's also important to say that this is a period when King George is a new king. He's a baby. He's twenty-one or twenty-two when he comes to the throne in 1760. And the simple fact of the matter is he just did not know what he was doing. England was actually as unstable in its politics as the colonies were.

DR: Who sent the troops over to Concord and Lexington? It was a massacre, and people were killed. That was in 1775?

DA: Exactly. But we skipped the Boston Tea Party of 1773. The Americans refused to unload the British tea because of the way the tax structure was working. They didn't want to pay. They were limited in their use of tea and other things that were coming through Britain. They couldn't just directly get tea from India and so forth. To protest this, the plan was to dump all the tea into the harbor.

DR: After the Boston Tea Party, the British were really upset. That's when they said, "We're going to send more troops over"?

DA: They're really worried about the amount of ammunition that has spread through the countryside and the colonial militias. They send troops to Lexington and Concord to try to secure these munitions, and there's an accidental shot that triggers other shooting.

DR: The thirteen colonies had never actually had a congress because they felt they were, in effect, arms of British territory. When did they decide to have a Continental Congress?

DA: In 1774. The Tea Party's in '73, then Britain closes the Boston port and imposes other kinds of onerous restrictions on the colonies. That's what motivates the Continental Congress.

DR: The delegates get to Philadelphia. They don't want to be independent. They say, "How can we save these colonies?"

DA: They work hard on reconciliation. They work hard on submitting petitions to the king. The entire case of the Declaration rests on the fact that they've been working really hard for years to make their case to England and to assert their rights as English citizens.

DR: The Continental Congress sent a petition to the king saying, "Your Parliament is treating us poorly, but we know you're going to treat us well." What did the king say about that?

DA: On multiple occasions they got insufficient responses from the king, but the most important one was in the Second Continental Congress. They send a petition in July 1775. They're getting to the end of their tether. Massachusetts is raring to go, ready for independence, but Virginia's dragging its feet. They decide to make one last effort to reconcile, and they hear nothing — nothing at all.

At the time, it takes something like six weeks for a letter to get across the ocean anyway, so they don't expect to hear immediately. They send the petition at the end of July. They get to September and they've heard nothing. They get to October, they've heard nothing.

The king completely disregards the petition. In October they start hearing news of skirmishes where British troops are attacking along the coast, so they take those actions on the part of the British military as their answer. They read the king's intentions from what they see in the actions of his military. At that point, John Adams is like, "Let's do it."

DR: John Adams says, in this Second Continental Congress, "What we need to do is be independent." Was that the majority opinion in the country?

DA: Things are tipping by the time we get to 1776, but it's that fall of 1775 that is the really critical point. The politics are complicated. You have John Adams driving politics in the North. You have Richard Henry Lee driving politics in the South. The two of them are early adopters for revolution, for independence, and they're trying to bring everybody else along.

What radicalizes the Virginians is that the governor decrees that any enslaved person who escapes from a plantation and fights for the British will earn their freedom. That is what commits the Virginians to wanting to declare independence. Their view is that the king is interfering with their rights of property, and they start to use that vocabulary, talking about the revolution.

So Adams and Richard Henry Lee are both driving toward independence, for different reasons. It's important to say out loud that Adams didn't own slaves. He thought enslavement was a bad thing. This country has always had multiple traditions operating at the same time. So John Adams writes this to-do list in February 1776, and on that to-do list he has both "Write constitutions for the colonies" and "Declare independence."

"Constitutions for the colonies" comes first. That's the important point in this story.

By this point, New Hampshire has no government. Their royal governor just ran away. They write to Congress and say, "What are we supposed to do?" And Congress says, "Write a constitution!"

So New Hampshire writes one, and by the time we actually get to June and July 1776, there's a lot of constitution-writing already happening. It's showing people what comes after the revolution that makes it possible for them to embrace it.

In June, Lee stands up and proposes independence. Not all of the delegations there in Philadelphia had the authority to vote. Because they wanted unanimity on the vote, they withheld voting until July so that people could go back and secure authority.

DR: They also decided to be prepared for a vote of independence. To do that, they wanted to have a document that would explain why. Who was put on the committee to draft that?

DA: Adams was super busy. He was on every committee, and Jefferson was a kid.

DR: He was thirty-three.

DA: Exactly. He lived on the outskirts of town, and he didn't like to socialize, and he didn't seem to have a lot of friends. Adams thought, "This guy knows how to write, and he's not very busy, so let's get him elected to chair of this committee."

DR: There were five people on the committee. The others were — ?

DA: Adams, because he worked the politics behind the scenes on the vote and got Jefferson elected chair by one vote. Adams came in second, then Benjamin Franklin, Roger Sherman of Connecticut, and Robert Livingston of New York. They worked together, and Adams and Franklin really made meaningful contributions to the text.

DR: Adams later said that he didn't think he should write it because he wasn't that popular and Jefferson was a better writer. What do you think really happened?

DA: I'm sure that was part of the conversation. Listen to who I named on that committee: Jefferson/Virginia, Adams/Massachusetts, Franklin/Pennsylvania, Sherman/Connecticut, Livingston/New York. One southerner, four northerners. The northerners were hotter on revolution than the South. They needed the Virginian to be at the head of making the case for independence as a part of uniting the entirety.

DR: Jefferson is given seventeen days to write. Does he spend every part of those seventeen days doing that?

DA: He goes out shopping, it seems, for ladies' gloves. He does mostly spend his time writing, but he isn't alone. He works with Adams and Franklin, and he's got materials to draw on. He has George Mason's work for the Virginia Declaration of Rights, which has a lot of related language and concepts. He almost certainly has a text [the Proclamation for the General Court] that John Adams wrote for Massachusetts in January 1776, which reads like a rough draft of the Declaration.

DR: Jefferson drafts this document, and then he shows it to the other members of the committee. They say, "We're going to edit this a lot, because we know you like being edited"?

DA: They do edit it in meaningful ways. Let me just give you a couple of the most important changes. *Creator* is a word that comes in from Adams and Franklin. There wasn't religious language in the version Jefferson wrote. That mostly comes in from Congress in its edits after the committee. *Self-evident* is another word that emerges from Franklin and Adams in their conversations.

The other really important thing that happens is in the phrase *life, liberty, and the pursuit of happiness.* What the philosophers of the seventeenth and eighteenth centuries delivered to the rights conversation was the phrase *life, liberty, and property.*

So what happened to *property*? Why did it turn into *pursuit of happiness*? Because of the royal governor's interference and promise of emancipation to enslaved African Americans who would join the British, Virginians had begun to argue for independence using a language of defense of property rights. So by the spring of 1776, the defense of property was connected to the defense of slavery.

Adams has been arguing that *happiness* is the concept to use. He puts out a pamphlet in April 1776 where he says that the objective for governments is the same as the objective for individual man, and that final objective is happiness. Adams was somebody who was against slavery. That phrase in the Declaration is an antislavery moment.

It's part of a compromise, because there was other language in the draft that was also antislavery, which Congress cut out. That cutting was the proslavery moment in the Declaration. It's important to recognize that the compromises and structure of the Constitution were already in play at the moment of the Declaration.

DR: So they submit this document at the end of June 1776 to the Continental Congress. The members come back and vote on July 1 and 2 to be independent. On the night of July 2, John Adams writes to his wife. What does he say to Abigail in his famous letter?

DA: He says, "No question as important as this has ever been debated in America or ever will be." He does think July 2 will be the day that everybody celebrates rather than July 4.

DR: When they take up the actual document that has been drafted by the committee, do they say, "This is wonderful, and we don't need to edit it"?

DA: No. The most substantial edits are two different compromises.

We can distinguish between good compromises and bad compromises. Compromise is a good thing. We've gotten really stuck in this country on this issue, because the compromise we know most about is the slavery compromise. Because it was such a bad compromise and did so much damage to so many people, it's very hard for us to see what a good compromise could be.

So how do we tell the difference? The good compromise in the Declaration is the compromise around religion. Congress added religious language. The document is very carefully constructed so that no particular doctrinal position is visible.

It has belt-and-suspenders language — in the beginning, the phrase *laws of nature, and of nature's God.* You could be a Deist or you could be an atheist and think there's a natural account about rights that is sufficient to justify the arguments of the Declaration.

That was a good compromise, because it incorporated all the different views about religion then in the colonies. To make a good compromise, you need the inclusion of all perspectives and voices.

Bad compromise — slavery. That left a lot of people out in terms of thinking about whether this was a workable compromise. My ancestors did not think it was a workable compromise.

DR: The words *slavery* and *slave* are never mentioned in the Declaration. In the debate on July 3 and July 4, I think in your book you say they made sixty-eight changes in the text given to them.

DA: They made a lot.

DR: What did Jefferson do while the debate was occurring?

DA: He suffered silently. He just listened and noted every change down as it went. The general accounting of it is that it was like watching your child being mutilated.

DR: Did he later send copies of his version and Congress's version to his friends, saying,

"Don't you think my version was better?"

DA: He absolutely did. Jefferson was not known for a small ego.

DR: The night of the fourth of July, they agreed on the text. What did they do to get people to know what they'd agreed to?

DA: Congress had its official printer, a man named John Dunlap, and he had two jobs as of July 4. The first was to produce a broadside — a poster. He produced about two hundred of those for distribution to the troops. It was also for distribution to foreign governments, as they were now in the process of trying to develop treaties with France and Spain, seeking resources and alliances. They also gave Dunlap the job of printing it in his newspaper.

DR: They printed up two hundred copies, of which I think there are only twenty-seven left. King George gets a copy. Does he say, "Hey, you convinced me, and now I'm going to change my position"?

DA: No. The British government doubles down. They're intent on maintaining control of the colonies. It's important again to recognize how much uncertainty and instability they had anyway.

We forget that King George was also the elector of Hanover. He was a German monarch as well as being a British monarch. So when he engages Hessian troops, German troops, to come fight here, it's not exactly calling in foreign mercenaries. He's using all the forces of both his regimes to try to control the colonies.

DR: When do the delegates actually sign the document?

DA: The signing doesn't start until August, and it takes some time to finish. Most of them do sign in August 1776.

DR: Why is John Hancock's signature so big?

DA: He was the president of the Continental Congress, so that was his job.

DR: Signing that document was treason?

DA: Any aid to the Americans had been designated as treason a couple years earlier. It wasn't just signing the document. Coming back to the difficulty of our original sin and the problematic nature of the compromise, even at that point, in 1776, they compromise over slavery out of fear. The fear is that they've now committed themselves to a treasonous battle that they cannot win if they split up. And so in the Continental Congress in July 1776, they basically decide to try to sweep the question of slavery under the rug out of fear.

DR: How could Thomas Jefferson write "We hold these truths to be self-evident, that all men are created equal"? Jefferson had two slaves with him when he was writing this. Did he think all white men were created equal? What was he thinking?

DA: That is super important, and there are a couple of different ways to get to the core of this. Again, if you go back and look at that rough draft, the passage that Congress cut out about slavery is one in which Jefferson was condemning the slave trade. He uses the same vocabulary for people from Africa as for the colonists. He refers to their sacred rights of life and liberty. And in that passage, he also condemns slave markets as places where men — and he puts the word MEN in all caps. So we know that he used the word "men" in a universal way to mean all human beings, because it's not just the case that in slave markets only males were sold. Women were sold too.

How do you explain the discrepancy in how power was organized? To answer that question, let's go back to the end of the second sentence:

That to secure these rights, governments are instituted among men, deriving their just powers from the consent of the governed, that whenever any form of government becomes destructive of these ends, it is the Right of the People to alter or to abolish it, and to institute a new government, laying its foundation on such principles and organizing its power in such form, as to them shall seem most likely to effect their safety and happiness.

Again, it's the last clause, the distinction between laying the foundation on principle and organizing the powers of government. What hangs on that distinction?

Abigail Adams wrote to John Adams. She was very excited about revolution, and she said, "What about the ladies? Where do the women fit in this account"?

Adams wrote back, and he said, in paraphrase, "The principles of life, liberty, and happiness, that's for everybody." As to how to organize the powers of government, he says, "We men are not going to give up our masculine system." That was his phrase, "masculine system." That was the distinction they relied on, but they actually did think of the principles as universal, pertaining to everybody.

Abigail writes back and she says, and again I'm paraphrasing, "Great that those principles apply, but you guys don't have a good track record, you husbands, at exercising power on behalf of wives effectively." She says, "If you can't do it, we women will," in her words, "foment rebellion for voice and representation."

In that moment, Abigail is making a philosophical contribution to the theory of democracy. It is not possible to deliver on those principles of life, liberty, and the pursuit of happiness for everybody if power does not include everybody.

DR: Some people would say that "We hold these truths to be self-evident, that all men are created equal" is the creed of our country in many ways, though we obviously haven't honored it completely. How important were the Declaration and that sentence outside the United States? Did it inspire other people to have revolutions or make declarations of independence?

DA: It's inspired the whole world. David Armitage, a historian, has written a beautiful book on declarations around the world. There are hundreds of them at this point, and they range from the Purna Swaraj declaration in India in the 1930s, which drew a lot on the text of the Declaration, to Ho Chi Minh using the Declaration in Vietnam. So there are

really quite variable cases for the use of the
Declaration.

CATHERINE BREKUS
ON RELIGIOUS FREEDOM

Charles Warren Professor of the
History of Religion in America,
Harvard Divinity School

"It's one of the biggest myths of American
history and American religious history that
the Puritans came here to create a new
world of religious freedom."

Religion is heavily intertwined with the
founding of many of the English colonies
established in North America throughout the
seventeenth century. The Puritans, Pilgrims,
Quakers, Catholics, Lutherans, Mennonites,
and Amish, among others motivated to create or build the American colonies, were
invariably seeking to practice their religion in
ways not permitted in their native countries.
The irony is that once in the colonies, these
seekers of religious freedom and tolerance
were not all that tolerant of those who had
different religious beliefs than their own. Native Americans, who had inhabited the lands

later occupied by the settlers, saw this quite early. The settlers made enormous efforts to convert them to Christianity. Indeed, the first Bible printed in the colonies was printed for the sole purpose of converting the Algonquin tribe.

One religious leader, Roger Williams, had to flee the Massachusetts Bay Colony in part because of his advocacy of religious freedom. He left and formed Rhode Island, where all religions were officially welcomed. My home state of Maryland was originally formed to provide a haven for Catholics, who were not welcomed in the other colonies.

It was recognized by a few leaders in some colonies that religious tolerance was a virtue and not a vice. Thomas Jefferson was one of the leaders of the Virginia General Assembly who in 1776 drafted a bill guaranteeing religious tolerance in the commonwealth — one of his proudest accomplishments — and James Madison was among the leaders of the assembly who pushed through its passage, albeit ten years later.

It was also Madison, as a member of the first Congress, who drafted and helped pass the initial Bill of Rights, whose First Amendment stated that "Congress shall make no law respecting an establishment of religion." And while Congress has generally, with the help of the courts, honored this commitment to religious freedom (e.g., prohibiting prayer in public schools), the story of religion in the United States has actually been one of intense disputes between religious groups.

It has also been a story at times of virulent prejudice against those who were not adherents of the dominant religion in the United States — Protestantism. This is not to say that the many Protestant sects did not have their own intrareligious disputes and disagreements. But for a bit more than the first half of the twentieth century, the anti-Catholicism and anti-Semitism of American society, notably led by the Ku Klux Klan, was an accepted fact of life, and a visible sign of religious-based prejudice.

Sometimes this type of prejudice was violent, and at times it was silent; but it was there. When John Kennedy was running for the presidency in 1960, his election was thought to be unrealistic by many, for he was Catholic. The only earlier Catholic Democratic nominee for president, Al Smith in 1928, was widely thought to have lost in no small part because of his religion.

In this century, especially after 9/11, the anti-Muslim feeling in parts of American society has also been very visibly and strongly held. The quite public and unapologetic effort by the Trump administration to effectively ban immigration from certain majority-Muslim countries for a period reflected, in the view of many, this prejudice.

Religion continues to be an important part of American life, though perhaps less so than in the earlier days of the republic. Attendance at places of worship, measured as a percentage of the population, is down, particularly in recent decades, though still higher than in most European countries (where religion has seriously receded in its appeal). A religious-affiliation survey conducted by the American Values Atlas in 2019 showed that almost 69 percent of Americans identify as Christian, about 1.3 percent as Jewish, 0.7 percent as Muslim, 0.8 percent as Buddhist, and 4.3 percent as some other religion, while almost a quarter — 24 percent — identify as "unaffiliated."

Through the help of the New-York Historical Society, I had a discussion on these subjects on November 20, 2020, with Catherine Brekus, a professor of the history of religion at the Harvard Divinity School. A nationally recognized scholar of the role American women have undertaken in religion, Professor Brekus is also a leading scholar on the development and importance of religion in the history of the United States.

DAVID M. RUBENSTEIN (DR): Who exactly were the Puritans, and why did they leave Europe and come over to what later became the United States?

CATHERINE BREKUS (CB): The Puritans came to the colonies from England, where they were being persecuted under Charles I. Remember that Henry VIII had broken from the Catholic Church during the Protestant Reformation.

There were religious wars in England from the sixteenth century on where, depending on the monarch, either Catholics or Protestants were being persecuted. Bloody Mary, the Catholic queen, tortured and imprisoned many Protestants. Then Elizabeth I, a Protestant queen, imprisoned Catholics. There was very little toleration for any kind of religious dissent.

Puritans objected to the Elizabethan Religious Settlement, a middle way between Catholics and Protestants, that allowed the Anglican Church to preserve certain Catholic customs like kneeling and priestly vestments. Puritans were called Puritans because they wanted to purify the Church of England. They refused to conform to Anglican worship, and, as a result, many were imprisoned or lost their lands.

The so-called Puritans didn't call themselves that at first. It was a term of derision. Some decided to flee from England and settle in Massachusetts Bay.

DR: When did they come over?

CB: The Puritans arrived in 1630. The more radical Pilgrims had already settled in Plymouth. The Puritans said that they wanted to reform the Church of England, but the Pilgrims said the Church of England was so corrupt that there was no way that it could be reformed. People just had to separate from it.

The Puritans put an ocean between themselves and the Church of England while continuing to say that they were not separating from it. In fact, they ended up creating their own church system in Massachusetts Bay.

DR: I've often thought it was ironic that the Puritans and the Pilgrims came over for religious freedom reasons, but when they got here, they didn't exactly let other people worship differently. Is that right? In other words, if you didn't agree with them, in what became the United States, they would treat you very poorly?

CB: Definitely. It's one of the biggest myths of American history and American religious history that the Puritans came here to create a new world of religious freedom. They came here because they wanted religious freedom for themselves, but once they got to Massachusetts Bay, they persecuted people of other religious faiths.

The Quakers, for example, were also part of the radical wing of the Protestant Reformation, but the Puritans objected to their decision to abolish the sacraments and an ordained priesthood. When Quakers started appearing in Massachusetts Bay, the Puritans literally put them on boats and deported them. Some refused to leave, or came back after being banished, including Mary Dyer, one of four Quakers between 1659 and 1661 who were hanged on Boston Common. So the Puritans were not religiously tolerant at all.

DR: Who was it that settled Virginia — the Pilgrims, the Puritans, or somebody else?

CB: The colonies were a patchwork founded by people of different religious faiths. The people who settled Virginia were Anglicans from the Church of England. Most of them were explicitly coming to Virginia for commercial reasons. They were hoping to make money, unlike the Puritans, who came mostly as families, not as twentysomething men hoping to make it rich in the New World. The Puritans hoped to find a place to worship freely.

The people who settled in Virginia had more commercial motives, but they also had sincere religious convictions, and they established the Church of England, meaning that only Anglicans were tolerated in Virginia. If you were not a Puritan in Massachusetts Bay, you could be imprisoned or fined or, if you were a Quaker, you could have one of your ears cropped. In Virginia, Anglicans did the same to people who were not Anglican.

DR: When did Catholics start coming over, and where did they come from?

CB: The first Catholic settlement was in Maryland, a fascinating story because most of the colonies were settled by Protestants. Early America had a definite Protestant bent that continued past the Revolution, but Maryland was different. It was founded by the Calvert family, a distinguished Catholic gentry family in England who hoped to make money while giving Catholics a place to worship freely. Catholics in England were not tolerated and could not worship in public.

After the Calvert family founded Maryland, they extended religious toleration to all Christians, not just Catholics. The first settlers of Maryland were Catholic gentry who brought Protestant servants with them, and Protestants actually outnumbered Catholics from the beginning. Lord Baltimore, George Calvert, wanted to protect Catholics' religious freedom by extending religious toleration to all Christians. He wasn't motivated by a desire to defend an abstract principle of religious toleration but by a fear that Protestants would ultimately end up oppressing Catholics. That's exactly what happened: by the early 1700s, Catholics in Maryland were forbidden to vote, hold public office, or worship in public.

DR: The Germans who came over, what religion were they?

CB: There were a number of small German sects like the Amish and the Mennonites who ended up in Pennsylvania. Pennsylvania was founded by William Penn, the wealthy son of an admiral in the British navy who converted to the Society of Friends, known as the Quakers because of their ecstatic worship in which they would tremble and quake. Penn decided to found a colony in which everybody would be allowed to worship freely, and dissenters from all over Europe ended up flocking to Pennsylvania, including Christians who belonged to small sectarian German groups.

DR: Where did the first people who were Jewish come from?

CB: There are a few scattered references to Jews in the records of different colonies in the early seventeenth century, but the first significant settlement came in what was then known as New Amsterdam, now New York.

New Amsterdam was the Dutch colony.

There was a group of Dutch Jews who had come from the Caribbean by way of Brazil, which had been a Dutch colony before the Portuguese conquered it. In the beginning, the governor of New York did not want to tolerate them, but under pressure from Jews involved in the Dutch West India Company, they were allowed to stay and to practice their faith in New York. And New York became, of course, a magnet for Jewish immigrants into the nineteenth and twentieth centuries.

DR: What was it that propelled people in Virginia to talk about religious freedom? Thomas Jefferson, James Madison, George Mason were all very interested in this. Why were they so interested, and what was their religion? Some people say Thomas Jefferson was a Deist. Can you explain what a Deist is?

CB: In the 1760s and 1770s, before the American Revolution, a number of elite men, including Thomas Jefferson, were influenced by their reading of Enlightenment tracts about the reasonableness of Christianity.

Jefferson was very suspicious of institutional, organized Christianity, which he called "priestcraft." He thought that religion was interfering with people using their powers of reason. When we say that Jefferson or other founders were Deists, what we mean is that

105

they did not believe in the Jesus of the Gospels but a more distant God who had set the world in motion and then stood apart from creation, sort of like a watchmaker winding a watch and letting it run.

Jefferson didn't believe in the efficacy of intercessory prayer, and he didn't think that Jesus had been the incarnate form of God. But he thought that Jesus was an exemplary person. You may have heard the story about the Jefferson Bible: Jefferson took a pair of scissors to the Gospels and cut out all the miracles of Jesus and left the ethical teachings, which he found admirable.

DR: The first Bible printed in the United States was a Bible designed to help convert Indians to Christianity. What religion did Native Americans have? Did the effort to convert them get anywhere?

CB: You're referring to the Eliot Indian Bible. John Eliot was a Puritan who became known later as the "Apostle to the Indians." One of the justifications for Puritan settlement was that they said they wanted to convert Native Americans to Christianity.

But the Puritans' evangelism was always accompanied by an attempt to take away Indian lands. That meant that many Native Americans were justifiably suspicious of missionaries.

Indigenous peoples already had their own religions, a variety of religions. They wouldn't have called their beliefs "religious" because there wasn't a word for religion in Indian languages. It was more like a way of life.

DR: What religions were slaves allowed to have, if any? Could they practice it, or they just were told that if they had a certain religion, they couldn't practice it?

CB: We know that enslaved Africans came to America with a number of different religions. Some practiced indigenous African religions. Some, from the Kingdom of Congo (in modern-day Angola), were Catholic. The Congolese king and many Congolese had converted to Catholicism in the fifteenth century. Based on descriptions of religious practices, we also know that some of the enslaved were Muslim.

In the seventeenth century, there was not that much interest in converting the enslaved. But around the middle of the eighteenth century, missionaries began a more active outreach to enslaved Africans. By the nineteenth century, during the 1820s and 1830s, plantation missions led to the conversion of significant numbers of enslaved Africans, but this was always in the context of what the slave owner would allow. Many feared that Christianity would make slaves rebellious.

DR: In the First Amendment, the first part of the Bill of Rights, there is a right to religious freedom. Why was there such a desire to have religious freedom? It doesn't seem like so many people in the United States were really practicing religious freedom.

CB: The First Amendment is one of the glories of the American system. "Congress shall make no law respecting an establishment of religion or prohibiting the free exercise thereof."

In some ways the First Amendment came out of the sheer multiplicity of Christianity in early America. Most of the founders were not devout Christians by any means. We've already talked about Jefferson being suspicious of institutional Christianity.

There were a number of dissenters who wanted religious freedom so that they could practice their religion freely. The Baptists were especially influential. In both New England and in the South, in the two decades or so before the American Revolution, Baptists were being persecuted for their faith by both Puritans and Anglicans. They were forced to pay taxes to establish churches that they didn't support, and rather than pay those taxes, they went to jail.

Historians usually account for the First Amendment by pointing to the alliance between Deists and religious dissenters who wanted religious freedom for practical reasons. Skeptics and dissenters came together around the idea that religion should be something that people were free to practice as they pleased.

What was really astonishing about the First Amendment is that, for the first time, it allowed people to not practice anything at all. At the time of the Revolution, nine of the thirteen colonies had an established church that people were legally required to pay taxes to, but now, on the federal level, there was no longer an established church. Someone could say, "I want to be president and I don't practice any religion at all." Not that this has ever happened. An avowedly atheist president is still too radical for our system, I think.

DR: After the Civil War and Reconstruction, the Ku Klux Klan emerges. It's seen as anti–African American but as also anti-Catholic and anti-Jewish. Was that an important part of American religious history — anti-Catholicism, anti-Semitism?

CB: Definitely. There were two Klans. The first was active during Reconstruction, explicitly trying to disenfranchise newly freed Black men. That dissipated and then was given new life by the racist 1915 movie *Birth of a Nation,* which depicted the Reconstruction Klan as heroes.

The Klan reorganized in the 1920s, and at that point it was not only a racist organization but also strongly anti-Semitic and anti-Catholic. In order to be a member of the Klan, you had to be a white Protestant man, and you took an oath of allegiance on a Bible draped with the American flag.

Both Catholics and Jews were suspected of not being true Americans. Catholics supposedly paid their first allegiance to the Vatican, to the pope, and so they couldn't be trusted to follow American laws. Remember that a deep vein of anti-Catholic hostility had existed since the time of the Protestant Reformation. Protestants had rejected the Catholic Church, and they become anxious in the 1830s when huge waves of immigrants, largely Catholic, began arriving from Ireland and Germany. There were also waves of Jews arriving from Germany and then from eastern Europe, and Jews were also seen as being a potential threat to the republic and the white Protestant identity of the United States.

DR: I worked in the White House for President Carter and he was a born-again Christian. When that was revealed during his campaign, many people in the United States didn't really know what *born again* meant, although it had been around for a while. What does *born-again Christian* really mean? Was it invented in the United States or did it come over from Europe?

CB: When people say they're born-again Christians, they mean that they belong to what historians call the evangelical movement, which we date from the eighteenth century. This transatlantic movement took shape not only in the American colonies but also in England, in Scotland, and in Germany. Evangelicalism was a kind of new form of Protestantism that emphasized the authority of the Bible and the importance of a personal experience of the saving work of Jesus.

We can imagine evangelicalism as in some ways a vector of the Enlightenment. The whole idea of a born-again experience was that you, as a Christian, could empirically know that you had experienced a change that made you a true follower of Jesus. This idea sounds like John Locke's epistemology. Locke asked, how is it that you know something's true? He answered that you know through personal experience, you know through empiricism. This is exactly what evangelicals said — you could know whether you were born again.

DR: One of your specialties is women and religion. What role did women in the United States play in the development of these various religions? Were they allowed to be very active?

CB: Women were the backbone of churches even in the seventeenth and eighteenth centuries. In 1692 Cotton Mather said there were far more godly women in the world than men. Church membership rolls even then were dominated by women.

Historians have wondered why this was the case. Why were there so many women involved in churches, especially since the Bible has been used to enforce women's subordination? There's a long history of Christians arguing that the Bible says that women must be subject to men. But women found many scriptural texts to be empowering. They used the same Bible to argue for their worth and dignity and equality.

Women were not ordained until the twentieth century, but they played all kinds of roles informally. They served as Sunday school teachers, as home missionaries, even as foreign missionaries. There were many Protestant denominations that would not allow women to be ordained in the United States, but they would send them off to be missionaries to the so-called heathen. Women became antislavery activists, inspired by their faith. There has been a very long history of women being the upholders of religion.

DR: Today, do Americans go to religious services or to our places of worship in greater numbers or lower numbers than before?

CB: We are in the midst of a significant shift on the American religious landscape. There have been a number of surveys that have shown an increase in what's called "religious nones." These are people who, when they're asked, say they have no particular religious affiliation. They make up almost a quarter of the population now, which is much higher than it was, say, twenty years ago. And that's especially true among younger people.

DR: Do people in the United States attend church or religious services to a higher extent than people do in Europe?

CB: Definitely. It's clear that religion is a more central part of life in the United States than it is in other Western countries. This is not true of, say, Africa or the global South, where Christianity is rising very rapidly. But the United States is unlike other modern Western nations in still having a very strong religious basis.

DR: When did Muslims come to the United States, and are they now an increasingly large percentage of people in the U.S.?

CB: Muslims are about 2 percent of the population, but they have become more visible since the 1965 Immigration Act. The Immigration Act of 1924 was highly restrictive.

It made it virtually impossible for people from Asia and Africa to enter the country, as well as people from southern and eastern Europe. But in 1965 those quotas were removed by the Hart-Celler Act. Since then there has been a real growth in the number of Muslims, Buddhists, and Hindus in America, and the American religious landscape has transformed in a much more pluralistic direction.

DR: What about atheism? Is that a very large percentage of the population in the United States, and have atheists not suffered some discrimination?

CB: It's a little hard to count atheists, because they get picked up by the category of the "religious nones," which includes spiritual seekers. Many "religious nones" believe in God, but they don't want to practice any kind of institutional religion. Atheists, in contrast, are people who are even more overtly skeptical of religion. Atheists have faced discrimination since the early nineteenth century, when unbelievers finally became willing to name themselves openly as atheists, perhaps because of the new climate created by the First Amendment.

DR: When I was in grade school, an atheist tried to get a case in front of the Supreme

Court saying that school prayer should be outlawed, and the Supreme Court upheld it. Was it a watershed moment in the history of religion in the United States when school prayer was no longer allowed in public schools?

CB: Yes. These cases in the early '60s continue to reverberate today. Public schools are not allowed to begin the day with prayer. For many white Protestants in particular during the early '60s, this seemed like a very threatening development that suggested that the country was changing. Some of their anger about the school prayer decisions helped to fuel the rise of the Christian right in the 1970s and into the 1980s.

The people most opposed to the school prayer decision were those who wanted to argue that the United States was founded as a Christian nation and that the nation was forsaking its original religious identity. We still hear this argument today, but the United States was not founded as a Christian nation. There is a difference between a nation that was founded at a time when most Americans were Christian and a nation that was founded with an explicitly Christian identity. God doesn't appear in the Constitution.

DR: In my lifetime, the most prominent religious figure in the United States has been

Billy Graham. How did he become such an important figure, advising or consulting with presidents? What was his religion, and what was he doing that made him so popular?

CB: Billy Graham was an evangelical. If you see pictures of him when he first started preaching, he looked like a movie star. William Randolph Hearst, the media mogul, admired Graham's opposition to communism and instructed reporters to begin covering his revival services. He was an extraordinarily charismatic preacher.

He built a very large following in these mass gatherings and, beginning with Harry Truman, he courted the attention of presidents. He became a frequent visitor to the White House as presidents realized that his presence could help them to clothe themselves in the garb of morality and to ally themselves with Christianity.

DR: As we look back on the history of religion in the United States, other than Billy Graham, who are one or two religious figures who had a particularly big influence?

CB: Someone you probably haven't heard of before is an eighteenth-century evangelist named George Whitefield. I sometimes say that he was the Billy Graham of the eighteenth century, but it would be more correct to say that Billy Graham was the George Whitefield of the twentieth century.

Whitefield belonged to the first generation of evangelicals. Born in England, he was a Church of England minister who traveled throughout England and Scotland and then up and down the American seaboard, sometimes by boat, sometimes by horse. He preached in Savannah, in Boston, in Charleston. Some historians have said that, even before George Washington, George Whitefield was the first intercolonial American hero. Everybody knew who he was.

DR: What was the justification that devout Christians used to justify slavery in those days?

CB: Slavery is often mentioned in the Hebrew Bible. Christians would point to particular texts and argue that if Abraham had been allowed to have slaves, then southern planters could also own slaves. This justification ignored the fact that slavery in the Bible is not race-based. War captives were taken as slaves, but there's nothing in the Hebrew Bible or in the New Testament that suggests that Africans in particular were deserving of slavery. Some justified African slavery on the grounds of a passage in Genesis that states, "Cursed be Canaan: a servant of servants he shall be to his brothers," but this passage says nothing about either Africans or black skin.

The argument over slavery often revolved around the question of whether the Bible justified it or not. Antislavery Christians argued that, even though Jesus hadn't said anything specific about slavery, his words "Do unto others as you would have them do unto you" implicitly denounced slavery.

DONALD E. GRAHAM
ON THE FIRST AMENDMENT AND FREEDOM OF THE PRESS

Former Publisher, *Washington Post*

"The First Amendment applies to the press, but it also applies to anybody. Someone speaking up and saying things the government doesn't like cannot be prosecuted for that, cannot be put in jail for that in our country. What's important here is not the rights of newspapers, not the rights of news organizations, not the right to broadcast, it's the rights of all of us."

It is safe to say that no government really likes being criticized by its citizens, and such criticism has cost innumerable people around the world their freedoms and their lives. In the United States, these kinds of criticisms tend to be protected by the First Amendment; and since the Bill of Rights has almost religious standing in America, the government has a much harder burden in trying to thwart or penalize the critics. In few other countries is "free speech" protected by the country's governing documents; and where it is so protected (e.g., Russia), the reality is much different.

The American concern about free speech preceded the First Amendment's adoption. In 1734, a British governor in New York did not like the criticism he received from a newspaper publisher and journalist, John Peter Zenger, and thus had him imprisoned for libel and ultimately placed him on trial. But a jury quickly acquitted Zenger on the grounds that what he had published was accurate.

The First Amendment — drafted by James Madison, approved by Congress, and ratified by the states — no doubt reflects the American view that free speech and a free press have social benefits far outweighing the angst of a criticized party, including the government.

There are exceptions to the concept that anyone can say or print anything. For instance, the courts have long upheld the view that publishing information that contains details vital to national security, particularly when it has been illegally obtained, does not deserve unwavering protection. The country's national security interests have been considered to have a higher societal value.

Over the past century, perhaps the most visible situation in which the U.S. government challenged the publication of what were seen as purloined, vital national secrets was the Pentagon Papers case. In 1971, the *New York Times* and the *Washington Post* published an internal, classified analysis — taken and leaked without authorization by a former Pentagon analyst, Daniel Ellsberg — of the U.S.'s involvement in Vietnam during the Truman, Eisenhower, Kennedy, and Johnson administrations.

The Nixon administration sued to stop further publication of the papers, following the initial stories. The U.S. Supreme Court ultimately upheld the publication, though both newspapers had taken serious legal risks by publishing the documents in the first place.

A few years later, the *Washington Post* backed two young reporters, Carl Bernstein and Bob Woodward, in their efforts to expose various illegal and unethical practices of the Nixon administration following the break-in at the Watergate offices of the Democratic National Committee. The administration repeatedly claimed that the *Washington Post* was printing inaccurate and unverified information about the activities that came to be known as Watergate.

The decision to back these two reporters, who were often using an unnamed source, dubbed "Deep Throat," for their information, again put the *Washington Post* in the crosshairs of the Nixon administration. While the reporters' stories proved largely accurate in the end, there was certainly a risk in publishing them.

With the Watergate and the earlier Pentagon Papers publication, much of the legal and financial risk was borne by the owners of the *Washington Post,* the Graham family. Katharine Graham was then the chief executive of the *Washington Post,* a position that her son Don ultimately assumed upon her retirement.

I have known and admired Don Graham for more than four decades, and greatly regret not pursuing the chance he gave me to buy the *Washington Post* in 2013 following the family's decision to divest the newspaper. But Jeff Bezos is obviously a deeper-pocketed, more tech-savvy owner and has done a far better job as owner than I ever could have.

I interviewed Don Graham virtually in November 2020 about the *Washington Post's* decision in the 1970s to pursue the publication of these controversial stories, and came away admiring even more the courage of his family in doing so.

DAVID M. RUBENSTEIN (DR): Your grandfather bought the *Washington Post* out of bankruptcy. What year was that?

DONALD E. GRAHAM (DG): Nineteen thirty-three. My grandfather Eugene Meyer became the first president of the World Bank in 1946.

At that time he obviously could not continue to be publisher of the *Post.* He had made my father, Philip Graham, deputy publisher when he returned from the war in 1945. In 1946 my dad became the publisher, and was the publisher until his death in 1963.

DR: When your father died in 1963, your mother became the president of the Washington Post Company?

DG: And publisher of the *Washington Post.* She continued as publisher from '63 to '79 and as CEO of the company until she stepped down in 1991. When my dad died in 1963, my mother faced an extremely difficult choice. I think most people expected her to sell the *Washington Post,* because no woman was running a company of comparable size in the United States. My mother, knowing what her father had put into the company, what her husband had put into the company, how hard they worked, how much they cared, made the very brave decision to try to take over and run it, with her four children cheering her on.

When we went public in 1971 as the Washington Post Company, I believe that she was the only woman CEO in the Fortune 1000. There were 999 guys and her. So she was in a very unusual position.

I became the publisher in 1979. I came to

the *Post* in January 1971 as a reporter. I worked as a reporter that year, and then as an editor, and then in almost every business department of the newspaper. I had about a year at *Newsweek,* which we owned at the time. I learned in a classic publisher's son way by delivering papers and selling ads and working in the production department and trying to learn the operations of the paper.

DR: Historically the *Washington Post* was the recipient of significant leaks from government officials. How did the *Post* assess, during your time there, whether that information was appropriate to publish — appropriate to publish because doing so would not endanger national security?

DG: The *Post* continually printed stories that came from classified government documents. As you know, many documents are classified for no particular reason, just because somebody could put a stamp on it. Senators, cabinet secretaries, many others in authority would tell things to reporters or get reporters documents.

The *Post* was meticulous about always trying to contact everybody and get their point of view before a story was printed. If we were working on a story, we would call the White House, the CIA, whoever else was involved and ask for their comment.

By the time I got there, Ben Bradlee, the executive editor, and later his successor, Len Downie — those were the two top editors I worked with in my many years on the paper — both knew a great deal about what the paper had published in the past. We frequently had complaints that printing a story would risk violating national security, when what was really meant was that it would risk political embarrassment to the president, the cabinet secretary, or someone else.

That was easy. There were times when our reporters had turned up information, and presidents or cabinet secretaries really wanted the *Post* to understand that they believed it might do some harm to national security. In those cases, Bradlee or Downie tried to talk to anyone with relevant information who wanted to say, "Here's the risk to national security." They would listen to all sides and then make a recommendation to the publisher.

Stories that reportedly had some risk to national security were something that Kay Graham wanted to know about. There was one rule between her and Ben Bradlee, which was: "No surprises."

There absolutely were occasions when the *Post* considered publishing stories and did not publish them, or did not publish pieces of them, because someone in the government said, for example, "If you publish this, you will risk someone's life. That could only have come from a particular source." I cannot ever remember printing a story where that was perceived to be a real, not imagined, threat.

DR: Did the president of the United States ever call the *Post* directly and say, "This is important to not publish," or would he usually have somebody call on his behalf?

DG: Presidents occasionally called. My mother in her autobiography, *Personal History,* describes the rich interchange that she had with President Lyndon Johnson, who hated being criticized. He hated our editorials about Vietnam and our stories about Vietnam, and argued extensively with her that the stories were hurting national interests.

My mother always reached out to people in any administration and told them that she was open to complaints about unfairness and inaccuracy. She did not, as far as I know, have any calls from President Nixon personally. There was one occasion described in her book when she had a call from President Reagan, but only one.

But it's quite a story. Bob Woodward, then and now the best reporter in Washington, had turned up a story about a CIA operation called Operation Ivy Bells. It was an attempt to intercept Soviet communications with their submarines in the Pacific.

Kay was taking a bath one morning, and her assistant came in and said, "Mrs. Graham, the president is on the telephone." So she, always ready for a challenge, got out of the bath, toweled off as best she could, picked up a pad and a pen, and listened to the president. The president said, "Kay, I'm afraid the *Post* is working on a story that is harmful to the national security, and Bill Casey is here."

Casey was then the director of the CIA. He spelled out his complaint in some detail. Then Reagan again said, "Kay, I'm concerned about the *Post* working on a story that's a threat to national security, and Bill Casey is here." And she realized that the president had gone through his three-by-five cards and was back reading the first card again.

She took the complaint very seriously. Woodward had been working on the story knowing that this secret about Operation Ivy Bells had been leaked to the Soviets by a spy inside the NSA [National Security Agency] named Ronald Pelton, who had subsequently been detected and arrested. So it was true that Operation Ivy Bells was the most secret project. It was also true that it had been compromised.

I got one call from a president of the United States in my time — from George W. Bush, when a very famous *Post* reporter, Dana Priest, a multiple Pulitzer Prize winner, was working on a story about secret CIA prisons for al-Qaeda detainees in other countries. President Bush was afraid that the story disclosed the names of the other countries and that that would end their cooperation with the United States. We printed that story. We did not print the names of the countries that were hosting those CIA prisons. I believed then and believe now that was the right goal.

DR: Should the press feel that its job is to protect national security in some way?

DG: The best answer I can give you is, "It depends." The most famous Supreme Court decision on the First Amendment refers to an outrageous example, trying to pick the most grievous possible threat to national security. It's an old decision. It refers to the movement of ships and men in wartime.

So if a newspaper were to publish that soldiers were traveling from New York to Europe on such and such a ship at such and such a time, they'd be alerting an enemy government that could try to sink the ship. The Supreme Court used that as an example of something that would not be permitted under the First Amendment. Direct, egregious harm to the country, in other words.

You couldn't be stronger in standing up for the right to free speech and the right to print than the *Post* was. Should we have listened to questions such as "If you print this story, might it result in the deaths of CIA agents or American soldiers?" You should listen to that, in my opinion. We did.

DR: When the government is calling up about national security, is it really more about political embarrassment than national security?

DG: Not necessarily. It depends on the president, depends on the situation. Let's take an example you and I both know well because of our age — the war in Vietnam. The government continually asserted that we were winning that war, that there was light at the end of the tunnel. Reporters, and this goes back to the Kennedy administration, kept writing stories that said that wasn't so. First President Kennedy, then President Johnson, then President Nixon complained bitterly to publishers about stories that basically said government officials weren't telling the truth.

History is pretty clear that government officials weren't telling the truth, or that perhaps they didn't understand what reporters knew from being in the countryside, that the enemy was a lot stronger than we thought they were. That's an example of government leaders complaining in good faith.

In the Nixon administration, I don't think their complaints were in good faith. President Nixon was desperate to keep the truth about Watergate from coming out, and repeatedly said that national security was involved, because indeed he had tried to get the FBI and the CIA to screw up the investigation in various ways.

DR: Let's talk about the Pentagon Papers case. When the *Post* received those papers from Daniel Ellsberg, were you more worried that they had been stolen from the government or that the publication of them would imperil national security?

DG: The latter. Remember the circumstances. Ellsberg, who in a sense was the author of the Pentagon Papers, one of their compilers, had leaked those papers to the *New York Times.* All of them. He also went through them with the *New York Times* and pointed to areas that he thought in fact would endanger intelligence-gathering sources and methods or in other ways compromise what he took to be actual secrets.

The *Times* had months and months to study the papers and prepare a series of articles for publication. They published two, and then were enjoined by a federal court from publishing any more.

At that point, Daniel Ellsberg called someone he knew at the *Washington Post* and gave us another set of the Pentagon Papers. They arrived on Ben Bradlee's living room floor early one morning, and Ben had every national security and foreign policy correspondent at the *Post* there ready to read them. We did not have months. We had part of the day to consider it.

Now, I have said that even Ellsberg thought that full publication of the Pentagon Papers would endanger sources and methods of intelligence-gathering, and I still don't know to this day what those parts were. But the Pentagon Papers were full of details unknown to the American public about the history of the war in Vietnam. On top of that, it was the story everybody in the United States was talking about.

The *Times* had published. It had been enjoined. The government was arguing that the publication of the papers would compromise national security. But it wasn't clear from reading the first two days of stories that there were any national secrets disclosed. There was a lot of diplomatic history and a lot of cases where presidents or secretaries of state or secretaries of defense had said one thing to the public while saying something else in private.

So Bradlee turned his reporters loose on this story. The first story that they wanted to publish had to do with dealings with Vietnam in the 1940s, and clearly did not involve any risk to national security. They were going to tell the story in multiple parts, and that was the first part.

Bradlee had in the lawyers who had represented the *Post* from a firm called Royall, Kegel, and Wells. Those lawyers looked at the stories not so much from a national security point of view.

Also, the *Post* had gone public that week. And just to help things along, the deputy attorney general of the United States called in our Justice Department reporter and said, "I want you to tell Mrs. Graham that if a corporation is convicted of a felony, such as violating the Espionage Act, it cannot own television stations." We at that time owned two television stations, which amounted to one-third of the value of our company.

So that was a pretty direct threat. The lawyers continued to read and make recommendations. Bradlee's writer Chal [Chalmers] Roberts wrote a story. Bradlee said, "I think this story has to run in tomorrow's paper." Businesspeople at the *Post* guided by the lawyers recommended against it. Mrs. Graham had to make the decision on the spot in a telephone call from Bradlee and the leaders of the paper. And she decided to print.

DR: When it was printed, what was the reaction of the government? Did they go into court to try to get an injunction against further publication?

DG: They did. They went before a judge in Washington, who denied an injunction. They then went to the Court of Appeals for the District of Columbia, which granted the injunction.

By then, one day had gone by. Courts worked a little faster in those days. We had printed, I believe, a second part of the story, and the appeals court decision came down during the press run. So some copies of the paper had been printed, but not all.

Gene Patterson, the managing editor of the *Post,* told me that was the only time that he went down to the press room, went into the foreman's office, and said, "Stop the presses." We ceased printing as soon as we had the order ordering us to desist.

DR: Then did it go to the Supreme Court?

DG: Yes. Our case was joined with that of the *New York Times,* roughly three weeks from the filing of the first complaint against the *Times.* The Supreme Court felt some imperative to decide the case quickly, as the lawyers for the *Times* and the *Post* certainly argued.

The Supreme Court ruled six to three that the government could not stop the papers in advance from printing a story except in the greatest imaginable circumstances. And it is the law of the land to this day. You get arguments about exactly what the decision says, but it said in this case the papers have the right to print the story, and we did.

DR: Did your mother ever tell you whether she had second thoughts or whether she came close to saying, "Don't publish it"?

DG: It was a very, very close call. The lawyers felt that with the company having gone public so recently, there was some legal threat involved in certain assertions we made. That threat, if it was a threat, never materialized. They also felt that, the *Times* having been enjoined from publication, we could be found in contempt of that court order for publishing.

That threat also never materialized. But it was a very close call for both Punch Sulzberger, the great publisher of the *New York Times,* and Katharine Graham. I think it was the best business day of her life that she made that decision.

DR: Let's go on to a couple years later, when two young reporters, Bob Woodward and Carl Bernstein, are assigned to follow a break-in at the Watergate Office Building. They ultimately produce a set of stories that win the Pulitzer Prize. Was it difficult for the

Post to go forward and publish those?

DG: It's very hard to describe how risky, how dangerous that period was. Certain things happened then that would be inconceivable today because of the Internet. Kay Graham had a farm in Virginia to which she often repaired for the weekend. I was with her at that farm on the night of June 17.

Howard Simons, the managing editor, called the next morning and said, "Kay, there's two great stories I've got to tell you about. First, there was a traffic accident in Alexandria and a car smashed the porch of a house and a copulating couple fell down from the second floor on top of the police car in full view of everyone on the street."

He said, "And second, there was a burglary in the Democratic National Committee headquarters at the Watergate, and they arrested five people in business suits, including a guy who used to work for the CIA."

That's how it began. I want to emphasize that no one at the *Washington Post,* not Bob Woodward, not Carl Bernstein, not Ben Bradlee, not Katharine Graham, in June of 1972, or when Bob and Carl began their reporting, had the slightest intimation that this would lead to the White House, that this would lead to the resignation of a president. I think that would have been regarded as ridiculous by any of them.

Knowing only that there had been a burglary at the headquarters of the Democratic National Committee under unusual circumstances, they wanted to know what had happened. They just took one step at a time, learning one fact after another, under demanding rules set up by Ben Bradlee.

Something that couldn't happen today was this: the *Post* would print a story, a further piece of information Woodward and Bernstein had learned in the course of the investigation. One tiny step at a time, beginning with how one of the burglars had a notebook in his pocket that included the telephone number of someone in the White House, Howard Hunt. Carl Bernstein called that number, asked to speak to Mr. Hunt.

The secretary said, "He's down the hall with Mr. Colson," one of the top aides to the president. He got on the phone and Carl said, "I want to ask you how your name came to be in the address book of James McCord, one of the burglars arrested at the Watergate." And Hunt said, "Oh shit," and hung up the phone.

That's where it started. It turned out that McCord had in his pocket money that was traced via serial numbers to a cash contribution someone had made to the Nixon reelection committee. That was interesting.

The stories turned out to be important because they were true. If the stories hadn't been true, it would have had grave consequences for the *Post*.

DR: At one point there was a story that Bob Woodward and Carl Bernstein published that was not accurate. Did the *Post* say, "We better stop with this story because we could have more mistakes and embarrass ourselves?"

DG: Months into the Watergate investigation, a grand jury had been convened. It had held hearings for months, and the *Post* had written story after story after story that turned out to be true. In one story, Bob and Carl wrote that a certain person in the White House had access to the fund that was used to pay the Watergate burglars and that there had been testimony to that effect in front of the grand jury.

What was *not* true was that there had been testimony to that effect before the grand jury. What *was* true was that that person had access to the fund. That was an embarrassing moment. However, by then Woodward and Bernstein had proven right on so many difficult stories, and they and Ben Bradlee immediately came to understand what the mistake was. No one thought about pulling back.

DR: There's a famous story where John Mitchell, the attorney general of the United

States, tried to send a message to your mother saying that some part of her anatomy would get into a wringer if she didn't stop this kind of publication. Did she ever feel threatened by that?

DG: Mitchell's statement may have been made while he was drunk, but certainly was made late at night to Carl Bernstein. No, she didn't feel threatened by it.

Two things that happened in the course of the investigation were very directly threatening. One was that friends of hers told her, "You have to be very careful. You have to assume that your phone is tapped." These were people in the White House.

Second, by then we owned four television stations. Two of them were in Miami and Jacksonville, Florida. People came forward in those areas to challenge our licenses. The groups in question were local Republican business groups, and it certainly looked to us to be possible that they had been encouraged to do this by the Nixon administration.

When the Nixon tapes became public, Nixon, sitting in the Oval Office, directs Charles Colson, one of his top aides associated with dirty tricks, one who subsequently went to jail, to "talk to our friends in Florida" and get them to challenge those licenses for the *Washington Post*. Had President Nixon not ultimately resigned, those challenges would have gone before the Federal Communications Commission, where the chairman, Dean Burch, was also the former chairman of the Republican National Committee. That remains to this day, as far as I know, the most direct assault on free speech. They wanted to take away those stations because they didn't like our coverage of Watergate.

DR: It's hard to believe, as we sit here talking, that these events occurred almost fifty years ago. In the ensuing fifty years, do you think that publishers have changed the way they look at publishing things that might affect national security or the way the president is perceived by the country? Do you think publishers are more willing to publish, less willing to publish? How has the world really changed in the last fifty years with respect to these First Amendment issues?

DG: Great news organizations like the *Washington Post* feel a duty to publish what they think is important to the public, and will run risks to do that. However, I think governments still feel the impulse to strike back when criticized, and I would say such an occurrence occurred this year [2020]. President Trump put out a tweet that Twitter chose for the first time to fact-check. Alongside his tweet, it published links to other sites that, in Twitter's opinion, suggested that Trump's tweet wasn't true.

Now, under the First Amendment, President Trump has a right to say what he wants, and Twitter has a right to run its site the way it wants. Twitter has an undoubted right not to publish a tweet of President Trump's. They don't have the right to alter it, to put words in his mouth, in other words. But they have the right to treat it as they see fit, not to run it, to run it, or to run it with a fact-check.

President Trump was furious. He immediately tweeted that what Twitter was doing was wrong. "We'll strongly regulate or shut them down" is approximately what he said.

Two days later, the White House published an executive order with three parts. First, government advertising would be taken away from social media sites that, in the opinion of the government, weren't fair to all sides. Second, the Justice Department was ordered to draft a bill to send to Congress, rewriting what's called Section 230 of the Communications Decency Act, which sets the legal standard for suits against social media companies such as Twitter. Third, the Federal Communications Commission, to which Trump had appointed the commissioners, would hold hearings on whether they ought to rewrite Section 230.

I don't know how much government advertising was subsequently taken away from Twitter or any other social media platform.

But that executive order invited the Justice Department, the Commerce Department, OMB [the Office of Management and Budget], and the FCC all to participate in this attack on Twitter. That is really something.

DR: What are the lessons that you've taken away from exercising the First Amendment rights the *Washington Post* has?

DG: The First Amendment applies to the press, but it also applies to anybody. Someone speaking up and saying things the government doesn't like cannot be prosecuted for that, cannot be put in jail for that in our country. What's important here is not the rights of newspapers, not the rights of news organizations, not the right to broadcast, it's the rights of all of us.

Governments are run by human beings. When people are criticized in ways that they think are unfair, they have an impulse to try to strike back. Those who care have a great need to keep reminding everybody in this country that one of the things that's special is the right of any of us to say what we think without risking attack by the government. I know that in the future, news organizations will stand up as strongly as ever for the First Amendment. And I know that courts are inclined to agree with them. I know that the citizens of this country also are on the side of everyone's freedom to say what they think.

MICHAEL BESCHLOSS ON THE PRESIDENTIAL ELECTION OF 2020

Presidential Historian

"We always have to be vigilant. Democracy is never safe. We can never take it for granted."

The events following the presidential election of 2020 were seemingly unprecedented: the losing candidate not only refused to accept the legally approved results but also tried to overturn those results through lawsuits, political pressure, untrue statements, intimidation of government officials, and the calling for a march on the Capitol to stop the official vote count.

How unprecedented was this? Had anything like this ever happened before? Who better to answer those questions than a scholar of the presidency, and I was fortunate to talk to a longtime friend who is one of the country's leading presidential experts. Over the past several decades, Michael Beschloss has become one of our best-recognized and most-

143

respected scholars of the U.S. presidency. And that is despite having a Harvard MBA — not the typical degree of choice for someone in his field. He is a best-selling author of ten books on the subject, including works on Franklin Roosevelt, Dwight Eisenhower, John Kennedy, and Lyndon Johnson, and he is a frequent television commentator on all matters relating to the presidency.

I have known Michael for many years — we both live in Washington and enjoy discussing the presidency whenever possible — and he is the person I invariably turn to when I have questions about the subject. I thought he would be the perfect person to discuss the impact of the events relating to the Capitol attack on January 6, 2021.

I had a virtual conversation with Michael on January 24, 2021, during which he related that there certainly have been other contested presidential elections. But in those elections, there seemed to be credible cases of some fraud — even if not enough to overturn the election outcome. But in none of those other elections, in his view, was the president engaged in efforts to incite violence to overturn the election, to get election officials to overturn the legally certified vote, or to have the vice president overturn the certified Electoral College vote.

For these reasons, he was not surprised that the House of Representatives impeached

President Trump. And while the Senate did not subsequently convict the president, Michael Beschloss felt that America's well-established commitment to democracy had passed a very serious stress test — to the country's credit.

DAVID M. RUBENSTEIN (DR): In the history of our presidential elections, have there been other times when the losing candidate contested the election's outcome in the courts or in Congress?

MICHAEL BESCHLOSS (MB): We have had contested elections in history where there was reason for one candidate or another to challenge the results. The year 1876 is the best example of that, where there were a number of states whose electoral votes were contested. It did go to Congress, and there was a process and the result was a compromise.

The good result is that there was a compromise that kept the country going. The bad part of it was it was a terrible compromise, which was to abruptly end Reconstruction and pull federal troops out of the South. As a result, Jim Crow was enforced in the South. A lot of the noblest hopes for the winning of the Civil War were dashed, and we had people suffering in this country, African Americans in the South, for over a century more as a result.

But there was a process that resolved the dispute. The difference between 1876 and 2020 is that in 2020 there was no serious reason to contest the results. President Trump and the people who worked with him were given opportunity after opportunity to show solid evidence of massive vote fraud, and they produced none. Yet they kept this process in limbo for two months plus and deprived the man who was actually elected, President Joe Biden, of a real transition, which will hurt the country, in my view, for years, because he was cheated of the full amount of information and time he needed to prepare for the presidency.

DR: Have other losing presidential candidates claimed that their loss was due to fraud?

MB: Yes. For instance, Richard Nixon lost the 1960 election by losing the electoral votes of Texas and Illinois. He lost Texas by 45,000 votes. He lost Illinois by 9,000 votes. And after the election, he seriously thought of trying to contest it and trying to get recounts in at least those two states.

He raised this possibility with Dwight Eisenhower, who told him to shut it down, that he would not support him if he did so, it was too divisive. Eisenhower told him that "no one" steals the presidency of the United States. Yet Nixon continued to tell friends,

"The election was stolen from me. I'm the person who was elected president in November, not Kennedy." He said that in private for the rest of his life.

But in public, the first week of January, it fell to Nixon, as the vice president and as president of the Senate, to declare the winner of the 1960 election. And he gave an absolutely elegant and statesmanlike and gracious talk in Congress, saying that Kennedy and Johnson had indeed been elected, and saying that one of the great features of democracy is that we have elections that are hard-fought, and once the decision is made, we unite behind the person who was elected.

In private, Nixon was graceless. But in public he did everything he was supposed to. And at least in public, Nixon was the model of the way that a defeated candidate should behave. However, Nixon's resentment and anger for the rest of his life, believing that the Kennedys had stolen the 1960 election from him, led directly to Watergate, because when he became president, it was his view that rules don't apply and that people on the presidential level do all sorts of things that cut corners. He felt that the Kennedys had done that and that FDR had done that, and so would he. The result was a lot of the offenses that led to the Watergate scandal and ultimately caused him to be forced from office.

The year after Nixon resigned, he encouraged Victor Lasky to write a book called *It Didn't Start with Watergate*. The thesis of the book was suggested by Nixon privately, and the thesis was that presidents had been abusing power and stealing elections long before the time of Watergate and that Nixon was unfairly singled out.

DR: When Al Gore lost the election to George W. Bush in 2000, he also had to read the results when he, as vice president, was the presiding officer of the Senate. Did he go around and complain that he had really won the election?

MB: Publicly he said, "George W. Bush is my president." And in the concession statement that he made on the night of the Supreme Court decision in *Bush v. Gore* in December 2000, he said — and the language is really illuminating here, this is a verbatim quote — "For the sake of our democracy, I offer my concession." Period. What he was saying was that he might have some private doubts over who was elected in the year 2000. But for the sake of our democracy, he said he was not going to contest a decision of the Supreme Court.

DR: When Gore read the results saying that George W. Bush had won, and when Richard

Nixon read the results that said John Kennedy had won, could they have said, "I don't really accept these results"?

MB: They could have absented themselves, as Hubert Humphrey did in January 1969. Humphrey was so broken up over having lost the election that he did not want to punish himself, and he found a reason not to be there. But Nixon and Al Gore had enough respect for our democratic process that they knew, in and after an election that was close and contested, it was essential for the losing candidate, who was vice president of the United States, to concede that indeed he and his running mate had lost.

DR: Has the Supreme Court ever gotten involved in these kinds of disputes?

MB: The Supreme Court got actively involved in 2000. It did so because it felt that that was the only way of resolving the dispute over the 2000 election peacefully. The result was a hotly controversial result, along party lines on the court, that to this day is one of the most debated and controversial things the court has ever done.

But the larger message from that episode is that the court ruled. A lot of people were angry. Some Gore supporters were saying they would never acknowledge George W.

Bush as president of the United States. One of them told me at the time that if he ever saw Bush, he would "moon" him. But Bush not only became president of the United States, he was treated as a full president, not one with a question mark or an asterisk.

DR: Have there been prior elections where the losing presidential candidate urged his congressional supporters or voters to help to contest the election?

MB: Again, 1876 is a classic case — 1876 was when you had Samuel Tilden winning the popular vote. Rutherford Hayes, the Republican, lost it. Both candidates refused to accept the result, and they pushed this dispute for months. The result was that a commission was appointed and a compromise was reached.

In our system, we usually prefer not to go to that extreme, because you never know quite how the system will operate. For instance, in 1968, George Wallace, the racist third-party candidate, ran for president against Hubert Humphrey and Richard Nixon. Wallace never thought there was much likelihood that he would win the popular vote, but he hoped to collect enough electoral votes in the South to throw the election into the House of Representatives and possibly force one of the major candidates to make a deal with him along the lines of the deal that was made in 1876 to stop Reconstruction.

DR: In the 2020 election, was there any real evidence, to your knowledge, of voter fraud?

MB: Nothing serious, and nothing that goes beyond any other election in American history whose results were immediately accepted by the loser and went uncontested.

DR: Why do you think so many people believed there was fraud? Do you think the members of Congress who supported looking into it really believe there was fraud?

MB: I think what was going on was this. Donald Trump is a survivor. He understood that if he lost the presidency for a second term, he would lose all sorts of legal immunity. If that happened, and the statute of limitations had not run out, he would be vulnerable to lawsuits and indictments, possibly hundreds of them at the same time. He also might be more vulnerable to financial demands made on him by people to whom he owes loans.

It's almost like something out of a novel. Trump had the most primal, personal, selfish reason to try to hang on to the presidency.

The interesting thing about Trump in that whole 2020 campaign was how little discussion there was by him of why he wanted a second term and what he intended to do for the country, what his agenda would be. Since reelection, for Trump, was as close to being a personal matter of life or death than we have ever seen in the history of the presidency, he was determined to do everything he could to hang on. The result was that immediately after the election, he claimed that he had won, although privately I presume he knew he had actually lost.

Trump tried to contest the results in a number of states, and charged vote fraud that was not there, lying during much of this time, and putting the country through the trauma of a period that was indecisive and unpredictable. Many people feared that he would abuse his presidential powers to try to get the United States involved in an unnecessary war, or foment domestic disorder that might let him use emergency powers, including martial law, to try to delay Biden's inauguration and overturn his election.

In retrospect, those things did not happen. We know that now. But at the time, it was impossible to be sure, and it was a very frightening period for many people to live through. Not to mention that this is a very complicated government. We are the world superpower, and we need every minute of that ten-week transition period for a new president to come in and make his appointments and plan his policies. Joe Biden and the country were robbed of that.

DR: You think it's ironic that this is one election where we didn't have any voter fraud?

MB: This was one of the most effective, cleanest elections in American history.

DR: Were you surprised about how easily President Trump was able to get many of his supporters to march to the Capitol and then to invade the building?

MB: I was surprised by his success in doing it. I was not surprised that he tried. I felt that he was so motivated to try to hang on to the possibility of a second term that he would almost do anything not to relinquish the presidency. As I've mentioned, I was worried about his access to nuclear weapons. I was worried about his ability to start an unnecessary war. I was worried about emergency powers.

Notice, throughout his presidency, the number of times in public that Trump would boast of his emergency powers, saying, "I've got powers that are secret that you wouldn't believe that I can't even talk about." Almost like a small boy. That's not exactly something that would instill confidence in Americans, having a president in a period like this who was desperately trying to hang on to his job.

His plan was clearly to incite an insurrection against Congress at the Capitol. If you read his speech of January 6, there's no other way of reading it. He's saying, "I'll even march with you."

They go up to the Capitol. For some reason we do not know yet, law enforcement lets them in. They go running into the Capitol, right to the places where the Speaker of the House was and where the vice president was, just as they were counting the ballots. We don't know enough yet to know whether this was a specific plan, but there's at least the possibility that they intended to grab the mahogany boxes with the ballots in them, and to go and kill the vice president and the Speaker of the House, as many of them were chanting. There was a gallows outside the Capitol that was designated for Vice President Pence.

And had the attack happened a couple of minutes sooner, before the vice president, the Speaker of the House, and other congressional leaders could be properly protected, they might have been assassinated or taken hostage. The mahogany boxes might have been taken hostage or burned. And we would be in a situation of chaos, which under certain circumstances might have absolutely jeopardized our democracy.

Do I believe that Donald Trump planned this out and abetted it and oversaw it? At this point we don't have conclusive evidence of that. Do I believe he would have welcomed it if it had resulted in his being president again? Absolutely!

DR: In hindsight, have you thought about how vulnerable the Capitol was, in the sense that had there been a foreign military force or really well-trained U.S. former military people with real weapons, what damage they could have done and how easily they could have killed so many people?

MB: This was a terrorist attack. And what is staggering is that only nineteen years after 9/11, when the Capitol was in danger of having a plane crash into it, we came so close. The real question is going to be, did we come so close because we had a president of the United States who wanted the attack to succeed? We don't know that yet. But it doesn't look great.

DR: What do you think countries around the world thought about seeing an invasion of the Capitol?

MB: Countries around the world were horrified by this, because one of the things they had counted on is the fact that, even though America has all sorts of political conflicts, you can rely on the stability of our democratic

155

system. What this showed was a scenario that was almost like the film *Seven Days in May* [1964] or some of the other books and movies that came out in the early 1960s about plots against the government. Those were scenarios that at the time were thought to be chilling but never quite plausible. The fact that this came so close does suggest that it nearly happened and it could happen again and that those founders were right who always said, "Eternal vigilance is the price of liberty." We always have to be vigilant. Democracy is never safe. We can never take it for granted.

DR: Were you surprised that the House voted to impeach President Trump over what happened at the Capitol?

MB: I was not surprised. I was shocked that so few Republicans supported the impeachment. Before the last four years, if you had told me that a Republican president was deeply implicated in an insurrection against the government of the United States that almost led to assassination and hostage-taking and overturning of a free and fair election and possible fracturing of our democracy, I would have said that members of his own party would vote to impeach him for that.

I was wrong. I would have underestimated

the degree to which a president like Trump can terrify members of his own party into supporting him through almost anything.

DR: As you look at our American legal and political system, what is it that you think prevented President Trump from being able to prevail in his effort to overturn the election? Was it the election officials in the states, members of Congress, the judiciary? Who do you think really deserves the credit?

MB: If you're looking at the positive side, look at the months between the election and the inauguration — the number of public officials who actually did take chances to stand up for what was right, secretaries of state in various states who may have been Republican Trump supporters but said, "I don't see any evidence of fraud," and who, as a result of their political courage, got death threats against them and their families, some of them from organizations that supported Donald Trump. Election officials in various states, those members of the Senate and the House who did speak out. Same thing with governors like the governor of Arizona, who refused to take a call from the president of the United States of his own party intended to pressure him into declaring the results of the Arizona presidential election invalid. There are a lot of individual profiles in courage, but the overwhelming verdict on this story, from my point of view, is that our democracy was very vulnerable.

DR: What have we learned, and what can be done in the future to keep this kind of fraudulent claim from gaining so much steam?

MB: I think the best thing we can do is to ask Congress, the courts, a presidential commission, or perhaps all three to look at the areas of American democracy, over the last four years and especially in the period between the 2020 election and the 2021 inauguration, where the system was in danger of failing, and to pass legislation or do other things that will make sure that nothing like that can ever happen again.

That happened in 1975, as you remember, after Watergate, but it was helped by the fact that there was a large Democratic majority and that most Republicans agreed that Richard Nixon had committed crimes that would have sent him to prison had he not been pardoned. That isn't the case now.

DR: Is our democracy, our system of governing, weaker or stronger now because of what occurred?

MB: I think our system of democracy is

stronger because of what we went through. But I hope that no one will see what happened and say, "This shows that we have a perfect system, because these attacks on democracy were defeated." If 2020 had been a different kind of year, without the tragic calamity of the pandemic and the widespread economic suffering that happened largely as a result of that, there's a very good chance that Donald Trump, despite his obvious threat to democracy, would have been re-elected.

So in many ways this was a close call, and rather than saying, "The system worked and isn't everything perfect?" what we should be saying is, "We almost did not make it. We almost did not get untied from the railroad tracks. Let us see what we can do in terms of new laws, new traditions, new regulations that can make sure that if a reckless, selfish, corrupt demagogue like Donald Trump is ever elected president again, God help us, our system will be better equipped to protect itself against that."

■ ■ ■ ■

2
SUFFERING AND
SORROW

■ ■ ■ ■

"Fourscore and seven years ago our fathers brought forth on this continent a new nation, conceived in liberty and dedicated to the proposition that all men are created equal. Now we are engaged in a great civil war, testing whether that nation or any nation so conceived and so dedicated can long endure."

— Abraham Lincoln, Gettysburg Address, November 19, 1863

PHILIP J. DELORIA
ON NATIVE AMERICAN HISTORY

Leverett Saltonstall Professor of History,
Harvard University

"There has not been a treaty made between the United States and American Indians that has not been broken by the United States."

From the time the early European settlers landed in North America, they acted as if the land they occupied was theirs — in part because a European royal leader had deeded it to them. These settlers saw the Natives they encountered as temporary — if not bothersome — occupants of this deeded land.

That the Natives' ancestors had lived on this land for centuries, if not millennia, was ignored. Indeed, the original sin of slavery to which African Americans were subjected was matched by the original sin of expropriation, deceit, violence, and murder to which American Indians were subjected by the early settlers (and their descendants).

The difference to some extent was that

African Americans were unwillingly imported into the colonies and then the United States, while American Indians were peacefully occupying the lands first settled by their ancestors. Indeed, when Christopher Columbus first arrived in the Western Hemisphere, there were already perhaps tens of millions of these Indigenous people on the continent, living in civilized, healthy, and prosperous ways, in several hundred different tribes.

How did these people lose their land, their lifestyles, their culture, and the bulk of their population over the ensuing several hundred years?

That is a complicated question, but the European settlers at first, and in time their American descendants, felt entitled to the land and its resources. They believed their civilization had a superior culture, religion, language, and life purpose. That entitlement gave the colonialists the belief that they were doing God's work in creating a country where whites of European descent controlled the Indians' fate.

Indians were given essentially no rights in the country created by the Constitution. They were not citizens, and they could not integrate into the society being built on the lands that their ancestors had long occupied. And agreements entered into between Indians and the U.S. government were repeatedly and violently broken by the government over a two-century period.

The result is that the Indian population today is modest compared to what it might otherwise have been. Fewer than five million Americans are considered Native. About half of that population lives on reservations, which are areas set aside by the U.S. government for Native Americans to occupy (but not own). Sadly, reservations have not been paradises; rather, they are well known for their intense challenges, including high alcohol, drug, poverty, and suicide rates.

This may be a difficult story for many Americans to believe. But the story is true. In recent decades, scholars have done heroic work in assembling the facts about the lives of Indians in the United States, long ago and now, and they have written eloquently about these facts.

One of the leading scholars of the Indian experience in the United States has long been Philip J. Deloria of Harvard University. I interviewed him virtually on September 4, 2020, in connection with a series at the New-York Historical Society.

DAVID M. RUBENSTEIN (DR): You are a professor of Native American history at Harvard, a university that has been around for almost four hundred years. In four hundred years, there had never been a tenured professor of American Indian history at Harvard.

Was that a surprise to you?

PHILIP J. DELORIA (PD): I'm not really surprised. We measure Harvard in centuries; we measure American Indian history, as an academic pursuit, in decades. It's part of the efforts of many institutions of higher education to take seriously Native American histories — not simply as something that sits within American history per se but as valid, separate, and distinct histories of their own, which intersect with American history but are also autonomous.

Native American history has been growing for the last fifty or sixty years. In the last two or three decades it has attracted much more interest, particularly as we've made arguments for the distinctiveness of the Native American experience and its centrality to the United States.

DR: When I was in school, we were told that Christopher Columbus didn't actually get to North America. He saw a few Caribbean Natives and called them Indians because he thought he was in India.

PD: That is why we call Native people Indians, yes. He ended up in the Caribbean. He did a number of voyages. We think about his first voyage and we think about discovery. But what's really interesting is to go back

166

and consider his relationships with the Indigenous people of the Caribbean.

One of the first things he did on his first voyage was to capture several Native people and take them back to Spain. His second voyage was quite explicitly a slaving voyage. He planned to capture as many Native people as he could — which he did — and bring them back to Spain to be sold in the slave markets.

When we think about slavery in America, we tend to think about it as a story of chattel slavery, of African slavery. But slavery actually begins in the New World with Columbus and the enslavement of Indigenous peoples.

DR: How many Native Americans were on the continent of North America around the time Columbus came over?

PD: These numbers have been debated. As we know, one of the things that Europeans brought was epidemic disease, which killed off many Native people — from 70 to 90 percent of the populations in some areas. It's an interesting history for us to think about when we're contemplating our own contemporary world, so vulnerable to pandemic.

Those population numbers have ranged from as high as 100 million people for the hemisphere to something on the order of 7.5 million people in North America. Scholars derive those numbers from many different methods, thinking about the carrying capacity of land, and social organization, and these kinds of things. A reasonable consensus for the population of the Americas in 1492 is around 50–60 million people.

One of the things we can say for certain is that the number of Native people here was dramatically reduced, to the point where environmental change actually ensued — the growing of massive forests, the proliferation of certain animal species. Many people have taken this as a marker of a moment when, literally, the planet changed because of human-caused effects.

DR: As you say, some people have said there were as many as 100 million Native Americans around the time Columbus came over. That went down to maybe 10 million. Was it the diseases brought from Europe that Native Americans were not able to withstand, or the Europeans killing them?

PD: It's pretty clear that epidemic disease is the major cause. But it's been very easy for people to say, "Oh, disease! What could anyone have done about that?" There's a way in which the language of disease, and the way we teach and talk about disease, is letting some other important factors off the hook.

One of the more interesting books of the last decade has been Andrés Reséndez's *The*

Other Slavery, in which he points out that when Columbus arrived in the Caribbean, it took almost twenty-five years for smallpox to arrive. And yet the amount of indigenous death in the Caribbean was extraordinary.

One of the things Reséndez has argued — quite correctly, in my view — is that slavery and violence and genocidal killing destroyed people before disease even arrived. And when disease does arrive, what do the Spanish do? They double down on the captivity, and the killing, and the violence against Native people. Jeff Ostler has extended this argument to other times and places: colonialism is the critical context for understanding Native population declines.

DR: Native Americans were thought to have come over when there was a land bridge between Russia and what's now Alaska. Is that correct? How long ago was it that they came?

PD: This has been one of the most interesting things that's been happening in our field. For a very long time we understood that, around 13,000 years ago, people crossed over the Bering land bridge, made their way through these ice-free corridors, through the glaciers, down into North America, and then spread across both the North and South American continents. That story has now been completely confounded by various forms of new archaeological and DNA evidence.

At the Monte Verde site in Chile, Tom Dillehay has discovered evidence of inhabitation 14,500 years back. That's a whole millennium of difference! Other archaeological and DNA evidence has pointed back to 20,000 years, and perhaps even longer, as time frames for the inhabitance of North and South America.

What we'll be thinking about, in the years to come, is how much further back, how much longer were Native people here? How many more people were here? What were the various routes of immigration to the continent? These things are going to get much more complicated and more interesting.

DR: The people that came over the land bridge, some went to Latin America and developed very sophisticated cultures in the 1500s and 1600s — the Aztecs, the Mayans, the Incas. Were cultures as sophisticated developed in North America at the same time?

PD: We tend to love old cultures that build big stuff made of stone that lasts a long time and is quite monumental. Archaeologists have argued that there are six independent vectors of civilization. Two of them are in the

New World, in Mexico and Peru.

But we should not ignore other societies — those who build (as my colleague Gustavo Verdesio characterizes it) in earth and clay. When we think about North America, we should always consider Cahokia [near present-day St. Louis] and the other mound-building Mississippian cultures. We should be thinking about the Chaco culture in the Southwest. All were capable of amazing kinds of technological achievements — the building of long straight roads, of monumental architecture, enabled by hierarchical social organizations.

It's been easy to think "history" and "prehistory" and to fail to do justice to the North American continent in terms of its own long and continuous past. One of the things that's really exciting in the field right now is the ways in which we're trying to bridge those kinds of divides. Juliana Barr, for instance, has reminded us of the ways that Chacoan culture or Cahokia culture, robust and active in the centuries before Columbus arrived, continued to have consequences after Europeans showed up. That history ought to be continuous rather than discontinuous.

DR: In the latter part of the 1500s and the early part of the 1600s, when settlers from England were coming to Plymouth Rock and Jamestown, how many different tribes were there of Native Americans in North America?

PD: There were hundreds of tribes and tribelets, and multiple forms of social and political organization. We think about nation states, and we think about tribes, and we are tempted to consider early Native social organization as being analogous to the nation. But if we imagine instead very dense and detailed kin relations that spread across geographies, and that took the form of political entities — confederacies, chieftainships, theocracies, alliances — we can imagine a village world that is also elevated in political form into larger kinds of structures.

Today, the media commonly uses "tribal" in a pejorative way that is actually offensive to a lot of Native people, to reflect a kind of crude, instinctual political clannishness. *Tribe* may not be the most useful word for thinking about the ways in which Native people had organized themselves prior to Columbus. But today, the tribal nation is in fact an important and legitimate form.

DR: When European settlers are coming to North America, at that time Native Americans are not one nation. They're different tribes or different groups. Did they have a common language? Did they fight with each other, or were they basically peaceful?

PD: Like any other place in the world, there was certainly conflict among different Native people. We mentioned slavery earlier. There are many different forms of unfreedom and enslavement across the diversity of North America.

There are interesting common languages. The Plains Indians' sign language functioned as a kind of lingua franca. Native people developed those kinds of language systems in many places. They also had diplomats who were quite capable of speaking five, six, seven, eight languages. So the network of Native people, even across language barriers in North America and in the Americas, was quite strong.

DR: In the United States, the tradition is that the settlers in Plymouth had a Thanksgiving with the Indians, who brought some turkeys and other gifts. Is there any truth to that myth?

PD: There was apparently food-sharing back and forth. But we can stop there. First of all, we should recognize that it's not that the Pilgrims land and they're the first white people that Indians have ever seen. The Indian people on the Atlantic coast had been dealing with European raiders and slavers and traders for a very long time, so they knew what was happening. The Wampanoags watched them for quite a while before reaching out, and they made an alliance with the Pilgrims in order to advance their own geopolitical interests. When the Pilgrims fired off their guns for a Thanksgiving celebration, ninety Wampanoags showed up. They thought the Pilgrims were under attack and came to hold up their alliance, not to share in a feast.

In most of these Atlantic places, when Europeans come and settle, there are a few years of adjustment, and then things really do start to fall apart. We can celebrate Thanksgiving as this dream of multicultural unity, but what we have to remember is these relationships often devolved into warfare. Throughout the 1600s, basically, there's a series of wars up and down the Atlantic coast, as Native people recognize what colonizers are coming to do, which is to take their land.

DR: Did the Native Americans say, "We've been on this land for thirteen thousand years or so. What are you doing here?" Or they did start trading and say, "You can stay here if you give us something"?

PD: There's a whole range of things that happened in those encounters. Many of the land contracts, the treaties, the agreements are situations in which Native people think they're just agreeing to share the use of the land, not actually making a legal transfer of ownership in a European sense. Most of those early agreements break down on the failure to share understandings about what exactly is being negotiated. And then those things tend to turn violent.

DR: Did the effort to get Native Americans to convert to Christianity get very far?

PD: There are many places where the Christian tradition is a useful thing for Native people. My own family is a Native Christian family of clergy.

When we think about conversion, we tend to think that people have left one system of belief and moved into another system of belief, and that's really not how it played for most Native people. Most were — and are — happy to keep multiple systems of belief going at the same time.

For Native people, efficacy really was the bottom line in terms of spiritual practice. There's plenty of evidence to think that Native people looked at Christians, and looked at the process of colonization, and imagined that there was some form of efficacy around Christianity. So you tend to get syncretic kinds of religious experiences.

DR: In the 1760s the French and Indian War — often called the Seven Years' War — occurred. What was that all about?

PD: It is another instance when two European empires clash and the Native people who are allies of those two empires become central to the whole experience.

The British have a model of colonial settlement, where they bring their own colonists, and they take over land, and they expand. The French have a quite different model, which relies almost entirely upon their Native allies. When you think about the map of New France, you should imagine small groups of Frenchmen trading up and down the Great Lakes and into the Mississippi area, accompanied by Indian allies.

So you've got two different systems of alliance that take shape around a European struggle. When the British end up winning the global Seven Years' War, or the French and Indian War here in North America, they have to then deal with their Native allies and with the allies of the French who remain their enemies.

DR: After the war is over, the British, to pay for their victory, started imposing taxes on the colonial settlers. That ultimately led to the Revolutionary War. What side did Native Americans take during that war?

PD: The last of the bill of complaints in the Declaration of Independence says that the king has brought on "the merciless Indian

176

savages, whose known rule of warfare is an undistinguished destruction of all ages, sexes, and conditions." Most — but not all — Native people sided with the British. And the Americans had a bad habit of killing Indian people at random, which tended to drive away even their own allies.

DR: The Revolutionary War is won by the colonies after a number of years, and then a new government is set up under the Constitution. At the Constitutional Convention, is there any discussion of how to handle Native Americans, and what their rights might be?

PD: So many of the legal histories of the writing of the Constitution pay not much attention to Native people. Yet they appear in the commerce clause, where Congress is charged to regulate commerce between the United States and foreign nations, among the several states, and with the American Indian tribes.

They also show up in the three-fifths clause, where we're told that the census for determining representation in Congress will take the shape of a math problem: to the "whole number of free citizens" add indentured servants. Then subtract "Indians not taxed." Then add "three-fifths of all other persons."

What does that mean, "Indians not taxed"? It suggests the ways in which Indians were, in fact, part of those discussions. If you can imagine an Indian not taxed, you can imagine an Indian who *was* taxed. That person presumably would have given up his or her citizenship in their tribal nation, and gone through a naturalization process to become an American citizen.

That tells you that Indians are put into the Constitution in order to exclude them. They're excluded because they are seen to be political entities in and of their own right. This is why treaties end up being the most important political relationship between American Indians and the United States.

DR: What about intermarriage and relationships between the Indians and the settlers? Were there a lot of relationships that led to children who were part Indian and part European? How were they treated?

PD: This is one of these things that we see much more in New France. My family, the Deloria family, was a mixed family of French men and Indian women. What you tend to see in the British colonies, particularly among those Native people who stayed behind, is intermarriage between Native people and African-descended people.

DR: The most famous Native American in the colonial era was Pocahontas. Who was Pocahontas, and did she really exist?

PD: Pocahontas did exist. She was a much younger girl than we imagine her being. She was likely caught up in diplomatic rituals and ceremonies involving her people and her parents. She did marry an Englishman, John Rolfe, who took her back to England, where she died.

Her cultural meaning has taken on so much more weight than the actual historical personage that she was. This is because there is this thing that happens with colonizing. You can see it in the dynamic of the Revolution. The colonizers, when they land in North America, they look back over their shoulder at Great Britain and they say, "We're not like them, we're new people. We're in this new land." At the same time they look west, out at Indian country, and they say, "We're not them either. We are civilized British people."

So you have figures like Pocahontas, Sacagawea [who accompanied the explorers Lewis and Clark], and La Malinche [an interpreter for the conquistador Hernan Cortés], who end up being critically important Indian women who figure in the cultural mythologies that sustain these kinds of settler societies. They allow settlers to claim a kind of authenticity or connection to the land through a metaphorical marriage.

DR: In the early 1800s, Thomas Jefferson is president. He completes the Louisiana Pur-

179

chase, which more than doubles the size of the country. Did he actually get permission from anybody in the Native American community to buy that land?

PD: This is a very familiar kind of story, right? European empires navigate and negotiate their own understandings of who owns what territory, and they never think that they actually don't own that territory at all.

This happens after the Revolution, and it certainly happens with the Louisiana Purchase. What it means is that the United States has to go out into this territory, which it now claims relative to other European nations, and figure out what's going to happen with the Native people who are actually there, who very much own the land and are quite willing and ready to defend it.

DR: The first president of the United States who was seen as a westerner and not part of the "establishment" was Andrew Jackson. He was widely seen as being very anti-Indian, and in fact drove a lot of the Indians out of the East Coast. Is that a fair characterization of his perspective?

PD: It is. Andrew Jackson is part of a much longer trajectory of the idea of removing Indian people from the eastern part of the United States, exchanging their land, and getting them to go west of the Mississippi.

Jefferson starts thinking about this in the late eighteenth century. But Jackson is the person who brings it to fruition through the Indian Removal Act of 1830; through military campaigns to move southern Indians and also midwestern Indians from their home territories to the west of the Mississippi River; and, by clearing these massive amounts of land, allowing American settlement but also, importantly, allowing the formation of American states.

The Northwest Ordinance sets out the terms through which a colony will become a state — sixty thousand free people. What that means is if you're a territory and you want to become a state, you need to get your Indian people out of there so that you can bring in more settlers. What that leads to is either removal — making them leave the state — or moving them onto reservation territories where they're contained and compressed.

DR: As the U.S. is expanding under what some people would call manifest destiny, we're moving across the continent, we're building a transcontinental railroad, we're looking for gold, we're looking for new places for cattle to graze. We're looking for new cities to build, more places where religion could be exercised the way people wanted to do it, such as the Mormons.

181

Very often you see this on television westerns when you're growing up — at least when I was growing up: the nice eastern settlers are moving west and all of a sudden they're being raided by Indians coming in with tomahawks. What was the real story?

PD: It's pretty much the other way around. These are Indigenous people who are in their home territories, and they look up and all of a sudden they're seeing a huge wagon train full of immigrants coming through their territory. They ride down and they say, "If you're going to cross our land, we're going to charge you a toll." Of course the settlers don't want to be charged a fee, and you get conflicts.

The story that we haven't really told is the story of what happens in the West during the Civil War. The Civil War is such an important watershed in American history, and it leads us to think about things only in terms of the North and the South.

But if we think about what happened in the West during the Civil War — the Minnesota uprising, and the resulting military campaigns across the Dakotas; the Navajo Long Walk, in which Navajo people were basically removed from their land and marched over to New Mexico; the Bear River Massacre [in present-day Idaho], in which three hundred people were killed by militia; the Sand Creek Massacre [in Colorado Territory] — there's so much violence that is militia-based and also state military–based that happens in the 1860s. This leads to a large number of clearances of Native people, and sets the stage for a really short burst in the 1870s and '80s where the United States Army comes in and basically mops up the rest of the West.

DR: When I was growing up and watching TV and movie westerns, the good guys were the settlers and the U.S. Army. Did the scriptwriters not know what the reality was?

PD: I think they just thought it was a better story. It plays into a whole set of American myths, which go all the way back to the founding colonies, of the frontier wilderness, of struggle with Indians, and that struggle making Americans into Americans. These are dueling notions, but they're all interlocked. The mythic potential of these stories is just so strong.

DR: During the 1860s, '70s, and '80s, a lot of treaties were entered into between the U.S. government, or states and territories, and local tribes or Indian groups. Who broke those treaties, typically?

PD: There has not been a treaty made between the United States and American Indians that has not been broken by the United States. Let's just be up-front about that. Sure, some of these things are complicated. There are moments when it's hard for Native people to restrain their young men, it's hard for Americans to restrain their young men. Next thing you know, you're in a fight and the treaty starts to fall apart.

But Americans have had a cynical view of their own treaties for a very long time. One of the things Jefferson says to William Henry Harrison goes something like this: "We can't let the Indians think about the future in the way that we're thinking about it. Make sure they're living in the present, so when we negotiate a treaty it feels like it's going to hold water, when we know that in fact over time it's not."

DR: Custer's Last Stand is a very famous thing in American mythology — that [General George Armstrong] Custer was there to protect the rights of the United States, and he was slaughtered by Indians. What was the reality in the situation there?

PD: Custer just goes looking for a fight. There's a series of fights between Lakota, Sioux people, and the American government — Red Cloud's War — that results in the Treaty of 1868, in which Lakota territory is codified. It's a quite extensive portion of land, and it includes the Black Hills [in the Dakota Territory]. In 1874, Custer leads an expedition into the Black Hills. They discover gold and, before you know it, there's a huge land rush.

The army refuses to enforce the 1868 Treaty, which would have required moving white settlers out of Indian land. In January of 1876, the government says, "Any Indian who's not at their agency is considered a hostile." This has nothing to do with the treaty. There's no reason why the United States should be able to make that kind of claim on Native people. That's just the pretext for a war. The military goes out. Custer wants the glory for himself. He rides ahead and attacks the largest Indian village ever assembled on the Great Plains, to his peril.

DR: What happened at Wounded Knee?

PD: In 1877, the government wages a winter campaign, which basically breaks Lakota resistance. Sitting Bull flees to Canada, Crazy Horse is killed. Then things settle down, and people are forced onto reservations.

Native people on reservations end up becoming dependent upon the United States — the bison fail, Indians are confined, and the government has promised rations, which it used to force Native compliance. The

United States is a trustee — it takes on those obligations through treaties — but it fails to uphold its end of the bargain. So Native people are starving in 1889, 1890.

They begin, on the Lakota reservations, doing a thing called the Ghost Dance. It actually comes from a prophet in Nevada named Wovoka. This is a dance of desperation. It's not a violent dance. But the agents who were there completely lose their minds about this. "The Indians are uprising!"

These are demoralized people, not particularly dangerous — but the agents call in the military. And what you have is the largest military mobilization since the Civil War. Trainloads of troops are coming in.

There is an attempt to disarm a Lakota band that has come down from Standing Rock and Cheyenne River Reservation to the Pine Ridge Reservation, and it goes awry. The army opens up with these Hotchkiss mountain cannons, which are horrific, powerful weapons. It's Custer's Seventh Cavalry basically taking revenge for the Battle of the Little Bighorn.

DR: How many Native Americans were killed at Wounded Knee?

PD: It's hard to know the exact number, but we think over three hundred people. People were chased for miles across the prairie.

These soldiers were giving no quarter. They killed women and children as often as they could. The stories that come out of Wounded Knee are just horrific.

DR: At some point the U.S. government says, "We're going to take the Indians who are left and give them some territory." Did the United States actually honor some of these commitments?

PD: It's useful to make the distinction: Was this land *given* them as a place to go and settle and be safe? There's a dimension to that when we talk about removal to Indian Territory, or what's now Oklahoma.

In most of these treaties, though, the land is *retained* rather than given. In other words, Native sovereignty on those reservations is continuous from before the United States until after the United States, and continues to be sovereign today. This is the reservation system. It goes all the way back to the late eighteenth century. It's really codified in the 1850s and developed in the post–Civil War period.

DR: How many Native Americans would you say there are in the United States today?

PD: It depends on how you count, but Native Americans make up something like 1.7

percent of the American population. And it is a growing population. Native American numbers bottomed out in the 1900 census, when there were about 250,000 Native people who showed up in the census. We're talking several millions today.

DR: What percentage of them are living on reservations, and how many reservations are there?

PD: There are 326 Indian land areas, with a range of names, that are administered as reservations. There are 574 federally recognized tribes at this point in time. But most Native people actually don't live on reservations.

In the 1950s, the United States started policies like Termination and Relocation, which brought many Native people into cities. Native people had been moving to cities and moving around for a very long time as well. People have connections to reservation home territories, and to urban, or suburban, or small-town kinds of places. There are a lot of connective webs across that geography.

The bottom line is that Indian people's unique political status, their self-determined management of sovereign Native lands, their resurgent demography and culture, and their control over significant natural resources means that Indian people are critical to the past and present of the United States. Native peoples make up 1.7 percent of the population, but Americans don't often give Indians even 1.7 percent of their attention. That ought to change, and the sooner the better.

Drew Gilpin Faust
on Death and the Civil War

Arthur Kingsley Porter University Professor of History, Harvard University; President Emerita, Harvard University

"We feel so strongly now that we are responsible for those who die in the nation's service. . . . This attitude is one that would have seemed very alien in 1858. It was really the Civil War that changed that attitude."

At the outset of the Civil War, many in the North thought the war might be over quite quickly, given its greater wealth, population, and military strength. Indeed, in the first battle of the war, Bull Run in Virginia, a number of northern civilians went to watch what they thought would be a festive quick victory for the Union troops. But the Confederate troops prevailed handily, presaging not a quick win for the Union but rather an epic four-year struggle (which could well at times have been won by the Confederacy).

190

That the war lasted so long obviously contributed to an enormous, unprecedented number of deaths. The war's length was not the only reason for the deaths of more than three-quarters of a million soldiers. Two other factors were also present. The traditional warfare tactics of straight-on soldier charges were now conducted with far more lethal weaponry than during the Revolutionary War; and medical treatments and capabilities were generally not helpful in later saving those injured severely on the battlefield.

In *This Republic of Suffering,* Drew Gilpin Faust, an eminent antebellum and Civil War scholar and former president of Harvard, addresses the relatively novel challenges during the Civil War of identifying the dead; burying them on the battlefield; reburying them in appropriate cemeteries when possible; and separating the Confederate and Union soldiers, who were never to be buried in the same cemeteries. During this interview, which took place on June 12, 2019, at the Library of Congress as part of the Congressional Dialogues series, Drew discussed the challenges that Union and Confederate soldiers and their families faced in dealing with the absolutely unprecedented levels of death during the Civil War.

There is no doubt that Drew's book makes one think much more about death and the manner in which it is handled — now or at any time. Her focus was on the Civil War, but similar issues have arisen in subsequent wars, though more modern medical relief and transportation methods have ameliorated some of the Civil War issues.

Dealing with large-scale death in the U.S. has occurred twice since the Civil War: during the Great Influenza of 1918–19 and during the COVID-19 pandemic. In both cases, though spaced by a century, the U.S. healthcare system, far more modern than it was in the 1860s, has struggled to deal with the human toll. One can only imagine how the citizens of the North and South struggled during the Civil War.

DAVID M. RUBENSTEIN (DR): In the Civil War, how many Americans were killed?

DREW GILPIN FAUST (DGF): There's been research since my book came out that indicates a higher death toll than the one I suggested in 2008. I talk about 620,000 dead. The number that now is agreed upon by epidemiologists and analysts and demographers is more like 750,000.

So it was about 2.5 percent of the population. That would be the equivalent of some seven million people today. Imagine if we had a war in which we had that kind of death toll.

DR: The Civil War lasted for four years. Why

were so many people killed in that war, while in the Revolutionary War, which lasted a lot longer, there were something like 6,800 American casualties?

DGF: There are a couple of explanations. One is that the Civil War was a war of mass armies. This was a war in which probably close to three million people served in military roles. So there were more people to kill.

That was part of it, but it was also the beginning of the era of industrialized warfare where artillery took on a really major role and where the range of firepower was much greater. All of those reasons contributed to an increase in the number of deaths.

DR: As many as 750,000 soldiers were killed. What about civilians?

DGF: We probably will never get an accurate number, but the impact on civilian populations was severe — the spread of disease, for example; the impact of deprivation, especially in the South; starvation, inadequate food; the effects of moving families around and what that did to mortality and morbidity. About two-thirds died from disease.

DR: In those days, we didn't understand germ theory. Your book points out that some doctors would operate for two days at a time but never washed their hands.

DGF: That, of course, spread gangrene and other kinds of infections.

DR: In the first battle, Bull Run, people thought the war would be over very quickly. People came out to watch it as an entertainment. How many were killed there, and when did people realize this was not entertainment?

DGF: If you look at the number of people killed at Bull Run/First Manassas, it's very small, actually. The death toll increases dramatically during the war. The Battle of Shiloh [in Tennessee], for example, was a shock, because it was multiple times the number of deaths of First Manassas.

DR: In the Revolutionary War, if an American soldier was shot and killed or wounded, there was time to take him off the battlefield and take him somewhere else. But there were so many people being killed during the Civil War that bodies would just lie there while the other soldiers went somewhere else. Is that what happened? A lot of soldiers were just left on the ground?

DGF: The scale of the Civil War was something that neither army was ready for and neither side anticipated, so the requirements for medical care were inadequate. For example, there wasn't a regular ambulance service, even in the Union Army, which tended to be better organized and better equipped, until the very last months of the war.

There was no provision for how to handle the dead, no grave registration services, no process of notification of families. It was all on a very informal basis until, toward the end of the war, there were the beginnings of what we might consider modern ways of identifying the dead and providing for them.

There were no dog tags. Soldiers did not carry any formal kind of identification. So, if there was a body on the field, you might find something on that body, an envelope with an address or a Bible with the name or some indication of who that person was, but that wasn't required. It was simply the decision of that individual. Increasingly during the war, soldiers carried things that they knew could identify them and ensure that their loved ones would be informed.

DR: In those days, how you died was considered very important. It was generally the norm, before the war, that 85 percent of people died in their homes. You died surrounded by your relatives, and you said, "Yes, I believe in God, and I believe in the afterlife." So there was a right way to die. Can you describe that more?

DGF: There was a concept of a good death, and a good death was good for several reasons. It involved your family. They knew that you died peacefully, but they also knew that you died with the appropriate expressions of fidelity to God, so they could believe they would be reunited with you in an afterlife. This is an overwhelmingly Christian concept. It was an overwhelmingly Christian nation.

The notion that someone would die who was not ready to meet his maker, had not shown that he was a believer, that was terrifying to families, because they thought that was obliteration. That person would never be reunited in another life with the beloved members of his family.

DR: What people would do, as you point out in your book, is if somebody died from a gunshot wound, soldiers who survived might tell their families that these people died praying to God, or that they died peacefully.

DGF: That's right. Walt Whitman [then a Civil War nurse] wrote a number of letters to families describing the deaths of their loved ones as he had sat by them in hospitals, and those letters are almost formulaic. They go through the elements of the good death, reassuring the family that the individual he witnessed dying had indeed done all the things that should console their families about their future.

DR: Throughout history, humans have thought that bodies are important. What did Civil War survivors do to make sure that their loved ones had an appropriate burial?

DGF: Burial on Civil War battlefields was an exercise in improvisation. There were no regular burial troops. Usually some unit was designated to do the burials. Often it was the unit that had not participated in the battle. Sometimes it would be an enemy unit, captives, who would be told, "You have to bury the dead."

Sometimes there were no shovels, no implements to do this work. And there were bodies that couldn't be identified, especially enemy soldiers, those who had lost the battle. The winners of the battle usually held the field, but the bodies of the losers had to be disposed of too. So they'd be buried in gigantic pits — just thrown into pits.

It was customary to bury your own dead in individual graves, to try to find some kind of identifying feature that you might write down. You might put a little marker on the grave. You might send something to a family member if you could get an address. You might find a bottle and put something in the

197

bottle and bury it with the dead person, so that when that individual was exhumed, there would be an identifying characteristic with them. But soldiers would also often have kind of makeshift funeral services or observances over the dead, readings from the Bible.

DR: Families who either could afford to, or were inclined to, would try to get their loved ones' bodies back for more appropriate burial. Did they go to the battlefield themselves? Did they send people? Were there services they could hire?

DGF: All of the above. Families tended to swarm to battlefields. There's a very famous story of Oliver Wendell Holmes Sr. rushing to the battlefield of Antietam [in Maryland] where he heard his son Oliver Wendell Holmes Jr., the future Supreme Court justice, had been injured. He goes down on a train from Boston, and all around him are families of individuals who have been reported as wounded or killed. People rushed to Antietam and rushed around the battlefield trying to get news of where their loved one might be, trying to engage a shipping company — families had to have means to do this, of course — to transport their loved one back to their hometown, and to find some kind of news that would enable them to come to a firm understanding of what had happened to their son or brother.

DR: Did embalmers say, "Hire me and I'll go embalm your loved one"?

DGF: It was a thriving business. A lot of embalmers had offices here in Washington, and they would say, "We'll go out to the Virginia battlefields and find your loved one and embalm them and they'll be safely shipped home." A lot of these people were a little crooked, and would sometimes claim they'd found bodies when they hadn't, or extort money from families. It was such a thriving business that General Ulysses Grant, at one point, was so infuriated, he banned all embalmers from his lines, because he felt they were exploiting families.

DR: If you were a Confederate soldier and you killed a Union soldier, would you just walk away?

DGF: Probably, if you killed that soldier, it was in the heat of battle, and you would be far away by the time the battle was over. If the Confederates, for example, held the ground, and it was covered with dead Union soldiers, it would be the responsibility of the commander of the Confederate unit to say, "How are we going to handle the dead?"

DR: Let's suppose you were an officer. Do you get treated differently when you're dead than if you're an enlisted person?

DGF: Absolutely. Why was that? Partly because your death would be more notable to those in your company. They would make a bigger effort to notify your family. But also it would be likely your family would either come or send someone or send money to have your body shipped home.

DR: The Union had roughly two hundred thousand African Americans who were fighting for the North after the Emancipation Proclamation. If those African American soldiers were in combat with a Confederate group and the Confederates killed them, did they give them a decent burial?

DGF: Often the Black dead were dishonored by the Confederates. There are examples of African American soldiers being left on the battlefield for extremely long periods of time to essentially disintegrate. There was a real degradation of African American soldiers by Confederates.

DR: When the war started, were there any government cemeteries where soldiers who had died could be buried?

DGF: The national cemetery system really emerges from the Civil War experience. What happens in the course of the war is a recognition that this notion of improvisation about the dead, a neglect of responsibility on the part of the government, simply cannot persist in a nation that is resting on the soldiers of the common people and on an ideal of democracy.

So there's an enormous shift in sentiment, even in four short years. As you know, Lincoln gave his Gettysburg Address next to piles of coffins that were being interred in a national cemetery that had been created there.

By the end of the war, there is a movement for reburial of the Union dead. Troops who are still serving from the war fan out across the South and locate more than three hundred thousand Union bodies and reinter them in seventy-four national cemeteries that are the creation of the Civil War. When we think about the national cemeteries that we know so well and often go to on Memorial Day, those really are the product of this changed attitude of the Civil War, where the government says, "It is our responsibility to care for those who lost their lives in our service."

DR: After the war was over, there were more national cemeteries set up. Would Confederate soldiers be allowed to be buried in the North?

DGF: Confederate soldiers were not buried in those cemeteries, and this excursion into the South to identify bodies was one that sought out only Union bodies. There are examples of the people looking for the Union dead and taking a Union body while leaving the skeleton of a Confederate soldier untreated and unburied.

It was hugely resented in the South, and it led to organizations led by southern women to identify the Confederate dead, to go out from Richmond and other sites where there had been extensive fighting, and to do, essentially, what the northern government did, but in a private way through these women's organizations. If you think of something like Hollywood Cemetery in Richmond, tens of thousands of southern dead were brought there. I think there are thirty-eight thousand Confederate soldiers in a cemetery in Petersburg, Virginia. That was the result of these organizations of southern women.

DR: How many soldiers were killed at Gettysburg during those three days of combat in July 1863?

DGF: It was about seven thousand.

DR: When President Lincoln spoke there in November, were all those bodies buried?

DGF: No, a lot of them still were piled up.

DR: You talk in the book about how the sixth commandment says we're not supposed to kill people. How did these very religious people in the South and in the North get used to the idea "I'm going to kill people"?

DGF: That was a question that interested me a lot. How do you train people to think that killing is okay? There was a lot of resistance to it, religious resistance, that then was mitigated by a sense that there were religious reasons to advance the cause of whichever side the individual was on. So God would permit it.

But then there was, sometimes, a reluctance to actually pull the trigger or to do whatever act it took to kill someone else. And so we see people who didn't fire their guns right or fired them in all directions.

DR: When the war was over and efforts were made to figure out who died and where they died, how many of the dead were actually identified?

DGF: Slightly less than half were identified, ultimately. There are huge numbers of unknown soldiers.

DR: The hospitals in which these soldiers were put — were they very sanitary? Were the surgeons that good?

DGF: We need to understand that medicine in the mid-nineteenth century was so far from what we understand or expect of medicine today. As you mentioned earlier, the germ theory of disease was not even understood. It was very hard to treat wounds without contaminating them with infection. It was not a pleasant thing to be in a Civil War hospital.

DR: Were soldiers afraid that they would be put with the dead and buried when they were still alive? Was that a problem?

DGF: That was something many soldiers were quite scared about, and there were stories about piles of bodies where someone started making a noise in the middle and was saved.

DR: Is that why they put bells in the coffins, so you could ring them?

DGF: That was a nineteenth-century practice that extended beyond the war.

DR: How did Arlington National Cemetery

come about? Were Union soldiers buried there as a way to punish Robert E. Lee?

DGF: Montgomery Meigs, the quartermaster general of the United States, was responsible for, among other things, burials and bodies. His son was, in his view, murdered by Confederate troops after he had already surrendered, so Montgomery Meigs was extremely bitter about the South. Part of the reason, I think, that southerners were not even considered for inclusion in the national cemetery system is that he would hear none of it. He also was the leading voice in saying, "Let's put a graveyard on the property of Robert E. Lee."

DR: As part of what we learned from that war, in future wars what did the U.S. government do? Did it require dog tags?

DGF: There's been a revolution, first in attitude. We feel so strongly now that we are responsible for those who die in the nation's service. We also feel so strongly, and I think comrades feel so strongly, about people serving with them that their bodies must be recovered, must be brought home.

This attitude is one that would have seemed very alien in 1858. It was really the Civil War that changed that attitude, and that then led to policies: dog tags or other identification is required so that an individual can be repatriated or the family can be informed. Then processes were put in place to inform families about the state of their loved ones and what happened to them. Also as much information as possible was developed about how soldiers led their last moments of life and how they died.

Grave registration units and the various bureaucracies that surround them were important too. It was often not even contemplated, except informally by a chaplain or by someone in a company or another military unit, to write down who had been killed. That kind of information wasn't typically available.

Now, of course, this is all routine.

DR: If you were an African American soldier fighting for the Union, could you be buried in a regular Union cemetery?

DGF: What you see in the early national cemeteries is segregation of Blacks and whites in those settings.

DR: The lesson you took away from your research is that we weren't really prepared for the enormous carnage, and therefore we allowed people to die without appropriate burials in many cases?

DGF: Certainly that was one lesson I took

away from it. In some ways, it's gruesome.

But for me, doing the research was inspiring, as I saw people struggling with such difficult circumstances and inventing ways to be human amid a context of inhumanity. Even within the impossible world that Civil War battles involved, you could do things to retain the important values that defined you as something more than simply an animal. Soldiers will say, "We can't throw these comrades in the ground like chickens. We need to do more than that." Seeing the human spirit triumph even under those kinds of conditions was very moving for me.

KEN BURNS
ON THE VIETNAM WAR

Documentary Filmmaker

"I've been drawn to stories that reveal us to ourselves. Who are we? Who are these strange and complicated people who like to call themselves Americans?"

America's successes in the Revolutionary War, the Spanish-American War, and World Wars I and II provided most Americans by the 1960s with a certain sense of power, if not omnipotence — i.e., "We've never lost a war." The War of 1812, despite the British destruction of the federal buildings in Washington, D.C., and the Korean War — where an armistice produced nothing close to a victory — were not seen, somehow, in the American psyche as "losses."

So when engagement in Vietnam began in the late 1950s, a series of U.S. presidents committed U.S. forces there for a variety of geopolitical reasons, including a desire to keep America from losing a war — even though it was widely recognized in the senior levels of the Johnson and Nixon administrations that the war could not be "won" in any military sense. This is made quite clear in the epic documentary on the war by Ken Burns (codirected with Lynn Novick).

Ken first came to widespread national attention and acclaim with his Emmy Award–winning PBS series *The Civil War* in 1990. That film, which took more than five years to finish, attracted PBS's largest audience ever, and showed the public a film style that has become synonymous with Ken Burns: frequent use of historic still photos, revelation of heretofore largely unknown facts or vignettes, lyrical and era music background, voice-overs by well-known individuals, and interviews with prominent individuals telling personal anecdotes.

The focus of this interview, which took place on November 28, 2017, at the Library of Congress as part of the Congressional Dialogues series, was another multi-evening series that Ken produced over a ten-year period and that PBS aired in 2017 — *The Vietnam War.* In the interview, he makes at least two critical observations: First, the U.S. government, during both Democratic and Republican administrations, throughout a war that resulted in more than 58,000 American soldiers dying, knew such a war could not really be won militarily; and, second, these administrations saw the war as really a domestic political undertaking rather than a military or strategic geopolitical undertaking. This is obviously disheartening for those who, like me, lived through this era, with all of its upheaval, turmoil, dislocation, and the deaths of friends and colleagues.

The debate and unrest over the wisdom or folly of the Vietnam War occurred almost continuously from the mid-1960s through the war's end in 1975. Those who did not live through that time cannot really imagine how divided American society became over the war. In some respects, it foreshadowed the divisiveness of American society in the following decades.

Today, nearly a half century later, it is difficult to find many Americans who feel the war was worth the human, financial, political, or military effort expended on trying to "win" it. It will be even harder to find such Americans after they have viewed *The Vietnam War* or listened to Ken talk about the film.

DAVID M. RUBENSTEIN (DR): What made you think the timing was right to do Vietnam? It's been a very controversial subject.

KEN BURNS (KB): I've never really considered timing in the choice of it. I've been drawn to stories that reveal us to ourselves.

210

Who are we? Who are these strange and complicated people who like to call themselves Americans? What does an investigation of that moment tell us about not only where we were, but where we are and, most importantly, where we may be going?

In late 2006, I was finishing up our World War II film. I turned to Lynn Novick, my codirector on that, and I said, "We have to do Vietnam."

A good deal of the cultural, political, social, sexual wars that we find ourselves afflicted with today seem to me to have their seeds in Vietnam. So Vietnam explains a lot about who we were, not only then but now.

DR: Did you have trouble getting Americans and Vietnamese to talk about the war?

KB: It was surprisingly easy. There were, of course, people who said, "I don't want to talk about it." I wish they had. They probably would have made the film better.

But we had a critical mass of Americans, more than fifty, of every possible stripe — from people who protested the war to people who were valiantly climbing up mountains in Vietnam and sacrificing, often, limb and almost life. And then people who came back from doing that and protested the war, and people who changed in every way.

We felt it was necessary to go deep into the

211

war's meaning; for too long Americans have not talked about Vietnam and, when we have, we've abstracted it. One of the ways we've abstracted it is by only talking about ourselves.

DR: What was the biggest surprise you uncovered in the research you did?

KB: The surprise of my own arrogance. I thought, having lived through the period, growing up in a college town where Vietnam was on everyone's minds and lips all the time, that I knew something about it. I learned that I knew nothing about it, nothing about it. Making the film was a process of unlearning — and a daily humiliation.

DR: If there is one message you would want to convey to the American people about Vietnam, what would you like them to take away?

KB: It's complicated. That's the message. When you're a filmmaker, when things are neat and the scene is working, the last thing you want to do is open it up and perhaps make it less "interesting." *Time* magazine had a famous internal joke, "That's a fact too good to check," meaning the story is just too good.

Wynton Marsalis, in our *Jazz* series, said something to me that has stuck with me forever. He said, "Sometimes a thing and the opposite of a thing can be true at the same time."

DR: Vietnam was controlled in the early '50s by the French. Then they lost control in 1954?

KB: They lost an epic battle at Dien Bien Phu in 1954. They'd been there since 1858.

DR: Did President Eisenhower ever think of sending American troops in to help the French?

KB: Very much so, as did President Truman. Charles de Gaulle had threatened that unless we supported the restoration of France's colonies in the post–World War II environment, he might be forced to go into the Soviet orbit. The American people had no idea about that.

DR: After Dien Bien Phu, did Eisenhower consider sending American troops in?

KB: Yes. And he, fairly wisely, didn't. He upped the number of what we called, euphemistically, "military advisors" there. He had inherited, I think, three dozen. By the time he left office, there were seven hundred.

But he was one of those promoting the

falling-domino principle, the idea that if you lost Vietnam, then you would lose Laos and Cambodia and Malaysia and Thailand and Burma and Indonesia.

DR: When President Kennedy came into office, there were roughly seven hundred American advisors there. What was his decision — to support the Vietnamese government?

KB: Kennedy saw things in the same sort of light. We're all being guided by George Kennan's notion of containment and that, in a nuclear world, one doesn't want to fight World War III. You want to fight a "limited war," as Kennedy called it, a "proxy war," as others were calling it.

And so he was gradually escalating the number of advisors. What we discovered from the printed record and from the audio records of Johnson and Nixon is that every single president involved, including Gerald Ford, presidents of both parties, made decisions with regard to national security and Vietnam and foreign policy based on domestic political considerations, i.e., "Will I get reelected?"

Kennedy had been humiliated at the Bay of Pigs in Cuba. He'd been humiliated by [Nikita] Khrushchev in Vienna. He had not been able to stop the Soviets from building the Berlin Wall. Eisenhower had asked him to intervene in an anticommunist insurgency in Laos and he'd refused. He said, "We have to draw the line in Vietnam or I do not stand a chance of being reelected."

DR: So he appointed Henry Cabot Lodge Jr. to be his ambassador there. Lodge was the person that Kennedy had defeated in the 1952 Senate election. There was a government run by President Ngo Dinh Diem. Did Kennedy support him?

KB: He had been our boy. The Geneva Accords that followed the peace talks after the battle of Dien Bien Phu divided Vietnam in half and agreed that there would be elections in two years. Everyone in the South and everyone in the North knew that Ho Chi Minh would be elected.

He had declared Vietnamese independence on September 2, 1945. When the Japanese were formally surrendering on the USS *Missouri,* he quoted Thomas Jefferson: "We hold these truths to be self-evident. . . ."

Eisenhower supported Ngo Dinh Diem, and Kennedy supported him until the chaos in South Vietnam became so great that the State Department and many factions within the government became undecided about Diem. When Kennedy was away from Washington, an undersecretary at the State Department, Roger Hillsman, drafted a cable that basically supported a nascent coup. Kennedy gave tacit approval to it while on vacation at Hyannis Port [in Massachusetts]. Other members of his administration signed on when they learned the president had.

DR: Kennedy didn't anticipate that Diem would be assassinated?

KB: Diem and his brother Nhu, who was a shadowy, strange, very dangerous man, took sanctuary in a church and surrendered, and were given assurances that they were going to get safe passage out of Vietnam. They were shot by the members of the coup.

Kennedy records this incredibly rueful Dictaphone entry in which he says, "I take full responsibility for the decision to go with the coup." He was very upset with the brutality with which Diem and his brother Nhu had been dispatched.

DR: Many people who supported President Kennedy have said that had he lived, he intended after reelection in '64 to pull all the American troops out of Vietnam. Is there any evidence for that?

KB: I'm in the business of what happened. Speculation's really fun: What if the Confederacy had won? What if the Germans had won? That's the province of fiction, and perhaps the fantasies of people.

What happened was that, when Kennedy was assassinated, less than three weeks after the coup, there were now eighteen thousand American advisors in Vietnam. His successor, Lyndon Baines Johnson, had an ambitious domestic agenda. He kept every single one of Kennedy's foreign policy hierarchy. And they, along with Johnson, plowed further into Vietnam.

DR: As you noted, when Johnson came into office, there were roughly eighteen thousand Americans there. When did he begin to increase dramatically the number of soldiers?

KB: He felt he could not act with any confidence until he had been elected in his own right. Barry Goldwater, who would be his opponent, was criticizing him for not being very clear-cut.

The Gulf of Tonkin event happens in the summer of '64. Johnson is decisive in his response. His already overwhelming poll numbers increase more. It took away one of the main arguments that Goldwater had.

Johnson had a landslide victory that fall, and by March of '65, he put boots on the ground. But he confided to Senator Richard Russell, his good friend, "I don't see any daylight here." Time and again we find, with all of the presidents from Truman on, that they and their closest associates know some hard and difficult truths, but they act as if the opposite is true.

DR: How many troops did Johnson authorize?

KB: Eventually we reach a peak of more than 540,000 ground troops in Vietnam.

DR: The antiwar movement grew, and ultimately in 1968 Johnson decided not to seek reelection. He tried to get a peace agreement, or at least a truce. What kept that from happening?

KB: There are a lot of reasons. In some ways, the Vietnam War had starved his ambitious domestic agenda, which had been hugely successful, second only to FDR's in terms of a successful legislative agenda that transformed American society. But then you had the Tet Offensive of 1968, which had been a terrible defeat for North Vietnam and the Viet Cong.

DR: Explain the Tet Offensive.

KB: The Tet is the Lunar New Year celebration, kind of like a New Year's Day celebration. There was a truce in the country, as there usually was. But for many, many months, Le Duan, the man who was actually running North Vietnam, had been building up troops to attack the major cities, the provincial capitals, and dozens and dozens of bases — more than 150 places simultaneously.

It was called the General Uprising and General Offensive. They presumed erroneously that the army of South Vietnam would collapse. It did not. They presumed that the people, weary of the corrupt South Vietnamese government, would rise up. They did not. And that their revolution would be triumphant. It wasn't. At least then. . . .

They were defeated within twenty-six days in every single one of the places they attacked, usually within a few hours, a couple of days, with the horrific exception of Hue.

DR: If the Tet Offensive militarily worked so well for SouthVietnam, why was it a public relations disaster?

KB: The U.S. government had been painting a rosier-than-accurate scenario for the American people, that there was light at the end of the tunnel. There clearly was not.

Americans saw images of the assassination of a North Vietnamese spy named Nguyen Van Lem by the head of the South Vietnamese police on the streets of Saigon. The war came into our living rooms with the Tet Offensive — not instantaneously, not live, but it was a huge public relations disaster.

219

Walter Cronkite came back and said, in essence, victory in a military sense is not possible.

Johnson didn't do well in the New Hampshire primary. Upstart Eugene McCarthy from Minnesota had gotten 40 percent of the vote when he had expected to poll far worse.

DR: I skipped over something very important — the Gulf of Tonkin Resolution. What was that, and why were we misled?

KB: A resolution giving the president far-ranging latitude to prosecute the war was something that LBJ and his staff had drawn up and prepared to send to Capitol Hill when they had the right sort of provocation. It gave the president more or less unlimited power to wage war without the congressional approval that you would normally have, as the Constitution would dictate.

He used a very murky event that took place in August of 1964. The United States military had been supporting South Vietnamese actions against North Vietnamese islands, in direct violation of the Geneva Accords. The tiny North Vietnamese navy came out to attack them. Two American destroyers were in the area in support of these clandestine operations that the South Vietnamese were launching. The North Vietnamese fired. Nothing hit. We fired. We missed them. Then carrier-based fighter planes destroyed the North Vietnamese ships.

We basically told them, "Don't do anything like that again," but anxious American sonar operators mistook routine North Vietnamese traffic chatter for an imminent attack. The attack never came, but because it was declared imminent, it must have happened, so Johnson ordered a retaliatory strike, and a few days later went up to Congress and got nearly 100 percent support on the Hill for his Gulf of Tonkin Resolution. Only two senators voted against him.

I needed to do that preamble. So [in 1968] there had been peace negotiations [in Paris] that had gone nowhere, and in late August, with Richard Nixon, the Republican nominee, comfortably ahead of his Democratic rival, Hubert Humphrey, with a very fractured Democratic Party coming out of a disastrous convention in Chicago, suddenly there's some real progress being made at the peace talks. Johnson sees that progress and he announces it, and Humphrey's numbers go up overnight.

It's decided to expand the talks to include the South Vietnamese and potentially even the Viet Cong, a four-way talk. Then Nixon personally intervenes and tells the South Vietnamese through intermediaries that, even though he knows that the U.S. has to get out of Vietnam, South Vietnam will get better terms if Nixon wins. So South Vietnamese President [Nguyen Van] Thieu announces that he is going to boycott the talks.

Johnson has picked this up through CIA intercepts and FBI wiretaps on the Presidential Palace in Saigon and the Vietnamese Embassy in Washington. He calls up Everett Dirksen, the Republican leader, and says, "This is treason." Dirksen said, "Yes, it is." Then Nixon calls up LBJ and says, "I would never do anything like that." And Johnson says, "Okay, Dick."

To this day one of the great mysteries of the war is why Johnson didn't use the information to Humphrey's benefit. Let's remember that in the vote — there was a third-party candidate, George Wallace — Nixon got 43.4 percent and Humphrey got 42.7 percent, a 0.7 percent difference. That bombshell happened on the eve of the election. If Johnson or Humphrey had released that information, it would have been an entirely different situation.

DR: In campaigning, Nixon said, "I have a secret plan to end the war in Vietnam," but he never revealed what it was. What was the secret plan?

KB: I don't really know what it was. But you have to understand that all of these presidents, worried about history and worried about domestic political considerations, didn't want to be the first president to lose a war. I think Nixon's "secret plan" was to keep the war going and then slowly change its course to be more about getting our POWs back than about "winning."

If you just said, "Quick, who's the president that lost a war?" Nixon doesn't come to mind. But he lost a war. A lot of it had to do with that interval of time between his election and his inauguration. If he'd walked into Paris on January 21, 1969, and basically accepted the terms then available, he would have gotten more or less what we ultimately got and there'd be 25,000 or 30,000 more Americans alive.

DR: At the peak of the war, how many American soldiers were there in Vietnam?

KB: Just over 540,000.

DR: How many men and women were being killed a week at the peak?

KB: It varied widely depending on the time of year and what would happen. I think the worst week was well above 2,000 killed.

DR: How many Americans were killed total?

KB: It's over 58,000 names on the wall at the

Vietnam Memorial, and, we believe, 250,000 South Vietnamese soldiers and one million — it's impossible to know for sure — North Vietnamese soldiers and Viet Cong guerrillas, and two million civilians, mostly in South Vietnam and North Vietnam, and tens of thousands, again unknowable, in Laos and Cambodia.

DR: Henry Kissinger is asked by Richard Nixon to start negotiating a peace agreement. Before the '72 election, Kissinger goes into the White House Press Room and says, "Peace is at hand." What was he talking about? Was there peace at hand?

KB: There were negotiations going on. Nixon worked shrewdly to check the antiwar movement by making the draft much fairer, with the lottery system rather than the deferments that placed the burden unnecessarily on poor, minority working-class Americans — Black and brown as well as white.

In August of '69 Kissinger went out on his own. I don't think William Rogers, the secretary of state, knew. Kissinger began meeting with Vietnamese diplomats secretly, apart from the peace talks where things had been stalled for months and months and months. In February of '70, he begins meeting with Le Duc Tho. They make some real progress, so that on the eve of the election,

Kissinger can say, "I believe I've got a good deal here."

And he does have a pretty good deal. The problem is that we've got an issue with our allies, the South Vietnamese. They don't want to go along with the things that Kissinger has agreed to, including allowing the North Vietnamese to stay in South Vietnam. And the Viet Cong, the North Vietnamese allies, are unhappy because they're not being consulted.

But Le Duc Tho and Kissinger feel they have something. It falls apart after the reelection of President Nixon.

DR: Ultimately it's renegotiated. What is the ultimate agreement?

KB: It essentially permits North Vietnamese troops to not have to leave the South, and permits us to get our prisoners of war back. As one journalist joked, "It looked as if half a million Americans went to South Vietnam to get 650 prisoners out." It was a good way to distract attention, as John Negroponte said in our film, from "how we bombed them into accepting our concessions."

DR: The POWs came back. Americans were very excited.

KB: The peace agreement was in early '73 and the prisoners came back in March, most of them.

DR: The agreement didn't hold very long. What happened?

KB: There were something like three thousand violations within a few weeks by both sides — South Vietnamese trying to reclaim territory that the North Vietnamese and Viet Cong had taken, and vice versa. Then they have this brutal, bloody civil war, until the sheer numbers of the North Vietnamese overwhelmed the South.

DR: Now, when Gerald Ford is president, there is the famous picture of the helicopter taking off from the American Embassy in Saigon. What was that all about?

KB: In the famous still photograph, it's not the last one taking off. That's one of many landing points in Saigon where American military personnel and civilians and some Vietnamese were ordered to go when all the other evacuation options had run out.

The last helicopter took off with a planeload of eight to ten marines who had been in the U.S. Embassy compound guarding staff. They were led by Master Sergeant Juan Valdez, whom we interviewed for the film. He was the last American out of Vietnam. At that point, the Republic of Vietnam had just a few hours to live.

DR: When it's all said and done, how much did the American people spend on the Vietnam War?

KB: Hundreds of billions of dollars in 1960–70 dollars [nearly a trillion dollars today].

DR: And the lesson you think Americans should take away from the war is what?

KB: I don't think we wanted to say what it was. Obviously, you want to tell the truth to the American people. You want to be more transparent than these administrations were. There are a whole bunch of lessons that could be — and I think to some extent were for a time — learned from Vietnam. The most important one is that we will never blame the warriors again. That to me is the single best thing.

DR: What's been the reaction to the series as you've gone around the country?

KB: Every day I've been out on the road, somebody has come up to me and said a variation of, "My dad/my uncle/my brother/my cousin/my grandfather never talked about the war, but we watched it together and now they're talking."

We say glibly, "Thank you for your service." Now that we have an all-volunteer army, where we have a separate military class that suffers its losses apart from the rest of us, it's a way to just end the conversation. But I say, "Welcome home. What can we do for you? Can we talk about this and have a conversation?"

And realize, with the Vietnam War, that the heroism occurred not just on the battlefield, but in moral decisions that people made around kitchen tables about whether to go or not to go. What we tried to do was honor as many of those perspectives as we could and just say that a thing and the opposite of a thing could be true at the same time.

JACK JACOBS
ON MILITARY SERVICE

Medal of Honor Recipient

"But the thing about fear in a situation like this is that it's a galvanizing element. It doesn't stop you from doing something. It makes you do the things that you need to do."

In his Gettysburg Address, Lincoln praised the young men buried in the surrounding cemetery for having given "the last full measure of devotion" to their country — i.e., they gave their lives.

While most people are generally prepared to support their country in some way — paying taxes, volunteering, working in government — many fewer are truly willing to die for their country. Yet those who serve in the military, especially in combat roles during times of war, must face the prospect of death every day, if not every hour.

What do they think about the realistic chance they could die as young men and young women? Would they die for anything other than their country — their state, their city or town, their school, their neighborhood? What is it about one's country that persuades young soldiers that the combat role they are committed to pursuing is worth their lives?

One person in my generation who volunteered for military combat in Vietnam was Jack Jacobs, a Rutgers graduate who shocked his Jewish parents by saying he was going to Vietnam and wanted to be in the infantry. When he was a young and relatively inexperienced soldier in Vietnam at the height of the war in 1969, his military team was ambushed by the Viet Cong, the South Vietnam combat arm of the North Vietnamese. In that battle, he was severely wounded in the head, yet managed to save the lives of many of his fellow soldiers, and to organize their escape through a dangerous helicopter flight.

Eighteen months later, to his surprise, Jack Jacobs was awarded by President Richard Nixon, in a White House ceremony, the nation's highest military award — the Medal of Honor. Unfortunately, many of the people given this award receive it posthumously. There are now fewer than seventy living recipients. Jack is one of them, and one of the two living Jewish recipients.

I met Jack when I was speaking to a class at West Point, where he has been a lecturer for many years. I thought his story was a compelling one about how young soldiers think about the prospect of dying, and what they do when that prospect arises, alongside the prospect of helping their comrades. So I asked Jack if I could interview him about his experience, which he has also described in an incredibly moving book, *If Not Now, When?*

The interview, done virtually on September 30, 2020, illustrates a vital and interesting aspect of the American experience: there obviously are people quite prepared to die for this country, and a great many have done so, as the following casualty numbers show:

Revolutionary War: 4,435
War of 1812: 2,260
Civil War: More than 364,000 Union soldiers
World War I: More than 116,000
World War II: More than 405,000
Korean War: 33,000
Vietnam War: 58,000
Various post-9/11 wars: 7,000

We honor these individuals, but often do not have a chance to ask them why they were prepared to make this sacrifice. Jack Jacobs provides telling insight into a combatant's look at potential death.

DAVID M. RUBENSTEIN (DR): As a young

231

man growing up in New Jersey in the 1960s, you were presumably not anxious to go to Vietnam and risk your life in the process. What prompted you to want to join the military and seek an infantry role in Vietnam?

JACK JACOBS (JJ): It all started with my father, who was dragged kicking and screaming into the army during the Second World War. Hated the army, hated being dragged out of college, hated getting shot at, hated the bureaucracy, and he got out of the army as soon as he possibly could, after the war was over.

Yet when he got to be my age, all he would talk about, and all of his friends too, was how proud he was in having saved the world, which that generation did. When I was going to college, I thought then — principally because of my father's service — and I still think today that everybody who is lucky enough to live in a free country owes it something in the form of service.

So I thought it was my obligation to go into uniform after I graduated from college. My whole objective was to go and do my bit for three years and then get out and go to law school, and instead I stayed for twenty years. The reason I did is because I love the people and I didn't want to leave them. Today, when people ask me, "What do you miss most about the army?" it's the people.

DR: What did your parents think of the idea of you, a nice Jewish boy graduating from Rutgers, going to Vietnam?

JJ: They were horrified. They tried to talk me out of it. They tried to talk me out of going into the army in the first place. They said, "That's not a good place for a nice Jewish boy. You should become a banker or something like that."

Twenty years later, when I was retiring from the army to go to Wall Street and become a banker, my parents said, "What are you doing that for? You have such a great career in the army." The lesson here is that you can't satisfy anybody, particularly your parents.

DR: Did you volunteer to go to Vietnam, or were you forced to go?

JJ: I volunteered. By that time, I thought I was going to be a pretty good soldier if I applied myself. I really thought that since we were in the middle of a war, the place for anybody in uniform was to be at the cutting edge of freedom. And so I volunteered to go to Vietnam. Thoughts about the political vicissitudes of being in Vietnam, the whole idea of a domino theory and all that stuff, when you're at the bottom of the military food chain, those things don't cross your mind.

DR: So you get to Vietnam and you realize it's not a panacea. There are lots of challenges. But you describe in your excellent book, *If Not Now, When?,* how one time you were in an encampment and all of a sudden you're attacked by the Viet Cong.

You have a head injury, and then it kind of blurs. But you go save some people, and you escape from what was going to be sure death. When did you realize that you were seriously injured? And what was your thought about self-preservation versus helping other people?

JJ: We had been in contact with a large Viet Cong unit during the Tet Offensive in 1968 for quite some time, and the enemy broke contact. We had an operation to go reestablish contact with the enemy. That included my battalion landing on the north bank of the Mekong River at dawn and moving north to where the intelligence said the enemy might be.

When you're in a situation like that where you don't know exactly where the enemy is, you have to apply yourself in the following way. You don't attack with your main body, because you lose all the optionality if you're engaged. You send the smallest possible unit forward to contact the enemy, and then you can maneuver around.

In any case, the scout platoon was supposed to be to the front and flanks, and I called back saying they were not to the front. To this day, I don't know where the scouts were, but they certainly weren't forward.

We walked into an enormous, L-shaped ambush of more than two hundred enemy soldiers who had had three days to prepare their positions. We got to within about fifty meters before they opened up the ambush. Almost all of the two lead companies I was with were either killed or wounded in the first ten seconds of the engagement.

Your first realization is that you're hurt but it's not that bad and that everybody else is hurt more badly. You have a lot of dead or wounded comrades.

And the notion that was expounded by Hillel, the first-century Hebrew scholar, actually came to my mind. It was, "If not you, who? And if not now, when?"

This was a genuine crisis. Something had to be done, had to be done right now, and if it's not done right now, everything is going down the tubes. And I thought I was the only guy who was in a position to do something to save these buddies of mine and to eliminate the enemy.

Then after a while I realized that I was really badly hurt and I was not going to make it through. Somebody asked me one time about fear in a situation like that, "Were you scared?" Absolutely. I was petrified — well, not petrified, because that suggests I couldn't move.

But the thing about fear in a situation like this is that it's a galvanizing element. It doesn't stop you from doing something. It makes you do the things that you need to do. In this case, fear was a useful emotion to have. But eventually I sat down to catch my breath and I had lost a great deal of blood and realized I couldn't get up again.

DR: You were injured in the head, is that right?

JJ: Yes, the least significant portion of my body.

DR: You had that injury, and then you realized that you had to save your colleagues. In this kind of situation, is it self-preservation, where you say, "I'm going to do whatever I can to stay alive"? What is the instinct that overcomes you and says, "I don't worry about myself so much. I want to save my colleagues"? Why would humans do that?

JJ: In retrospect, it didn't go through my mind at the time. But if you ask anybody who's been in difficult situations in combat, he would probably say that those things are not mutually exclusive — that saving your buddies, doing something that other people might think is valorous, is not completely different from self-preservation.

You're in a bad situation. If you don't do something, everybody is going to die, including you. I think that really is the distinction between something that is a crisis and something that's just lousy. One of the things that distinguishes good leaders from leaders who are not so good is the capability to distinguish between a situation that's a crisis and a situation that's just lousy.

Because you do different things. You commit resources in a crisis you wouldn't commit otherwise.

That's something that's useful to know, not just in combat but in just about every other walk of life. The notion of self-preservation and the notion of doing something for others coalesce, particularly in crisis situations.

DR: You were injured. If you had just stayed there, on the ground, did you think that maybe the Viet Cong would go away thinking you were dead and everybody was dead?

JJ: No, I had already been in combat for six months and I knew that that wasn't going to happen. The enemy was going to prevail and everybody, all of us who were caught out in the open, were all going to die.

DR: How did you manage to get a helicopter

to come and help pick up you and your colleagues?

JJ: My boss, Major John Nolan, and my other NCO [noncommissioned officer], who was with the battalion headquarters, Ainsley Waiwaiole from Maui, came to the rescue. Half of us made it back to a hospital and managed to survive.

Somebody asked a Medal of Honor recipient one time, "What about your valorous acts on that day?" He echoed the feelings of other people who have received any kind of valorous award: "There were lots of brave people on that day, many of whom didn't come home, and I wear the award for all of them."

But that's how I made it out of there — I was rescued by my boss, who called in a helicopter in a hot landing zone. The helicopter was getting all shot up as we were pulling out of there, and I don't remember much of it until I woke up in the hospital sometime later.

DR: You helped get some of your wounded colleagues onto that helicopter?

JJ: They said I did. I don't remember it.

DR: You go to the hospital. They try to patch you up. You've got some serious wounds. After how many weeks were you able to get out of the hospital?

JJ: It was a couple of weeks. I was supposed to be evacuated, but I escaped and went back to my unit. Not recommended for anybody. My unit was astonished that I showed up.

DR: What about your parents? How did you tell them that you were wounded, almost died, and that you were going back into combat?

JJ: You've got to remember that communication wasn't at all like it is today. I remember not getting paid for months and didn't realize that I hadn't been paid for months because I hadn't received any mail for months, until I finally got a load of mail with my wife telling me, "We've got no money. Where is the allotment that's supposed to be coming?"

I wrote a letter back to my parents from the hospital, saying I'd been wounded but don't worry about it, it's just a minor thing and I'm going to be just fine. They never did know the extent of my injuries until I finally got home.

DR: Did you get shrapnel in your head? And do you still carry that with you?

JJ: Yes, I still have shrapnel in my head. My

wife tells me what I really should be doing is wearing an armband that says NO MRI because I've got so much in there.

DR: Do you go through metal detectors when you go to an airport?

JJ: They're not as sensitive as they used to be. When they first came out, I'd set them off all the time. Now it's less of a problem.

DR: You describe in your book how somebody calls you about eighteen months after this event and asks you some questions, and you're worried that maybe you did something wrong. You had no clue that you were going to get any kind of award?

JJ: I got a call from some colonel in Washington. My company clerk calls into my office, says, "Hey, sir, there's some colonel on the phone. Wants to talk to you." Colonels don't talk to captains. I thought maybe it was a gag call, except back in those days phone calls actually cost money.

Anyway, I pick up the phone and this guy says, "I am Colonel Schmidlapp" or whatever it was. "Were you in the Kien Phong Province on 9 March 1968?" "Yes, sir, I was." "Is your service number OF108672?" I said, "Yes, sir, it is." He said, "You'll be hearing from us," and hung up the phone.

I was completely nonplussed. I was trying to think about what I had done, what happened, did I do anything wrong? When you've got hundreds of people shooting in every direction, just about anything can happen. It's totally out of control, and I thought perhaps I had done something wrong.

In any case, I didn't get any sleep for twenty-four or forty-eight hours, and then I got a phone call from a different colonel. He said, "I'm in charge of Army Awards Branch. Congratulations, you're going to receive the Medal of Honor. You may not tell anybody except your immediate family. One of my people is going to call you up and make arrangements for you and your family to come to Washington for the ceremony at the White House. Congratulations again. Out here." And hung up the phone.

That was the entirety of the conversation. It was a total surprise to me for sure.

DR: You didn't think it was a prank or anything?

JJ: It was clearly not a prank when this guy with a sonorous voice identifies himself as head of Army Awards Branch and says you're going to get the medal. I was shocked.

DR: When you eventually call your parents and tell them this and they go to Washington with you, are you kind of feeling on cloud nine?

JJ: I am indeed. I'm vindicated. I shouldn't have gone into uniform. I shouldn't have gone to Vietnam. And something positive has come of it in the end. It's *naches* [a proud moment] for them.

For me, it was bittersweet, because I had lost so many friends, both before that battle and in that battle, and a lot of them were killed subsequent to that battle. More bitter than sweet. But I was very proud of having worn the uniform. That's what I was most proud of.

DR: You had this ceremony at the White House with President Richard Nixon. How was that?

JJ: The most shocking thing about it was I don't remember much of the ceremony at all, to be honest with you. I remember more about the battle, about which I don't remember everything, than I do about the ceremony.

We had a reception in the East Room and then we went into the Oval Office with Nixon and Stanley Resor, who was secretary of the army; Melvin Laird, who was secretary of defense; and the president's aide. Nixon said, "Won't you sit in my chair, and you can make believe you're the president."

It was a beautiful day on the ninth of October 1969. When we came out of the White House, out to the Rose Garden, they had built up a platform. There were four of us from the army, from different actions, who were being decorated in this same ceremony, and we marched up there.

The most shocking thing was the sea of people in front of us. They had opened up the White House grounds for just about anybody who wanted to come watch the ceremony. Government employees, passersby, homeless people, anybody who wanted to walk onto the White House grounds and watch the ceremony could do that. There were people as far as you could see. You couldn't even see the fence around the White House.

My enduring memory was of that sight — not of the president, of the White House, but of all those people.

DR: What rights does one have as a Medal of Honor recipient?

JJ: A small stipend from the Veterans Administration, which at the time was $100 a month. That's basically it. You go back to whatever you were doing.

DR: When you're the Medal of Honor recipient, how does one let people know that without appearing to be bragging about it? Do you just drop it in conversations?

JJ: No, I don't tell it to anybody. I think most recipients do the same thing. The only reason people would know is if someone were billed as the attraction at some charitable or other kind of event as a Medal of Honor recipient.

My wife was the British exchange officer to the Seventh Infantry Division at Fort Ord, California, when I was a battalion executive officer there. We met and I asked her out. We'd gone out a number of times before one of our other colleagues told her that I was a Medal of Honor recipient. I hadn't told her. I didn't tell anybody.

DR: If I had been the recipient of a Medal of Honor, it would probably take me about two seconds to tell somebody.

JJ: I bet you wouldn't. The first event I ever attended with other Medal of Honor recipients was in Houston right after the award ceremony. At that time there were more than 350 recipients, and probably 300 of them or more were there at the dinner, including recipients from the First World War.

At the end of the dinner, Jimmy Doolittle [a Medal of Honor recipient from World War II who led bombing missions over Japan] came up to me and put his arm around my shoulders and said, "Young man, come with me," and he took me to a corner of the ballroom. I'm a newly minted Medal of Honor recipient. This is Jimmy Doolittle.

And he put his arm around me and he said sternly, "Young man, let me explain something to you. You're no longer Jack Jacobs. You're Jack Jacobs, Medal of Honor recipient, and you'd better comport yourself accordingly. Do you understand what I am telling you?" I said, "Yes, sir, I sure do."

DR: Here's a question I've thought about for a long time. Nobody ever says, "I'm prepared to die for my neighborhood. I'm prepared to die for my high school. I'm prepared to die for my state. I'm prepared to die for my fraternity." Why is it that people are prepared to die for their country, whereas they're not prepared to die for virtually anything else?

JJ: First, I think it's commensurate with wearing the uniform in the first place, performing any kind of community service. The motivator is being part of something bigger than you are.

The second thing, I think, is optimism that it isn't going to happen to you. I'm prepared to die for my country. I'm prepared to die for my colleagues. They're also prepared to die for their country. They're also prepared to die for me. But it isn't going to happen. The perception that it's not going to happen figures heavily.

The third thing that motivates people to do things they otherwise wouldn't do is the notion that the other guy would do it for you. And he would, too. I've seen it time and time again. You don't think you're going to die. You are part of something bigger than you, and somebody else would do it for you too.

■ ■ ■ ■

3

RESTORATION AND
REPAIR

■ ■ ■ ■

"What, to the American slave, is your Fourth of July? I answer: a day that reveals to him, more than all other days in the year, the gross injustice and cruelty to which he is the constant victim. . . . There is not a nation on the earth guilty of practices more shocking and bloody, than are the people of these United States, at this very hour."
— Frederick Douglass, "What to the slave is the Fourth of July?," July 5, 1852

HENRY LOUIS GATES JR.
ON RECONSTRUCTION

Alphonse Fletcher University Professor and Director of the Hutchins Center for African and African American Research at Harvard University; author of *Stony the Road* and other books

"But after Black people were freed and then Black men had the right to vote, the genie was out of the lamp, and you had to try to put the genie back in the lamp again. You had to convince Black men and the larger society that they were not only inferior, they were subhuman."

As the Civil War was moving toward an end in which the Union would clearly be victorious, attention shifted to how the Confederate states would be reintegrated into the Union, and also to how the emancipated slaves would be treated — legally, politically, socially, and financially.

Had Lincoln lived, it is likely that these issues, collectively labeled Reconstruction, would have been handled more skillfully, equitably, and judiciously. But even with Lincoln there was no easy answer. His Reconstruction plans would not readily have enabled southern whites or freed slaves to quickly adjust to the new economic, social, and political realities.

The whites wanted to return to their prewar economic and political power, and could not truly accept the freed slaves as "equals." And the freed slaves had expectations of economic and political power that would have been hard to realize, even under Lincoln.

As events unfolded, Lincoln was assassinated on April 14, 1865, before ratification of the Thirteenth Amendment freeing the slaves, the Fourteenth Amendment giving former slaves citizenship, and the Fifteenth Amendment giving these new citizens the right to vote. Those amendments, and the 1866 Civil Rights Act, were intended to put the original sin of slavery behind the U.S., and to usher in a new era.

But Andrew Johnson, a native of Tennessee, had neither Lincoln's credibility and political skills, nor his concerns about the rights of the freed slaves. And as a result, the anti-Black actions taken in the South meant that Reconstruction essentially devolved into a return to the pre–Civil War economic and political structure in the old Confederacy, minus only the legality of slavery.

Jim Crow laws, regular lynching of Blacks, and the rise of KKK groups in the South thwarted the ambitions and expectations of freed slaves. And it turned out, as well, that many northern abolitionists and strong opponents of the Confederacy did not actually feel that Blacks were equal to whites. To many of those opponents of slavery, fighting slavery did not translate into supporting equality. That reality became apparent as Blacks, frustrated with the violence against them and the lack of social, political, and economic progress in the South, migrated to the North and often found, to their surprise, many similar challenges.

In truth, the best of intentions that some in the North had to make Reconstruction a time to right earlier wrongs and to produce post-war healing backfired terribly. From the end of the Civil War until the civil rights revolution of the 1950s and 1960s, the South was essentially unreconstructed, and the North was far from a paradise for most African Americans.

The sad story of Reconstruction and its aftermath has been vividly recounted in *Stony the Road* by Henry Louis (Skip) Gates Jr., following a PBS documentary he earlier produced on the same subject. Skip Gates, a professor at Harvard University and the director of its Hutchins Center for African and African American Research, is the acknowledged dean of African American scholarship. He is the author or coauthor of more than twenty books, the editor of twelve books in the general area of African American scholarship, and the recipient of nearly sixty honorary degrees.

To the general public, Skip Gates may be best known for his work on public television over the past quarter century. He has produced more than twenty films for PBS, many dealing with the genetic and other roots of African Americans. I thought he would be the perfect person to discuss Reconstruction and its aftermath, and we did so in a January 22, 2021, interview facilitated by the New-York Historical Society.

DAVID M. RUBENSTEIN (DR): If Lincoln had lived, would Reconstruction have become more successful than it was?

HENRY LOUIS GATES JR. (HLG): One of the things people forget is that one of the crucial elements in the rollback of Reconstruction was a conservative Supreme Court, and many of those justices had been appointed by Abraham Lincoln. That is almost never talked about. There was a series of Supreme Court cases that severely restricted the applicability of the Fourteenth Amendment's equal protection clause to the rights of Black Americans. I'm thinking of the Civil Rights Cases in

254

1883, which quite disastrously declared unconstitutional the Civil Rights Act of 1875.

That was the last thing that the great Charles Sumner, one of my genuine heroes, wanted to see passed by the Congress before he died in 1874. It was passed in 1875, and guaranteed equal enjoyment of public accommodations, et cetera, et cetera.

It would take a hundred years for us to get those rights back that had been guaranteed in 1875. It was the conservative court, among other things, that helped undermine the impact of the Fourteenth Amendment and then the Fifteenth Amendment. And we know that the court in *Plessy v. Ferguson* sanctified "separate but equal" as the law of the land in 1896.

I was thinking about this when I was listening to Joe Biden's inauguration speech, which moved me very much by its sincerity. We would have to fact-check this, but I think he was the first president to use the phrase *white supremacy* ever in an inaugural address. I almost fell out of my chair. When you and I were teenagers, *white supremacy* was used by George Wallace and Orval Faubus [governor of Arkansas during the Little Rock school crisis].

It actually originated in 1824 — that's the first known usage of the phrase that I'm aware of — but it really became an ideology during the rollback of Reconstruction, which is called Redemption. Reconstruction was ended because of the Compromise of 1877, because of a series of opinions by a conservative Supreme Court, and because of the first Great Depression, which is now called the Great Panic of 1873. Then, after 1890, former Confederate states beginning with Mississippi held new state constitutional conventions and, without ever using the word *Negro* or *Black,* rewrote their constitutions in a way that would undercut the Fifteenth Amendment, which gave Black men the right to vote.

And if you want to know how effective that was, in Louisiana, which was a majority Black state, there were 130,000 Black men registered to vote in 1898. By 1904, that number had been reduced to 1,342.

South Carolina, Mississippi, and Louisiana were majority Black states. Georgia, Alabama, and Florida were in the high 40 percent range. So there were six states that together constituted a mini Black republic. And Black men in the former Confederacy got the right to vote before Black men did nationally through the Fifteenth Amendment, which was ratified in the 1870s. Southern Black men did because of the Reconstruction Acts, which Congress passed in 1867, that gave them the right to vote.

The summer of 1867 is a great story. It's the first "Freedom Summer." There was a massive attempt through Black churches and by former abolitionists to register all of these formerly enslaved Black men plus free Black men in the South. Some 80 percent of eligible Black male voters in the former Confederate states registered to vote, and in 1868, 500,000 of them cast their ballots, the lion's share of them for Ulysses S. Grant.

Grant won the presidency overwhelmingly in the Electoral College but only by 300,000 odd votes in the popular vote. So, in effect, Black men had elected a president.

This scared the daylights out of the new representatives of the former Confederacy but also out of white, so-called liberal people in the North. This was too much Black power. That's why, eventually, Black males in the South were disenfranchised.

You could say that Joe Biden's defeat of Donald Trump was the fourth Reconstruction defeating the third Redemption. Donald Trump was redeeming the country from the Reconstruction politics of Barack Obama and Joe Biden through the Black vote. The Black vote and the Black church were crucial to Biden's victory, as you know, because when Biden came out of New Hampshire, nobody thought that he would be sitting in the White House today until Congressman Jim Clyburn pushed the button and mobilized the Black vote in South Carolina. That created a domino effect, and Biden emerged as the victor. This shows the inherent power of the Black church still to this day.

DR: Let me go back for one second. The general view is that Lincoln would have had a better Reconstruction for Blacks. His successor, Andrew Johnson, was very anti-Black. Had Johnson been more sympathetic to the Black position, would it have made a difference?

HLG: Andrew Johnson was a nightmare. He took away the "forty acres and a mule" order that General [William Tecumseh] Sherman had issued — Special Field Order Number 15 — in January of 1865, which redistributed land, from the Georgia sea islands down to Florida, to the formerly enslaved people who lived there.

They were given the redistributed land from their former masters, and they lived on it and worked it for months. And Andrew Johnson sent General Otis Howard, a white man for whom Howard University is named, down to tell these poor people face-to-face that they had to give that land back in the fall of 1865. So there was no hope. Andrew Johnson was a racist man. He wanted to roll back Reconstruction as quickly as he could. That's why they had to impeach him, so that there could be Radical Reconstruction by the Republican Congress.

DR: Johnson stays in office but he's not reelected. Beginning in the 1870s, powerful whites in the South said, "We can regain our power by disenfranchising Blacks." That went on for a long time. When did the idea of Jim Crow laws come along?

HLG: Lincoln said he was for the limited franchise for Black men, for his Black warriors, his Black soldiers. He really thought the main reason for the Union victory was the fact that the Emancipation Proclamation included the provision that Black men could carry arms and fight. That was quite radical. He authorized Black men, if they were in the Union Army, to kill white men. That was unheard of.

But in that speech, he said he believed that Black men should have the right to vote, the men who had served the cause of the Union in the Civil War. Lincoln said "the very intelligent Negroes," so he was not for giving all Black men the right to vote. He wanted to start with that limited group of people. I'm sure that Lincoln was a very cautious politician, and he knew it was a radical idea. Without the Radical Republican Congress, it never would have been ratified.

Here's something people don't realize. Freed Black men in the South got the right to vote before Black men whose families had been free for a century in the North. Until ratification of the Fifteenth Amendment, Black men could only vote in five of the six New England states, not in Connecticut. And in the state of New York, only if they satisfied the $250 property requirement.

Jim Crow became formalized after the Mississippi plan caught fire starting in 1890. The Mississippi plan was the state constitutional convention movement that disenfranchised Black people.

DR: Who was Jim Crow?

HLG: Jim Crow was a white man, a minstrel who was very popular. That was his stage name in the 1830s. There was a dance he created called "Jumping Jim Crow." Blackface minstrels were one of the most popular forms of entertainment, if not the most popular form of entertainment, in America even through the Civil War. So he was a minstrel character, and that name, for reasons that no one knows, affixed itself to what the Supreme Court called "separate but equal."

DR: Now, the whites were trying to regain their power in the South. They passed Jim Crow laws, and a lot of Blacks began to leave and go to the North. And they discovered there that life wasn't all that much better.

HLG: We tend to forget this, but until 1910,

90 percent of the Black community lived in the South. That changed with the Great Migration, which continued until 1970, when reverse migration took effect. More and more Black people moved from the North to the South than the other way around.

Charles Blow, the distinguished *New York Times* columnist, has a new book, *The Devil You Know,* that calls for Black people to reclaim their entitlements to the South, moving back to the South. Look at Georgia. Think about that tremendous power base that manifested itself in the general election of 1868. Then think about this election. Stacey Abrams pulled it off. Raphael Warnock becomes a United States senator from Georgia. That's because of the old Black community and the recent migration of Black people from the North to the South.

DR: You point out in *Stony the Road* that the upper class of the Black population began to say, "They're making fun of us. They're calling us minstrels, or saying we're not very smart. We actually are better than the average. We are the New Negro." Can you explain what that meant?

HLG: That was the Black elite. Remember, there had been prominent free Black communities in New York, Philadelphia, Baltimore, and Boston as well as, interestingly enough, New Orleans and Charleston.

In 1860, there were more free Black people living in the slave states than in the North. There were 262,000 living in the slave states and 222,000 living in the North, which always surprises my students. You can take my family as an example. Two of my [great-great-great-great-] grandparents, Joe and Sarah Bruce, were freed in 1823 in Hardy County, Virginia, and were given one thousand acres of land. What are they going to do, give up that land and become homeless in Boston? That would have been stupid.

So the old Black elite in the North, when the Great Migration began, as Zora Neale Hurston put it, classed themselves off from these former sharecroppers. These were agrarian rural people moving up from the South, as opposed to the Black people who have had a long history of free ancestry, who were very well educated, very well spoken. They invented, starting in the 1890s, a metaphor, a trope, an image of themselves: "We are the New Negroes, not the old Negroes. The old Negroes were the sharecroppers, the recent descendants of slaves. We are the descendants of free people. We have more in common with the white elite than we do with the Black poor or the Black working class."

DR: As this was going on, you point out in

your book, Blacks were being demonized in ways that were practically worse than during slavery.

HLG: It was true. If you own somebody, you don't need to remind them or yourself that they are a subspecies. That's not to say that intellectual racism didn't obtain during slavery. It did.

But after Black people were freed and then Black men had the right to vote, the genie was out of the lamp, and you had to try to put the genie back in the lamp again. You had to convince Black men and the larger society that they were not only inferior, they were subhuman.

DR: The Black elite, as they moved forward, became reasonably prosperous. But when the civil rights movement came along in the 1960s, its leaders said, "Why don't you help us? You're not really doing much. You're not really helping poor Blacks." Was that a problem?

HLG: Here's what happened. The idea that one class of Black people, an old aristocracy, would be treated differently under the law — that they could create a class within the race that would be given equal access to the right to vote and economic opportunities — was dispelled by *Plessy v. Ferguson* in 1896. If

263

you have a law that says "all Blacks shall" or "all Blacks shan't," it doesn't matter if you've been freed for two hundred years or fifty years. It doesn't matter if your grandparents or your great-grandfather fought in the American Revolution, as [my forebears] did, or if they were living in Africa and came here just before the slave trade ended in 1808. All Black people, whether they had a PhD or could barely read and write, were equal, or unequal, before the law.

This created one big class of people, but we always have had classes within the race, like every other group. Before the law, before the larger white society, we were all of one class. It's a paradox, but it always existed. Behind the color curtain, Blacks had upper-class people, middle-class people, working-class people, and lower-class people. W. E. B. Du Bois, in fact, in his seminal study *The Philadelphia Negro,* published in 1899, identified five classes within the African American people.

We've always had a really tough class structure. Sometimes it was confused with color. If you were mulatto, if you were light-complexioned, if you had straight hair, that put you in a higher class. If you had more, quote-unquote, African features, it was a nightmare. Really.

That began to change with the civil rights movement. No one thought the movement would begin in the South. There was always a history of protest in the North, starting with the abolitionist movement.

But Martin Luther King Jr., who was a third-generation pastor at Ebenezer Baptist Church, only left the South to go to Boston University to get a PhD and then hurry back to the South. He starts the scene, and Rosa Parks starts the civil rights movement that emerges from the heart of the Confederacy, Montgomery, Alabama, with a bus boycott that shocked everybody.

James Baldwin writes about this. He's living in Saint Paul de Vence in the South of France. He's so ashamed when he sees those children integrating Central High School in Little Rock in 1957, when President Eisenhower sends in the National Guard, he comes back and joins the movement, and the upperclass Black people from the North all have to go south to help their brothers and sisters fight. That's in the belly of the beast.

Because, as you know, those guys weren't joking. They were stone-cold racists. George Wallace stood at that door and said he would never embrace the desegregation of the University of Alabama. Orval Faubus said the same thing with Central High School. You know the story as well as I do.

DR: Where did the title *Stony the Road* come from?

265

HLG: "Stony the road we trod, Bitter the chastening rod" — that is one of the verses of "Lift Every Voice and Sing," the Negro national anthem. I happen to love that song, though I have to say Bill Clinton and the late Vernon Jordan are the only two people I know who know all of the verses. But that's where it came from, and it's a beautiful song.

DAVID W. BLIGHT
ON FREDERICK DOUGLASS

Professor of History and Director of the
Gilder Lehrman Center for the Study of
Slavery, Resistance, and Abolition at Yale
University; author of *Frederick Douglass:
Prophet of Freedom* and other books

"Some of the most powerful, sometimes
beautiful, harrowing aspects of Douglass's
autobiographies are the ways in which he
reconstructs those years of his youth, and
what this system of slavery was doing to
him, not so much physically as psychically
and mentally. Douglass always argued that
the worst impact of slavery was on the mind
and not on the body."

Until the civil rights revolution of the 1960s
and the rise to national and global promi-
nence of Martin Luther King Jr., the most
prominent African American in the country's
history was, without doubt, Frederick Douglass — a man who had been born into slavery, was essentially orphaned as a little boy,

and yet, in time, rose to be the most distinguished and respected abolitionist seeking the end of slavery.

When that goal was achieved, Douglass became the most visible freed slave working to provide African Americans with equal rights and opportunities. He lived to see that dream partially realized and then betrayed; but his impact on American society, and on the long struggle to correct many of the country's legal and social flaws, was enormous, indeed without peer during his lifetime.

Few would have predicted this from Douglass when he was a youth. Slaves were not supposed to learn how to read, but he did so, somewhat surreptitiously. He ultimately escaped from his Maryland slave owner and moved north, and developed his writing and oratory skills to such a level that he could make a living as a public speaker, typically attacking slavery and racism in American life.

He became influential enough to meet several times with Abraham Lincoln. And after slavery was abolished, Douglass continued his fight for social justice and equality as a best-selling autobiographer, newspaper editor, traveling orator, and, ultimately, federal government official. He was the first African American confirmed by the U.S. Senate when he was appointed by President Rutherford B.

Hayes as the marshal for the District of Columbia.

For many whites, Douglass was a mystery. How could a Black man learn to read and write and speak publicly so well? For many Blacks, Douglass was also a mystery. How did he avoid being seriously harmed (though he was attacked physically from time to time)? How did he not get killed for his socializing with white women, including his second wife, or for his decades-long efforts to change the laws of white society?

These questions, and so many others, about the courageous and pioneering life of Frederick Douglass are answered as best as they can be in a Pulitzer Prize–winning book, *Frederick Douglass: Prophet of Freedom,* by David Blight, a Yale scholar who has devoted virtually his entire academic life to the study of slavery, abolition, emancipation, and Reconstruction.

In this interview, conducted on February 12, 2020, as part of the Congressional Dialogues series at the Library of Congress, Professor Blight brought to life the remarkable life of a man many had known a bit about, though few had realized just how extraordinary was his life or his impact on American society. Blight's broad knowledge about Douglass was aided immeasurably in this book by a treasure trove of Douglass family records and letters not previously available to any scholar.

I had long wanted to interview this great scholar of Frederick Douglass and that period. The interview with David Blight lived up to all of my expectations.

DAVID M. RUBENSTEIN (DR): Let's go through Douglass's life, because people may not be that familiar with it. Where was he born?

DAVID W. BLIGHT (DB): He was born at a horseshoe bend along the Tuckahoe River, on the Eastern Shore of Maryland. His father was white, he knew that. The two principle candidates are his two owners, Aaron Anthony and Thomas Auld.

His mother was a woman named Harriet Bailey, who was owned by Aaron Anthony. She had five children between roughly the age of eighteen and thirty-one, when she died. Douglass saw her last when he was six years old.

DR: Then what happened?

DB: He was dropped off at the Wye House Plantation on the Eastern Shore when he was six. He lived there until he was nearly eight. He was then sent by his owner to Baltimore to be the playmate of his owner's brother's son, Tommy Auld.

DR: He goes to Baltimore and one of the most important things in his life happens: he is taught to read. It was illegal for slaves to learn how to read. Why was that? And why was he taught to read if it was illegal?

DB: Literacy is power. Literacy is a means to potential dignity. And it's the potential of escape. Teaching a slave to read was illegal in virtually all slave states. However, that didn't stop some people from either allowing or teaching slaves to read.

Douglass's mistress in Baltimore was a woman named Sophia Auld, the wife of Hugh Auld, and for nearly two years, when Douglass is seven, eight years old, she teaches him his alphabet, reads the Bible out loud with him. He learns to read from his white mistress, until her husband came in one day and said, "You will not teach that slave, because if you teach him to read, he will next want to write, and then he will want to escape." Douglass once said, "That was the first abolitionist speech I ever heard."

DR: As a teenager, he's sent back to the Eastern Shore. Why is he sent back?

DB: He's sent back first because his owner died. This is one of the most horrifying things about slavery. An owner dies, the slaves are going to be sold off. After just one year in

Baltimore, Douglass is sent back to the Eastern Shore, because old Aaron Anthony had died, and all of his twenty-five or thirty slaves were being divided up.

But Douglass had the great good luck of being sent back to Baltimore. He will spend nine of his twenty years as a slave in Baltimore, and it has everything to do with why we even know about him.

Baltimore was a city, a big maritime city. In the year Douglass escaped, 1838, it had about three thousand slaves, but it had seventeen thousand free Blacks. It was a very large, and very active, and vibrant free Black community, with churches and debating societies.

He lives within that community as well as living as a slave. He works on the docks, works in maritime trade. He becomes a caulker, and he has a vision of the world, in Baltimore Harbor, of all those ships always going in and out of the town.

All the money he earned down on the docks went to his owner, which was one of many causes of a building rage inside of him. And again Douglass is sent back to the Eastern Shore. He does brutal farm labor, and he becomes a disgruntled, despairing teenager. He was made to work as a fieldhand.

Some of the most powerful, sometimes beautiful, harrowing aspects of Douglass's autobiographies are the ways in which he reconstructs those years of his youth, and what this system of slavery was doing to him, not so much physically as psychically and mentally. Douglass always argued that the worst impact of slavery was on the mind and not on the body.

He was hired out by Auld, his owner, who couldn't handle him anymore. Auld hired him out to a man named Edward Covey.

If you ever read Douglass's narrative, Covey is an unforgettable character. He was himself a slaveholder, but a smaller farmer. He was well known in the area for punishing and breaking recalcitrant slaves. Covey, let's just say, beat the dickens out of him weekly for months.

Douglass ran away at one point. He ran back to his owner and said, "This guy Covey, he's a devil, he's killing me." Auld said, "You must deserve it," and sent him right back. The way Douglass tells the story — Douglass is a very crafty writer, let's remember that; all great autobiography is good storytelling — he went back, and when Covey came after him with whip and boards, Douglass took him on and fought him, physically.

Douglass says the fight lasted two hours, but I doubt that. And Douglass tells us that he busted Covey. He beat him up, and Covey never again laid a hand on him.

Douglass makes that story into the pivot of his autobiography. He makes it into a kind of a resurrection story. He's resurrected from his bondage through violence, through standing up in self-defense.

DR: Eventually he goes back to Baltimore?

DB: First he is rented out from Covey's farm. He's eighteen and he's rented out to a guy named [William] Freeland, a much different master. One of the most fascinating things about Douglass's autobiography is that it's not just about the horrors of slavery. It's a fascinating analysis of the slaveholders' minds. He gives you portraits of very different kinds of slaveholders, very different kinds of people.

Freeland didn't beat his slaves. But it was when he was with Freeland that Douglass organized what he called his band of brothers. He'd read the Bible out loud with them, because he was the only one who was literate. He would practice oratory with them.

But they also launched a plot of escape, and they got caught. Douglass was marched in chains with three of his buddies to the Talbot County Jail in Easton, Maryland, and jailed for two weeks.

This is crucial, because it is the luckiest break of his life. For two weeks Thomas Auld left him in his jail cell. He expected to be sold south, which is the worst possible fate. You could die getting there. You'll never see your kinfolk again. Douglass had no less than fourteen brothers, sisters, and cousins sold south during his twenty years as a slave in Maryland.

But Thomas Auld lets him out and says, according to Douglass, "You're not a very good slave. I'm sending you back to Baltimore. If you behave, I will free you on your twenty-first birthday."

But Douglass didn't believe him. He will escape when he's twenty.

DR: He meets a woman name Anna, whom he later marries, and who is illiterate. How did she help him escape?

DB: Anna Murray is about three years older. He meets her in Baltimore, probably at a church. She's born free out on the Eastern Shore, about three miles from where Frederick was born.

They fall in love somehow. Anna did remain illiterate, a nonreader and nonwriter all of her life, through their forty-four years of marriage. That's a very complicated story. One of the biggest challenges a Douglass biographer faces is finding Anna. But I think I managed to, to some extent.

She became a companion in his escape plot. They planned it together. He escaped in August of 1838 dressed as a sailor. He borrowed an old sailor's maritime ID papers. Douglass didn't look anything like this guy.

He's twenty years old. He escaped with about three dollars that Anna gave him and his copy of the *Columbian Orator* in his other pocket, which is this magical book that he discovered when he was twelve years old. It's a manual of oratory.

He took three trains and three boats from Baltimore to the Lower West Side of Manhattan in thirty-eight hours. He gets a letter back to Baltimore. Somebody tells Anna, "He's in New York City, go."

Anna had her bags packed, and her escape takes the same bravery that Douglass's did. Because if she gets caught, her fate is going to be just as bad as his. Anna, by the way, had a good job for a free Black woman — the best deal she could get. She was a domestic servant in a white person's home, a safe job. [A free Black woman with a domestic job was the best she could ever aspire to; free Blacks lived circumscribed lives, with no civil or political rights and very meager wages. Frederick must have represented high hopes and better days ahead for Anna.]

But she got on the same train, the same three ferryboats across the Susquehanna, the Delaware, and the Hudson, and joins him in New York City. They were married in the home of a former fugitive slave.

Douglass had no plan when he gets to New York City. He was told, "Go to New Bedford [Massachusetts]. It's a safe haven for fugitive slaves, and you'll get maritime work." It was the whaling capital of the United States.

He begins to preach at a small AME Zion church, a Black church, in New Bedford. At age twenty-one, he registered to vote. I found it in the New Bedford City Hall Manifest of Voting Records. There he is, in 1839, registered to pay a $1.50 poll tax. In Massachusetts, you had to pay a tax. There he is, Frederick Douglass, on the voting roll.

DR: He's speaking as a preacher, getting a good reputation.

DB: He's discovered in New Bedford preaching in this AME Zion church at the age of twenty-one, twenty-two. He learns his homiletics there. He learns how to preach to the text on a Sunday.

He's discovered doing this by some white abolitionists from up in Boston who are close associates of William Lloyd Garrison, the leading abolitionist of the time. Garrison created the American Anti-Slavery Society and published the longest-lasting antislavery newspaper, the *Liberator.*

They invited Douglass out to Nantucket in August 1841 for an abolition convention. It's the first speech he ever gave to white people, and he tells us that he quaked in his shoes. What they basically asked him to do was "tell your story." And he did. He told it three times in a day and a half.

He was immediately hired by the Garrisonian abolitionists in Boston. They launched him that fall, 1841, as an itinerant abolitionist orator, all over New England at first, and then all across the North. By 1842, he was becoming the star of the abolitionist circuit. He's twenty-three, twenty-four years old.

DR: At that point, he decides to go for a couple of years to England and Ireland. Why?

DB: He writes that first autobiography [*Narrative of the Life of Frederick Douglass, an American Slave*] in the winter of 1844–45. That first autobiography is basically Douglass summing up, putting into story form, all the stories he's been telling out on the circuit.

It was explosively successful. He had already planned to go to the British Isles under the auspices of the Garrisonian abolitionists. They funded the trip, primarily. He also took boxes full of this book. He couldn't keep it in print. He had a second and third edition published in Dublin, Ireland.

That *Narrative* will sell thirty thousand copies in the first five years. That's good today. If you can sell thirty thousand, you're doing fine.

DR: I thought one of the reasons he went was because the publicity he was getting for his autobiography made him fear his slave owner would come try to get him.

DB: His abolitionist friends were, in some ways, I think, more concerned than he was. He is a fugitive slave, still. He can be captured at any time, and returned to slavery, by law. In fact, he spent nine years as a fugitive slave.

So he goes first to Ireland, spends four months. Then into Scotland. He loved Ireland, although he arrived there right at the beginning of the famine. He said he saw poverty there, starvation, much, much worse than he'd ever seen in southern slavery, although he would not let the Irish abolitionists say that they were enslaved to the British worse than African Americans were enslaved in America.

In Scotland, he arrives during a classic Scottish ecclesiastical war. The Church of Scotland is at war with itself over money that had been raised in the American South [from proslavery supporters]. It was perfect for Douglass. His favorite speech in his first three years out on the circuit was a speech he came to call the "slaveholder sermon." Douglass was a great mimic. He was a performer. He would get up on a stage and he would start mimicking a slaveholding preacher: "Slaves be loyal to your masters," as the Bible instructs in one instance.

But he arrives in Scotland and they're having a war over religious hypocrisy, his favorite subject. By the time he leaves Scotland, six months later, they're writing poems and children's songs about him.

DR: Why is his name Frederick Douglass?

DB: When he and Anna arrived in New Bedford — this is when they escape out of New York — they spend the night with the Johnsons. The next morning, Mr. Johnson, who is himself a former fugitive slave, says, "You've got to change your name." Mr. Johnson had just read Sir Walter Scott's epic poem *The Lady of the Lake.* Scott was really popular in those days. And Johnson said, "There's a great heroic character in that story. His name is Douglas. It's a powerful name."

That's how he became Frederick Douglass, but he added an *s.* The Douglas in the Scott poem has only one *s.*

DR: How does he become free and stop being a fugitive slave?

DB: A group of British abolitionists, led by two sisters up in Newcastle upon Tyne, raised the money, did the correspondence with Thomas Auld back in Maryland, and arranged for the purchase of Douglass's life.

DR: For how much?

DB: Seven hundred and sixty-six dollars. It was £150 in British sterling.

DR: Eventually he comes back to the United States. Why does he move to Rochester? Not that it's not a great place to be.

DB: It's a great place if you want to be an abolitionist. Rochester was out at the end of the Erie Canal. It was a big, booming town, known to be an antislavery enclave, and Douglass didn't know about the winters there yet, I guess. He moved his whole family — his wife and now five children — out to Rochester.

His British friends who purchased his freedom also sent him back to America with about $2,000, serious money then, to launch this newspaper called the *North Star.* It will be the longest-lasting Black antislavery newspaper of the nineteenth century.

DR: He's also going around the country making speeches. Is he well received everywhere?

DB: Yes and no. He's a big ticket on the abolitionist circuit, but he's also a target. It was one of the ways he made a living, but we shouldn't romanticize this. He was lucky if he got $50 for a speech in those years. Later on, after the Civil War, he'll get $100, $150 a pop.

But the newspaper nearly died every year. It just wasn't well funded. He had between four hundred and seven hundred subscribers. That's not a lot of people, although with a newspaper like that in the 1840s, one person might get it but show it to six neighbors.

DR: So he can barely make a living doing this. He had a white woman helping him raise money and do some of the editing. Wasn't that controversial?

DB: Yes. Her name was Julia Griffiths, one of the most important friends Douglass ever made. She was British. He met her in England. One Douglass biographer years ago said it was love at first sight. We don't know that, especially for him.

Julia Griffiths was a brilliant woman. She was about three years older than Douglass, came from an abolitionist family in England. Extremely well educated, but there was no career open to her.

She helped raise a lot of money for him, and she came over to the U.S. in 1849 with her sister. Her sister married Douglass's printer, and Julia moved into the Douglass home in Rochester, which Anna Douglass ran.

Anna was a thoroughly talented domestic woman, famous for her garden, famous for her cooking, for her rectitude, and for being a temperance woman. Julia lived in Rochester with them for six years, 1849 to '55, crucial years in Douglass's life. She became his assistant editor on this newspaper. She was his principal fund raiser. She was a very close personal confidant. And she helped him with his writing. He needed an editor. It blew up in controversy.

DR: There was another woman from Europe who also became very close to him. What happened to her?

DB: Julia went back to England in 1855, right after the publication of Douglass's second autobiography, *My Bondage and My Freedom,* which is his long-form masterpiece. A German woman named Ottilie Assing had been living in the States for about three years. She was a journalist, a German Jew, although a ferocious atheist. She came to the U.S. to cover the American abolition movement.

She took the train out to Rochester, New York, basically knocked on Douglass's door in 1856. For the next twenty-two years, they had a friendship-relationship on and off, which included the very complicated problem of Ottilie Assing coming many summers to Rochester and living for as much as three months in the Douglass home with the family.

The problem, though, is that 99 percent of

what we know about it comes exclusively from Ottilie Assing in the two-hundred-some-odd letters that she wrote to her sister in Europe, all of which I had translated. Every letter he wrote to her, and he did write her a lot, was destroyed.

DR: So, as Princess Diana said, there were three in that marriage.

DB: The exact nature of that Assing relationship was my second biggest problem in this book, but I treat it seriously.

DR: John Brown is an abolitionist, interested in military insurrection. What is his relationship with Frederick Douglass?

DR: Douglass was fascinated with John Brown from the day he met him, this steely-eyed, radical, biblical, Old Testament abolitionist who wanted to find some way to cause whatever breakup he could in the slave system, if not the whole country. A fellow radical abolitionist.

John Brown had this idea that he was going to create manned forts in the lower part of the northern states, and they were going to funnel slaves out of the upper South to these forts and then further north, and thereby damage the slave system. Not a very reasonable plan. But Douglass was interested.

You have to understand what happened in the 1850s. The United States tore itself to pieces. The political parties tore themselves to pieces, the union tore itself apart. From the Compromise of 1850 all the way to secession, abolitionists got more and more desperate, especially after the Dred Scott decision [by the Supreme Court].

Because if you were Black in America the day after that decision, you lived in the land of the Dred Scott decision, which said, "You have no future here." So, when Brown was talking about some kind of insurrectionary strike on the South, Douglass listened. However, by 1858, when he learned that Brown's real scheme was to attack Harpers Ferry, the largest federal arsenal, Douglass said, "This is suicidal, this is crazy."

DR: John Brown does attack Harpers Ferry, he's captured, ultimately executed. Why does Frederick Douglass flee the United States? He wasn't involved.

DB: He wasn't at Harpers Ferry, but unfortunately, in this big trunk of material the government found that John Brown left behind were lots of letters from Frederick Douglass. He was, in a sense, not only complicit, he was easily a coconspirator. He knew where this was going to happen. He didn't know exactly when. Right after the raid, he was in Philadelphia giving a speech, and he had to escape for his life back to Rochester.

DR: Let's go forward to 1860. Abraham Lincoln is running for president, nominated by the Republican Party. Was Douglass in favor of Lincoln?

DB: Yes and no, depending on which week you asked him. In the 1850s Douglass becomes a thoroughgoing political abolitionist. But he just was never sure how to own up to this new Republican Party. He cheered the fact that they opposed the expansion of slavery, but he always wanted them to go further.

In the first year and a half of the war, Lincoln had no more ferocious critic among abolitionists than Douglass because of the policy of returning fugitive slaves, if possible, to the Confederates, and because the war was quite explicitly not being prosecuted against slavery.

Lincoln had good reasons for this, let's make no mistake. But in 1861, Douglass called Lincoln the most powerful slavecatcher in the land. Douglass will not really change his tune on Lincoln until the preliminary Emancipation Proclamation.

DR: That's issued in preliminary form in September of 1862, and in final form on January 1, 1863, including the provision, in effect, that Blacks could serve in the Union Army.

DB: In fact, it ordered it.

DR: When Lincoln was president, he met with Douglass on three occasions. What was the nature of those meetings?

DB: The first meeting was Douglass just going to Washington in August 1863 without an invitation. They'd been recruiting Black soldiers since January '63, but it came to be obvious that Black soldiers were serving with terrible discrimination, unequal pay, inferior equipment, brutalization, never allowed to be officers with commissions.

Douglass had recruited a hundred members of the famous Fifty-Fourth Massachusetts Regiment. But he quit recruiting in July of '63, and he went to Washington. First time he'd ever set foot in Washington, D.C. He went to the White House. He just got in line.

You've probably heard the famous story of the lines that would form at Lincoln's White House. People would wait and try to see the president, and the poor man would sit there and meet them all.

Douglass got in line, and he was admitted to the president's office. He spent probably forty-five minutes that first meeting with Lincoln, and he protested these discriminations against Black troops. Douglass left that first meeting with no promises, but he did come away from it awed by Lincoln. In speeches he said that he'd never been in the presence of a powerful white man who treated him so fairly.

DR: Second meeting, he wasn't treated as well.

DB: The second time is August of '64. Lincoln is up for reelection, but it doesn't look like he's going to be reelected. The war is in hopeless stalemate in Virginia, in Georgia, and a lot of other places.

Lincoln invites Frederick Douglass to the White House. He needs the greatest Black spokesman in America. He looks Douglass in the eye and asks him to be the principal agent of a scheme — think back to John Brown now — that would funnel as many slaves as possible out of the upper South, to behind Union lines, into some kind of legal freedom before Election Day.

Douglass had no idea what he was supposed to do. All Lincoln told him was, "The War Department will help you." He went back to Rochester, he started firing telegrams and letters off to his friends, telling them about this scheme, even though he had no clear idea what they were supposed to do.

But he was saved by history, because within two weeks was the fall of Atlanta. Douglass never had to put that team together.

DR: Douglass sees him the final time after Lincoln's inaugurated a second time. Lincoln is assassinated not too long thereafter. Ultimately the Thirteenth Amendment is passed. Slavery is over. Is Douglass's mission in life gone?

DB: For a while he thought it was. In his third autobiography [*Life and Times of Frederick Douglass*], the chapter about the end of the war is called "Vast Changes." He opens with a paragraph — classic Douglass, if he wasn't quoting the Old Testament, he was always quoting Shakespeare — he opens with a paragraph in which he says, "Othello's occupation is gone." That comes out of a soliloquy where Othello is lamenting the loss of his army, his horses. But Douglass really probably was worried that "they don't need me anymore."

DR: He does have a meeting with Andrew Johnson. How did that go?

DB: It was the worst meeting between an African American delegation and an American president ever held. It's in February 1866, during the Joint Committee on Reconstruction, which is holding hearings on what to do about Reconstruction in the South. The

Republicans have called a halt to Andrew Johnson's attempts to reconstruct states.

Douglass had no invitation. He went to the White House with a delegation of twelve other Black leaders. One was his son. Johnson preached at them for forty-five minutes. He told them their presence in this land was the cause of this war. He said, "You will never have any kind of civil and political liberty and equality in this country." Then, as they were leaving, Johnson was overheard [saying] — Douglass heard him say it — "That Douglass is just like every other N-word I've ever seen. He will sooner cut your throat than not."

But Douglass was Douglass. He took this delegation back to a hotel here in the District. They issued a press release. They told the world what had just happened. It was splashed in the papers the next day.

Then he went to his desk, and he wrote a whole new speech, "The Perils to the Republic." And he took it on the road, during the midterm elections of 1866, all over the North, and he skewered Andrew Johnson.

DR: Ultimately, he moves from Rochester because his house is burned down. Where does he move?

DB: He moves right behind the Capitol on F Street. He then bought Cedar Hill, land up in Anacostia, in 1878 with a big loan from a good friend, Robert Purvis.

DR: He gets an appointment as U.S. marshal for the District of Columbia. Was that the first time a Black person had ever been confirmed by the United States Senate?

DB: Indeed it was. In 1877 Rutherford Hayes appoints Douglass marshal of the District, which was like being a glorified sheriff of the District of Columbia. It was an important federal post, much more important than you might think, because in the Black press, all over the country, this was hugely celebrated. It also had a salary — the first salary he ever made in his life.

DR: Does he believe in nepotism at this job?

DB: He makes eight appointments as clerks in the marshal's office. The first four are his four adult children. There were nine or ten D.C. newspapers then, three of them Black, five of them white. Everybody is charging him with nepotism. Finally he goes and meets the press one day and says, "Okay, it's nepotism. My kids need jobs."

DR: His wife of forty-four years dies. Does he remarry?

DB: Anna died in 1882, after long illness. They had four surviving adult children, twenty-one grandchildren. By the 1880s, there were always a variety of other hangers-on around Douglass. All of them are financially dependent on him for lots of reasons. It's one of the most complicated aspects of Douglass's life.

Anna dies in the summer of '82 and Douglass has an emotional breakdown. He went up to Poland Spring, Maine. He spends two months there by himself, and he writes some priceless letters to his daughter — priceless because of how he opens up about the nature of his life, how he opens up a little about Anna.

Douglass, in his 1,200 pages of autobiography, never says anything, or almost anything, about his family. There's one mention of Anna in 1,200 pages.

Fourteen months after Anna died, he married Helen Pitts. A woman twenty years younger. A white woman. It became the most scandalous marriage of the nineteenth century.

DR: What does he say about it?

DB: He says it's nobody's business, even though everybody made it their business.

DR: One of his parents was white.

DB: He would joke about it. Douglass became brilliant at converting racism into humor when he had to. What do you do with the absurdity of racism sometimes but find some way to laugh at it if you can? Otherwise you'd go crazy. He said, "In my first marriage I honored my mother. In my second marriage I honored my father."

Most importantly, Helen was a very well-educated woman, a Mount Holyoke graduate. Came from a staunch abolitionist family in western New York.

DR: Douglass was at the Seneca Falls Convention in 1848, and he was a big believer in women having the right to vote. Except when the Fifteenth Amendment came around, he had to choose: Do you want to let women and Blacks vote, or just Blacks? Why did he say he didn't want women to be in the Fifteenth Amendment?

DB: He wasn't the one who said women shouldn't be in the Fifteenth Amendment. That was done for him by Congress. Everyone with one eye open knew that if you put women's suffrage in the Fifteenth Amendment, it never passes.

But back to Seneca Falls, briefly. Douglass was the only male speaker. He was one of twenty-two men who signed the Declaration of Sentiments.

Douglass was all-in for women's rights, including women's economic rights. But when it came to the Fifteenth Amendment, he had a terrible falling out with Susan B. Anthony, Elizabeth Cady Stanton, and a few other great leaders of women's suffrage.

DR: You say in your book he was the most-photographed man of the nineteenth century. Why did he never smile?

DB: I think Douglass smiled a lot, just not on camera. You had to sit for way too long to be photographed. Douglass used this modern new invention to create his own image. He manipulated photographers. His sternness in many of his photographs had a lot to do with how he wanted to present himself. There is one late photo of Douglass in old age where he is cracking a smile.

DR: When did he die?

DB: In 1895, at the age of seventy-seven. He had a heart attack. He had heart disease for some time, though I can't prove that. There was no cardiology yet. Douglass died of a heart attack in early evening on a day in February 1895, just after returning from downtown and attending a women's rights convention. Eulogies and tributes appeared in all parts of the country for many weeks.

ELAINE WEISS
ON WOMEN'S SUFFRAGE

Journalist; author of *The Woman's Hour: The Great Fight to Win the Vote* and other books

"One thing we have to understand is that the idea of women's rights actually stems from the abolition movement. . . . The idea of all humans having the divine spark and having the right to freedom and a voice in their government really comes out of abolition."

Thomas Jefferson's eloquent rhetoric in the Declaration of Independence's preamble had two glaring omissions, one unstated and one stated. The unstated omission was that the "all men" who were to receive the blessings of "Life, Liberty, and the pursuit of Happiness" were to be white men. The stated omission was that women were not entitled to these same blessings.

So it was not a surprise that when, eleven years later, the Constitution was drafted by fifty-five white men and ratified by the states' white men shortly thereafter, the system of slavery was essentially endorsed by the document. Nor was it a surprise that no words in the Constitution, or the subsequently adopted Bill of Rights, referred to the rights of women.

The Seneca Falls Convention in 1848 adopted a resolution, though not without dissent, supporting women's suffrage, and that is often seen as the unofficial launching pad for the women's suffrage movement in the United States. That a constitutional amendment granting such a vote was not finally ratified until August of 1920 — more than seventy years later — demonstrates how politically controversial women's suffrage turned out to be. What was the controversy?

Of course, those who have power generally are not in favor of surrendering it. And thus the men in the country did not see how their power or ability to control political or social events would be helped by allowing women to vote.

In the face of these arguments, the suffragist leaders — Susan B. Anthony, Elizabeth Cady Stanton, Alice Paul, Carrie Chapman Catt, Julia Ward Howe, Lucy Stone, Sojourner Truth, among many others — worked tirelessly to develop the requisite political support for a constitutional amendment after their earlier legal efforts had failed to persuade the Supreme Court that the existing

Constitution already permitted women to vote.

The effort to get Congress to pass the requisite constitutional amendment was a hard-fought political undertaking, not aided by the fact that a fair number of women, including some prominent figures, initially opposed the amendment. But Congress finally approved what became the Nineteenth Amendment in June of 1919.

Three-quarters of the states — thirty-six out of forty-eight at the time — had to ratify the amendment. So the political arguments that had been raised by both sides in the halls of Congress were then shifted to the houses of the state legislatures. The outcome was hardly a foregone conclusion. Many southern states in particular opposed the amendment, arguing in part that the amendment would disrupt the southern way of life by giving Black women the right to vote.

By August of 1920, thirty-five states had approved the amendment, but the number of states likely to approve was dwindling. One southern state, Tennessee, was thought to be a possible supporter, and the combined lobbying forces of both sides moved to Tennessee as its legislature began to consider the amendment.

What happened there is retold in great novelistic style by Elaine Weiss in *The Woman's Hour,* one of many interesting books that

were published around the centenary anniversary of the Nineteenth Amendment's
ratification. Weiss is a well-respected journalist and media commentator specializing in issues relating to women's rights and political
activities.

I interviewed her about the battle for suffrage for the New-York Historical Society on
September 25, 2020. In recounting the vote
in the Tennessee legislature, Elaine Weiss
helps to remind readers that the right to vote
is seen by Americans as a necessary prerequi-
site to meaningful citizenship.

DAVID M. RUBENSTEIN (DR): It's hard to
believe women didn't have the right to vote
for so much of our country's history. We'll go
through that, but let's talk a little bit about
your own background. What prompted you
to write this book?

ELAINE WEISS (EW): I'm a politically aware
and engaged American woman and voter, and
I realized I did not know how it was that I, as
an American woman, had obtained the right
to vote. I knew that it was not in the Constitution when our country began, and then at
some point it was. I asked some friends, who
are very well-educated men and women, and
they also looked at me kind of blankly and
shrugged and said, "Oh, Seneca Falls."

I realized we really don't know this. It's not

in our popular sense of our history. I wanted to explore it. While beginning my research, I came upon a report in the Library of Congress that explained how a bequest to the suffrage movement in 1914 had been spent. It described the ratification fight, because that's how some of the money had to be allocated, and it talked about the last state to ratify, which was Tennessee.

The story that this little bureaucratic report in the Library of Congress described was so dramatic and almost wild that I knew that this was a great story. What I realized is that by focusing in on this last battle in Tennessee, in the summer of 1920, when the Nineteenth Amendment was being decided, I could tell a larger story about democracy, about voting rights, and about the history of women's struggle for this.

DR: What was the principle argument that men used against giving women the right to vote?

EW: In this crusade for the vote, we're asking men to share power. There's a natural opposition to that, not only in the political classes but in American homes, because men were used to women having a subservient role. It's in much of our religious tradition, certainly in our civic tradition.

Men said, "Women are too fragile. They're

not bright enough. Women can't handle the rough and tumble of politics. They can't conceptualize public policy."

They were using this rather patronizing idea of what women could and could not do in order to say, "She can't deal with important issues like who to vote for and what our nation's policies should be."

The other argument was that if a woman was able to vote, she might think she was socially equal too. And this was going to disrupt what they considered the natural order of things, which was patriarchy.

So men used a variety of descriptions of women to advocate that they shouldn't be able to vote. Clergymen used the idea that this went against God's plan, because he had made Adam to be dominant over Eve, and to question that was an abomination. So you have interesting approaches that men took besides just raw political power.

DR: Why did some women not feel they should have the right to vote?

EW: There were organized groups of women, even in 1920, who opposed the idea of women's suffrage. In the beginning of the movement, in the mid-nineteenth century, almost everyone was against this idea. It was considered a radical idea. The great majority of American men but also American women thought it was just too outrageous, this idea of women voting.

Slowly, slowly, the suffragists worked for decades to change hearts and minds about this, to change attitudes about what woman's role should be and what her rights should be. By the dawn of the twentieth century, when the suffrage movement is beginning to make some real headway, that's when you see women organizing and saying, "We don't want to vote. It would be a burden upon us."

Their reasoning often was: "This is going to disrupt the American family. It's going to upend gender roles. Husbands and wives are going to argue and divorce will boom, because there'll be disruption in the home."

There was an idea that this was going to cause women to abandon the family. The anti-suffrage women call the idea of suffrage "the moral collapse of the nation." They see it in what we call culture-war terms, that this is going to affect private life as well as public life.

DR: One of the most progressive women in American history, certainly in the twentieth century, is thought to be Eleanor Roosevelt; yet early in her career she was opposed to women's suffrage as well. How can that be explained?

EW: That was quite a shock when I came

upon that in my research. Eleanor Roosevelt exemplifies a certain stratum of American woman who was very comfortable, comes from wealth, comes from connections. The status quo is just fine with them. Why shake things up?

A lot of the antisuffrage leadership comes from wealthy women whose husbands are congressmen, senators, mayors, professors, presidents of universities, who see no reason that uneducated women, factory women, women of all different classes, whom they consider below them, should have the right to vote.

Eleanor Roosevelt in 1920 is a thirtysomething young mother with five little children. Her husband's a very ambitious politician. In fact, he's running on the Democratic ticket for vice president in 1920, and yet she's not sure how she feels about women's suffrage.

She was never an antisuffragist in that she didn't join them, though they courted her. She doesn't join them, but she's so insecure about what her role as a political wife should be that when New York women gain the right to vote through referendum in 1917, and can vote in 1918 for the first time, she refuses to vote.

After ratification in 1920, she joins the League of Women Voters, and she becomes a protégé of the great suffrage leader Carrie Chapman Catt, and she begins becoming much more politically engaged. She serves on the League of Women Voters for many years.

So we see this evolution of her political consciousness. It's really fascinating. Uncle Teddy's in the White House. She didn't really need to influence anyone else. But she comes to learn how important the vote is.

DR: In United States history, there's always a racial overtone. What is the racial overtone here? Is it that with Black women and Black men voting, there might be too many Black votes in the South?

EW: It becomes one of the pivotal issues when it comes to ratification. Race was always part of the women's suffrage movement, from the very beginning. One thing we have to understand is that the idea of women's rights actually stems from the abolition movement. The women whom we consider the foremothers of this movement — Elizabeth Cady Stanton, Susan Anthony, Lucy Stone, and Lucretia Mott — are all abolition workers before they become suffrage workers. The idea of all humans having the divine spark and having the right to freedom and a voice in their government really comes out of abolition.

These are twin causes from the 1840s until after the Civil War. Then there's a rift. The powers that be say, "Women cannot get the vote, only Black men will be accorded the vote by the Fifteenth Amendment," and the suffragists feel betrayed.

DR: A hundred years after the ratification and certification of the Nineteenth Amendment, what does history show us? Do women vote in roughly the same percentages as men?

EW: They vote in larger percentages.

DR: And in the United States, there are more registered women voters than registered men. Is that true?

EW: We do know that women surpass men's participation in voting, so I would say yes, because you have to be registered first. And that gap has been growing in the last few decades.

DR: There was a concern initially when this ratification effort was under way that women would vote much differently than men. They would, for example, be against railroads. The railroad industry was against women getting the right to vote because it was thought that somehow women would take away their power in the Congress. As it turned out, do women vote that much differently than men?

EW: For the first fifty years, they voted very similarly to men. The suffragists had both promised and threatened an organized women's vote that would reward its friends and punish its opponents. That never really developed.

When politicians realized that women were not voting as a bloc, not punishing those who had been against suffrage or the Nineteenth Amendment, they began to ignore them. And so what you do see is that participation of women does not equal that of men until around 1960. Then by 1980, which is the first time we're measuring this in a more modern way, we see women's participation surpassing that of men. That's been growing ever since.

DR: Let's go back to our country at the beginning. When there were just thirteen colonies, did any let women vote?

EW: New Jersey did allow women to vote when it became one of the original thirteen states. What's so interesting about that is that women in New Jersey did vote from about 1789 until 1807, when the powers that be realized that they were voting out some of the rascals and voting in some reform candidates. Politicians didn't like it, so they changed the state constitution, and New Jersey women lost the right to vote.

Sometimes a school board in certain districts allowed women to vote on school matters. That was the domestic domain of women, so it was considered okay. But for the most part it was prohibited by state constitutions.

DR: Did England allow women to vote before that happened in the United States or not?

EW: It was a little bit before. The U.S. and U.K. suffrage movements were very much sister movements. They moved in parallel. There was a lot of communication between the leaders. Some of the leaders actually joined together and formed an International Woman Suffrage Alliance. This was not just an American idea, it was a concept that was spreading around the world.

Great Britain did give women the right to vote in early 1918, while World War I is still raging. But it did not give all women the right to vote — only women who had property and paid taxes and were over thirty years old.

I was really puzzled by the thirty-years-old requirement. Then I read an account that this age requirement was put in because Great Britain had lost more than a million men in World War I, and they felt if they allowed all women over twenty-one to vote, there'd be an imbalance. There'd be too many women voting. So it's not for another decade — 1928 — that all British women over the age of twenty-one get the right to vote.

DR: The beginning of the women's suffrage movement in the United States is often thought to be the Seneca Falls conference in 1848. No disrespect to Seneca Falls, but it's not a major city. Why didn't they have this in Boston or New York or Philadelphia?

EW: There's a really simple answer to that. It's because Elizabeth Cady Stanton lived in Seneca Falls. Now, women's rights was something that had been talked about for decades. It didn't just pop up at Seneca Falls. But this was the first publicly announced conference dedicated to the idea of women's rights.

DR: The suffragists would say, "Why don't we use the Fourteenth Amendment as a justification? Let's go to the voting booths and vote." Then they would take it to the courts and see if the Supreme Court would uphold it. What happened to that effort?

EW: The suffragists used many different strategies and methods. One of them was to use the courts to try to get women's rights acknowledged.

It launches in the 1870s after American women are left out of the Fifteenth Amendment, which only covers the newly freed

Black men. The suffragists decide to conduct civil disobedience. Susan B. Anthony and Sojourner Truth and more than two hundred other women in several elections in the 1870s, but specifically the 1872 presidential election, go to the polls and demand to be registered and to vote. They're trying to test the law that under the Fourteenth Amendment, as citizens of the nation, they already possess the right to vote and they just have to exercise it.

Susan Anthony gathers her sisters and some friends in Rochester, New York, where she lives, and they march down to the polling place and they vote. The authorities come after Anthony as the face of the movement, and they arrest her. She is charged with illegal voting in a federal election. She brings her case to the public and says, "Is it a crime for a U.S. citizen to vote?"

And of course she is convicted. She refuses to pay the fine. She wants to bring this to the Supreme Court. She wants to go to prison. The judge does not allow it. He doesn't want a martyr in prison. So she never pays that fine, but other people do bring a case to the Supreme Court.

It's decided by the Supreme Court in 1874 that women are citizens but they are nonvoting citizens. At that point the suffragists realize they're going to have to do something different, and they draft an amendment to the Constitution.

DR: As I understand it, there were two strategies. Strategy one is "Let's try to get a constitutional amendment." That would solve everything. But there was also an effort to go state by state and get a state legislature to approve the right for women to vote in that particular state. Why did the effort to get a constitutional amendment prevail and the effort to get the vote approved in each state not prevail?

EW: The suffragists pursued a double-track strategy throughout. They begin with a state campaign in Kansas in 1868. They realize it's going to be a huge undertaking, but they try. There are scores of these campaigns in almost every state, and sometimes multiple tries. Oregon has five attempts. New York has three attempts before it was successful.

It's very slow going. Congress sits on this amendment that's introduced in 1878. They do not act on it for forty years.

In the meantime, the suffragists are going state by state and trying to convince the men of each state that they should share power with women. They are successful in some of them, mostly in the West.

They go to Theodore Roosevelt and they say, "What will it take for you, Mr. President, to support this federal amendment?" He says,

"Bring me another state." Basically he's saying there have to be enough states who have allowed women to vote so that they're voting for their representatives. If there's that kind of pressure, then Congress will begin to listen.

So it's really this double-edged campaign where they're trying to get enough states to put pressure on Congress to make it a political reality that women can vote. When New York State does pass women's suffrage in 1917, that's a game changer. Now the politicians can't really ignore it anymore. It's not a coincidence that soon after, in 1919, at the conclusion of World War I, is when the amendment finally emerges from Congress.

DR: By 1920, when the Nineteenth Amendment is passed, how many states allow women to vote at that time?

EW: About fifteen already have given women full suffrage. There's another group of states that, almost as a prevention against the Nineteenth Amendment, have given women what's called limited suffrage. You can vote for president or the presidential electors, but you can't vote for your congressman, your senator, your mayor, your governor, your state legislators.

There was something called the suffrage map, which was like a crazy quilt designating which states gave which kind of suffrage. But by 1920, almost nine million women are able to vote. So now the pressure is on.

DR: You mentioned World War I. Was there a feeling among men that women had done a terrific job in helping the war effort and maybe we should thank them by giving them the right to vote?

EW: Yes. Women participate in the war effort in ways they've never been allowed to before. They're not only nurses, rolling bandages for the Red Cross, they are also in the mines, they're in the fields, they are working in munitions plants, they are making airplanes and tanks and ships.

They are doing what was considered men's work. This whole idea that women are too fragile, too temperamental, too weak to have the vote is really blown out of the water when you see women in uniform, working in the mines. World War I makes a big difference in how men view women, and those old canards just don't work anymore.

DR: When was the first time that there was an actual vote on the floor of the House of Representatives or the Senate on the Nineteenth Amendment?

EW: Over forty years, it's actually voted down either in committee or on the floor twenty-

311

eight times. It's finally passed by the House in January of 1918.

The Senate will delay for another eighteen months, and they will humiliate President Woodrow Wilson, who goes before the Senate and begs them to pass this amendment as a war effort.

And the Senate votes it down again. It's not until June of 1919, a good six months after the war is over, that the Senate relents and finally there's congressional passage.

DR: To amend the Constitution, you need two-thirds of each house and three-quarters of the states. We had forty-eight states then, and needed thirty-six states to approve. Relatively quickly some states were saying, "We want to be the first." Who was the first state?

EW: Wisconsin and Illinois kind of tie. They had a race, and they both sent their ratification certifications on fast trains to Washington, and one got a little delayed.

So yes, there is this race to be first, and sometimes it passes unanimously and the legislators get up and sing "America the Beautiful" or "The Star-Spangled Banner." In other places it's really close. In New Jersey it was extremely close. Then in other states, like Delaware, it fails.

DR: Thirty-five states approve it within a number of months, and it's generally thought that a thirty-sixth state will approve it at some point. Why was Tennessee, a southern state, thought the most likely to be the thirty-sixth state?

EW: By the summer of 1920, thirty-five states have ratified, but there are a few outstanding. In two northern states, Vermont and Connecticut, the governors refuse to even call their legislators in for a special session to consider the ratification.

One of the things the Senate did spitefully was that, by dragging their feet and not allowing the amendment to go out to the states until the summer of 1919, they knew that most legislatures would not be in session the following year. Most state legislatures then did not meet every year. So thirty governors would have to be convinced by the suffrage advocates to bring their legislators back from every corner of the state for a special session.

Governors were very reluctant to do this. It was a bit expensive: the legislators had to be paid per diems. Some governors thought they might be impeached if legislators came back, because there were other issues that might come up.

It's politically dangerous for some governors to do this, and so they don't want to do it. In Vermont and Connecticut, there are corporate interests who are threatening the governors and saying, "You better not do this," and so they refuse. There are a few other states outstanding, but they're also southern — North Carolina, which everyone assumed would reject the amendment, and Florida, where the governor refuses to call the legislators back.

So it turns out that Tennessee is the last best hope, even though it's a very dangerous place, because it is a southern state and it is going to be riven by the racial issues. Suffragists are not pleased that that's their final, best chance.

DR: The suffragists and some of the anti-suffragists descend on Tennessee. They take over the hotels, they start lobbying.

The governor was supportive, but he said, "Not right now." Is that right? He wanted to wait until he got renominated?

EW: I wouldn't say he was that supportive at the beginning. He didn't want any part of this.

He's up for a very difficult primary challenge, and then he has to run for reelection. He's not very popular. The last thing he needs is a divisive debate about women's suffrage.

There's also a part of the Tennessee constitution that might make it more difficult for the state to consider ratification — a waiting period, so to speak. The Supreme Court wipes that away in June of 1920, and suddenly there are no more excuses. So the governor has to call his legislature back, but it's only after his primary. Then there's a very limited amount of time for the suffrage supporters to actually get to work.

DR: Which chamber takes it up first, the Tennessee Senate or the House?

EW: The Senate takes it up. There were rancorous debates, but the Senate actually does pass it with a pretty comfortable margin. As you said, everyone descended on Tennessee, not only the suffrage leaders but also anti-suffrage leaders from all around the country, the corporate interests, and the political operatives from the different political parties. And not just the Democrats and Republicans. There were some minor parties involved. Also the presidential candidates or their representatives, because it's a presidential election that fall. So it's a wild time in Nashville.

DR: The Speaker of the House in Tennessee comes out against the amendment?

EW: He flips. At first he says he's going to support it. His intention, he tells the suffragists, is to be the great champion and bring it through the House.

But he flips right on the eve of the opening of the special session. It's very peculiar that he does this. The historical assumption is that he has been pressured or induced by the railroad industry, because he will soon have a very lucrative job with the railroads.

DR: There's a motion to table, which means to not vote on the amendment, and the vote is forty-eight to forty-eight. It's obviously close. What is the ultimate vote?

EW: It gets kind of messy. It does come down to this tie, forty-eight to forty-eight. A few legislators were absent. There's a young delegate, the youngest representative in the legislature, a twenty-four-year-old freshman delegate from a little hill town in East Tennessee, and he has been voting with the antisuffragists all this time. He wants to duck. He's up for reelection. He is reading law to become a lawyer under his mentor, who is a rabid antisuffragist. It just would be safer for him to go with the flow and vote this down.

Personally he does feel that women should have the right to vote, but politically it's very dangerous for him. He's wearing the red rose in his lapel, which is a symbol of antiratification, antisuffrage. The suffragists wore yellow roses in their lapels and on their dresses.

It comes down to this tie, and young Harry

Burn realizes he can't duck, that actually his vote matters. He can break that tie.

It's one of the great romantic stories in American history. That morning, he has received a letter from his mother back home in East Tennessee. She's written to him and said, "I've noticed you've not been supporting suffrage. Do the right thing, Harry, and be a good boy and vote to ratify." In that moment, when he realizes he can make the difference, he can kill the amendment or pass it, he has his mother's note in his breast pocket, and he changes his stance and he votes aye.

DR: So it passes?

EW: Yes. Then what happens is the Speaker of the House, using a parliamentary maneuver, changes his vote to aye. He is very much against ratification, but by doing that, he can trigger something called reconsideration. He puts the vote in limbo, and at any time in the next seventy-two hours he can call the House together again, whoever is there, and reconsider it. He's buying himself some time to twist arms and kill the ratification. And all hell breaks loose in Nashville.

DR: But in the end, the amendment passes again?

EW: It does. He isn't able to shake that very

tiny majority, though they try through threats like blackmail and fake telegrams that "your house is burning down, you better leave Nashville." There's a lot of dirty tricks going on during those three days.

DR: You pass an amendment and it's certified by the governor, then it has to be sent to the United States secretary of state so he can officially certify it. Did they send a person on a train to Washington, D.C., to get the secretary of state to sign it?

EW: There were a lot more shenanigans between that vote on August 18 and August 26, when it finally arrives in Washington. The antisuffrage lawyers are successful in getting a series of injunctions that at first freeze the governor from certifying. When he finally is able to certify it, they put it on a train and it chugs its way up to Washington.

Meanwhile, the suffragists are following it, hoping they can be there when it is signed. It arrives in the middle of the night in Washington.

The Post Office is the hero of the story. They have their employees waiting for that mail train, and they're told, no matter what time it is, take that certification envelope and bring it to the secretary of state. They do that at like four in the morning. He receives it, he has it checked over by his attorneys, and he signs it because he doesn't want any delay. He signs it basically in his bathrobe in his own house, with one witness.

DR: And that's August the twenty-sixth?

EW: That's the twenty-sixth. So that's the day it is proclaimed as the Nineteenth Amendment to the Constitution.

Jon Meacham
on John Lewis
and Civil Rights

Historian and Biographer; author of *His Truth Is Marching On: John Lewis and the Power of Hope* and many other books

"The world he was fighting to change sixty years ago is in some ways resurgent, and the lessons and the strengths he brought to the fight bear our attention."

John Lewis lived two storied lives: one as a very young civil rights leader in the 1950s and 1960s, and one as a selfless congressman widely seen as "the conscience of the Congress" from the late 1980s until his death last year from pancreatic cancer. During both of these lives, Lewis, a sharecropper's son from Alabama, repeatedly showed physical and moral courage, as well as an unyielding dedication to the mission of improving lives by having America live up to the promises made in the Declaration of Independence and the Constitution.

Lewis's life in Congress lasted more than

three decades. While there, he had the universal respect of his colleagues, and was a key voice on civil and human rights initiatives. But it was John Lewis's life as a civil rights activist for a decade that will forever be seen as his most historic legacy.

It was during that time that he was one of the leaders of the dangerous Freedom Rides; that he was imprisoned for leading countless civil rights and voting rights demonstrations; that he was the youngest featured speaker (at twenty-three) at the historic March on Washington in August of 1963; that he was physically beaten into unconsciousness while nonviolently protesting; and that he led over the Edmund Pettus Bridge in Selma, Alabama, two marches that ultimately helped persuade Congress to pass the Voting Rights Act of 1965.

It is this period of Lewis's life on which Jon Meacham, a Pulitzer Prize–winning biographer, focused his attention. In retracing Lewis's steps, Jon vividly captured the challenges, risks, and courage involved in the life of this heroic civil rights leader. Jon was also able to interview Lewis about his early civil rights activities, and many of those interviews occurred while John Lewis was courageously fighting cancer.

I have interviewed Jon Meacham in person on a number of occasions, but did so this time virtually from our respective homes for a New-York Historical Society program on September 11, 2020. The interview, like John Lewis's life, was quite riveting, for Jon was able to eloquently capture the civil rights icon's humanity, courage, leadership, and humility.

DAVID M. RUBENSTEIN (DR): Your books are often about people who are not alive when you started writing about them. What prompted you to write a book about John Lewis?

JON MEACHAM (JM): I was standing on the Edmund Pettus Bridge in Selma in March of 2020 with my family and about a thousand other people. It was John's last trip there, and that was fairly evident. He'd been diagnosed with pancreatic cancer the previous fall.

I'd known him for about twenty-eight years. I always thought I would write about him, but I wasn't sure when. I thought I had another decade or so, because I thought he would keep going. I was standing there watching him, and he had, because of the cancer, lost a lot of weight. So he was physically more like the John Lewis who had been on the bridge on Bloody Sunday in 1965, more like the Lewis of the Freedom Rides and the sit-ins of 1960, '61, '62.

I realized, as he was speaking, that his life

and message are exactly the antidotes to where we are now politically. He spoke of faith, both in God and in America, both secular and sacred terms. And I thought, "This is a story that needs to be told as much as possible. Not because it's a fairy tale, not because it's uncomplicated, but because it *is* complicated." The world he was fighting to change sixty years ago is in some ways resurgent, and the lessons and the strengths he brought to the fight bear our attention.

DR: He had already written an autobiography. When you told him about this, did he say, "I don't need any more books about me"?

JM: He was very generous. He has a really excellent autobiography, *Walking with the Wind,* published in 1998. What I told him was that I wanted to do a kind of theological view of what had brought him to the bridge.

That was the fundamental question: Why was he on that bridge on Sunday, March 7, 1965? There were a lot of other places he could have been. What was it about him, his character, his background, his vision of the world that put him in the maelstrom of history?

He said, "Call anytime." We talked probably a dozen times, from early March until the third week of June. He died on July 17.

I don't always do this, but in the three

decades or so that I'd known him, whenever we'd spoken, I tended to keep notes on it, because he was a very astute student of history. John was one of the great listeners of all time. Howard Baker once said that the art of politics lies to some extent in the art of listening eloquently. And John Lewis did that.

And when he spoke, he did so with this prophetic voice, this deep voice. And we argued for twenty-eight years about a very fundamental point, which was that John Lewis believed that if you and I put our hearts and minds in the right place, if we oriented ourselves correctly, we could bring about the Kingdom of God on earth. That the vision of Isaiah, the vision of Micah, the vision of the Christian New Testament could come into actual, tangible reality.

I don't believe that. I think that we're too frail, too fallible to do it, but John Lewis did believe it. I wanted to explore the experience of someone born in a segregated society who faced white-sanctioned, state-sanctioned totalitarian violence. What made him think that perfection was possible? That was not an angle of vision that he had spent a lot of time contemplating himself, so he was very welcoming to that theme being explored.

DR: Did he live to see a draft of your book?

JM: He read it. I was touched by that. He

contributed an afterword. I wanted him to have the last word, because this is an appreciative account.

There may be warts to John Lewis, but if so, they're pretty minor. They're mostly about pride and ego, more than anything else, which is another reason I wanted to do it. You and I know a lot of folks who had exemplary early careers who tended to take care of themselves as life went on. They started out doing good and they ended up doing well. John Lewis didn't do that. He stayed in the fight, he stayed in the arena. And I wanted to explore what the roots of that had been.

DR: You really don't go into his congressional career, which was more than three decades. You wanted to focus on the civil rights struggle and his involvement in it?

JM: I did. I wasn't that interested in his congressional career, honestly. It was interesting in that he continued to speak out on national issues, but markup sessions in the Age of Clinton were not something that I wanted to spend a lot of time on.

This was really my opinion and my understanding of what religious faith can do in our politics when it is marshaled and managed by people of goodwill. That was a very particular point I wanted to make.

DR: Some people today may be familiar with him as a member of Congress, but many people may not be familiar with exactly what he did during the civil rights struggle. Where was he born, and did he come from a prominent family?

JM: No. He was born on February 21, 1940, in Pike County, Alabama, the great-grandson of a slave, a grandson and son of sharecroppers. Pike County is about fifty miles from Montgomery — red clay, Black Belt Alabama. Eight or nine children in the family.

He overcame a childhood stutter by preaching to the chickens in his farmyard. He took care of the chickens for the family. It was one of the ways his theological vision became manifest as he would baptize them and marry them. Once, when he was baptizing one, he drowned it, and that was a problem. He said his first act of nonviolent protest was refusing to eat chicken at dinner. He thought it was the death of one of his soulmates.

His father was, as I say, a farmer and drove a school bus. His mother had jobs around town. It was a classically poor life, economically poor, in a segregated county, in a segregated state.

DR: How old was he before he saw a white person?

JM: About fourteen or fifteen, when he went into town. The mailman was the white person.

He applied for a library card and was refused. When the *Brown* school desegregation decision [*Brown v. Board of Education,* decided by the Supreme Court] came on May 17, 1954, he expected his new white friends to come to school with him. He was sitting there waiting for what Dr. King and James Lawson called "The Beloved Community" to come into effect.

The media coverage of the civil rights movement was hugely important. He read about *Brown* in the newspaper that his grandfather subscribed to. He saw the pictures of the lynching of Emmett Till in Money, Mississippi, in 1955. He read about Autherine Lucy, the woman who attempted to desegregate the University of Alabama at Tuscaloosa. He heard Dr. Martin Luther King Jr. on the radio coming from Montgomery.

He had an innate revulsion against segregation. That was one tributary of his life. The other tributary was seeing that the world beyond Troy, Alabama, was quickening to the same cause. And those two tributaries merged when he came to Nashville.

DR: He came to Nashville to go to a seminary, is that correct?

JM: Yes. American Baptist Theological Seminary is up on a hill over the Cumberland River, not far from where I'm sitting.

DR: When he came there, all of a sudden he got involved in civil rights protests. What propelled him to do that? Were his parents supporting him to do that or not?

JM: No. One of the things about John is his life was quite biblical. He was not John Lewis when he was growing up, he was Robert Lewis or Bob. When he came to Nashville, he became John Lewis.

[In the Bible] Abraham was renamed. Elijah was renamed. Peter was renamed. When you receive new work, you're renamed. He had to walk away, to some extent, from his family of origin to take up that cross and that course. He comes to Nashville in the fall of '57, during the Little Rock Nine experience over in Arkansas. He's at American Baptist, which is a Black school, run by the white Southern Baptist Convention to train Black ministers. It's very modest, two or three buildings up on a hill called the Holy Hill. So, as in the Bible, he went to a mountaintop to receive this new work.

He encountered Kelly Miller Smith, the pastor of the largest Black church in Nashville, who had helped bring in a man named James Lawson. I think Lawson may be the most important living American about whom not enough people know.

Lawson was a Methodist minister. He was a conscientious objector during Korea. He went to jail for refusing to be drafted into the conflict. He went to India, he met with Gandhi's lieutenants. Gandhi was dead by then, but Lawson saw that the tactics of nonviolence that had worked so well in India could be applied to the segregated order in the South.

He had come back to the United States and ran into Martin Luther King. When King realized that Lawson had both a theological background in the American church and the experience of knowing what Gandhi had done, he said, "You're exactly the kind of person we need in the South." And so, under the sponsorship of the Fellowship for Reconciliation, Lawson comes to Nashville.

Kelly Miller Smith recommends John Lewis go to these Tuesday-night workshops in the basement of a little brick Methodist church not far from the college. In those sessions, Lewis begins to really absorb the philosophy and the tactics of the nonviolence that he would carry to his grave.

DR: In all the protests that he was involved with, all the times he was hit by police, did he ever fight back?

JM: Only once, in Selma, before Bloody Sunday. Dr. King had come to town. He was desegregating the Hotel Albert, the old downtown hotel in Selma, and a white supremacist came up to King, struck him, tried to kick him in the groin, and Lewis reacted for the first and only time in that long life of civil disobedience by throwing his arms around the guy. He embraced him in a hug.

King was so important to Lewis. They were about twelve years apart in age. He was not quite a father figure, but he was very much an elder brother and could really do no wrong, in Lewis's eyes. The love was such that Lewis was forced into that one instance of retaliatory action. And even that was a hug.

DR: So he gets involved in protests that are starting in Nashville and other cities to desegregate luncheon counters. Why did he choose that area to protest?

JM: The lunch counter was the public-facing facility in heavily trafficked department stores. We lose this now in the age of Amazon and Uber Eats and all that. But department stores were enormously important, because that's where, in Black communities, you went and you got your Sunday clothes. It's where you shopped. You could go in and spend your money, but you couldn't go in and have a hamburger or a Coke.

It was this flashing red light for people about their second-class citizenship. Their money was good enough, but they weren't good enough. It was also somewhat more straightforward than trying to integrate a school.

When you look at the civil rights movement, you see that the degree of difficulty rose. They start with public facilities in department stores, they move to interstate travel with the buses, and ultimately reach the schools and the ballot box. It was very carefully planned. These were not spontaneous demonstrations. They knew to dress well. They knew to go and buy something, so they were paying customers. They were to say "sir" and "ma'am," very carefully calibrated.

It also had an economic effect, because the department stores depended on these folks for a huge part of their income. Before they were fully ready to launch the all-out effort in Nashville, students in Greensboro [North Carolina] acted more organically. They sat in at a Woolworth's, I think it was.

Then a minister in Greensboro called James Lawson and said, "What can the students of Nashville do to support the students of Greensboro?" At that point, all these separate movements that had been taking shape in the South more or less rose up simultaneously.

A Nashville sit-in was Lewis's first arrest. And interestingly — again, biblical — he felt, as he put it, free. The freest he'd ever felt was when he was put in the paddy wagon in downtown Nashville, which was the way Saint Paul felt, the way Silas felt, the way the New Testament folks felt when they were imprisoned for the faith. They felt that they were actually fulfilling their mission in life.

DR: What were the Freedom Riders, and why was John Lewis indispensable to that effort?

JM: Imagine how important buses were in the 1940s, '50s, and early '60s. People — particularly people without great means — were not jumping on airplanes. The way folks got around was on buses and trains. There'd been a Supreme Court decision, the *Boynton* decision, that had ordered the integration of interstate travel facilities, but nobody was paying any attention to it.

And so the Freedom Rides took shape in May of 1961. They were going to send integrated groups of protesters on Greyhound and Trailways buses into the segregated South to both integrate the buses themselves and, also as important, the restrooms, the lunch counters, the facilities that were downtown, and the bus stations — sixty or seventy years ago, the bus stations were pretty important cultural landmarks in these different southern cities. It would be as if they were integrating airports now.

In May of '61, this was Lewis's first trip to Washington. He spends the night at a Quaker meetinghouse. They have what they jokingly but mordantly called a Last Supper at a restaurant in Cleveland Park in Washington. First time he met Stokely Carmichael.

They get on the buses and head south. And he's beaten in Rock Hill, South Carolina, by a Klansman, man named Elwin Wilson, who, in 2009, moved by the election of Barack Obama, reaches out to John Lewis to say, "I'm the one who beat you in Rock Hill, South Carolina, in 1961, and I want to apologize." And John accepted his apology, forgave him, and they became friendly. Again — biblical. Jesus told us to love our enemies. Who does that? Well, John Lewis did.

DR: The Freedom Rides resulted in the president of the United States sending his people down, through the Justice Department, to make certain that violence wasn't out of control. Is that right?

JM: Yes. They got to Montgomery and Birmingham and ultimately Jackson, Mississippi, and that's when the trouble truly started. There was an enormous amount of violence. Lewis was knocked to the pavement. John Seigenthaler, the personal representative of the president of the United States and the attorney general, a Nashville newspaper man, was also knocked unconscious.

We're still not quite sure how long John Lewis was out. He ends up in Jackson, Mississippi, and is sent to Parchman, which is the penitentiary in the Mississippi Delta that William Faulkner described as "Destination Doom."

We've all seen many of the images of John Lewis and his colleagues being struck, being hit, bleeding in the streets. But I submit, and he agreed, that he was actually in more physical danger when he was in police custody. He was arrested forty times in the course of the movement. But imagine, when the cameras weren't there, how much danger those "outside agitators" were in, and the remarkable physical bravery of this young man.

He starts when he's twenty during the sit-ins in Nashville, he's twenty-one during the Freedom Rides. He's twenty-two and twenty-three during Freedom Summer and when he addresses the March on Washington. He's twenty-five when he's on the Pettus Bridge. He's just so young, which is another biblical parallel — "and a little child shall lead them." He was more than a little child, but he was incredibly brave physically.

DR: I guess it's biblical that he was in the prison forty days and forty nights?

JM: Yes. It goes on and on. It's fascinating. I

argue in the book that he was a saint, and it's not to make a stained-glass figure or say that he should be removed from the ordinary run of human experience, but saints aren't saviors. Saints are just believers who are a little more virtuous than the rest of us.

DR: After President Kennedy is assassinated, President Johnson comes in and the 1964 Civil Rights Act is passed. Why didn't John Lewis say, "I've gotten a lot of things done. I'll go get my college degree and get a job doing something else"? He wanted to pursue voting rights?

JM: Two things happened in 1964 that don't get a lot of attention anymore. One was the treatment of the Mississippi Freedom Democratic Party at Atlantic City during the Democratic Convention.

Johnson does a brave thing. He passes the civil rights bill when he didn't really have to. He could have waited until after the '64 election. It was signed the first week of July in '64, but Johnson — an amazing politician, as we know — saw the white backlash coming. Having signed the bill, he wanted to shut down as best he could the movement of the South to the Republican Party. He would slow it, but he couldn't stop it. One of the ways he wanted to slow it was by refusing to seat an integrated delegation at the convention.

The other delegation, called the regulars, was the all-white segregated one. When we look at 1964 results, we think it's crazy, but Johnson believed that the whole South could go for Barry Goldwater. He was egged on by John Connally of Texas. I heard him on tape.

Neither delegation is seated. The whites leave, and Johnson, even when the whites walked out, would not seat the integrated delegation.

Until I was dealing with John on this, I didn't appreciate this. It was the first big break in the civil rights movement between the people who thought that the power structure could be brought into harmony with the ideals of the movement. Suddenly they saw that they couldn't count on the politicians in Washington.

They had come through a couple of years where they had done great education. They had been brave. The Kennedy administration had moved slowly, but had gotten there. Johnson had pushed the bill through, but then they realized there was a limit to that progress.

That was one of the moments when Lewis realized, "The only way we're going to be fully engaged as citizens is if we can vote for these folks and if they are accountable not simply to white people but to us." That's when the push for voting rights really took shape.

DR: So John Lewis stays involved and he begins one of three marches across the Pettus Bridge. The first march, he's the leader. He's walking as the head person, although he's still very young. What happened when he walked across the big bridge?

JM: They started at Brown Chapel AME Church, which is where the memorial service was held for him in July of 2020. The plan was to march from Selma to Montgomery. The idea was to march that fifty-four miles or so to end up at the Alabama State Capitol, George Wallace's Capitol, where Jefferson Davis had been sworn in as president of the Confederacy in 1861, and to present the demands for voting rights to the government.

Lewis is at the front of the line with Hosea Williams. Andy Young is back at Brown Chapel. They have medics on hand because they anticipated some trouble. They get to the top of the bridge.

It's a big bridge. You're pretty high up there. The Alabama River is brown and swirling. They get to the top and they look down and they see, as John said, a sea of blue. It was Alabama state troopers and also posse men, deputized white supremacists from Jim Clark, the Dallas County sheriff, who were determined that they were going to teach these agitators a lesson.

The marchers get to the foot of the bridge. They asked for a moment to kneel and pray. The Alabama official says, "There'll be no word, there'll be nothing." Then the tear gas comes and the beatings start.

DR: Lewis is hit over the head and knocked unconscious for a while?

JM: He is. He doesn't remember how he got back to Brown Chapel. The tear gas is something that I hadn't fully appreciated until I read the FBI reports. The FBI had lots of people there. They weren't helping, of course, but they were watching, and the FBI reported everything as you know. It was particularly difficult, tear gas.

DR: They have another march, which Martin Luther King leads over the bridge. What happens when he gets to the place?

JM: He stopped. This is one of the great weeks in American political history. When you do projects like this, you realize there are these inflection points that could be an entire book themselves.

June 11–12, 1963, could be a book. Wallace stands in the schoolhouse door in Tuscaloosa, Kennedy gives the speech on civil rights, and

Medgar Evers is assassinated in Jackson, all in the span of a day.

The time between Bloody Sunday — March 7, 1965 — and Johnson giving eight days later the great voting rights speech "We Shall Overcome" is also a fascinating slice of American history, because Johnson wanted both sides to submit ultimately to his authority.

He brought George Wallace up and gave him the Johnson treatment, loomed over him, said, "George, what are you doing down there?" He forced Wallace to say that he would allow a safe march from Selma to Montgomery. At the same time, Johnson is forcing King and others — John Lewis is in the hospital — to submit to Judge Frank Johnson's orders, that they would wait for the injunction against the march to be lifted.

DR: There's a third march over the bridge, which is the one that's going to be allowed. On that one, even though John Lewis was physically impaired, he does walk the entire way to Montgomery?

JM: He walks the fifty-four miles. He can do about seven or eight miles a day. Then they drive him back, he sleeps, and they drive him back again. It was an incredibly important march to finish, and they do end up at the Capitol. They do end up giving important speeches there. That was the force that ultimately led in August to the Voting Rights Act.

DR: After the incredible courage that John Lewis has shown throughout this early part of his life, he is voted out as the head of the Student Nonviolent Coordinating Committee, and Stokely Carmichael replaces him. Why were people upset with him after all the courageous things he had done?

JM: Nonviolence was out of fashion even when white people thought it was in fashion. One of the things about the reaction to John's death I thought was so fascinating is that almost no one addressed this tension. Dr. King and Lewis and their adherents who wanted to turn the other cheek, who wanted to use nonviolence to make the long and slow struggle for justice, were running into an immense amount of pressure for the conversation and the tactics to move from "Love thy enemy" to Black Power, to a more — and I use this word advisedly — proactive, more aggressive way of trying to address the issues of social, political, and economic injustice.

The borders between these philosophies are more porous than the popular version has it. But John Lewis was seen by May of 1966 as too close to the White House. The Sunday-school piety of the King-Lewis movement was falling out of fashion.

DR: For the rest of his life he's valued for what he's done and has a lot of very important jobs, but the greatest things he did were probably in his twenties. Did he regret that he lost this position? Do you think the rest of his life was as valuable as what he'd done in his twenties?

JM: He never really got over losing to Carmichael. It was very difficult. He went into a kind of self-imposed exile for two years. Then he came back in '68 and was working for Robert Kennedy, for that presidential campaign, both when Dr. King was killed and when Senator Kennedy was killed.

No, he saw his life as a series of sequential chapters that were about bringing the Declaration of Independence into fuller realization and trying to bring about that beloved community. I don't think he had a hierarchy of satisfaction about what he'd done.

If anything, I think the steadiness of purpose that he brought to his work is something that almost befuddled me. What does he do at the end of his life? He's standing at Black Lives Matter Plaza. He's talking to President Obama on a virtual town hall about the murder of George Floyd. And so his life was of a piece.

■ ■ ■ ■

4
INVENTION AND INGENUITY

■ ■ ■ ■

"We choose to go to the moon. We choose to go to the moon in this decade and do the other things, not because they are easy, but because they are hard, because that goal will serve to organize and measure the best of our energies and skills, because that challenge is one that we are willing to accept, one we are unwilling to postpone, and one which we intend to win, and the others, too."
— John F. Kennedy's moonshot speech at Rice University, September 12, 1962

BHU SRINIVASAN
ON 400 YEARS OF
AMERICAN CAPITALISM

Writer; author of *Americana: 400-Year History of American Capitalism*

"My view of American capitalism is that it's more like an operating system, rather than a rigid ideology. It requires adjustments, updates, patches, safeguards, and constant iteration to work properly."

Few would disagree that the U.S.'s remarkable rise from an eighteenth-century collection of thirteen British colonies to the greatest economic power in the world by the end of the nineteenth century was due in part to a capitalist approach that was (and remains) uniquely American: decisions about capital creation and investment are principally the province of the private sector and markets rather than government.

It is perhaps not surprising that America began as a capitalist country, powered initially by British traditions; but the country's capitalist approach was later fueled by a combination of entrepreneurial instincts, European trading relationships, a growing immigrant population, and slave labor in the southern economy. But why did this American-style capitalism not go the way of so many other European or Latin American economies, where socialism or even communism became commonplace, with central governments playing a much more significant role in the economy?

There is no simple answer. But surely a large part of the answer rests on these factors: a large immigrant population; seemingly unlimited natural resources; the decentralized (in the early years) governmental system; and, very importantly, the continued succession of entrepreneurial wizards who helped create the cotton gin, steam engine, telegraph, distributed electricity, railroads, airplanes, automobiles, radios and televisions, computers, transistors, semiconductors, Internet, e-commerce, and social media, among some of the best-known products or services invented or enhanced significantly in the United States.

American capitalism tends to provide great wealth for the inventors or the enhancers of these kinds of devices and services, and these wealth creators have subsequently often been lionized, in part because of their creativity, in part because of their job and wealth creation, and in part because of their philanthropy.

And even though it is increasingly recognized that American-style capitalism has the downside of creating or enhancing income inequality and reducing social mobility, the U.S. is not likely to soon materially change its centuries-old love affair with capitalism.

That this style of capitalism does not transfer perfectly to other countries is not seen as a major concern. And that significant social unrest may well result if larger and larger parts of the population are left behind also seems, regrettably, not to be a major concern for significant parts of the American population.

The American style of capitalism resulted from an unlikely confluence of historical, cultural, and economic factors swirling together in ways no one could have predicted. Countless efforts have been made over the years by historians and economists to describe how this confluence occurred, and many have contributed to our understanding.

But just a few years ago, another unlikely event occurred. A young businessman and immigrant from India, Bhu Srinivasan, decided to leave his business career behind to research and write a history of the four centuries of American capitalism.

A first-time author tackling such a detailed and complicated subject might not have been expected to produce a book admired and lauded by both scholars and business leaders.

But, after seven years of detailed research and writing, that is what happened.

I had the opportunity to interview Bhu Srinivasan virtually for a New-York Historical Society program on September 18, 2020, and could see how his passion for detail and history, and his clear understanding of business and economics, produced such a significant — and readable — work.

DAVID M. RUBENSTEIN (DR): What propelled you to want to write a four-hundred-year history of American capitalism?

BHU SRINIVASAN (BS): Immense curiosity. I came to this country in 1984, when I was eight years old. My mother was doing her postdoctorate degree. Obviously our migration to this country was stimulated by economic opportunity. Once we arrived, a lot of our movements were commercially oriented. That was the backdrop of my American experience.

As I entered adulthood, had children, and had some commercial success myself, I started reflecting on the backdrop. How far do these economic motivations go back in shaping the American trajectory — to the Pilgrims, for instance, or to the Virginia Company?

You can trace it back all the way to four hundred years. The Virginia Company was a company, after all, a for-profit company. Even the Pilgrims on the *Mayflower* were backed by shareholders back in England.

DR: Let's suppose somebody says, "I'm not sure I want to read a four-hundred-year history of American capitalism." Could you summarize what is so essential or distinctive about American capitalism? How would you contrast it with, let's say, European capitalism?

BS: I don't think that there is a lot of relevance between American capitalism and European capitalism. European society has multiple languages, multiple cultures. What we think of as Europe today is a fairly new thing — common borders, a common currency. These are very recent developments. Even Germany was divided into two countries until not so long ago.

For centuries, they were weighed down by tradition, aristocracy, war, geographic shape-shifting, redrawing borders. You're looking at the Franco-Prussian War, World War I, the Spanish Civil War, World War II, postcolonial retrenchment for France and Britain. You have a number of different things happening in Europe that don't translate very well to thinking about the American experience.

DR: What would you say are the two or three

most seminal events that propelled American capitalism forward to the state it is in today?

BS: The major thesis of my work is that America was shaped by discoveries and deployment of what I think of as next big things. The voyages to the New World, to America itself, were the next big things of that era. Some of these discoveries, like Eli Whitney's cotton gin, are accidental and incredibly significant. The young man, after Yale, goes to the American South to take a tutoring job, and ends up staying at a plantation over a few days.

The cotton gin seemed like a very simple device. You basically put cotton into this small, circular contraption where you remove the cotton seed from the cotton fibers. That sets off a big boom in cotton, because while it was very easy to grow, separating the seeds from the fiber was very laborious at that time.

This happened in the early 1790s, when Whitney invented the cotton gin. The Louisiana Purchase happens in 1803. These things are unrelated but they converge — the fertile soil of the Mississippi Delta coupled with the easy extraction of cotton fiber from cotton seed.

You have a ready labor source in American slaves who are able to produce immense amounts of cotton. For much of the eighteenth century, the big cash crop was tobacco, but that was not the case post-Revolution. At the same time, you're looking at the Industrial Revolution in England, where cotton cloth really becomes the first global consumer commodity where you have an industrial layer that has to be applied. So you're able to get cotton cloth, when a change of clothing is this very rare and luxurious thing, and all of a sudden it becomes a more affordable commodity. It starts with Black hands touching cotton in the Mississippi Delta, and the device that made it possible was Eli Whitney's cotton gin.

Similarly, the telegraph, when Samuel Morse stumbled onto this in the 1830s, was a very significant thing. When George Washington died, it took seven days for that news to travel back from Washington to New York. With the telegraph, they're transmitting details from one of the nominating conventions in 1844 within seconds. You're looking at light speed for information transmission, whereas before, the physical speed of mankind was how fast information could travel. It was like magic. There just was no reference point for how such a thing could be possible. People were bewildered and awed by that. It suggested immense possibilities and sped up commerce.

The third seminal event is a political event that shaped the American Century. The rise of Teddy Roosevelt as president in 1901 was fairly significant. This happens with the death of William McKinley, who had defeated William Jennings Bryan both in 1896 and 1900. In a simplistic sense, McKinley is the market's candidate, Bryan is the people's man, a populist.

Upon McKinley's assassination in Buffalo, New York, Teddy Roosevelt becomes the youngest president in American history. He turns out to become this highly energetic mediator between powerful business interests and labor unions, between the consumer and businesses. He uses the power of U.S. Navy contracts to end child labor. Within months of assuming the presidency, he makes the argument that since the corporate form itself is a creation of the law, meaning that the idea of limited liability does not exist in nature and only exists because the government recognizes it as such, it made little sense to him that the government should not have any regulatory authority. His presidency set the trajectory for American capitalism in a big and underrated way.

DR: Which two or three or four individuals would you say are really responsible for the powerful growth of American capitalism over the last four hundred years?

BS: My view of American capitalism is that it's more like an operating system, rather than a rigid ideology. It requires adjustments, updates, patches, safeguards, and constant iteration to work properly. If one person didn't exist, it doesn't mean that the trajectory of American capitalism would have been altered that dramatically.

That said, I think Henry Ford is very significant. In 1914, when he basically comes out with a $5 workday — for a full day of work, an eight-hour shift, you get $5 — it was double the prevailing wage. Black men included. The announcement was stunning. It was front-page news. It leads to this equation that, to some degree, still awes me.

The reason why that's significant is because you could have a recently arrived immigrant, as many were, who works ninety days and could theoretically accumulate $450, which was the price of a Model T that year.

That's an amazing thing. That doesn't happen in China today. If somebody is earning $250 a month making iPhones, three months of labor gets you a new iPhone. Whereas in 1914, three months of labor was the equivalent of a brand-new Model T. That remains stunning. I've always believed that the automobile was the ultimate symbol of American industriousness and wealth in a staggering way — it closed the loop on the American producer and the American consumer, making the workingman one and the same.

DR: If you could have interviewed one or two or three of these famous people you've written about, who would you like the most to have interviewed?

BS: Andrew Carnegie is at the very top of the list. He was a child laborer when he arrived in this country. He's thirteen years old. The family is displaced by the Industrial Revolution in Scotland — his father was a weaver. They migrate to the United States and end up in Pittsburgh.

Andrew immediately has to abandon school to go work in a boiler room. I'm not talking about a boiler room where you cold-call grandmothers to sell questionable securities, but one where a small boy is feeding coal into a furnace all day. He gets into the telegraph office, where he's a messenger boy, and ultimately rises to the Pennsylvania Railroad as an executive, and has these side ventures. And he keeps making his way in the world. This diminutive man just dominates the steel industry, completely ruthless, utterly brilliant.

Then in 1901, when J. P. Morgan decides to buy Carnegie Steel, along with some other steel companies, and form U.S. Steel, Carnegie immediately starts giving away most of his money from the sale. He stayed true to that creed he put out in his book *The Gospel of Wealth.* Whether they know it or not, it becomes the instruction manual for men like

Warren Buffett, Bill Gates, yourself. I've always believed this paradox also describes and explains American capitalism in a lot of ways.

DR: Let's talk about the periods of history you've divided your book into: the beginning of the country up to the Civil War, from the Civil War up to the early part of the twentieth century, from the early part of the twentieth century up to the latter part of the twentieth century, and then on to the present.

Let's go through each of those periods briefly. It's been thought by some historians that the person most responsible for our American capitalism was Alexander Hamilton, the first secretary of the treasury. He was very much focused on having a kind of financial system that was opposed by Jefferson. Do you think Hamilton deserves the credit he's received?

BS: To some degree. But my view is that capitalism is an action game — it is event-driven. And the interests of states and the federal government were at odds many, many times in that era. For instance, in 1824, you had *Gibbons v. Ogden,* the Supreme Court decision that affirmed that the right to regulate interstate commerce belongs to the federal government.

The Erie Canal, for instance, was a project

that was entirely financed by bondholders in the state of New York. It was guaranteed by the state itself. It opens up the Great Lakes, connects the American interior to the Eastern Seaboard, the Atlantic Ocean. Same thing with all these canal systems that connected other bodies of water and made all this American land more useful — the individual states did this. The federal government had a very difficult time coming up with money for any of these massive public improvement projects.

The secretary of the treasury under Thomas Jefferson, Albert Gallatin, had a plan to fund a series of canals in 1806, with one major canal to do what the Erie Canal ultimately did. But at the end of the day, the states did not want one state to be favored. Where would you build this large canal? Would you put it in Virginia? In Maryland? In New York? You'd end up favoring one state or the other.

So it's very hard for me to give too much credit to the foresight of the framers in this particular respect, because there were such conflicts. Federal efforts shape capitalism in different ways, but they just couldn't have foreseen the consequences of the Louisiana Purchase, which was a federal expenditure under Jefferson. This certainly shaped the contours of American capitalism, as the best cotton-producing region was the Mississippi Delta, which extended and deepened American slavery. They couldn't have foreseen the incredible accidental benefit of the Mexican-American War, which brought California into America and the greatest gold discovery of the time almost days later. At the time there were exactly fifteen slave states and fifteen free states; admitting California as a free state, the thirty-first state, required the Compromise of 1850.

The reaction was severe. The Whig Party self-destructed. You have the Supreme Court's *Dred Scott* decision. And you have the assertion of states' rights versus federal authority, all on the issue of slavery, tearing apart the country. Aside from moral questions, slavery was a most commercial of institutions that only ended with a bloody civil war. The Civil War is what enabled the federal government to assume the importance that it has today.

So the unified evolution of American capitalism really didn't happen until after the Civil War. Alexander Hamilton was certainly very influential. But the narrative should be about the discoveries, accidental events, unforeseen consequences, and how all these things worked together, how they played out. It's very difficult to trace much of it to the foresight of one individual or even a collection of individuals.

DR: In grade school, you learn this myth — I

guess it's a myth, and maybe you can tell me it's not — that people came to the United States, or what became the United States, for religious freedom. But you point out that a lot of these things were commercial ventures. Companies were formed to come over here and get some wealth and then send it back to the people who had invested. Can you describe what that was all about?

BS: Once you start stripping away the mythology and ideology and you really dive into the letters and financing documents leading up to the *Mayflower*'s voyage, for instance, you see they're not talking about God as much as they're talking about contractual terms. It's a commercial negotiation. That's one of the things that drew me to the structure of the book.

The *Mayflower* was a huge commercial endeavor. It was costly. They had British financiers, and capital from men known as "adventurers" — quite literally, the provenance for the modern idea of venture capital — is what financed it. The Pilgrims sold shares. Either you could work for your shares or you could just buy them. Same thing with the Virginia Company, which had a very similar structure.

DR: If there had not been slavery, do you think American capitalism would have developed differently?

BS: That's a huge question. Obviously, it is impossible to separate slavery from the history of American capitalism.

Initially, slavery was not as essential to the growth of the U.S. economy until cotton became this immense cash cow for the South, requiring an increasing need for slaves to harvest it. And as the overseas demand for cotton increased, the southern economy became far wealthier than its population or other natural resources would have made possible.

And sometimes, numbers tell the best story. On the eve of the Civil War, there were about 30,000 miles of railroad track. The biggest system at the time, the Illinois Central, cost about $25,000 per mile to build, give or take — labor, steel, land all included. This implies that the entire value of the railroad infrastructure of the United States had a cost basis of $750 million or so. Based on data from slave auctions, we know that the value of the average slave across age and gender was about $700 or so in 1859. The 4 million slaves in America were declared to have a value of $3 billion. One of the southern states even cited this exact dollar value in their reasons for secession. Another claimed it was $4 billion.

At the same time, the northern economy went into overdrive during the war effort.

The Pacific Railway Act was passed, creating the transcontinental railroad, during the Civil War. Land-grant colleges too. The telegraph became instrumental for modern warfare. Even the dollar became temporarily de-coupled from gold during this time, the Greenback Era. It is very difficult to separate slavery and its aftermath from the story of American capitalism.

DR: Let's go to the post–Civil War period. Of the things you write about that are very significant to the further growth of American capitalism, one of them is oil. Why was oil so important, and when did it really get discovered?

BS: In 1859. Even before this, oil was known to exist; it would seep out of the ground in some places, but you couldn't extract it at scale or at will. In Titusville, Pennsylvania, a businessman known as Colonel Drake drills down fifteen or sixteen feet with a small steam engine.

All of a sudden it's a gusher. It sets off this enormous speculative activity, where men rushed to the oil fields of Pennsylvania right during the Civil War. You have this activity in the North that's almost decoupled from the world altogether. Oil then goes on to light homes. This is obviously long before the automobile. That was the real change in

American homes. Instead of candles, you're able to have cheap lighting. Later, obviously, it didn't hurt the American automakers that there was a domestic oil industry to power all these cars.

DR: Speaking of oil, you write about a man named John D. Rockefeller, who was not from a wealthy family. What did he do to become the wealthiest man in the history of our country, as measured by the percentage of GDP he had?

BS: He probably understood economies of scale better than anyone who's ever existed in this country. He was derided as a bookkeeper. His detractors would say he was just that. But he was an incredible organizer of talent, of capital, of subsidiaries, all the things you need for industrial scale.

He was also one of the largest users of the trust mechanism. At that time, one corporation couldn't own shares in a corporation in another state.

The only way you could do that is to have a trust. You take your shares, put them into a trust, and the corporation in another state would put theirs in a trust as well. The trust beneficiaries would be the shareholders on a pro rata basis. John D. Rockefeller and Standard Oil executed that in a very large way before anybody else really knew how to do that. That's what he brought to the table.

DR: Let's talk about railroads. Why were railroads so important to the development of American capitalism?

BS: When the transcontinental railroad was completed in 1869, you can imagine the symbolism and implications of this vast country being connected. Throughout the nineteenth century, America seemed like a blank canvas that could be filled in. What the pioneers had done in settling land, you could now connect. Unlike industrialization in England, the transportation infrastructure in America itself was the industrial catalyst. It dramatically reduced the price of commodities, of natural resources, since transportation was a major cost. Railroads also enabled the idea of mail-order catalogs, so a consumer in a small town had access to the same goods as in a major city.

DR: Let's talk about electricity. When it came along, in the first couple decades or so of the twentieth century, it wasn't as if everybody had it. Who was most responsible for electricity getting developed in the United States?

BS: Certainly Thomas Edison — everybody knows that. But there were a number of people before Edison who had experimented with electricity.

Electricity took some time to really take hold in the home, primarily because you had cheap alternatives. You had gas infrastructure in a lot of the major cities and urban environments, and you had plenty of oil from Standard Oil.

So electricity as infrastructure for the home didn't take off until maybe 1910, 1920. But there were other things like streetcars that took off. Electricity had a lot of uses in industrial settings. Department stores had ample electric lighting, office buildings had lighting and elevators.

DR: World War I comes along. How did it affect our capitalist approach?

BS: The construction of planes, certainly, climbed from a few hundred annually to tens of thousands. Radio technology matured on the battlefield and the oceans. But there is one thing that World War I really moved forward — the income tax.

The income tax required a constitutional amendment. In 1895, the Supreme Court had ruled such a tax unconstitutional, because it could put a disproportionate burden, on a per capita basis, on certain states versus other states. The Sixteenth Amendment is what made the income tax possible when it was ratified by the states in 1913. With the income tax, it soon became clear that you could use it to finance the American entry into World War I.

The next thing you know, tariffs on imports and the taxes on alcohol and tobacco were not nearly as important. Right after World War I, you have Prohibition, and Prohibition would not have been possible if the government had not figured out that the income tax was extremely effective at raising revenue, far superior to the tax on alcohol.

DR: Let's skip forward to World War II, which obviously has a major effect on the United States and the capitalist system. You mentioned Henry Ford. Automobiles became much more prevalent after World War II?

BS: You had well over ten million automobiles in the 1920s on American roads. During World War II, the automakers put out maybe a couple of hundred consumer automobiles for the consumer market over a three-year span — not a couple hundred thousand, a couple *hundred.* You're talking about an entire full-scale nationalization of every automobile factory in America to build tanks, to build the Liberator planes. All industrial capacity was essentially converted for the purposes of war. But after World War II, the one-car household often became a two-car household with the move to suburbia.

And then there were the R&D efforts during the war, which seeded a lot of future industries. There is this very interesting article published in 1945 by a man named Vannevar Bush, who headed scientific development during the war, in which he is fearful that all these wartime discoveries, all this knowledge, are going to be lost, because there is no effective way to keep track of it all. And he outlines a physical retrieval system for information that, decades later, Tim Berners-Lee, who invents HTML and the World Wide Web, credits for aiding his thinking.

DR: You mention in your book the impact of radio and cinema that arose before World War II. How important was the postwar rise of television to the growth of American capitalism?

BS: Radio was the first time in human history when you had millions of people doing something, listening to a hit show or a World Series game, for instance, at the exact same time.

In the 1930s, film was one of the few green shoots during the Depression. You had big films like *Gone with the Wind.* You had sound coming to film for the first time in the late 1920s, then hugely prevalent after that.

But television put a window on the world inside almost every home in this country. The adoption rate was very, very fast. It changed politics; it was considered a deciding factor in the Kennedy-Nixon election, given how photogenic and smooth Kennedy was.

In the 1950s, it gave rise to professional football, a sport perfect for TV. Pro football was not commercially viable before; teams played so few home games, attendance revenues were insignificant. TV rights fees changed that. Football is still the most expensive programming on TV. And there was a certain intimacy about TV stars who came into your living room on a weekly basis — Ronald Reagan, for instance, who hosted the show *General Electric Theater* for much of the '50s.

DR: How important were computers to the growth of American capitalism?

BS: Tremendous. Punch-card computing can almost be traced back to the eleventh census of the United States, all the way back to 1890.

A man named Herman Hollerith receives a contract from the federal government to take all this census data and put it on punch cards. They had figured out a way of putting electricity through the holes of the punch cards to tabulate them, to count the results and sort data fields mechanically.

Hollerith then becomes part of a company called CTR, Computing-Tabulating-

Recording. CTR hires an executive named Tom Watson Sr. who had left, under murky circumstances, a company called NCR, National Cash Register. Watson figures out that the punch-card business is where the future is and renames the company IBM [International Business Machines].

And IBM has a huge punch-card business in the '30s for everything from the Soviet five-year plans to the Nazis to every American company — companies like Time Inc. that are managing huge subscription rolls. This was well before electrons, transistors, and semiconductors were used in computing.

And again, the earliest user of the next wave of computing is the government. The Cold War saw no expense spared in the 1950s, nor did the space program in the 1960s. Both were catalysts for further commercialization.

The impact was huge. In the '60s, you had mainframe computing touch every industry in terms of managing inventory, managing supply chains. Sam Walton of Walmart was one of the very early users of computers. He was well known for investing heavily in technology. Ross Perot became computing's first billionaire; Electronic Data Systems had its IPO in 1968. Intel was founded the same year, so that was certainly a seminal time for computing.

DR: You talk about the importance of start-ups to American capitalism, particularly in the last few decades. The start-up phenomenon is a uniquely American kind of thing.

BS: When I say "start-up," I mean a particular type of business where venture investors are willing to tolerate losses for a long time in pursuit of hypergrowth. The other thing is that up-front capital costs for your average software start-up are insignificant compared to what industrial capitalism required.

Look at a company like Airbnb or Stripe or Dropbox. These are companies that are worth tens of billions of dollars now.

But these three were ventures backed by Y Combinator [a well-known seed investment company] that got started for $100,000, $120,000. There is no better example of how the venture model operates. As the companies progressed and met milestones, more capital was added by other venture funds, and they became these gigantic hits within a decade. All of these companies rely on some form of virality or network effects (or both), which are economies of scale on steroids. This just does not happen in any other setting. Imagine building a viable first version of your product with $100,000, then with additional rounds of capital, that becomes worth $10, $50, $100 billion less than ten years later. It's not possible for such an inexpensive funding model to propel hits at this scale in hardware, for instance.

When I say "start-ups," I largely mean software start-ups now. It's not unique to the United States anymore. India and China are right up there, and they're creating very big hits as well. But this model has pretty severe limitations. You are not building viable models of rockets, surgical tools, or robots that do the dishes for $100,000.

DR: You describe another period when finance is very important, where high-yield bonds propelled the advent of private equity. How important was all that to the growth of American capitalism?

BS: It was very important to industrial capitalism. You saw this era of conglomerates in the late '60s and '70s, and a lot of wealth started accumulating inside these corporations. You had all sorts of companies buy all sorts of disparate assets, like Coca-Cola buying Columbia Pictures. Private equity at that time found corporate America largely to be stodgy.

Then private equity and leveraged buyouts entered that business, which you know well, and started cleaning up and instituting some operating discipline. I write in the book that private equity is almost the last cycle of capitalism, whereas venture financing is at the very embryonic stages. When you have a public company that is not very efficient, that's when private equity steps in.

DR: How important has the Internet been to the growth of American capitalism? What about the ubiquitous smartphones that everybody has?

BS: Smartphones are very important, obviously, to the United States, but almost more important to India and China.

In 2007, when the iPhone came out, that was the first time you saw China manufacture a product known to the world as being of extremely high quality. That "Made in China" badge was no longer about inferior goods. If they can manufacture something to Steve Jobs's exacting standards, they know what they're doing. The world then took notice. That was a seminal moment for the rise of Chinese capitalism.

At the same time, my family, when we were in India, did not have a landline telephone. The vast majority of Indians today who have a mobile phone have never had a landline in their lives. The smartphone is the first time they've ever had access to the Internet. They didn't have desktop computers or laptops or television, in the vast majority of cases. So it is a substantial leap.

Both of these things are extremely important — for growth in India, certainly in terms of the consumer Internet and consumer economy; and for China, in terms of manufacturing, allowing them to move up the value chain. China now manufactures all kinds of things, from drones to boring machines. They certainly moved up from making shoes and plastic toys to a completely new era of precision manufacturing.

DR: Having studied four hundred years of it, do you think that American capitalism is going to prosper and do well in the next fifty years or so compared to the Chinese form of capitalism? How do you compare the two?

BS: There's a giant question mark. The communists seem to be very good at capitalism. There is still a giant portrait of Chairman Mao that hangs over Tiananmen Square. China is one large consumer market. It's now the largest market for automobiles. It's the largest market for European luxury goods. It has a lot of internal momentum, and that's something that America has never faced. Americans have never faced a competitor that has a larger consumer market than we do, that produces a greater variety of consumer goods than we do. And on top of that, China has its own online companies that are worth hundreds of billions of dollars, like Alibaba and Ten Cent.

The Chinese were a factory to the world,

but now they're a factory to themselves. It's going to be very challenging for America to meet that challenge head-on.

Think about your small thousand-dollar drone. That's not going to be manufactured in the United States. This small drone has sophisticated flight capabilities, sophisticated sensors and cameras. You weaponize that, you have next-generation infantry for a few thousand dollars. Momentum begets momentum, and China is in a period where all of their accumulated advantages of the past two decades are compounding quite quickly.

Our big mistake is leaving the bulk of our economic policy to be determined solely by the impulses of the consumer market. Consumers think on very short-term horizons. They just want the cheapest products and services at good quality, and lots of them. And I think entrepreneurs and the marketplace can satisfy this, but it is not enough. Citizens need their government to think on a generational basis in terms of economic policy, just like we do for defense or clean air or even national parks.

WALTER ISAACSON
ON AMERICAN INNOVATION

Author of *The Innovators: How a Group of Hackers, Geniuses, and Geeks Created the Digital Revolution* and many other books

"Curiosity leads you to be interested in all sorts of disciplines, which means that you can stand at the intersection of the arts and sciences. To me, that's where creativity occurs — at that intersection."

Americans have always seemed to be innovative, inventing equipment, tools, processes, and services that have helped the country meet its needs, grow its capabilities, and, as a by-product, increase its wealth.

Nowhere has this been more true than in the technology sector since World War II. Engineering skills developed in the military and in academic life, combined with a renewed and increasingly driven entrepreneurial instinct, sparked a tech boom that changed the world in ways that once seemed unimaginable.

While the computer's forerunner was actually invented by a British woman, Ada Lovelace, in the nineteenth century, the computer was improved and enhanced dramatically by a number of large American companies, principally IBM in the 1950s and '60s. But the computer, initially quite large and cumbersome by today's standards, spawned — most especially in the newly named Silicon Valley area of Northern California — a whole variety of products that revolutionized the business world as well as life itself.

Transistors, microprocessors, computer software, personal computers, smartphones, search engines, social media platforms, and artificial intelligence, among other tech innovations and inventions, created infinite new ways to solve problems, get information, communicate, conduct business, and live.

And the geniuses, entrepreneurs, and technology creators who produced this revolution became household names for their creativity, drive, wealth, philanthropy, and, in some cases, eccentricities and lifestyles. David Packard, Walter Hewlett, Robert Noyce, Gordon Moore, Andy Grove, Steve Jobs, Bill Gates, Jeff Bezos, Sergey Brin, Larry Page, Mark Zuckerberg, and Elon Musk, among others, became tech and business icons as they helped shape the modern world.

Were they geniuses? Did they get lucky? What were their secrets? There is no simple answer, but Walter Isaacson provides perceptive insights into these questions in his book *The Innovators.*

Walter is an extraordinary writer, while also having many other legendary intellectual skills. He has focused his best-selling books on individuals who could fairly be seen as geniuses — Henry Kissinger, Benjamin Franklin, Albert Einstein, Steve Jobs, Leonardo da Vinci, and, most recently, Jennifer Doudna (recipient of the 2020 Nobel Prize in Chemistry for the CRISPR gene-editing process).

Those individuals, as well as the many individuals described in *The Innovators,* have several things in common. One is that they tended to build on what had already been discovered or invented — virtually nothing was created out of "whole cloth." And two, they often worked as part of a team. Lone, madcap geniuses tended to be an image rather than the reality.

This interview took place virtually on October 5, 2020. I have interviewed Walter about almost all of his books. How he wrote so many of them while having a full-time job like chairman and CEO of CNN or president and CEO of the Aspen Institute is something I cannot really understand. He says he writes at night and is not distracted by television.

He does not own one. If I had only known that was the secret to great writing.

DAVID M. RUBENSTEIN (DR): In your research and writing about great innovators like Leonardo da Vinci and Franklin, Einstein and Jobs, have you found any common traits? Do they tend to be the leaders, the loners, often associated with individual creativity and genius? Or is the reality more of a collaborative effort?

WALTER ISAACSON (WI): There are two interrelated traits that are common to all the innovators I've written about. The first of these is curiosity — pure and passionate and playful curiosity about everything. Like Benjamin Franklin, as a teenager, going over to England for the first time and measuring the water in the ocean because he's trying to figure out how does the Gulf Stream work. Or Leonardo da Vinci, my favorite, who in his notebooks writes things in the margins like "Describe the tongue of the woodpecker."

Who wakes up in the morning and wants to know what the tongue of a woodpecker looks like? A curious person does. And that's Leonardo.

Einstein and Leonardo both wrote in their notebooks, "Why is the sky blue?" Now, we all see blue skies, but we forget to be curious about "Why is it blue?" And of course Steve

Jobs had a voracious curiosity.

The other thing about their curiosity was that it crossed all sorts of fields. Whether it was Steve Jobs being curious about calligraphy and coding or Leonardo being curious about art and anatomy, they wanted to know everything you could know about everything knowable.

That curiosity leads you to be interested in all sorts of disciplines, which means that you can stand at the intersection of the arts and sciences. To me, that's where creativity occurs — at that intersection. People can have a foot both in engineering and in the humanities or in science and the arts.

So, a wide-ranging curiosity, one that allows you to see that patterns exist across nature and how those patterns ripple, whether it's Leonardo da Vinci's spirals of water becoming the curls of hair of the *Mona Lisa* or Steve Jobs understanding the beauty of calligraphy and ingraining that in his first Macintosh.

DR: Is there something about the way the U.S. developed from its early days that encouraged innovation or creativity?

WI: Ingrained in the DNA of our country is that the people who came here were either pioneers or refugees. They were the second and third children who had to strike out on

377

their own. They were people escaping oppression and looking for freedom. They were going on an errand into the wilderness.

They are people who are used to uprooting, changing their minds, and being part of a frontier. Whether that was the literal frontier that existed until around 1900 or things like the electronic frontier, people in the United States were more willing to uproot from their Old World and take the risks of embarking on an errand into the wilderness.

DR: In recent decades, the science and technology worlds appear to be dominated by American companies. Is that because the U.S. seems to be more encouraging of innovation than, to mention one area, Europe?

WI: It's partly because the U.S. has less regulation and allows more freedom, and the fields in which there was less regulation were the ones where the most innovation happened. We think that the U.S. is the most innovative because we look at things like the Internet and computers and social networks and social media, which tended to be rather unregulated things. In fields that are more regulated, whether it be physical things like batteries and nuclear power or air travel or even, to some extent, pharmaceuticals, the U.S. doesn't have quite the same advantage.

Secondly, the U.S. is better at allowing

people to take risks. Especially out in Silicon Valley, if you haven't failed two or three times, nobody's going to take you seriously. Whereas in Europe, if you fail once or twice, you're probably not going to get your foot in the door looking for financial backing.

DR: When did American leadership in such areas, like computers and semiconductors, really start?

WI: It happens right after World War II. During the war, Germany, Britain, and the United States were all developing digital computers, mainly to calculate missile trajectories and other wartime needs.

As Leonardo da Vinci knew from working for the warlord Cesare Borgia and the duke of Milan, war tends to stimulate technology. And that's what happened with computers.

But the genius in America is that right after World War II, leaders like Vannevar Bush came up with the concept that we had to have science as the next frontier. They said that there was going to be a three-way partnership between universities, government, and corporate America, that the new types of labs for computers weren't going to just be done in the government, the way the atomic bomb was done with the Manhattan Project. We were going to have places like RAND and Bell Labs, and the government was going to create the National Science Foundation to give grants to universities to do research.

ENIAC was really the first general-purpose computer, invented by the War Department and the University of Pennsylvania during World War II. That spins out into a private company, which becomes UNIVAC and eventually Unisys and Sperry Rand. The ability to have that three-way partnership distinguished the United States from other countries.

DR: What was the impact on innovation from returning World War II veterans who had technology training?

WI: I'll tell a personal account. Innovation in America is not just done by huge companies; it's about thousands of foot soldiers in the progress of innovation.

My father left Tulane his senior year, with six buddies from engineering school, to make sure they could join the navy before the end of World War II. They were trained in radar and supply chains and even refrigeration and sent to the South Pacific.

When my father got back in 1947, he became an electrical engineer, because he had been trained. He invented new ways to air-condition department stores and movie theaters in New Orleans with his buddies.

And he was just one of tens of thousands of

returning World War II veterans who got their technology training but also learned to take risks that you have to take during wartime. He became a great innovator as well as a small-business owner in New Orleans.

DR: Did the growth of venture capital after World War II, and particularly from the 1960s onward, have an impact on fostering innovation?

WI: When we think of great innovators we often think of scientists or engineers. But one of the most important inventions that happens in the 1960s is venture capital. It's people like Arthur Rock, who had worked for investment banks in New York, who decides to go west and invest in new ventures.

Up until then you had the Rockefeller family, Laurance Rockefeller and his siblings, doing things like Venrock. But you didn't have firms that raised capital and said, "We're going to bet on new entrepreneurs." So, if you look at great innovators of the digital revolution, Arthur Rock and his successors really came up with a new invention, which is raising capital funds. Getting people to have equity stakes in new ventures that hadn't yet started up. Being angels for entrepreneurs.

Rock helps Robert Noyce and some of the rebels at Fairchild Semiconductor start what becomes Intel. That led to the birth of a venture capital industry, which was one of the ingredients that made Silicon Valley the cradle of innovation more than even Boston or New York.

It almost echoes Florence five hundred years earlier, when the Medici family and others invented new ways of doing double-entry bookkeeping, so they could do debit and credit financing. That provided funding that helped the Renaissance flourish.

DR: What were the big advances in computers in the post–World War II period?

WI: The biggest advance was the realization that computers should be personal. In World War II, there were these huge computers, like Colossus that Alan Turing worked on in Bletchley Park in England, or ENIAC at the University of Pennsylvania. After the war, companies like Sperry Rand and Digital Equipment Corporation thought that computers were going to be huge machines owned by corporations and the government and maybe universities.

What happened in the early 1970s, because of a confluence of forces, is that a group of people — hobbyists and hackers and rebels, computing-power-to-the-people types — decides, "Let's make the computer personal." That mind-set coincides with Intel creating microprocessors that allow people like Steve

Wozniak and Steve Jobs to say, "We can make our own personal computers."

What distinguished the United States in its digital revolution from other places is that great entrepreneurs snatched computing power from the big corporations and turned it into personal computers. The advent of personal computers enabled creativity, entrepreneurship, and innovation in garages and garrets and dorm rooms around America from then on.

DR: You think if they didn't have garages, Silicon Valley would never have gotten anywhere?

WI: Larry Page and Sergey Brin knew the Wojcicki sisters, who had two things: they had a garage, and they had a friend who was in the venture capital business. This program Page and Brin created called PageRank eventually became Google.

DR: What led to the development of transistors? What was their impact?

WI: During World War II, most of the computers used vacuum tubes, which only you and I are old enough to remember. They were like lightbulbs, and they burned out, and you had to replace them, and they were hot, and they used electricity.

Right as the war was ending, people who had been engaged in the war effort, who had worked at Bell Labs, came back. They were given the task of figuring out how to replace vacuum tubes so that the Bell system could amplify phone calls from coast to coast without having all these vacuum tubes that would burn out.

What allows Bell Labs to invent the transistor is that it was a place that mixed everybody from theorists, to practical engineers who had come back from the war, to experimentalists, to pole climbers with grease under their fingernails who strung phone lines, to people who understood how to turn something into a business. So in December 1947, a theorist like William Shockley, who understood and could visualize how electrons danced on the surface of semiconducting materials such as silicon, could pair with an experimentalist like Walter Brattain, who could take a chip of silicon and germanium and a paper clip and solder it together and put it underwater and see if it all worked.

The transistor allows the digital revolution to happen, just like the dynamo or the steam engine allows the Industrial Revolution to happen. The invention of the transistor is the key thing, because the transistor is simply a tiny on/off switch.

The digital revolution is based on the theory that information can be encoded as zeroes and ones — in other words, it's on and off — and that you can build circuits that can manipulate this information and say "Yes, no, if this do that," based on zeroes and ones. To make that work you needed an on/off switch that was tiny, and that's what the transistor was.

DR: What led to the development of semiconductors? How did that speed up technology development?

WI: One of the distinguishing things about U.S. antitrust law and patent law is that it incents a big corporation, like the Bell system, to take a patent but license it out rather freely so that they wouldn't be accused of an antitrust violation. Everyone from Fairchild Semiconductor to Texas Instruments, which originally was an oil field company, decides to license the transistor.

They try to figure out how to make the transistor better. At what becomes Intel and also at Texas Instruments, they realized that you could etch many components, including transistors, on a single chip of silicon. That becomes the microchip, which is the next great advance in semiconductors. Underlying that theory is the same simple on/off switch. Semiconducting materials such as silicon can be juiced up in ways to become on/off switches.

DR: What is a microprocessor? Is that the same as a microchip?

WI: No. A microchip is when you take a lot of transistors, say, and etch them on a chip. But at a certain point in the 1970s, Intel figured out a way to take this chip and to put together all of the components you might need for a circuit — transistors and resistors and capacitors — and etch them all on the same chip.

The subtle but huge breakthrough is that instead of just making this as a special-purpose chip, like for a calculator for a specific company, Intel made it so that those chips could be reprogrammed. You could take a chip that had all these components on it and program it to do whatever you want.

That becomes a microprocessor, which is the kernel of a computer. Back in the early days of computers, these processing systems were huge. But after Intel invents the microprocessor, it becomes the heart of a computer on a chip that you can put in the palm of your hand.

DR: When did the first minicomputers begin to replace the large-scale computers that IBM had developed?

WI: In the early '70s, after Intel creates the idea of a microprocessor, people like Ed Roberts, who ran a hobbyist company in Albuquerque, say, "I can use these types of microprocessors and make a kit so that hobbyists can build a computer." That becomes the Altair, the first personal computer. It was just done for hobbyists and hackers. Didn't have much use.

As soon as Bill Gates saw that on the cover of *Popular Electronics,* he and his friend Paul Allen said, "We're going to create software for this Altair." In the meantime, at the Homebrew Computer Club up near Palo Alto, people like Steve Wozniak and Steve Jobs were hanging out. They said, "We can use this tiny microprocessor from Intel and we'll build our own computer." And they built the Apple I and then the Apple II.

So hackers and hobbyists, as well as sort of these hippie-like *Whole Earth Catalog*–reading people, ranging from Steve Jobs to Ed Roberts, who wanted to take computing power away from the big companies and give it to the people, then the peace movement, free speech movement, power to the people — they all jell in places like the Homebrew Computer Club in the early '70s.

And the hackers and the hobbyists and the Homebrew types all start building their own computers. Out of that comes the Apple I, the Apple II, and eventually the Macintosh, but also many other computers.

DR: You mentioned Bill Gates. What led to his company becoming the dominant software producer for computers? There were many other companies producing software in the early days of the so-called software revolution.

WI: Bill Gates had a singular insight, one of the most important, innovative insights in the business of technology, which is that it was not going to be about the hardware, it was going to be about software. And that eventually, whether you were Dell or Sperry Rand or IBM, the hardware would be pretty interchangeable, but whoever made the operating system software would be at the lead of innovation.

Early on, when they were big computers owned by grand corporations, it was boys with their toys. The men made the computers and then they hired women like Grace Hopper and the six women who programmed ENIAC, thinking that programming was just a clerical thing that women could do. But when the inventors of ENIAC eventually create the company UNIVAC, they're smart enough to hire Grace Hopper and the women who did the programming. And they create things like COBOL.

There was a struggle between who was going to be in control, the hardware manufacturers or the software writers. Then Bill

Gates, with help from his father, who was a great lawyer, figured out a way to write and adapt an operating system for a personal computer, and then not sell that software to IBM but instead give them a nonexclusive license to it. The software company, which becomes known as Microsoft, becomes more powerful than the hardware companies such as IBM and Dell and DEC.

DR: Who really invented the Internet? The French had a predecessor called the Minitel. Why did that not take off around the world?

WI: With all due respect to Al Gore, the Internet has many inventors. The reason the French system didn't catch on is that it was a centralized system. One of the rules of innovation in the digital revolution is empower the fringes and decentralize and distribute authority.

What happens in the United States is that the Defense Department is trying to create a system to link the research computers at the various universities they were funding so that they could time-share. They tell the professors at these universities, "You have to figure out a way to link to our network."

The professors do what they always do. They delegate that task to their graduate students. About thirty of them joined together to invent what becomes known as ARPANET, the predecessor to what is now the Internet. It was based on a system called packet-switching, which meant that, unlike Minitel in France and unlike the phone company in the United States, there were no central hubs in which the information was controlled by whoever ran the system.

In a packet-switch network, the information is all broken up into small packets. It scurries through a web, with address headers so it knows where to go and how to re-assemble itself when the packets get where they're supposed to be.

It means that every single node on that network has the power to create and store and transmit and forward information. It becomes a web in which there's no central control mechanism.

Later, at *Time* magazine, we once wrote that that was done to survive a nuclear attack from the Russians. If you have a centralized system and you take out one of the hubs, you can screw up the whole network. But with the Internet, if any one of the thousands or millions or billions of nodes gets knocked out, the information just knows how to route around that.

That distributed system, where every node has equal power to create information, is at the heart of the Internet. It's not centrally controlled, unlike the systems that were being developed by British Telecom or Minitel by the French Telecom.

DR: What role did Marc Andreessen and the company Mosaic that he helped to create play in fostering the widespread use of the Internet?

WI: Mark Andreessen's contribution was huge. The World Wide Web, which is a set of protocols for easily navigating the Internet, had been created at CERN in Switzerland by a guy named Tim Berners-Lee. But what turns out to be the most important element for that is the piece of software called the browser that allows a normal person to easily navigate the web.

When Mark Andreessen was at the University of Illinois, a big, corn-fed Iowa guy, he does what great innovators do. He combines a feel for technology, because he was a great computer coder, with a feel for the humanities.

He knew how people interface with great products. He created the Mosaic browser, which had wonderful technical features and was done in a smart way. It was made public. It was made free. It was almost as if it were more open-source than proprietary.

So everybody got to use the Mosaic browser, and it caught on. That not only made the browser important, but it caused the web, the World Wide Web, to be the best way to navigate the Internet.

Only people like me, who are early Internet geeks, remember that it wasn't inevitable that websites with hyperlinks and hypertext were going to be the way the Internet became easy to navigate. There were things like Gopher and Veronica and Archie and Send and Fetch and all these other ways to navigate the Internet.

But the Mosaic browser becomes the popular user interface. Just like Steve Jobs took the personal computers of the early days that were for hobbyists and hackers and said, "I'll make an easy graphical user interface and make it easy for people to interface with their computer," Mark Andreessen had the same innovative spirit. He says, "I'll make it easy for people to interface with the World Wide Web." And the way he did it was so that you could hop around anywhere.

DR: What led to the development of the smartphone?

WI: Steve Jobs's great innovative genius was connecting our technology to us as humans, which is what he did when he created the Macintosh, which is easy to use. When he comes back to Apple in the late 1990s, after having been fired from the company twelve years earlier, he and his brilliant team sit around grousing, "Our cell phones suck. It's not intuitive. There's no screen on which to see things."

He made one of those great creative and innovative leaps. Having been in the business of personal computers, he said, "Let's reinvent cell phones and do for them what we did in the early days of computers, which is make them intuitive and easy to use." He had already invented the iPod, which had a way to put a thousand songs in your pocket. It was just a beautifully intuitive music player.

He said that if the people who made cell phones figured out a way to make them easy to use and to put music on them, it would kill the iPod. So he decided he was going to create a cell phone that was an easy-to-use music player, a cell phone, and also an easy-to-use personal assistant and computing device — all three rolled into one.

In a stroke of genius that he did not know was a stroke of genius initially, he creates a place where people can put apps. When he eventually opens up the App Store to outside developers, you get things from Amazon to Uber to Airbnb.

DR. What was the innovation that led to the widespread development of e-commerce?

WI: Unlike some of the other entrepreneurs like Steve Jobs or even Bill Gates, who came at it from inventing a product, Jeff Bezos came at it from a business and finance mind-set as well. He figured out how you could do an easy-to-use online store.

That coincides with the explosive growth of personal computing and then the advent of smartphones. By the late 1990s, when Amazon is coming along, it coincides with a period when everybody is getting easy-to-use personal computers and easy-to-use access to the Internet.

In the beginning of the 1990s, an ordinary citizen could not go on the Internet. You could go on an online service like America Online or CompuServe. But those were walled gardens that had their own ecosystems.

Al Gore gets made fun of, but the most important innovation in the early '90s was the Gore Act [the High Performance Computing Act of 1991] and a subsequent act the following year [the Scientific and Advanced Technology Act of 1992], which opened up the Internet to people who want to dial in and use it for personal or commercial reasons. He invents things like the ".com" address, which means that you don't have to be at the university or a major corporation to get on the Internet. You can create your own business.

Gore opening up the Internet to things like dot-coms in the early 1990s, the spread of easy-to-use Internet interfaces such as Mark

Andreessen's Mosaic web browser — all of this laid a fertile field for a guy like Jeff Bezos to come in and say, "I'm now going to create a store that will sell books on the Internet, and I'm eventually going to make it an everything store." E-commerce is one of those things that was largely driven by one great, creative visionary, and that was Jeff Bezos.

DR: What was the innovation that led to the development of social media?

WI: The first insight into social media, I think, was Steve Case at America Online. This is before the Internet was opened by the Gore Act. People would go onto services like America Online or CompuServe or Prodigy. Those services had information you could get — stock prices, sports scores, weather, news.

What Steve Case realized with America Online was that community and social networking were the killer app — not only inventing that wonderful phrase "You've got mail" but creating easy-to-use bulletin boards and chat rooms and instant messaging services all embedded in the early AOL. That caused the rise of bulletin boards on the web.

When the web takes off in the 1990s, it leads eventually to services like the WELL and other online communities. Then it gets driven by various entrepreneurs who create things like MySpace.

Then, famously, Mark Zuckerberg is in a dorm room at Harvard trying to create a college facebook service where you can connect with other people at your college. Zuckerberg ends up winning because he makes his the best and the easiest to use.

There's also a network effect. If you're on AOL and your friends are on CompuServe, it doesn't quite work. Once somebody has the place everybody wants to go to, it goes into hyper growth mode, because everybody wants to be where everybody else is. Facebook won that race.

Facebook did it by creating a better product. They did it by doing things that can be a bit harmful, like becoming addictive or incenting people to send out things that enrage or incite them.

But it was mainly done by creating a product that made it easier for people to connect. Once again, it was led by the type of person who would connect technology to humanities, who understood "Hey, a like button will work" or "A share button will work."

DR: Two final questions. Do you see any signs that innovation is slowing down in the U.S. compared to China or other countries?

WI: There is a danger. Part of it is that the

four or five big technology companies, Facebook, Amazon, Apple, Google, maybe Microsoft, have such control in their particular fields.

Since the invention almost twenty years ago of things like Facebook, Google, Amazon, and others, we haven't had as much innovation in the digital technology realm. I don't believe you have to break these companies up, but I do believe a little more antitrust enforcement, where these big companies can't favor their own products over those of new innovative entrepreneurs, would be healthy, so that we'd have a greater market for creativity and innovation.

DR: How important is a country's culture or government to the advent of innovation?

WI: It's absolutely critical whether it's a culture that allows failure; a culture that celebrates success and creating a business; a culture that can regulate with a soft and sensitive hand instead of an iron fist; a culture that knows how to protect intellectual property but not allow patents to get in the way of innovation.

These all require delicate balances. It's not to go hell-bent for or against regulation, or for or against intellectual property; it's understanding the delicate balance. Ever since the Patent Act of 1790 and the antitrust enforcements against Standard Oil, we've gotten the balance pretty much right in this country.

I fear that the hyperpartisanship we have now could cause the culture of America to lose that ability to say it's all about balance or nuance when it comes to government, academia, corporations, and entrepreneurs all being part of an ecosystem that can flourish.

David McCullough
on the Wright Brothers

Historian; author of *The Wright Brothers*
and many other books

"Then I began to understand what kind of
human beings they were and what they
were up against when they set out to
achieve this immensely exciting mission,
which no one in history had ever been able
to do. How did they do it? Why was it they
who accomplished this?"

Many of the world's most singular and transformative achievements have been the work
of the most unlikely of individuals. That was
certainly the case with manned flight.

For millennia, humans dreamed of following birds and flying from destination to
destination, saving time and energy. And the
greatest human minds, like Leonardo da
Vinci, developed possible ways to achieve that
feat.

But no human was actually able to do this
until two unknown brothers, operating out of

a bicycle shop in Dayton, Ohio, showed the world how planes that they had designed and built could indeed take humans off the ground — and, importantly, also bring them safely back.

That Wilbur and Orville Wright, with no formal engineering or aeronautical training and no college degrees, did this, with their own limited funds, after years of experimenting on the isolated beaches of windswept Kitty Hawk, North Carolina, is truly remarkable.

But as remarkable as that accomplishment was, it seems just as remarkable that the Wright brothers were unable to convince the U.S. government to support their efforts or, later, even to affirm their success. Indeed, it was the French government that lured the Wright brothers to Paris to show their feat, and it was there that they demonstrated their invention to large French crowds, who were utterly amazed. Acceptance in the U.S. came a bit later, a bit to the brothers' chagrin.

Without doubt, one of America's most distinct contributions to human progress during the twentieth century was the invention of the airplane. And what better person to chronicle this contribution than America's most beloved historian, David McCullough?

Over the past five decades, David has written best-seller after best-seller about such historic American creations as the Brooklyn

Bridge and the Panama Canal and such American leaders as Teddy Roosevelt, John Adams, and Harry Truman. David has now written more than a dozen books, all of which are still in print.

For the quality of these and other books about America, David McCullough has won every award an American citizen can win: two Pulitzer Prizes, two National Book Awards, the National Humanities Medal, the Presidential Medal of Freedom, and more than fifty honorary degrees.

I have had the privilege of interviewing David on many occasions, and he is always as enthusiastic and voluble in describing his subject as someone who is speaking about the subject for the first time. That was true as well in this interview about the Wright brothers, which took place as part of the Congressional Dialogues series at the Library of Congress on June 24, 2015. The secret to the brothers' success, in David's view, was that they never gave up. They failed repeatedly but kept tinkering and experimenting and reinventing.

They would not accept failure — but for reasons unrelated to a desire for fame or money. Those were of no real interest to them. They simply wanted to prove humans could build and safely fly planes.

David suggests, though, one other reason for their success. They loved to read. They had grown up with books and were always reading. And they were reading the classics of literature and history. David suggests that this informal liberal arts education the brothers gave themselves, in both their youth and their adulthood, produced manned flight as much as did their self-taught engineering and mechanical skills.

As a believer in the value of the social sciences, I found David's point highly encouraging. But I found it highly discouraging that I had not figured out how to use my own social sciences background anywhere near as productively as did the Wright brothers.

DAVID M. RUBENSTEIN (DR): You can pick any subject as a historian. Why did you pick the Wright brothers?

DAVID MCCULLOUGH (DM): I was working with the collection of Edith Wharton letters that are at Yale University in the Beinecke Library, and I came across a letter that she wrote to a friend of hers, describing how she was coming back to the Hôtel de Crillon on the Champs-Élysées in Paris, and stepped out of her beautiful chauffeur-driven limousine and noticed a lot of people on the sidewalk were looking up into the sky. She looked up, and there was a Wright biplane flying over Paris.

Wharton went on to describe beautifully —

as she, one of our greatest writers, could do — the thrill of that image in detail. Then she said, "Imagine. I've seen the first airplane ever to fly over Paris." In fact, it was the first airplane ever to fly over any city up until that point, and it was being flown not by one of the brothers but by a French aristocrat, the Comte de Lambert, who had been taught by Wilbur Wright how to fly that plane.

Then I found out that Orville Wright was also in France at that point, and that Wilbur Wright had been there almost a year before. I thought, "What in the world are the Wright brothers doing in France? They're meant to be back in Ohio in their bicycle shop."

At that point, about all I knew about the Wright brothers was that they were bicycle mechanics from Dayton, Ohio, who invented the airplane. It's what we all learned in the five minutes that they're given in high-school history classes.

Then I began to understand what kind of human beings they were and what they were up against when they set out to achieve this immensely exciting mission, which no one in history had ever been able to do. How did they do it? Why was it they who accomplished this? Two men who'd never been to college, never even finished high school, but who were thoroughly, as I soon found out, well-educated on their own, in everything — including, I must emphasize, the liberal arts.

Although they grew up in a house that had no running water, no indoor plumbing, no electricity, no telephone, it was a house full of books. Their father, an itinerant minister, insisted that they be readers, so they grew up reading Dickens and Mark Twain and Hawthorne and the poetry of Virgil and Plutarch's *Lives* and Thucydides and history and natural history and philosophy and theology.

They had a full liberal arts education. I hope that some of the people in education today, and the parents who are advising their children, and the students who are making decisions about what they're going to do with their time in college, will keep in mind that these brothers, who cracked one of the most impossible technical mysteries of all time, had a liberal arts education. And it carried them further in their work and in their imaginative and creative thinking than they would have gone otherwise.

They were also taught by their father to write the English language correctly and effectively. They were incapable of writing a dull letter or a short one.

DR: If the Wright brothers were here tonight, is there a question you would like to ask them?

DM: There are so many questions. I'd like to talk with Wilbur more about art and architec-

404

ture. He was fascinated with the paintings in the Louvre when he first got there. He'd never been in an art museum in his life.

He loved walking through the city of Paris and looking at the architecture and the way the public buildings are set off by open space in front of them. He wrote these marvelous letters home to his father and his sister, particularly about the nave of the great cathedral at Le Mans and how it reaches up and up toward the sky and, as you get up in the upper clerestory it's all lighted, with light coming through stained-glass windows. He describes this reaching for the sky.

And, of course, that's just what he's doing, reaching for the sky. The fact that this architecture is moving him this way — Wilbur was a genius. I don't think there's any question about it. Orville was clever and mechanically ingenious.

DR: Their father is a traveling minister. The mother dies relatively young. There are a number of children. Wilbur is four years older than Orville.

What is it that made them interested in flight? What is it about flight that made the Wright brothers interested in devoting their entire life to it?

DM: Reading. Wilbur Wright was hit in the face with a hockey stick as a teenage boy

405

playing hockey with some of the neighborhood fellows. It knocked out all his upper front teeth. He was badly beat up and in extreme pain for weeks. He also slipped into what we today would call a depression and went into a self-imposed seclusion in this little house they grew up in.

He wanted to go to college, he wanted to go to Yale, and he almost certainly would have. But all talk of college ended, and it was a swerve in his life that caused him to start reading about, among other things, ornithology and aviation.

While it was the most painful and demoralizing blow in his life, and the swerve was something totally unexpected, it was what set him on the path to what he did with his life. Their father raised them to have purpose in life, have a mission, a quest, to accomplish something worthy, to make the world a little better than it was before you came along. This was all heading in that direction.

Now, the question was, who hit him in the face and did he do it intentionally or was it accidental? The boy later became one of the most notorious murderers in the history of Ohio, who killed his mother, his father, his brother, and an estimated twelve other people. He grew up right around the corner. He was known as a neighborhood bully. Whether he did it intentionally or accidentally, we still don't know.

But we do know it changed Wilbur's life, changed history consequently, and it reminds us that this wonderful neighborhood that the Wright brothers grew up in, small houses on a little back street in Dayton, Ohio, wasn't just a Norman Rockwell setting for a *Saturday Evening Post* cover. You had great genius, great ambition to excel, in the same neighborhood with outright evil.

History reminds us of that very often. Just as the plane they invent will go on to be used as one of the deadliest weapons of all time, as demonstrated in World War II. The devastation was unimaginable to anybody, let alone the Wright brothers. Wilbur never lived to see that happen. He died in 1912.

DR: Wilbur and Orville decided to work together to see if they could actually make something fly, but there were people who tried to make things fly before the Wright brothers. They didn't invent the idea of trying to get off the ground, right?

DM: No. We could go back to Leonardo da Vinci. Earlier, people were jumping off of towers, covering themselves with feathers and jumping to their deaths. There were a number of crackpots still, proclaiming that their device would take them into the sky. The Wrights were thought of as very nice fellows, gentlemanly, well-dressed, polite, but weird,

407

and maybe a little off their rocker. Nobody took them seriously, not in Dayton, not in the federal government.

DR: There was a man who was the secretary of the Smithsonian, Mr. Langley, after whom Langley Field [in Virginia] is named. He was an early pioneer. What happened to his efforts?

DM: There are two very important things to understand about the Wright brothers. They invented the plane. But also they invented how to fly it. They were the first test pilots, if you will.

Wilbur gave a perfect analogy. He said, "There are two ways to tame a wild horse. One is to sit on the fence and study its every motion and write notes about it, then retire to a comfortable chair at home and write a thesis on how to tame a wild horse. The other way, which is our way, is get on a horse and ride it."

Now, Samuel Langley invented what he called his aerodrome. It looked like a giant insect. It was launched from the top of a houseboat on the Potomac River.

DR: How far did it fly?

DM: It had cost $70,000, which doesn't sound like much today but was a fortune then. Fifty thousand was public money, Smithsonian Institution money. Twenty thousand was donated by some of his wealthy friends, including Alexander Graham Bell.

It took off from the top of the houseboat, went straight up and straight down into the river. Twice. It was a humiliating thing, to say the least, and embarrassing because of all the public money spent. But Langley never ever considered flying it. He had somebody else do it, a man who barely got away with his life.

DR: The Wright brothers, knowing of Mr. Langley's interest in flight, wrote a letter to the Smithsonian, saying, "Can you send us all the information you have?"

DM: That's where it really began, when Wilbur sat down at his sister Katharine's little slant-top desk in the front parlor of the house at 7 Hawthorn Street and wrote a letter to the Smithsonian, saying, "I'm very interested in the possibilities of flight, and I think it can be accomplished."

He added a kind of P.S., saying, "I'm not a crank. Take me seriously." He was serious, all the way along. Always. They sent him volumes of material, including a bibliography, a reading list of material there that they printed.

DR: He read a lot of this material, and then

they did some experiments. They decided they needed to find a place to actually do the testing of a glider. Why did they pick Kitty Hawk?

DM: Because of the presence of strong winds. They had figured out, by studying soaring birds, that birds could get up into the air and hang up there without flapping their wings. The notebooks of their observations of soaring birds are extraordinary. One of the great lines in Wilbur's book is, "No bird ever soared in a calm."

In other words, you need that wind. You don't want, in the old Irish saying, to have the wind at your back. You want to head into the wind. That's how you get up. The wind will lift you, just as they felt that adversity will lift you. No bird ever soared in a calm. They faced adversity of a kind that would make all of us give up not very far into the project.

DR: They had a bicycle store. They're making bicycles, but they decided to pick up, both of them, and go to Kitty Hawk. Were there any hotels there?

DM: Nothing. There were no roads, no bridges, very few people. But they got the wind and then some. They also got sand to land on, soft landings. Very, very advantageous, to say the least, because they would crash many times. And there were very few people to be coming around all the time bothering them with questions and curiosity.

DR: How did it work the first year they went there?

DM: They were working with gliders, not a powered airplane yet. They're trying to learn how to glide, and they invented what they call "wing warping," which was their version of what soaring birds do with their wings. They would go up and down on the beaches, doing this and imitating the birds.

They're wearing their suits as if they were back in Dayton, Ohio, starched shirts and neckties, and the local people thought, "Are they crazy?"

Until they saw how hard they worked. One of the men who became very helpful and instrumental in their work on Kitty Hawk, John T. Daniels, said, "They're the workingest boys I ever knew in my life."

DR: They had some experiments the first summer. They made some mistakes, they came back another summer. Eventually they started to do motorized flight. How did they know how to make an engine?

DM: They found out that all the data accumulated and published and taken as gospel by people like Langley was all wrong. As Orville said, "It was worthless."

What were they to do? They weren't learned scholars at MIT or Rensselaer Polytechnic. They said, "We'll make our own data." So they built their own wind tunnel, models of which are in the Wright Cycle Shop, which is in the wonderful Henry Ford Museum in Dearborn, Michigan, as is the house with all its possessions.

They built a wind tunnel, with a regular fan on one end, and they made all different shapes of wings and the camber or the upper curvature of the wing out of little hacksaw blades. They spent hours and hours, for months, making all this new data, which was right because it was based on their experiences flying, none of which their predecessors had had. That alone was a huge accomplishment.

Then they realized they wanted to put a motor on the glider, but there were no motors available from any of the automobile motor manufacturers that were light enough in weight or strong enough for their purposes. So they thought, "We'll have to build a motor." They'd never built a motor before in their lives. They had a wonderful machinist, Charlie Taylor, who worked with them, and he'd never built a motor in his life.

They built it out of aluminum. First time

anybody had thought of building an engine out of aluminum, which they obtained from a tiny little start-up company in Pittsburgh called the Aluminum Company of America, Alcoa.

The first one they built cracked. Instead of saying, "Well, I guess it won't work," they said to Alcoa, "Another one." And the other one did work, and not only did it work, it supplied more horsepower even than they expected. That's what made possible the first flight, on December 17, 1903.

DR: They went back to Kitty Hawk, and they flew the first time with a motor flight and a pilot? And that was the first time man had controlled flight ever?

DM: Yes. If you read how long the flight was and how much time it consumed, you'll think, "Oh, come on" — 120 feet in twelve seconds. But they knew they'd done it. It was a bitterly cold day, December 17, wind blowing. Langley had just done the nose dives of his machine into the Potomac River, so it was up to them to show they could do it.

Langley had spent, as I said, $70,000 on his machine. They had spent, in total, less than a thousand dollars, because they'd built and done everything themselves in their spare time with what little money they had from the profits of their bicycle shop.

Before the day ended, Wilbur had flown [a distance of] 800 feet. So they absolutely had done it. But they also knew that their wing warping wasn't as good as it could be, because they couldn't bank and turn sufficiently to claim that they had a practical airplane yet.

One of the scenes that I dearly love is, here they've done this thing nobody in the history of the world had ever done, and done it under the most adverse conditions imaginable. They're four miles out from Kitty Hawk, four miles out from any civilization at all. They're out in the middle of a sand desert all by themselves.

They went back into their shed to get warm and made themselves some lunch, probably Campbell's soup. They did the dishes before walking the four miles into town to send a telegram back home that said, "We've been successful."

They knew they would be successful, and they also knew they had much more work to do, because they had to create a practical plane. That took them two more years. It wasn't really until 1905 that they had a plane that could take off, land, bank, turn, fly in a circle, fly in a figure eight, skim along eighteen inches or two feet above the grass, with perfect control.

They were brilliant pilots. They were like acrobats or star athletes, and could perform with that machine as nobody on earth could perform.

Still, our government here took no interest. None. They wouldn't send anybody out to see what they were doing. This was all going on in a cow pasture outside of Dayton. It's still there, by the way, exactly as it was.

DR: They went three summers to Kitty Hawk. Then they went back to Dayton. They found a pasture that somebody let them fly on, but they didn't want people knowing much about it. Why was that?

DM: They didn't want people that would come out and disturb them, distract them. Because, as I said, they were gentlemen, and if somebody wanted to ask them a question, they'd stop and answer the question. It wasn't like they were hiding things. Anybody that took a serious interest was perfectly welcome to come out and watch.

DR: And did the U.S. government come along and say, "We now have a great plane, let's buy one"?

DM: No. The U.S. government took no interest whatsoever in coming to Dayton to see this phenomenon, and when the Wrights offered to bring the plane [to Washington, D.C.] to demonstrate it, the government slammed the door in their faces about three or four times. They got sick of that, understandably.

When a French delegation showed up in Dayton, keenly interested in what they were doing, and told them, "If you come over to France and show us there, there'll be a big market for your airplane," they didn't want to do that because they were devout patriots. But they decided, "Let's do it."

So Wilbur crossed the Atlantic. The plane was shipped over. And on August 8, 1908, the eighth day of the eighth month of the eighth year, the world saw, for the first time, that human beings can fly. At Le Mans, the racetrack town southwest of Paris. There were only about two or three hundred people, maybe not even that many, in the little grandstand at the racetrack that day. But within a very few days thousands of people were coming from all over France and all over Europe, and Wilbur became the hero of the day.

In fact, he became the most popular American in France ever until then, except Benjamin Franklin. Just as Franklin insisted on wearing his fur hat around Paris and remaining an American, the Wright brothers and their sister Katharine, when she came over, were absolutely 100 percent Middle West Americans, and the French loved it. They adored her, in particular, because she had opinions and would express them, as they said, in a good midwestern American way.

She took France by storm. They adored her. And because she had pretty good Latin in the Dayton high school, she picked up French just like that, whereas the brothers spoke hardly a word.

DR: When Wilbur made the successful flights, people in France who thought initially the Americans were lying or bluffing were convinced. What did the U.S. government decide to do?

DM: They suddenly woke up and said, "Hmm, maybe we ought to have a look."

Orville brings the plane down to Fort Myer, across the river [in Arlington]. Half of Washington poured across the river to go see. All of Congress went over there. The cabinet, the Supreme Court, the president of the United States, all went across to see this miracle.

And Orville continued to break records. He was breaking records here at the very time that Wilbur was in France breaking records there — the two of them, these unknown brothers, in the two great capitals of the civilized world, the stars of the moment, the most famous people on earth at that time.

And then, tragically, Orville had a very serious mishap and crashed at Fort Myer. His passenger that day was a young army lieutenant named Thomas Selfridge, and he was killed — the first fatality in the history of aviation. Orville was nearly killed. Broken bones in one leg, ribs sprained. But even more, his spirit had been absolutely crushed.

Katharine got a telegram that same day [in Dayton]. She called the principal of her high school [where she taught] and said she was taking an indefinite leave of absence. She packed, she was on the next train that same day, arrived the next morning, went over to Fort Myer, and stayed with her brother for the next six weeks, living with him right in the hospital, to be sure that he got proper care from everybody involved, and doing everything she could to lift his spirits.

They were worried he was going to die. They were worried that he'd never walk again and that he'd never fly again.

She got him through it. He said later he wouldn't have made it if it hadn't been for her. She got him home, which was no small task, because he was in terrible pain all the time, walking on a cane — hardly walking at all.

She stayed with him for the next months there in Dayton, looking after him every single day, and then took him on a ship over to France to join Wilbur, and he not only started walking again, he later came back to Fort Myer and flew again.

Now, Katharine and Wilbur insisted that he

418

not do that. There was the psychological burden of going to the place where this terrible accident had happened. It would be too much for him. But he said, "No. I have to go back and do it where that happened."

He arrived, he flew again, and he again broke all kinds of world records. It's one of the most phenomenal comebacks in our American story that I know of.

DR: Their father had said, "I don't want Wilbur and Orville to fly at the same time." But what happened at one point after this accident?

DM: In May of 1910, the brothers announced a hometown air show. By the way, they never changed. They never got full of themselves. That wasn't how they were raised. You don't get too big for your britches. They remained exactly as they'd always been all their lives, no matter how famous or how wealthy they became.

But when they knew they had achieved this high purpose they'd set out to achieve, they decided to stage a hometown air show, and invited anybody in Dayton that wanted to come out to Huffman Prairie to come see them fly. Thousands came out to witness it. Beautiful day.

And then, for the first time, Orville and Wilbur went up together. They'd never done that, because they knew that they could get killed any time and every time they went up.

They went up fifty to a hundred times in a year. Their courage, their plain bravery, was extraordinary. But they were also very careful. They weren't daredevils. They weren't showing off. They were trying to achieve something and not get killed in the process. So they went up together only once.

DR: And they took their father up?

DM: Katharine had gone up with them in France, and she was a sensation. In order to keep her long skirts from blowing up and embarrassing her, they tied a rope around that part of the skirt, and one of the famous Paris designers saw that and quickly adapted it and caused a fashion sensation throughout Paris.

The only one who hadn't gone up was their father, and so Orville said to him, "Would you like to go up?" Now, he's eighty-two years old. No one even close to that age had ever gone up in an airplane.

He said, "Sure." This wonderful old minister went out, climbed aboard — there are no seat belts or anything, they're sitting in little upright camp chairs — and took off. The whole flight around the field, the father kept saying, "Higher, Orville, higher."

DR: Orville Wright was the younger brother, but Wilbur Wright got ill at one point. And what happened?

DM: They both hated business. They hated money talk. Money was not ever the center of their focus. And they hated lawsuits. They did set up a Wright airplane manufacturing company, which was instantly successful, and the legal issues began to really play on Wilbur. You could see it in his face. He lost weight, he got very pale, and his strength was obviously in decline. He contracted typhoid fever and died in his mid-forties, much too soon.

It's a little like a Greek tragedy, because their father had warned them, since they were little children, "Don't drink dirty water." And of course that's where typhoid fever comes from — bad water. It was a real loss.

Orville lived on until 1948. If I had grown up in Dayton, Ohio, in the same neighborhood, I could have known Orville Wright. Think of that. I was fifteen in 1948. He might have been that nice old gentleman around the corner.

DR: Did the family ever get wealthy from their enormous invention?

DM: They got wealthy, but they did not get wealthy the way so many people are wealthy at that time. The robber barons, the ultra-rich, were far wealthier than they were.

DR: Where is the original plane now?

DM: The original plane is in the Smithsonian. It was smashed up so it had to be completely reconstructed, but it's there.

The first human being to take off in an airplane, Orville Wright, and the first human being ever to set foot on the moon, Neil Armstrong, both came from the same section of southwestern Ohio. Think of that. Another wonderful point is that when Neil Armstrong landed on the moon he was carrying a little swatch of the canvas from the original plane that flew at Kitty Hawk.

DR: What would you say is the most remarkable thing that you learned about these individuals? What would you say is the most remarkable thing that you uncovered in writing the book?

DM: They wouldn't give up, no matter how many setbacks. We don't talk much about failure with our young people today.

There's all kinds of ways to go through failure. One is you get knocked down, you lie there, you cry and you whimper and you lapse into self-pity or you blame other people. The other is you get up on your feet again and you learn from your failure. What went wrong? How can we fix that? Let's do it again, only this time let's do it right.

I found some very marked similarities, though they were very different human beings in different ways, between the Wright brothers and Harry Truman. They remained modest all their lives, they had excellent manners, they never got full of themselves, they were loyal to their hometown, loyal to their families. They came from very modest beginnings and they were knocked down many times and they always got back up.

There are very similar parallels between Truman's famous '48 whistle-stop campaign and the Wright brothers' determination to fly. There was something in that age, that time, the way people were raised at home, not just at school, that mattered powerfully.

And, of course, it was a time excitingly full of innovation — the automobile, the light-bulb, the telephone, the bicycle, the escalator, the elevator, the skyscraper, all coming of age. Dayton, Ohio, had more patents issued to it on a per capita basis than any other city in the country. It was kind of the Silicon Valley of our country at that time in mechanical/technical innovation. It's where the cash register was invented and made by the National Cash Register Company.

All kinds of things were being made on almost every street downtown. It was kind of a renaissance of its kind. We had Theodore

Roosevelt in the White House, we had no debt — none. We had a surplus. We were setting out to build the Panama Canal with perfect confidence we could do it, and we did — the greatest achievement this country had ever undertaken in terms of cost and risk and difficulty.

The attitude was one that the future was exciting and the possibilities were infinite. The spirit of the country was high. That's what we need to recover. We need leadership that will lift the spirits of this country, lift the spirits patriotically.

DOUGLAS BRINKLEY
ON THE RACE TO THE MOON

Katherine Tsanoff Brown Chair in
Humanities and Professor of History at
Rice University; author of *American
Moonshot: John F. Kennedy and the
Great Space Race* and other books

"How do we all work together for a grand
objective?"

In 1957, the United States was shocked when
the Soviet Union launched Sputnik 1, the
first satellite to orbit Earth. Was the U.S. too
far behind in the race to control space to even
catch the Soviets, let alone ever beat them?
Many in the U.S., and in the world, thought
so.

President Dwight Eisenhower quickly approved the creation of the National Aeronau-
tics and Space Administration (NASA) and
authorized the recruitment and training of
astronauts, and the American government
began to play catch-up. But before the world
could see the American progress, the Soviets

succeeded in launching, in 1961, a manned satellite — putting the first man, Yuri Gagarin, into space and into Earth orbit. The U.S. seemed to be falling further behind.

The following month the United States did manage to put a man, Alan Shepard, into space, but it was only a fifteen-minute suborbital flight. However, America did finally get an astronaut, John Glenn, to orbit Earth in February of 1962, and that event — followed by a ticker tape parade in New York and enormous public adulation for Glenn — probably gave President John Kennedy the confidence to visibly push an idea he had originally spoken about in 1961 to Congress: send a man to the moon before the end of the decade.

When this ambitious idea was first presented to Congress on May 25, 1961, it was given only modest public attention and was not really very high on Kennedy's New Frontier agenda. But in September of 1962, Kennedy made his famous "Moonshot" speech at Rice University, where he firmly committed the U.S. to land a man on the moon and return him safely by the end of the decade. As he famously said, he wanted to, among other reasons, pursue these tasks "not because they are easy, but because they are hard."

At the time, the American public's general sense was that President Kennedy and his team had the drive and focus to make this awe-inspiring task possible. Within his administration, however, this time frame was seen by virtually all of Kennedy's advisors as technically unrealistic and prohibitively expensive.

These concerns were buttressed by another not insignificant problem: there was no real scientific rationale for men, as opposed to robots, to get to the moon by the end of any decade. All of that was beside the point to President Kennedy. He felt a political need, as the records now show, to beat the Soviets in the space race, and this seemed the best prospect, in part because the Soviets seemed then unfocused on this particular space achievement.

As we now know, Kennedy's goal was achieved, but the president tragically did not live to see it. Since that time, long-range goals that seem to be out of reach have come to be labeled "moonshots."

As the fiftieth anniversary of the original moonshot approached in 2019, countless books were published on the details of the actual Apollo 11 mission and its heroes. But there was one extraordinary book published then, *American Moonshot* by Doug Brinkley, that focused on man's centuries-old quest for flight and space travel, and the various decisions made by President Kennedy that led to this historic flight.

Doug Brinkley is one of the country's leading historians, having written more than twenty-five well-received history books on a wide array of subjects. I have interviewed and talked to him many times about our shared interest in American history; this interview took place on April 30, 2019, at the Library of Congress as part of the Congressional Dialogues series. The knowledge he brings to any discussion of his book subject is awe-inspiring.

I should add that the fact that politics drove the moonshot goal does not, in my mind, diminish the boldness of the goal or the enormity of the achievement. It was one of the epic scientific and technical achievements of mankind's long history on Earth, and a testament to American boldness, skill, leadership, and innovation.

DAVID M. RUBENSTEIN (DR): How long did it take you to write this book?

DOUGLAS BRINKLEY (DB): I started my journey to writing *American Moonshot* as a kid who grew up in a town on the Maumee River called Perrysburg, Ohio, which is near Toledo. I was eight and a half years old when Neil Armstrong and Buzz Aldrin walked on the moon.

Armstrong was from Wapakoneta, Ohio, which wasn't too far away from where I grew up. He became my boyhood hero. I started collecting anything and everything I could about NASA. My family would go to Cape Canaveral, and finally, in 2001, I was able to do, for NASA, the official oral history of Neil Armstrong.

It was right after 9/11. I thought the interview would be canceled in Houston at the Johnson Space Center, but George Abbey, who was running it for NASA, chipped in and said, "Mr. Armstrong doesn't cancel anything." Armstrong flew his airplane from Cincinnati and landed there at Houston. I got to spend eight hours with him, including six hours on tape.

DR: Was he as good as his image?

DB: The big thing about many of the astronauts, but particularly Neil Armstrong, was that he was an engineer first and foremost. Obviously, he was one of the greatest pilots who ever lived. He was a true Korean War aviation hero, shot down under enemy fire, a great survivor and all of that. But he used to say that we underappreciate engineers in the United States, that we don't celebrate engineers in history enough.

I struggled with interviewing Armstrong because I'm a historian, a humanities person. I was trying to get him to open up. He was famously skittish of the news media, to put it mildly. Charles Lindbergh's baby had been kidnapped, so he was worried that something would happen to his family.

But at one point, I said, "Mr. Armstrong, in the days leading up to Apollo 11, did you ever just go out and look at the moon, and think, 'My God, I'm going to be standing there looking down at blue-green marble Earth?' " And he said, "No."

That was the extent of it. He wasn't being difficult, he just didn't think like that. It was a mission, something to be accomplished, and he accomplished it.

DR: Who actually selected him to be the first man on the moon? Why was it him and not one of the two others?

DB: Armstrong was picked — it's ironic, because he did have a great career as a military pilot — because he was a civilian. In 1969, with the Vietnam War going on, it was preeminent that the first person on the moon was a civilian, that it didn't look like the United States was militarizing the moon.

Also, everybody liked Neil Armstrong. Among the astronaut corps he had no enemies. He could be very quiet and self-effacing, and NASA publicity people recognized, with a name like Neil Armstrong and the background that he had, he would be the perfect kind of quintessential American. I think NASA and the Nixon administration were correct to pick Armstrong as the first.

DR: Buzz Aldrin was going to be the second man on the moon. Did he lobby to be the first?

DB: Buzz Aldrin really wanted to be first. He didn't get that slot. People think Buzz is a pugilist, that he fights and is a rough-and-tumble kind of character. He's actually utterly brilliant. He did his doctorate in engineering at MIT. He's not just a rough-and-ready guy.

That said, if you get to know Buzz Aldrin, the big thing about him is that his moonshot is the Mars shot of the future. Anytime you talk to him, it's about going to Mars and how there's no coordinated leadership to go to Mars by 2040. He's still banging the drum of being a space explorer, and wants to be remembered in history as promoting going to Mars.

DR: Was there any infighting as he was trying to lobby to be the first man on the moon?

DB: Just massive disappointment, wanting to be first. But Armstrong did something special, which was that the photographs we see of astronauts on the moon are Neil Armstrong taking photographs of Buzz Aldrin.

Incidentally, one of the greatest things our country did, fifty years ago this summer, is right when they're running out of fuel and time and they're getting ready to leave the lunar surface and get on to the *Eagle,* you can hear, if you listen to the [recordings], Armstrong say to Aldrin, "Did you leave the packet?"

He put something down on the moon, and what was in that packet were medals honoring the three astronauts who died at Cape Canaveral in the Apollo 1 disaster of 1967 — Gus Grissom, Ed White, and Roger Chaffee. And medals to honor the Soviet cosmonauts who died in their race to get to the moon, as a way for the United States to honor Russia because without somebody to compete against, without the Russian technology to spur the United States forward, we never would have gone to the moon.

DR: Did NASA tell Neil Armstrong what the first words on the moon were supposed to be? If not, where did those words come from?

DB: Neil Armstrong wrote those words and invented the words himself — the famous "That's one small step for man, one giant leap for mankind." He test-marketed the phrase at a kitchen table with his brother. And his brother said, "Wow, pretty hard to beat that."

If any of you want to play a futile game, try to come up with your own best line. It's kind of hard to beat the line that Armstrong came up with. Nobody knew officially what he was going to say — at least we don't think anybody knew.

DR: There was some confusion about what he actually said. Did he say, "This is a small step for man" or "for *a* man"?

DB: It should be "a man," and that's what Armstrong meant. But if you listen to it, you won't hear the "a." A lot of times people will put brackets around it to insert the "a." But others say that he said it, but it's just that the telecommunications didn't come across clearly.

DR: When they came back, they landed in the ocean and were quarantined. How long and why were they quarantined?

DB: They were quarantined immediately for fear that they might have been contaminated or contracted some unusual virus or bacteria on the moon. Nobody believed that to be the case, but we were erring on the side of precaution. They were held in quarantine twenty-one days.

But what was very interesting to me writing my book was that right when we rescued the

Apollo astronauts from the ocean and they went on the USS *Hornet,* Neil Armstrong, Buzz Aldrin, and Michael Collins spoke to then-President Nixon. It was a moment filled with American pride. That summer, there were some talks led by Daniel Patrick Moynihan of New York and Bill Moyers, LBJ's speechwriter, of PBS fame later. They were lobbying the Nixon administration to name the rocket the *John F. Kennedy,* to go to the moon.

Nobody in the White House cottoned to the idea of giving JFK credit for the moonshot. Bryce Harlow, Eisenhower's former White House assistant, fumed about the federal government having "gone far enough" in "Kennnedyizing" NASA space ventures. White House advisor John Ehrlichman warned that if Nixon "fell prey" to naming the rocket after JFK "the next step will be renaming the moon" after Kennedy "because NBC thinks it would be a good idea."

So Nixon never invoked John F. Kennedy's name. But at NASA Mission Control in Houston, Texas, the second the astronauts were rescued to be put in quarantine, on the big screen at NASA was John F. Kennedy's May 25, 1961, afternoon pledge to Congress, when he famously first put out they were going to put a man on the moon by the end of the decade. And on the screen, after the Kennedy quote, they put in big letters: "Task Accomplished July 1969." And that day at Arlington National Cemetery, a citizen put a card on JFK's grave that said, "Mr. President, the *Eagle* has landed."

DR: Most of your book is not actually about the flight to the moon, the Apollo 11 mission. It's about the effort to get there, the pledge by President Kennedy to get there, and the whole history of the search for what was on the moon. Where did the moon originally come from?

DB: Most people believe that it's actually a part of Earth, and it came out of a collision with another planet. It's eerily similar — the dust, the rocks that we brought back — to compositions found here.

DR: As long as men and women have been on Earth, they were looking to the moon and saying, "How can we get there?"

DB: It was an age-old desire to get to the moon. The tides are dictated by the moon, our calendar by the moon.

I found out in my research that the great French novelist Jules Verne, right after the American Civil War, in a novel, *From the Earth to the Moon,* predicted the first humans on the moon would be Americans and they would leave from Florida. It took eight days for Apollo 11, and Verne has that in his book too. He was eerily prescient.

And by the twentieth century, particularly by 1903, once Orville and Wilbur Wright leave Kitty Hawk, North Carolina, and we're in the aviation age, people were looking more and more to the skies, and more and more literature started being written about going to the moon.

DR: Who was Robert Goddard?

DB: Dr. Goddard taught at Clark University, and was America's only really top-tier rocket scientist of the 1920s. He would go into a cabbage field in Auburn, Massachusetts, and launch liquid-fuel rockets, very primitive deals. He'd get written up for noisemaking, and he got hassled by the authorities quite a bit.

They tried to then control him by putting him on an army base in Massachusetts. That didn't work. So Dr. Goddard moved to Roswell, New Mexico. They weren't crazy in New Mexico, the ranch hands, about all those weird objects in the sky they thought were aliens. It was Goddard doing rocket experiments in Eden Valley, as they called it. We tested most of our rockets after World War II at the White Sands Proving Grounds in New Mexico, due to the proximity of Goddard and also the excellent weather conditions there for conducting sky experiments.

DR: During World War I, was there any effort to have rockets that could launch against an enemy?

DB: We were so far behind on rockets, nobody in the Wilson administration took it really seriously in World War I. In the 1920s and '30s, while we're doing a lot of great things with military aviation, we're neglecting the idea of rockets and missiles.

The country that wasn't neglecting it was Germany, first in the Weimar Republic and then when Adolf Hitler came into control. Rocketry in Germany was a big, big deal.

DR: There was a person leading that program for the Germans named Wernher von Braun. He developed missiles that could actually go all the way from Germany to England?

DB: Dr. Wernher von Braun was a genius rocket scientist of unbelievable magnitude, but he also did not flee Germany when Hitler came in, and instead took money from Hitler to test his rockets. They built the Peenemünde base along the Baltic, where they started testing what Hitler called the "vengeance weapons," V-1s, V-2s, and V-3s.

It is Wernher von Braun from Nazi Germany, in the middle of World War II, who's able to fire a rocket over sixty-two miles up, which means breaking Earth's gravity grip. It's the beginning of humans being able to go into and out of space.

Then he built this V-2 rocket that could arc upward around 210 miles. V2s launched from Holland rained down on London during World War II. Some of the rockets went astray, some were duds. But in late '44, early '45, the V-2 was quite a sophisticated missile developed by the Germans.

DR: When World War II was toward the end and it was clear the Nazis were going to lose, did Wernher von Braun say, "I made a mistake. I was on the wrong side"?

DB: Von Braun recognized that Hitler was doomed and he started hedging his bets. He forged some documents, took the V-2 missile blueprints, designs, and materials, and put them on train cars. He snuck out of Peenemünde with 137 Nazi engineers. They constituted von Braun's top rocket scientist team.

Von Braun's team hid in the Bavarian Alps. Von Braun was determined to surrender to the U.S. Army, because his rockets were built by Jewish slave labor at the Dora campus, a subcamp of Buchenwald, under the most heinous conditions you can imagine. There were also some Italian POWs put to work, but mainly Jewish people.

He was worried he'd be tried for war crimes in London, because he'd almost destroyed their city. And nobody wanted to live in Russia or work for Joe Stalin.

So von Braun decided to cut a deal with America. He sent his little brother, Magnus von Braun, out on a bicycle. A private in the army from Sheboygan, Wisconsin, ended up training a gun on him, and Magnus said, "My brother is the great rocketeer Wernher von Braun."

Army intelligence checked it all out, and they found out it was true. Under a thing called Operation Paperclip, we brought all of those Nazi German rocket scientists to live in Fort Bliss in El Paso, Texas, as prisoners of peace, and to start building rockets for the U.S. Army out there, working in West Texas and New Mexico.

DR: Not all the German scientists came here. A number of them were captured by the Russians. Then the Russians started developing their own missile technology?

DB: That's right. With von Braun, we had the future genesis of missiles, but the Red Army had also been able to capture a lot of engineering blueprints and Nazi rocketeers.

The United States kept thinking Russia was behind in technology. We underestimated them. From 1945 to '49 is the only time in

U.S. history that a country has a nuclear monopoly. But by 1949 the Soviets get the atomic bomb and Russia develops the R-7, the world's first ICBM [intercontinental ballistic missile].

By the time of the Korean War, we are recognizing slowly but surely, "Uh-oh, the Soviet Union is ahead of us on missiles." So we send Dr. Wernher von Braun and his ex-Nazi rocket team to Huntsville, Alabama, to take over the Redstone Arsenal, and we start building rockets for military purposes and space exploration out of Huntsville, which overnight becomes Rocket City, U.S.A.

DR: The United States, despite that effort, is shocked in 1957 when Sputnik is launched. How big was Sputnik?

DB: You hear so much about Sputnik in October 1957. It's the size of a beach ball. But it created a lot of commotion, the *beep-beep-beep,* the signals we picked up.

It happened on Dwight D. Eisenhower's watch. But Eisenhower was telling the truth in saying, "Let's not overreact to Sputnik." U.S. satellite technology was moving in a very good direction, and that's true.

But the Democrats saw this as an issue to hammer Eisenhower with. By late '57 and early '58, John F. Kennedy is talking about the missile gap with Russia, the space gap.

440

Lyndon Johnson is maneuvering in the Senate to create NASA.

In 1958, as a result of Sputnik, Eisenhower creates NASA as a civilian space agency. Guess who didn't like the idea of NASA? A lot of army generals, air force birds, navy people, because they're like, "Why are civilians going into space?" But the point for both Eisenhower and Johnson in 1958 was not to be seeming to militarize science and space exploration.

DR: The Soviets were the first to launch somebody into space as well — Yuri Gagarin. What year was that?

DB: Yuri Gagarin goes into space in April 1961, and John F. Kennedy starts promoting space in various ways. I have quite a letter that he wrote to a young person at Princeton University. A student wrote to him, and Kennedy says, "We've got to find a way to leapfrog the Soviets' program instead of going, 'You put Sputnik, we put Explorer, you put a dog in space, we'll put a monkey in space.' "

I went back and watched the four Nixon-Kennedy debates, and you could see John F. Kennedy scoring body blows on Nixon on two points. One is when Kennedy says to Nixon, "You told Mr. Khrushchev last year in your kitchen debate that the United States is number one in kitchen appliances and color television. I'll take my TV in black-and-white. I want to be number one in rocket thrust."

Then, in another debate moment, Kennedy says, "If Nixon is elected, I envision a Soviet flag planted on the moon. I want an American flag planted on the moon." So the campaign grabbed hold of the moon in '60, but here in April '61, the Soviets put Gagarin in space on Kennedy's watch, not Eisenhower's, and he is concerned and angry.

John F. Kennedy did not like losing. He was a cold warrior. He never lost a political election in his life. He won Congress in 1946, '48, '50. He won in the Senate in 1952 and '58, and he won the presidency in '60. In one story, when he's playing chess with an aide of his, Kennedy is about to get checkmated and he knocks the whole table over and says, "I guess we'll never know who won."

He liked to win. And beating Russia became preeminent.

DR: When he became president, he selected as the head of NASA James Webb. Who was he?

DB: James Webb is a genius technocrat marine from North Carolina. He had an early understanding of radar, which emerged out of World War II. Many people said they didn't want the NASA job. Kennedy and Lyndon

Johnson insisted that Webb take it.

And Webb, in the 1960s, is a mastermind of congressional appropriations. He was able to raise $20 billion, or $185 billion in today's terms, to go fund the Apollo project to put a man on the moon by the end of the decade.

DR: Our first man in space was Alan Shepard. How long was he in space, and when did that happen?

DB: Alan Shepard goes up on May 5, 1961, as a direct response to Gagarin. Kennedy played it so that if Shepard died in space — he went up for fifteen minutes that day — if he died, Lyndon Johnson was going to get blamed. But when instead Alan Shepard was a huge success, it became like folklore overnight. JFK saw the media raves, how the whole country prayed for Alan Shepard.

There's a direct correlation between Alan Shepard, May 5, 1961, and Kennedy's speech to Congress on May 25, '61. Shepard, a great American hero from New Hampshire, came from a family that was on the *Mayflower,* and he was one of the most interesting of all the astronauts to read about.

DR: Kennedy makes that speech before Congress, but it wasn't only about the moon. Was the moon the major part of that speech or it just happened to be mentioned?

DB: It was a major part. But when Kennedy came to Capitol Hill to give in effect a "second inaugural" address, when he did the moon thing, he got very light applause, no cheering. When he left in the limo to go back to the White House, he told Ted Sorensen, his speechwriter, "I bombed." He thought it would go over bigger.

But Kennedy was wrong. The next morning, the *Washington Post* said it was great. Many Republicans said, "We'll fund going to the moon. It's an American objective."

At NASA, everybody said, "Kennedy's nuts. We have no way to get to the moon." McGeorge Bundy, the national security advisor, had the temerity to go to JFK and say, "This is a grandstand ploy by you." And Kennedy said, "Mac, you don't run for president in your forties if you don't have a certain kind of moxie."

DR: Where did the idea actually come from? Did somebody go to Kennedy and say, "You should do it by the end of the decade"?

DB: That's the key question. Probably Wernher von Braun.

Jack Kennedy's brother Joe Kennedy died in World War II in a navy aviation accident as a hero. They took a B-17 plane and flew it over the English Channel, aiming to go into France to blow up places where we thought

444

V-1, V-2, and V-3 parts were. Instead Kennedy's plane blew up in the sky. He basically died taking out von Braun's hardware.

And here it is 1953. Jack Kennedy and Wernher von Braun are judges for *Time*'s Person of the Year together in New York, and they get along fabulously. Kennedy didn't hold his Nazi past against him, because they were twentieth-century men. Kennedy trusted in von Braun, and von Braun said, "We can go to the moon."

DR: It turns out that the Soviets really didn't have a plan to get a man on the moon, is that right?

DB: They were trying to get to the moon, but they didn't know how to do it. They didn't have the technology they were bragging about.

In 1958, a guy named Jack Kilby and others at Texas Instruments down in Dallas created the transistor and the microchip, modern computers. NASA was the first beneficiary of new American computer technology in the sense that they were able to adapt it and adopt it. The timing worked really well for von Braun, Kennedy, the Cold War, computer chips, radar. What Kennedy did in a genius way was sell going to the moon like nobody's business.

DR: Was there any scientific reason to have humans go to the moon versus just have a spaceship go there?

DB: When we land on the moon with *Eagle,* Neil Armstrong had to make a radical landing so we didn't go into a crater, which a robot would not have been able to do, most likely, at least not in those days. Then, at one point, a valve part was broken, and Armstrong jammed a pen into it and saved the day. There are practical reasons humans are the greatest computers of all.

Besides that, people don't care as much about a robot or mechanical rovers. Humans, heroes going to space, is what the American people were funding.

Kennedy framed it as beating Russia with the first human being going to the moon. He framed it in sports metaphors, and basically said, instead of a proxy war like Korea, what if we're in a good healthy science competition to see who can go to the moon first?

DR: As the race to the moon is going forward, did people come in to President Kennedy and say, "We can't do it, it's not worth it, it's too expensive"?

DB: Yes. Once Kennedy said we were going to the moon, at some meetings — and we have the Kennedy tapes to listen to, they're spectacular — he will say, "So is going to the moon the number-one thing?" They'll say, "It's a lot of things. We want to do science and we want to do this satellite." And he said, "Those can wait six months. I'm telling everybody we're funding this to go to the moon."

Kennedy sticks with it. He calls the sky the new ocean, the new sea to be explored. And it's not just going to the moon, it's all the satellites we're starting to put up, like Telstar in 1962, where we can start beaming images from the U.S. to Great Britain, or meteorological satellites. Kennedy would go all over giving speeches about spin-off technology, including in medicine — things like CAT scans, MRIs, affordable walkers, kidney dialysis machines, heart defibrillators. The technology that spun off from funding NASA hit the medical sector.

DR: Speaking of technology, did those astronauts really drink Tang?

DB: You hit the real key question. They drank Tang, but NASA did not invent Tang for the astronauts. It was a product on its own that capitalized on space mania. Everything started being marketed as "the new space age," including Tang.

DR: The most common question asked of

447

astronauts, certainly by children, is, "How do you go to the bathroom?" What did NASA come up with for the astronauts?

DB: Kathryn Sullivan, the first woman to walk in space, said the single most asked question is, "How do you go to the bathroom in space?" And it's not a pleasant story to tell you. Now they're finding ways to do it, but in those days, if you had to go, you would just go into a bag or tube or on yourself.

DR: John Kennedy has to go to Texas for the reelection campaign. As he's getting ready to go, he tours the Johnson Space Center in Houston?

DB: He goes regularly to Texas. Albert Thomas was the congressman from Houston, and he was the head of congressional space appropriations.

Kennedy is worried, with civil rights in the South, with James Meredith integrating Ole Miss, with problems in Alabama, that a lot of those conservative southern Democratic senators were going to denounce his Justice Department. So, as a trade-off for being quiet, so to speak, they would start getting big contracts in places like Houston, Huntsville, Biloxi, Hampton [Virginia], Jacksonville.

Kennedy saw space as a way to create jobs in infrastructure and technology. FDR had the TVA and Grand Coulee Dam. Eisenhower had the interstate highway system and Saint Lawrence Seaway, which connected the Great Lakes to the Atlantic Ocean. That's a big part of all this.

DR: Did Lyndon Johnson lobby to have NASA headquarters put in Houston?

DB: Lyndon wanted it desperately in Houston, and he got it. So much money went into Houston. Remember, Kennedy barely won Texas by a hair in 1960. So he was looking at '64, running for reelection, and he needed Texas. Getting money into Houston was a big deal.

DR: On his last day, in Dallas, did he not want to have an astronaut with him?

DB: Gordon Cooper, one of the Mercury astronauts. There were six Mercury missions in the Kennedy years, and all six were successful. Cooper was going to come with Kennedy to Dallas, but he was detained for a NASA exercise and couldn't be with Kennedy.

When Kennedy was shot in Dallas, he was on his way to give a speech about space and technology, how we were beating Russia, why NASA was paying off. In the mid-'60s, NASA was getting about 4.4 percent of the federal budget annually. Today it's a third of one percent or something like that. They used to say in NASA, "No bucks, no Buck Rogers" — meaning going to the moon is expensive.

DR: One of Kennedy's great legacies is the effort to get mankind to the moon, and that did succeed before the end of the decade. When did "moonshot" become part of our language?

DB: My book is called *American Moonshot,* and the phrase now means a lot of things. It really means can-do-ism, engineering excellence, and the private sector, Congress, the White House, universities, all working together for a big goal, a moonshot goal, short of war.

Everybody has different views of what the moonshot should be right now, but the actual phrase comes from baseball. There was a batter named Wally Moon for the Los Angeles Dodgers who would hit these towering home runs in the Los Angeles Coliseum. Then Vin Scully, the radio announcer, would say, "There goes the moonshot, over the left field fence." In the late '50s, that term "moonshot" started tracking. And in Houston, newspapers started calling it Moonshot Command Center.

Today, Joe Biden talks about a cancer moonshot or, as I said, Buzz Aldrin talks about Mars as the new moonshot. There are people who think the new moonshot should be an Earth shot to deal with climate change. But it's still part of our national discussion. How do we all work together for a grand objective?

Dr. Francis S. Collins on the Human Genome Project and Scientific Research

Director, the National Institutes of Health; Former Director, International Human Genome Research Institute

"We are making progress at a pace now that would have been unimaginable a few decades ago, and that's going to continue."

The biotech revolution of the past several decades had its original roots in the pea plant crossbreeding experiments of an Austrian monk, Gregor Mendel, in the 1850s and 1860s, though his value was not recognized until many decades later. Mendel was uninterested in promoting the fact that he had effectively discovered heredity. Not an unimpressive accomplishment for anyone, let alone a scientifically untrained monk.

By contrast, the value of what Francis Crick and James Watson discovered in their Cambridge University lab in 1953 was recognized immediately as truly historic. They discovered the double-helix structure of DNA, and thereby the structure of life itself. The result for those two scientists was not only international acclaim, including a Nobel Prize, but the beginning of a global race to determine how best to understand and use genetics to enhance health, cure illnesses, and extend life.

Part of that race involved sequencing all of the genes in the human genome and thereby giving the world the first complete genetic picture of a human. The U.S. Human Genome Project, begun in 1990, was funded largely by the federal government and was initially led by none other than the now legendary James Watson. But in 1993, he was succeeded by Dr. Francis Collins, a medical doctor and geneticist, who led the international project to its successful conclusion in 2003. (There was a race to map the human genome, and a private sector effort was led by Craig Venter. In 2000, President Bill Clinton announced that both efforts had succeeded essentially simultaneously in completing a draft map.) For this effort, Dr. Collins was later given the nation's highest civilian honor, the Presidential Medal of Freedom.

The American-led effort to map the human genome was breathtaking not only in its complexity, but also in its success. The result was a whole new world in which genetic solutions could improve the human condition. One might think that was enough of a lifetime accomplishment to enable Francis Collins to run a few victory laps and settle easily into a less demanding life.

But Francis Collins is no ordinary human or scientist. Homeschooled until the sixth grade by parents who were generally viewed as somewhat counterculture, he has lived in several worlds: the world of music (he has long had his own rock band); the world of genetics and medicine; the world of improving health care in the developing world; the world of religion (he is a born-again Christian who has written a book explaining why science and religion are compatible); and the world of ethics and privacy.

As if that were not enough for one person to do, he has led the largest biomedical research and funding complex in the world for a record length, beginning in 2009 and continuing into 2021. He is a rare person whose talents and skills are considered so vital to the country that he was appointed to lead the National Institutes of Health (NIH) by President Barack Obama and then reappointed by President Donald Trump, and later by President Joe Biden.

As director of the NIH, Dr. Collins has led efforts to enhance the country's capabilities in precision medicine, oncology research, and opioid mitigation. Too, he led the institutes in working to deal with the COVID-19 crisis of 2019-'20. (Dr. Anthony Fauci directs the

National Institute of Allergy and Infectious Diseases, one of the NIH's twenty-seven institutes and centers of medical research under Dr. Collins.)

I have known Dr. Collins for many years and have interviewed him on a number of occasions. This interview took place in September 2017 at the National Institutes of Health.

DAVID M. RUBENSTEIN (DR): What is the human genome, and why do we care about your having codiscovered it?

FRANCIS COLLINS (FC): The genome is basically the entire instruction book, written in the language of DNA, for an organism. Animals, plants, bacteria, they all have a genome. Ours is pretty big.

If you think of DNA as a language, it's an interesting one. It has just four letters in its alphabet, which we call A, C, G, and T. They're abbreviations for chemical bases.

Our genomes are six billion of those letters. You get three billion from Mom and three billion from Dad. That's a lot, although it's pretty amazing to contemplate that that's a bounded set of information sufficient to build a human being from a single cell.

DR: Why is any human being better off because we now have mapped the human genome?

FC: The whole thing got finished in 2003, and there were some silly comments: "Medicine will be transformed in the next two weeks because of this." Of course not. Six billion letters, you don't really know the language, it's going to take a while to figure it out.

What's happened over the years since then has, however, been transformative in medicine, and particularly in cancer. If you develop that terrible disease, you want to know exactly what misspellings have happened in the genome of those cancer cells that are causing those good cells to go bad. That's now affordable because of the genome project, and it pretty much has changed everything in terms of the way in which we approach the diagnosis and treatment of cancer.

DR: Today it's the case that anybody can have their genome mapped for less than $1,000. Have you had yours mapped?

FC: I had a sampling of it done. I was writing a book about personalized medicine and I wanted to use myself as a guinea pig. One thing I did learn was that my risk of diabetes was substantially higher than the average person based on my genetic inheritance, and that was sort of a shock, because that's not something that's run in my family.

But my family are all pretty lean, athletic people, so maybe they managed to avoid it. I learned this at a point where I was not lean and athletic. I was indulging in too many muffins and honey-buns and not doing any exercise, and I was getting chunky. That genetic information was enough to motivate me to change all of that, to lose thirty-five pounds, to get into an exercise program. I'm a different person now than I would have been if I had stayed on that same path.

DR: Muffins and honey-buns are not healthy for you is what you're saying?

FC: They are not healthy for anybody, I'm afraid.

DR: Somebody might say, "The man who is running the NIH must come from a family of medical professionals and scientists, because this is one of the most important scientific jobs in the world." You were raised on a farm. You were homeschooled?

FC: I was. Not because my parents were religious in their persuasion at all, but because they thought the county schools where I grew up in the Shenandoah Valley of Virginia were not up to their standards in terms of what they thought their four boys should have as far as education that would get them excited about learning. But my mother was incredibly gifted as a teacher. She was a polymath. What she really gave us was this excitement about learning new things, which I carry with me to this day.

DR: You did this until the sixth grade, and then you went to school?

FC: We moved into town. My grandmother, who lived about seven miles away, had a stroke and needed somebody in the house. I think my mom was a little tired of teaching these four boys at that point and figured, "The public schools in the city of Staunton are probably up to a better standard."

DR: Did you realize that after homeschooling you were ahead of everybody else or behind everybody else?

FC: I was ahead. I ended up two years younger than everybody else in sixth grade, and that was maintained all the way through. I graduated from high school at sixteen because my mom got me started in this particular way of learning quickly.

DR: I graduated at sixteen too. I wouldn't recommend it necessarily, because you're a little bit younger than your friends when you go to college.

FC: The social part of it is a little conflicting.

DR: You went to college at the University of Virginia. Were you an academic superstar there?

FC: I was a bit of a nerd. I got excited about science in high school. What got me interested in science didn't come from my family — no scientists, no physicians for generations. It was a tenth-grade chemistry teacher. I majored in chemistry at UVA because I had figured that's what I wanted to do based on the course I had from John House in tenth grade at Lee High School in Staunton, Virginia.

DR: You then went to Yale to get a PhD in what?

FC: Chemical physics. Quantum mechanics. It was mathematical physical science.

DR: You've got a degree from the University of Virginia, you have a PhD from Yale. You're ready to get a job, right?

FC: You would think so, wouldn't you? But I had made this mistake of narrowing my focus at a very early stage. I thought life science was really messy and not very interesting. It seemed very descriptive. I couldn't perceive there were a lot of principles, partly because it wasn't taught very well. So I avoided biology or biochemistry or any of those things in college. I took straight chemistry, physics, math, that was it, likewise in graduate school.

But here I was as a graduate student, working late at night. There was another guy one floor above me who was also there in the middle of the night, working in a lab on the chemistry of DNA. I had no idea about this stuff.

The more I read about it, and talked to him about it, and began to read articles about it, the more excited I got. This was an area of science ready to burst forward with all kinds of potential. Frankly, I was feeling a little bit lonely, and a little bit like what I was pursuing wasn't going to be my way of making the world a better place, and maybe there was something else I could do.

This was a pretty dramatic change of heart. I had had no inkling of being interested in biology or in medicine until I was already a second-year graduate student. And yet it became more and more compelling.

DR: You got your PhD at Yale, and then you said to your parents, "Guess what, I'm going to go to medical school"? Did they say, "We've given you enough degrees already"?

460

FC: Fortunately for them, they hadn't paid for any of my education. I was the youngest kid, and the money kind of ran out before they got to me. Fortunately tuition at the University of Virginia was about $900 a year, so I could make that money in the summer. For Yale I had an NSF scholarship. Thank you, National Science Foundation.

To go to medical school was going to be a challenge, because I was already married and had a kid at that point. But the University of North Carolina offered an occasional medical student a Morehead Foundation opportunity to have their fees and tuition paid for, and even a little bit of a stipend.

As a medical student I was trying to figure out, "How do I put this all together — my love for digital information, for mathematics, which is what I got out of chemistry and physics, with this messy thing called medicine?"

Where does it all come together? In genetics. DNA is digital information. It's something you can compute on. It also is fundamental to life and it's fundamental to medicine. So by the time I was halfway through my first year as a medical student, I knew I wanted to be a medical geneticist.

DR: When you were younger, you were an agnostic. Now you have become very involved in religion, and you've written books about it. How did you transform yourself into somebody who's a committed Christian?

FC: It does seem like an odd story, doesn't it? My parents were not opposed to religion, they just didn't think it was particularly relevant, so I had no religious background.

So I was an agnostic. But by the time I got to graduate school, I was shifting even more to being an atheist, and I would not be too comfortable keeping quiet if somebody was talking about the supernatural. All that mattered was nature and how you study it and how you describe it.

Then I went to medical school. That third year of medical school, you're thrust onto the wards, and you're sitting at the bedside of wonderful people, many of whom are not going to survive, and you start to realize that your own thinking about life and death has been pretty unsophisticated compared to the reality of what these people are facing.

I realized that I was a scientist, I was supposed to make decisions about really important questions based on evidence, and I'd never really considered whether there might be evidence supporting the idea that there really is a God. I just assumed the answer was no. That was a bit unsettling, but it seemed like something that I shouldn't ignore. It took me a couple of years of fighting against that, trying to prove that this was all wrong and that I could stick with my agnosticism, but ultimately I realized I couldn't, that it was so compelling.

DR: The Bible would say that maybe the earth is a couple thousand years old. Scientists would say it's much older, five billion years old. How do you reconcile those two different strands of thought?

FC: A lot of people are tripped up by what they interpret as a conflict between a literal interpretation of Genesis 1 and 2 and what science teaches us very convincingly about the age of the universe — almost fourteen billion years — and the age of the earth — almost five billion years. But you know what? That idea that there's a conflict is a fairly recent arrival on the scene, based on an insistence of an ultraliteral interpretation of Bible verses that were almost certainly not intended to be read that way.

I wrote a book, *The Language of God,* about this perceived conflict, because for me there really has never been a discrepancy between what I know as a scientist — if you're going to ask me a question about nature, science is going to be the answer — but also as somebody who's interested in questions that science can't answer, like "Why am I here?"

DR: At the National Institutes of Health, you

have twenty-seven institutes, and they do research. If somebody has an acute problem that can't be solved elsewhere, they can get into the National Institutes of Health hospital?

FC: It's called the NIH Clinical Center, and it's the largest research hospital in the world. People come to that hospital to participate in clinical trials that are experimental. Many of the people who come there have exhausted all of the other opportunities for any kind of help for whatever it is that ails them.

The taxpayers pay the whole cost, and we think that's the right way to do this. The people who come there trust in us to do the best we can to find an answer for something that doesn't have answers.

DR: In the business world, biotech medicine and other companies in the health sciences can get a lot of venture capital funding. Why do we need the government to still provide research money?

FC: The private sector does do an awful lot of the good stuff that results in America leading in biomedical research. They are our partners, and important ones. They actually spend about twice what the government does in this whole ecosystem of biomedical research.

But the private sector has to focus on things where their shareholders are going to see that there's some possibility of a profit. Most of the things that you now see that are getting to profit would never have gotten there without the government having invested first in the basic science that it takes to make those discoveries.

DR: Give me one or two examples, if you could, of something that you or your predecessors funded that became very helpful to the health of individuals.

FC: There's a long, long list of examples. Let's just take what's happened with heart disease. Death rates from heart attack are down by more than 70 percent. Why is that? Part of that is our funding something called the Framingham Study in Massachusetts, which taught us what the risk factors are that you could actually interfere with. We didn't really know how important hypertension and high cholesterol were and how critical it was to treat them until that came along. Part of this is also drugs, statins, the most commonly prescribed drug these days.

DR: Do you think it's possible to eliminate all heart problems by diet, exercise, and statins?

FC: There again, heart disease has a strong genetic component. Cholesterol is certainly a big risk factor. It's particularly important for somebody who's had a heart attack and doesn't want to have another one to get on a statin and to really manage their cholesterol very tightly.

But people are different. We still have this need for individualized data. We are about to launch a program to enroll one million Americans — one million — in a prospective long-term study of health and illness, which will begin to give us some answers to those questions. Ask me again in ten or fifteen years, I think I'll have a better answer about what works, and what works for which person.

DR: President Nixon famously said, "We're going to have a war on cancer," and we're still fighting that war, though we've made a lot of progress. Do you think within fifty years or a hundred years it's possible to eliminate all the various things that are called cancer?

FC: I think we'll get very close to that if you'll give us thirty to fifty years, because we're already making remarkable strides. And what we have been able to do, which was not possible when Nixon declared the war, is to develop some really good weapons to figure out how to go after this disease.

466

We also have the ability to diagnose it earlier and earlier, and that's obviously an important part of making sure that it's curable. But of the big, exciting developments, one is the fact that every cancer has DNA mutations in it that are driving those cells to grow when they should not. We can now say for that individual which genes are driving that malignancy and which drugs we have that work for that pathway.

So instead of chemotherapy, which is a form of carpet-bombing the situation, we now have smart bombs that go after that particular cancer with fewer side effects. Then we have immunotherapy, activating the immune system to tackle a cancer.

DR: As people live longer, one of the side effects has been more prevalence of Alzheimer's, or dementia. Do you think we have any progress being made on Alzheimer's, and what do you think causes it?

FC: This is a huge challenge. We now have more than five million people affected in the U.S., and that's going to go up as our average age goes up. We have an enormous investment in this at NIH, and are working closely with the private sector in a partnership to try to come up with ways to prevent or at least delay the onset of this.

Clearly some of the factors are genetic, and

we now know about more than a dozen places in the genome where a little change in the spelling will increase or decrease the likelihood of this disease. But some of it is still a bit of a mystery. What is it that triggers it? Can we come up with a solution? I'm guardedly optimistic, based on the things we have learned about what's going on at the molecular level. But it's not right around the corner.

DR: Why should somebody go through the agony of medical school and then work for the government or do things relating to health care but not making lots of money by the standards of Wall Street? Why should somebody come and work at NIH or become a medical doctor or a researcher?

FC: It really comes down to this: what is it that we all hope to do in that brief time that we're here on this planet? Right now I would say medical research is very much near the top of the list of opportunities that people have to make a difference, because it is such an exciting time. We are making progress at a pace now that would have been unimaginable a few decades ago, and that's going to continue.

So if you want to spend your time working hard but feeling as if you made a contribution to help people who are suffering, this is a great way to do it. And money alone is probably not going to give you that same satisfaction.

It's also an adventure, it's also like a detective story. Scientific discovery is one of those amazing moments where you learn something that nobody knew before, and that's such a rush. You don't get to have that experience in a lot of other professions.

What I worry about, though, is that this current generation of budding scientists is feeling pretty anxious about whether there is a career path for them. We've gone through a tough time in terms of support of biomedical research in this country, and we're not done with it yet.

DR: What would you like to see as your legacy when you ultimately do retire from this position? Would you like to do something else in medical research? Would you like to ride your motorcycle? Would you like to start a rock band?

FC: It's hard to think about doing something else after you've had the chance to do this. I would think it would be something involving science. It might also be something involving this conversation about science and faith. It might involve some music, yes. But some mix of those — God willing that my health holds up and I don't crash my motorcycle.

DR: Would you ever consider the highest calling of mankind: private equity?

FC: I don't think I have the skills and talent to be much use there.

DR: I'm sure you'd do very well.

■ ■ ■ ■

5
CREATION AND CULTURE

■ ■ ■ ■

"Here in the United States, hopefully, what we're building are not just pyramids, are not icons to one pharaoh. What we're building is a culture and a way of living together that we can look back on and say, [This] was good, was inclusive, was kind, was innovative, was able to fulfill the dreams of as many people as possible."
— Barack Obama, "Exit Interview with Doris Kearns Goodwin," September 21, 2016

WYNTON MARSALIS
ON JAZZ, AMERICA'S
NATIONAL ART

Musician and Composer; Artistic Director,
Jazz at Lincoln Center

"The music has three fundamental elements.

"The first is improvisation, which is our kind of individuality and what we believe in. We have rights and freedoms that are about the individual.

"Then swing, which is about nurturing common ground, finding balance with other people, working out an agenda as you go along under the pressure of time.

"And then the blues. And the blues is an optimism that's not naïve. The blues also implies an acuity. That's a democratic thing."

Every culture tries to convey the essence of that culture through music. In the United States, our culture has produced a variety of musical forms over the centuries. But one particular type of music — jazz — for more than a century has probably been the most

475

distinctively American form of music. It was initially created by African American musicians in New Orleans; expanded upon by African American and white musicians in Chicago, New York, and Kansas City; transformed into a variety of styles (swing, bebop, soul, gypsy, Latin, and big band, to mention a few); and popularized around the United States, and in time the world, by such legendary performers as Duke Ellington, Louis Armstrong, Count Basie, Dizzy Gillespie, Sidney Bechet, Benny Goodman, Charlie Parker, Thelonious Monk, Sarah Vaughan, Milton and Harold Batiste, Wayne Shorter, Earl Hines, Miles Davis, Ella Fitzgerald, Jelly Roll Morton, Billie Holiday, Dave Brubeck, and Herbie Hancock.

In recent decades, the royalty of the jazz world could fairly be said to be the Marsalis family: the late Ellis Marsalis Jr., a jazz pianist and educator from New Orleans, and four of his six sons — Branford, Wynton, Delfeayo, and Jason — all of whom carved out niches for themselves in the world of jazz.

Wynton, perhaps the best known of the sons, was actually trained initially as a classical musician, schooled briefly at Juilliard, and considered making a career in that genre. And he did begin his career that way, winning Grammy Awards two years in a row for classical music performance as well as jazz in 1983 and 1984. But, in time, the family tradition prevailed, and Wynton devoted himself and his trumpet primarily to the world of jazz and, like his father, to the world of jazz education.

For his jazz recordings, Wynton Marsalis has won six Grammy Awards. He was also the first jazz musician to win a Pulitzer Prize for musical composition. He is one of the very few Americans to be awarded both the National Medal of Arts and the National Humanities Medal, and he is a 2021 inductee into the prestigious American Academy of Arts and Letters. And to give jazz a prominent and permanent home in New York City, Wynton Marsalis helped to create and continues to lead Jazz at Lincoln Center.

While Wynton Marsalis's first love is educating young people about the power, beauty, and wonders of jazz, he has a relentless performance schedule in New York, throughout the U.S., and around the world, while also managing to compose and proselytize about the magic beauty of jazz. During the COVID-19 lockdowns of 2020, Wynton found traveling and performing in person a bit more challenging. So he became a master at plying his many jazz talents virtually. And it was virtually that I had a chance to interview Wynton from his home in New York on October 25, 2020, for my *Peer to Peer* Bloomberg TV show. Just listening to Wynton talk about his life in jazz, and jazz's meaning to his life, made me feel that I have missed a fair bit in life by not trying to better appreciate jazz.

DAVID M. RUBENSTEIN (DR): Do you get tired of people calling you a jazz legend?

WYNTON MARSALIS (WM): I like the word *jazz.* I don't like *legend.*

DR: Sadly, your father passed away in April of 2020 at the age of eighty-five because of COVID. It must have been a very sad loss, because you were very close to him.

WM: Me and my brothers, we loved him so much. He was such an example for us. He was such a kind man, and a man with a large worldview, and also a large person. He didn't do small things.

He was very philosophical. He wasn't a touchy-feely type of person. There wasn't a lot of hugging and "I love you" going on. But there was underneath a lot of resolve and seriousness and deep love, not just for us. He had many students who loved him and loved to tell stories about him.

DR: Your father was a prominent jazz pianist based in New Orleans. He had four sons, all of whom are jazz musicians?

WM: He had six sons, and four are jazz musicians. One of my brothers is severely autistic, and another is not a musician. That's the one who actually is the most like him.

DR: When you were growing up, you looked up to your father. Was he somebody who said, "I want you to be a jazz trumpet player"?

WM: No, he didn't push any of us into anything. My father really struggled when I was growing up. He was trying to play modern jazz in the era of segregation, in clubs, with a populace that didn't like that style of music.

So much of my experience was going to sparsely populated clubs with him in colorful areas. I loved to go because I was always the only kid in the room. It started when I was three, four, five years old, and it continued till I got into high school and started to work myself.

But I always went with him and identified with his struggle, because he continued to play even though he didn't get audience support. He was not well known. He wasn't famous. He struggled financially. He never complained. He was very high-minded in his belief in jazz and in his belief in the necessity of it as a tool for healing people and raising consciousness.

DR: When you were growing up, you experienced racial discrimination. It was a segregated area then?

WM: Segregation, discrimination, racism — that was just a part of life. This is not philosophy I'm talking now. It's just how it was. Your neighborhood looked a certain way. The white neighborhoods were a certain way. Black people generally lived in our area on one side of the railroad tracks. We still had ditches in our streets.

Any type of systems always worked against you. It was just what the system was. You didn't have distance from it. When you grew up in it, it was very much a fact of life. I fought with it a lot and had a lot of problems in that system.

But most people adapted to it and were okay with it. They didn't like it, but sometimes you're in a bad situation. In this case we're talking about racism. It could be anything. It could be a health situation. The degree to which you're willing to fight against it is based on your ability to accept the pain of fighting against it.

DR: Are you surprised about the Black Lives Matter situation? Here we are in the year 2020, well past the time that you grew up, and we still have racial problems of the same type.

WM: We're not anywhere near advanced past what I grew up with. So no, I'm not surprised by it. We have a segregation in our systems in general.

DR: Today, you're recognized all over the country and around the world. Do you still feel you are not treated the same as you would be if you were white?

WM: Yes, I feel that. I feel it in terms of the kind of intellectual patronization that I receive, the low-level criticism of our music. I'm subject to things — of course, nothing like what I grew up with, nor do I make a habit of complaining about it constantly, because I'm also treated with so much respect by so many people that for me to complain would be past gratuitous. It's not a part of what I talk about.

But if you ask me the question directly, yes, I would say I've been treated unfairly by newspapers like the *New York Times.* The way Jazz at Lincoln Center has been covered is abominable. Even though we get articles, those articles are always very poorly researched. The writers oftentimes, down through history, lack the intelligence and depth of engagement with the form to be qualified to speak on it in the paper of record. Because it's jazz, it doesn't matter.

That's only in direct response to your question. I don't want to confuse it with when I was growing up, or the situations that I found myself in, or my father's situation, or my grandfather's. I'm very, very grateful for how I've been treated by people all over this country.

DR: Many African Americans of your age and my age have told me that they have given their children the so-called talk about being very careful about how they interact with the police and to be careful to not do anything that would be misinterpreted by police. Have you had that talk with your own children?

WM: Of course. I just give them examples where I was not as mindful of my mouth in an instance when I didn't have the power. I always tell them, "Deal with them like you would deal with a dude in the street with a gun."

That does not apply to certain people. But it's been that way for a long time. For my kids, it was never a big dramatic thing to tell them something that's a fact of living in this country.

But my kids have had run-ins. I've had run-ins. There's a level of compliance you have to follow, just as you would have to do if you were on the street. It's shameful that you have to be that way with police officers. But that's the environment that we live and have been raised in.

DR: There's a story that your father had you sit down with, I think, Al Hirt and Miles Davis, and they said, "How would you like to play the trumpet?" and they gave you a trumpet.

WM: My father was playing with Al Hirt, and Al Hirt gave me a trumpet for my sixth birthday. Before Al got me a trumpet, my father was talking to Miles, and Miles said, "Don't get that boy a trumpet. It's too hard." So that is a true story.

DR: As you grew up, you were actually a classical musician more than a jazz musician. When you went to Juilliard, you were interested in classical music?

WM: I grew up always wanting to play jazz. But jazz was much more difficult to learn, in that time especially, than classical music. Because my father was a jazz musician, I was always around the music. I was raised in the culture. I love the musicians.

My father was a modern jazz musician. He wasn't playing New Orleans jazz. But at a certain time, when I was maybe ten or eleven, he started to play New Orleans music.

It was difficult at that time for a person my age and my generation to figure out what it was, because it was not a part of the American mythology. Whereas with classical music, you had competitions and classes you could go to, so you could get a track record on your résumé. It will say that when I was fourteen, I won a competition to play the Haydn Trumpet Concerto with the New Orleans Philharmonic.

I was playing jazz the whole time. But what could I say that I did? That I played in a club called Tyler's Beer Garden on a Wednesday.

My sensibility was always that of a jazz musician, because that's the environment in which I was raised. From birth, I always loved my father and the other musicians. And they were living very difficult lives. I always wanted to help them and do whatever I could do to become a good enough musician for them to respect me.

I had to be able to swing and play on changes and improvise for them to have a certain level of respect for me. But I later developed a love for classical music because a guy gave me an album of the great French trumpet player Maurice André. When I saw it was a classical record, I was disappointed. When you live in segregation, you think classical music is for white people.

The guy — it was a white guy — went in the back of the streetcar, where white people didn't really go at that time, to give me that record. He put his trumpet case down by mine. He was a college student, and I was twelve, thirteen years old. I read the back of the album, and it said that Maurice André's family were coal miners. "Man," I thought, "I've got to hear a coal miner's kid play a trumpet."

When I went home to put it on, man, the playing was so unbelievable and beautiful. So I started to learn these concertos off of the record. Because I was trying to learn John Coltrane's solos and Clifford Brown's and Miles Davis's songs. I learned those off of the record. I learned the concertos the same way.

So I loved classical music after I encountered it. But I always came at it from the standpoint of a jazz musician.

DR: You're the only person to ever win a Grammy in jazz and in classical music in the same year. That must have been pretty impressive.

WM: I didn't really know what the Grammys were. There's a funny story about my father. He went to the Grammys. He was not into those kinds of things. He sat through the whole show.

At the end of the show, I won. I was back in the hotel with him and my mother. My daddy looked at me. He said, "So that was the Grammys, huh? Don't get me wrong. It's

485

great that you won. But you don't think this means you can play, do you?" I started laughing, because I was, like, twenty-two.

I knew what he was saying, because I still, of course, had a long way to go to learn how to play. No way was my father ever small, so I didn't take it as an insult. He didn't care about awards and all of that. I said, "No, man, I was raised by you. I'm not looking at it like that."

DR: Explain why jazz is so popular. It's one of the most unique American forms of music. Classical music came from Europe, but jazz was invented in the United States. And it's a classic American kind of invention, I would say.

You make it sound, in your book [*Moving to Higher Ground*], like it's almost a religious experience to play jazz and to understand jazz. Can you explain why jazz is almost like a religion to people who care about it?

WM: Jazz is our national art form. As such, it objectifies a lot of our basic principles.

In different periods, different times, people are good at different types of arts. We know about the Dutch masters and the great playwrights of the Elizabethan period, the great Greek playwrights, the French Impressionists. I could go on and on about the German symphonists in the classical style.

486

America was blessed with a group of musicians and the social conditions that produced this music.

The music has three fundamental elements. The first is improvisation, which is our kind of individuality and what we believe in. We have rights and freedoms that are about the individual.

Then swing, which is about nurturing common ground, finding balance with other people, working out an agenda as you go along under the pressure of time.

And then the blues. The blues is an optimism that's not naïve. The blues also implies an acuity. That's a democratic thing.

I'm giving you a thumb line of what jazz is. I'm giving you a thumbline understanding of the music.

Now, suffice it to say that everything in the music ties into things that we do, down to the three branches of government. How to amend the Constitution is like adding to an arrangement. I could go on and on.

These are not superficial things that are contrived. They come out of the American way of life. This is going to be a longer answer. But it's important, because the central question of jazz's position in our country concerns the relationship of slavery to the American identity and our mythology as a country.

Black Americans by and large in our country have little or no knowledge of jazz. And jazz is the greatest achievement of the Afro-American culture in the context of American culture, meaning it's Afro-American but it applies to all Americans.

Our poor public education system makes sure that a certain group remains ignorant. And the average white jazz writer is actually a rock fan who has for a long time wished that jazz would be something else without Black folks at the core of it, that maybe jazz would just die away. That's why, if you study jazz, there's a long-standing tradition of article after article, and decade after decade, saying, "Is jazz dead?"

Now, all of this investment in the destruction of jazz is to further obscure a big lie that jazz uncovers. It's important to look at this, because it's a serious thing to consider if we are to transform our nation.

If we say our nation is based on human freedom, and we are the first on earth founded on the glorious celebration of human freedom, dignity, and life, how do we then reconcile and correct the systemic dehumanizing ownership and brutalizing of a large underclass of people for free labor because of their skin color? It's too much injustice to correct.

So we're forced to say that those people are responsible for the problem. They're less than human. It's just their condition. But if it's not their condition, it means that our mythology and belief about ourselves is not true.

DR: If I were to go to listen to a Tchaikovsky concert or a Beethoven concert, it's going to be mostly sounding the same no matter where I'm going to listen to it, no matter what orchestra. They might play it slightly better, slightly different, but basically you know what you're going to get when you sit down. A jazz musician can expand on what has been composed and play it differently every different time? Is that part of what jazz is all about?

WM: That's the improvisation part. You have a lot of latitude to do things. That's like the way Americans conduct business — all the innovations we have, the freedom we have to speak, the fact that we think we can step into a space and use our personality to transform a tradition.

Yes, we have that freedom. But balancing that freedom is that we have the responsibility to extend a courtesy and an understanding to other people who have those freedoms, and nurture that common space.

DR: When you're playing jazz in a concert, and one of your musicians is improvising, do you know when he's going to end or she's going to end?

WM: You know when they're going to end because we play on a cycle. We play on a form, a harmonic cycle that goes around and around, in most instances. There are many types of jazz, but in most instances we're playing on a chord progression that repeats.

When you get to the top of that repetition, you start listening for "Is this person going to stop playing?" They normally will indicate to you when they're getting ready to stop. But sometimes they keep playing too long. Then there are certain cues that take place on the bandstand to let you know it's time for you to stop soloing.

DR: In your book on jazz, you talk about some of the greats you either played with or who influenced you. I'd just like to ask for your brief comments on some of them. First is Louis Armstrong. You originally thought he was, as you say, an Uncle Tom. But you obviously changed your view.

WM: Yes. It's hard for later generations to understand the challenges of an earlier generation, and the norms of show business, and what Louis Armstrong did. Now I understand more of his genius and who he was and what he played.

When I look at the movies he made or the positions he took, I still don't necessarily like that. I don't like a lot of what Black people

490

are in any of the American movies of the 1930s and '40s and '50s. A lot of it now has that same destructive mythology.

Later I learned and understood who Louis Armstrong was as a musician. That's a totally different story. That man was a genius of such magnitude you could lie about how great he was and you still wouldn't be saying enough.

DR: You're a composer as well as a performer, educator, conductor, and so forth. One of the great composers in the jazz world was Duke Ellington. Did he have any influence on you?

WM: Duke's intelligence, his dedication, over two thousand pieces — I love him.

Because I grew up also listening to classical music, I love Beethoven. The first symphonic piece I ever played was Beethoven's Fifth Symphony. How Beethoven tied all the themes together — Duke Ellington wrote a piece that's called *A Tone Parallel to Harlem,* and it uses the same basic concept, very little thematic material and a lot of development.

I go back to when I first heard Beethoven's music and began to study it and listen to his symphonies and think about how he developed material. And I tie it to Duke Ellington's developmental concerns and the things he did, albeit in another style of music. I love many other composers in the jazz tradition and in the classical tradition. Russian composers I love — Stravinsky, Shostakovich. I could go on and on.

DR: What about Dizzy Gillespie? Was he an influence on you?

WM: That was my man. The thing about Dizzy Gillespie that hit me first was the depth of his intelligence. I met him when I was fourteen. And when he started talking — oh, the way my daddy and other musicians listened to him. He's part of the reason that we developed Jazz at Lincoln Center.

DR: You began playing jazz there in the late 1980s. That evolved into Jazz at Lincoln Center.

WM: We wanted to fill a space in American arts and provide enough education and music and advocacy for us to have our native art form when it came time for us to address our mythology and correct it, so that we could move forward as a nation.

We've succeeded beyond our wildest imagination with the volume of concerts we've been able to do. We built three concert halls in the middle of Manhattan on Fifty-Ninth Street, the House of Swing. We put on concert series over thirty years. We have twelve education programs. Even since this pandemic began, we've put out over five hundred or six hundred pieces virtually.

From the beginning, we had three tenets: no segregation, no generation gap, and all jazz is modern. We've continued to live that credo through all of these years.

DR: When Lincoln Center opened in the 1960s, people thought, "Okay, this is opera, symphonic music, classical kind of music." What did people say when you said, "We need to do more jazz at Lincoln Center"?

WM: We had a lot of support from the top of the organization. The Constitution was not written with the rights of Afro-Americans and Native Americans in mind. But the Constitution can be amended, and it has been amended. And me and you are sitting here talking right now.

DR: What do you enjoy the most now? Is it composing or is it teaching? Is it conducting or playing?

WM: It's all the same to me. I taught some of my students at Juilliard last night and we were talking about a chapter of Albert Murray's book *The Hero and the Blues*. We're on Zoom, I'm going back and forth with forty young people and they're talking about what things mean and what does it mean to be in the moment. So for me it's all a blessing. I feel grateful.

DR: Is jazz popular outside the United States?

WM: Jazz has never really been popular. It's not popular like funk was popular, like rock and roll is popular. Jazz is meaningful and it's necessary. Those who are interested in that like jazz. Those who are not, they don't like jazz. We need to teach our kids about the music. It is a national art form.

DR: What is it that you would tell people about why the jazz experience as a listener is so compelling compared to other forms of music?

WM: Because it has a development section. You have to follow what musicians play from one point. Jazz is the music that's most in the world like conversation. You interviewing me — we're not really conversing, but I'm reading you. Like when I gave you that one real long answer, you gave me a couple of, "Okay, man, I'm getting ready to come in here."

Jazz is a music that prizes individuality. You have a lot of great individuals you can interface with, from Lester Young to Billie Holiday to Chick Corea and Herbie Hancock. You have great groups you can love that play in different forms. And you have the whole Afro-

Latin form of jazz that takes you everywhere from Brazil to Cuba to Puerto Rico. It integrates your citizenship in and your understanding of the world.

Most importantly, it gives you tremendous pride in being American. We didn't have to denigrate or cut anybody down or do anything negative to anybody to create this. It's a nonpredatory form. It's a symbiotic form. You can be as rich as you want to be in jazz and nobody else has to be poor. I'm going to do this till I die if I can, the Good Lord willing, if people will have me. I've been blessed to do something and get unbelievable support from people.

DR: If you could play with any two or three jazz musicians — without offending anybody you don't mention — who are the ones you'd like to play with the most?

WM: I always say Count Basie's band in 1937. One of my great mentors was Sweets Edison, and he was a member of Count Basie's band in 1937. This man was the epitome of soul. Anything that could produce something as soulful as Sweets, I want to be a part of that.

RITA MORENO
ON THE ACTOR'S LIFE

Actress

"How many times in my life have I said, 'I'll never work again'? How many times do actors say that to themselves? Over and over. It's as though you somehow never learn that particular lesson, because show business is so bizarre, it's so odd, it's so demanding, it's so mean."

One creative cultural area where Americans have been at the forefront for over a century, even before recorded sound ("talkies") was possible has been the motion picture. From a base in Southern California, often referred to as Hollywood, entrepreneurs built studios, and young men and women came there to develop their acting skills, with the hope of becoming a star — a Clark Cable, Cary Grant, Jack Nicholson, Paul Newman, Sidney Poitier, Katharine Hepburn, Elizabeth Taylor, Marilyn Monroe, or Meryl Streep.

Some motion picture stars also become

stars on Broadway or on television.

Few of those actors or actresses were at the top of their profession for seven decades and still performed in their late eighties. And fewer still were awarded all of the most significant awards of their profession: Emmy, Grammy, Oscar, Tony, Kennedy Center Honor, and Golden Globe. And even fewer have also been awarded two of the highest awards a president of the United States can bestow on a performing artist: the National Medal of Arts and Presidential Medal of Freedom.

Actually, there is only one living person who has done all of the above, despite the fact that she suffered a great deal of discrimination in her career because she was Puerto Rican. That person is Rita Moreno, who first came into American consciousness as the Academy Award–winning Anita in the epic *West Side Story* movie of 1961. But that role did not free Rita Moreno from being typecast as the typical barefoot actress playing roles that Hollywood and Broadway thought appropriate for a woman of Latin descent.

In time, because of her considerable skills as a dancer, actress, and singer, and a larger-than-life personality combined with extraordinary beauty, Rita Moreno overcame prejudice and showed the full array of her talents through every medium available to performing artists.

She also led an at times tempestuous life. The longtime lover of Marlon Brando, she once came close to committing suicide over Brando's infidelities.

I first came to know Rita Moreno when the Kennedy Center awarded her a Kennedy Center Honor in 2015, and I found her to be the most pleasant and engaging of persons, with no Hollywood star airs or pretensions. She had led a full life as a performer but still seemed to relish the thrill of entertaining others.

This interview, done on April 29, 2017, as part of the center's Profiles in Creativity series, only summarizes some of the highlights of an exciting professional and personal life. The love of her life was actually not a famous performer, but a medical doctor, Leonard Gordon, to whom she was married for forty-five years until his death, and with whom she had one daughter, Fernanda, to whom she is very close. For those who want to learn more about this gifted woman, I highly recommend her autobiography, *Rita Moreno: A Memoir*. As in the interview, so too in the book, no holds are barred.

DAVID M. RUBENSTEIN (DR): You've now been in show business for more than seventy years. An incredible career. You've won all the kinds of awards, every award you can possibly win — the Presidential Medal of Freedom, the National Medal of Arts, every award. Why do you think you've been so successful? You had good genes? You worked harder? You're smarter? You're more talented? What do you think was the reason?

RITA MORENO (RM): Why do I think I've been so successful? I have no idea. That's for you to say! Why do you think I've been so successful, seriously?

DR: You worked very hard, you had a lot of innate talent, you practiced when you were very young, and you were really driven. How about that?

RM: Here's the thing. I know a lot of people who did all of those things and haven't gotten as fortunate as I. I know a lot of people who deserve all of the attention in the world, all kinds of honors, and don't have them. I really think at a certain point it's in the lap of the gods. I do.

DR: Let's think of it another way. You've been in show business for seventy years. Many people your age are spending time with their grandchildren — you're doing that too — but they're not competing actively in the performing arts world. You are now filming a new show for Netflix, *One Day at a Time* [it ran for three seasons starting in 2017, the year of this interview]. You must feel young there because Norman Lear is the producer and he's ninety-four. Why have you decided to continue your career? Not that everyone doesn't want you to do it.

RM: Because I love it! I love what I do. Look at me eighty-five, for God's sake. I have an album out, in Spanish, which is produced by Emilio Estefan. I have a book out, which I know you've been carrying around. I have all of these things going for me. What an astonishing life I have. I wake up humming.

DR: You should bottle that. That's pretty impressive. But let me ask: You've won all these great awards. Which one surprised you the most?

RM: The Oscar. At the time that the Oscars came along, I was doing another crappy film in Manila in the Philippines, where I was playing yet another dusky maiden, a guerrilla girl in World War II. Then to my astonishment I got nominated and I was flown into Hollywood for the night.

I was really pretty sure that Judy Garland was going to get it, because number one, it was Judy Garland playing a dramatic role in a film called *Judgment at Nuremberg*. I thought, "I don't have a chance."

But I wanted to be there just in case, and

they called my name. I damn near wet my knickers. I could not believe it! I had flown in, I was exhausted with the time change. You saw that really thrilling and touching speech: "I don't believe it." I've always wanted to make up for that. I think I did when I got the wonderful Screen Actors Guild Life Achievement Award.

But the best part of that night is that as I got off the stage, Joan Crawford was there. She was the cohostess, and I think Rock Hudson — yes, he gave me the Oscar — Rock Hudson was the other host. And she, Joan Crawford, liked to drink. Vodka was her drink, and she had a Pepsi cooler in her dressing room because her husband was Mr. Pepsi, I forget his name, a very famous man. [It was Alfred Steele.]

She had been spiking her Pepsis with quite a bit of vodka. When I got offstage and into the wings, she was drunk as a skunk. A photographer came over to take a picture. She saw the photographer and she grabbed me and hugged me. She was built like a linebacker.

She's got me in this grip like this and the photographer says, "Can I see Miss Moreno's face, please?" She really was crushing my face against her bosom, such as it was. "Oh no," she says, "she's so upset." She wanted the picture, right? I'm saying, "I'm not upset, I'm not upset!"

It ended up that they had to wrest me from her grip. She would not let me go! They wanted to take me to the press room because I just won this amazing Oscar, this girl that half the world hadn't heard of.

DR: Let's go back to the beginning of your life. You were born in Puerto Rico, and your mother was only seventeen when you were born?

RM: I think she was about seventeen.

DR: You were living happily in Puerto Rico for five years or so.

RM: It was lovely. I was born in Humacao, and then we lived in a town called Juncos, which is right close to the rain forest. It was an idyllic life for a little girl. The fragrances — I mean, you can imagine, it's just pure paradise, Puerto Rico. I used to play with these teensy little frogs that were no bigger than your thumbnail called *coqui* because they made that sound. *Coqui! Coqui!*

It was a wonderful life. Then my mother decided that we needed to have a better life. She left me with my father, whom she had divorced, and she took a ship to New York City, and worked in sweatshops as a seamstress. She made enough money at some point to go back to Puerto Rico to get me and bring me back to the United States for this better life that she thought about.

DR: You went on a cruise liner, which is a very big ship.

RM: You know what, the funniest things happen. God's editing room sometimes does some interesting things. The moment we were out at sea we had a huge, really nasty storm. And everybody came from the hold where we were, which of course was not smart, because that's when you really get sick.

The trip took about three days longer than it should have because of this awful storm. We approach the United States, and there is this enormous green lady holding the biggest ice cream cone I have ever seen.

DR: You had a luxurious apartment waiting for you?

RM: Yes, of course. In a place called La Bron — the Bronx.

DR: With lots of your relatives?

RM: Yes, it was wonderful. It was a four-bedroom apartment, but each family had a room, and my mommy and I had one room also.

It was really very tough. It was very difficult. And it was cold. I had never seen a tree without leaves on it. I remember, in the bus on the way to La Bron, I said to my mommy, I said, "What happened to the trees? There's no leaves!" She said, "It's called winter."

That's when I learned that there was another different kind of weather. We didn't have that in Puerto Rico. We had the rainy season, and we had hot and we had balmy, but we didn't know about winter.

DR: Eventually your mother worked hard enough and you got your own apartment.

RM: We got our own apartment. We slept in one little small iron bed. And she sent me to kindergarten. I didn't know a word of English. This was before the Puerto Rican diaspora. So there were very few Hispanic kids in kindergarten. That's when I really began to understand that this was not going to be an easy life.

DR: There was discrimination. People called you names.

RM: Oh my God, I got called names. On the way to school, usually on the way back for lunch, on the way back from school in the afternoon. There were gangs, and I would do a zigzag route to our apartment building

504

because these little gangs would gang up and call me names like "Spic" and "garlic mouth" and "gold tooth."

I was very young. I didn't understand why that was happening. When you're very young like that, you are tender and you tend to believe what people tell you, and if they say you're not worthy and that you don't have value, you believe that. So I grew up feeling that way about myself. I never told my mom about those nasty occasions.

DR: Your mother decided that you might get some dance lessons and you became a child dancer?

RM: A friend of hers, Irene Lopez, was a Spanish dancer and she saw me bopping around the apartment one time and she said, "I think Rosita might have some talent. Can I take her to my dance teacher?" My mom said yes, and Irene took me to a man named Paco Cansino, who it turned out was Rita Hayworth's uncle. He was kind of royalty in dance circles. That's where I learned to dance professionally.

DR: You started getting some gigs. You were doing bar mitzvahs.

RM: I did bar mitzvahs! I did weddings, all kinds. Jewish, Catholic weddings. I was what, eight, nine, ten?

DR: When you get to the ripe old age of about thirteen, you're doing Broadway.

RM: Yes, my very first theater experience.

DR: And what was that like?

RM: It closed overnight. One show. It was a shock. I found out that all of that kind of magic can go away literally overnight. We rehearsed for about three and a half weeks. We opened, and the next day they said, "Don't come in."

DR: After that show lasted one performance, you began to go back and do more of your dance routines in various places, but then somebody got you an interview with Louis B. Mayer.

DR: What happened was an actual talent scout came to see a dance recital by our dance school, which is what they did in those days. They would go to all kinds of places and see if they could find new talent.

He saw me and he thought I might very well have a future. He said, "The time isn't right just now, but I'll stay in touch with you, and when the time is right I'll call you again." He was with MGM Studios — the studio of my dreams, because that was the studio that had all of the great, great musicals.

Sure enough, about six months later, he called my mom and he said, "Louis B. Mayer is coming to town and I would like Rosita to meet him." We did all that we could for me to look like Elizabeth Taylor. Little girls like me had no role models whatsoever, so I chose Elizabeth Taylor.

We went to the Waldorf Astoria Hotel to meet him. We never even heard of that hotel. He had the penthouse. We didn't know what that meant.

So my mother gets in the elevator and she doesn't know what to do. So she goes to the desk, she says, "We are supposed to see Louis B. Major, what do we do?" He said, "Penthouse, P-H."

Ah, okay. So we go up and it opens at his penthouse and there he is, all five feet four inches of him. You know, like the fellow in *The Wizard of Oz*, because that's the studio that made *The Wizard of Oz*.

It didn't take long. He looked at me and he literally turned me around, took my hands in his, and he said, he actually said, "Why, she looks like a Spanish Elizabeth Taylor! So how does a seven-year contract sound to you, young lady?" I flew, I just flew. It was the dream come true.

MGM — you have to understand what a studio that was then. It was it for musicals.

That was the studio. Fox made musicals, Warner's made musicals, but nobody else had Gene Kelly under contract, nobody had Ann Miller, nobody had Judy Garland. That was MGM.

DR: So you had a contract and you went out to Hollywood. You're what, seventeen or eighteen?

RM: I was seventeen. In fact they had to give me a guardian because I wasn't eighteen yet.

DR: You go out and you show up in the commissary and you see Clark Gable.

RM: Oh my God, I see all of them start sauntering in like real people. It was just astonishing. I'm looking at the steam table, all these exotic foods like roast beef. I was brought up on rice and beans. And who is there? Elizabeth Taylor! I thought I had died and gone to heaven. It was so thrilling.

DR: You made a couple of movies on your contract.

RM: I made a couple of movies there with Mario Lanza, who was the tenor of the time. He was actually quite wonderful.

DR: The eater and drinker of the time as well.

RM: Big drinker, big. He used to eat three pizzas for lunch. He really did have a beautiful tenor voice.

DR: So this is working out well. You have a contract for seven years. All of a sudden they don't renew your contract.

RM: I did three films there. I did *Pagan Love Song* with Esther "The Backstroke" Williams. I lied. They said, "Can you swim?" and I said, "Yes."

I had lied through my teeth about being able to swim. I suddenly thought, "I'm going to drown. I just better go in the hotel pool and start trying to do something." I didn't dare tell anyone, so I couldn't have anyone teach me.

Believe it or not, one night I dreamt that I could swim, and I went into the pool the next day and I could do the backstroke. So in this big swim number with Esther at the head and all of these beautiful Polynesian-looking people — I'm supposed to be a Polynesian girl — there's all of these people doing this graceful breaststroke and I'm doing the backstroke. But it's the only way I didn't drown. Probably nobody noticed because there were tons of people doing this

DR: Whatever reason they didn't renew the contract, it wasn't because of that, right?

RM: They didn't know what to do with me. In those days, what are you going to do with this Puerto Rican girl? The fact that I didn't even look exotic didn't seem to matter. I had this name. Which was changed, of course.

DR: You might describe that.

RM: Moreno was my stepfather's name, so it was Rosita Moreno, and they took me to Bill Grady, a casting director, who said, "You've got to change your name, kid. It's too Italian." They suggested some really hilarious names. The only one I really remember was — even I, as shy as I was, turned it down — Orchid Montenegro. It might have gotten me some jobs. Who knows?

I didn't tell my mother I'd lost my contract for a couple of months. I would just go in the closet or in the car and cry and cry. Because it was as though Mr. Mayer was Daddy and he said, "We don't want you anymore."

Finally I told my mom, and it was a very scary time. How many times in my life have I said, "I'll never work again"? How many times do actors say that to themselves? Over and over. It's as though you somehow never learn that particular lesson, because show business is so bizarre, it's so odd, it's so demanding, it's so mean.

I started to do television, doing westerns, and I started to do westerns outside of

MGM. And boy, if you've ever worn buckskins at five in the morning on location in Kanab, Utah, you could die from the cold.

DR: While you were shooting something, somebody took some photos of you and *Life* magazine had you on the cover.

RM: That was 1954, and it was at the time when Desilu, the Lucille Ball company, was beginning to branch out to do four-camera shows, comedy shows. They were doing a pilot with Ray Bolger, and they had me do a dance number with him. He wasn't really a dancer. He was a hoofer. There's a big difference. And he kept stepping on my feet and just killing me.

Life magazine was doing a layout on these new shows. The editors at *Life* said, "Who's that girl? Take some pictures of her." They were thinking of doing a layout on young Hollywood.

Life magazine never had actors or actresses on their covers. They had political figures, they had presidents, they had people like that, but rarely show-business people. They said, "You're going to make the cover in two weeks, unless President Eisenhower gets a cold."

DR: He didn't, and you got on the cover and everybody saw it. Darryl Zanuck of 20th

Century Fox said, "Can she speak English? Let's line her up."

RM: I got a contract with 20th Century Fox.

DR: Did they produce the movie *Singin' in the Rain*?

RM: That was MGM. That was the other picture that I made at MGM. That's one of my favorite movies ever, ever. It's a classic.

Gene Kelly put me in a nontraditional part. I had a red wig and I could actually use makeup of my color for a change instead of that brown stuff they always used to put on me. I thought, "Oh, my career is made. I don't have to speak with an accent anymore, blah, blah, blah." Didn't happen. Rita Moreno was a Hispanic name, and that's what they saw.

DR: You developed a relationship with a lot of people in Hollywood. You wrote about that in your book, and we'll talk about a few of them. One of them was Marlon Brando, who was the love of your life at that period of time.

RM: Well, he was the lust of my life. Big difference.

DR: He seemed to have an insatiable appetite. He had a lot of different women, and wasn't

512

monogamous exactly. That produced some depression.

RM: One time I found some lingerie that obviously was not mine. We had an eight-year relationship. I went home that day just weeping and distraught and devastated and wounded and angry and hurt, and didn't know what I was going to do because I thought, "I cannot live without him." It was one of those dreadful, tumultuous relationships.

The very next day I get a phone call. "This is Colonel Parker. I handle Elvis Presley. Elvis spotted you in the commissary at Fox the other day and he liked what he saw. He would like very much to meet you. Would you like to meet him?"

I thought of that rotten underwear, and I said, "Yes, I would." So I went out with Elvis, who was darling. The best part is that despite the fact that there was no social media then, it got out immediately. He took me to this very famous nightclub called the Moulin Rouge, and it was everywhere. It was in [the *Hollywood*] *Reporter,* it was in *Variety,* it was in the gossip columns. Rita Moreno, Elvis Presley.

And of course Marlon heard about it and he got furious. He threw chairs. Which was wonderful. That's the kind of relationship that one was.

DR: Because of your relationship with Marlon Brando, at one point you tried to commit suicide.

RM: It was one of those relationships where one person fed the other. It was just a nightmare. I really wanted to end it and didn't know how. I ended it five, six different times, and I'd go back, and I'd go back. The last time I went back, I felt so awful about myself — how could you treat anyone so badly, how could I treat myself so badly? — that I tried to end my life. I almost succeeded too. I took sleeping pills. His assistant came in, and she couldn't wake me up. That's when she called the police and an ambulance.

DR: You came to the famous March on Washington in 1963, the civil rights march. What was that like?

RM: Harry Belafonte felt it was important that there be a Hollywood contingent. He wanted Dr. King to know that there were people in Hollywood in films who thought a great deal of him. So Harry invited a number of us. Sammy Davis, Diahann Carroll, James Garner, myself — I don't remember who else, but there were some pretty fabulous people.

We sat no more than fifteen feet from Dr. King where he was speaking. I get such goose bumps just talking about it still. There was a moment when Mahalia Jackson said, because he was reading from a text, she said to him, "Tell them about the dream, Martin, tell them about the dream!" I mean, I could just cry. That's when he started to say, "I have a dream." I was there! I was there. Ah!

DR: So as you look back on your extraordinary career, what would you say is the legacy that you would like people to think about you?

RM: I would like people to think of me only in one way: *she never gave up.* Perseverance.

MARK BRADFORD
ON THE VISUAL ARTS

Visual Artist

"I have markers laid down along the way.
And I have a loose structure that I start off
with. But then you always have to let the
painting win. You have to let the material
win."

For centuries the art world looked to Europe
for inspiration, creativity, genius, and un-
matched masterpieces. But around the
middle of the twentieth century, America
developed its own distinctive visual art styles
— from abstract art to pop art to street and
graffiti art, among other uniquely American
art forms.

The great American artists — Jackson Pol-
lock, Georgia O'Keeffe, Andy Warhol, Keith
Haring, Jasper Johns, Helen Frankenthaler,
Frank Stella, Robert Rauschenberg, and Roy
Lichtenstein, among others — became the
leaders of the global visual arts world.

More recently, one of the most distinctive

of the current generation of visual artists is Mark Bradford. From a young age until adulthood, he worked at his mother's beauty parlor — and, without the money for paint, learned how to take materials used in the beauty parlor to create art that told a story quite different than what others had ever done.

Today, Mark Bradford is at the pinnacle of the U.S. art world, and has officially represented the U.S. abroad, a few years ago at the Venice Biennale. His expressionistic works of art use paper or materials other than paint to provide a unique texture, meaning, and depth. They often reflect the urban environment he knows from having lived much of his life in Los Angeles.

Mark Bradford's works also reflect a deep sense of history and its impact on current America. And they send a message that makes the viewer think about life in America — the challenges and the opportunities relating to class, race, gender. That message is frequently communicated through a grid that reflects city life or a set of figures designed to evoke important moments in history.

Unlike some abstract artists, Bradford is quite willing to explore the meaning of what he has put on canvas (or other material). Bradford has, not surprisingly, been the recipient of a MacArthur "genius grant."

I interviewed Bradford virtually in January

2021; he was in his Los Angeles studio, preparing to work on another history-related creation. One of his most famous works in that genre is his epic recounting of Pickett's Last Charge from the Battle of Gettysburg in a commission for the Hirshhorn Museum in Washington. The work consists of eight separate paintings, each of which is more than forty-five feet long, completely filling one of the museum's large circular floors. Although the Hirshhorn — part of the Smithsonian — is free to visitors, almost any price would be worth paying to see this monumental work, and to hear about its meaning from its gifted creator — an American original for sure.

DAVID M. RUBENSTEIN (DR): When you were growing up in Los Angeles, did you have any plans or dreams about what you might want to do when you became an adult?

MARK BRADFORD (MB): No, I did not. My dreams were basically kids' dreams, playing, doing whatever was in front of me.

DR: How did working in a beauty shop as a young man inspire you to be an artist?

MB: Because inside the beauty shop there was nothing but creativity. Women would come in and they wanted to look like Farrah

Fawcett, and you would try to do the best that you could to make them look like Farrah Fawcett. I was always aware that my mom was pulling things out of the air. It was magic. In that way, creativity was something that I used every day. My mother would say, "Mark, take these wigs in the back and do something." I would pull something from the air. That was creativity for me, and I never associated creativity with being an artist.

DR: Were there things from the beauty parlor that helped you to create your initial works of art?

MB: End papers [used to wrap hair ends during perms] are the first thing I started using when I got out of grad school.

DR: When did you realize that you wanted to be a full-time artist?

MB: In grad school. I really thought I could do it, finally.

DR: What did you learn at the California Institute of the Arts?

MB: I learned that there was a whole history of people thinking and doing for generations what I was thinking and doing. I discovered a whole tribe of people.

DR: When you finished your formal education, did you have a style in mind? How did you develop that style that you now have, which is so distinctive?

MB: I didn't have a style in mind, but I did know that I wanted to connect the social and art history in some form.

DR: Was it hard getting started as an artist? Did you have to do other jobs as well to pay the rent, or your success happened from the start?

MB: It was hard. I worked in the hair salon for the first six years of my career, but I just took whatever I could get. I would show where I could show. And yes, I struggled, I was on the bus. I worked in the hair salon and I was an artist in the evenings.

DR: How long does it typically take to produce a work of art? Do you work on one at a time or many at a time?

MB: I work on many at a time. I would say that to really produce a work of art I'm comfortable with takes me about sixteen months to two years.

DR: Where do you typically get your inspiration from for a work of art?

MB: I don't know where it comes from. A conversation I have with someone, a book that I'm reading, a social project, the news, history. It can be a little detail. I'm like Sherlock Holmes and I'll follow that detail until it opens up a larger area, and a larger area, and a larger area.

DR: When you start a work of art, do you know how it is ultimately going to look when it's completed? Or is there a fair amount of improvising?

MB: I have markers laid down along the way. And I have a loose structure that I start off with. But then you always have to let the painting win. You have to let the material win.

DR: Sometimes, in the old days, Leonardo and other artists would paint over things they had already painted. They didn't like what they originally painted, I guess. Do you ever do that, or that doesn't happen anymore?

MB: All the time. If you run an X-ray of my paintings, you will see paintings on top of paintings on top of paintings. You know how you can tell, in a painting of mine, is by the weight of it. If it's really, really heavy, you can tell there's about five or six paintings under there.

DR: Do you ask friends or others to look at your completed work to see what they think? Or do you not need that type of affirmation?

MB: I ask everybody from the mail lady to the curator and everybody in between.

DR: And if they say they don't like it, what do you do? You say, "You don't know much about art"?

MB: No, I ask them why.

DR: When did you first realize that your art was sufficiently attractive to art collectors, both individuals and museums, and you could make a comfortable living doing this?

MB: When I sold my first work, I didn't know if I could make a living, but I certainly knew that instead of working in the hair salon five days, I could drop it down to three.

DR: When did you realize you could not only make a comfortable living but also could become a nationally and globally recognized artist?

MB: Never.

DR: You're very well known.

MB: But I never had that idea. But the real marker that I can remember is when I represented the United States in Venice [the Venice Biennale exhibition in 2017]. I really knew that was a mark.

DR: What does it feel like to work on something for quite a while, maybe a year, eighteen months, then you sell it quickly and realize you might never see it again?

MB: The operative word is *quickly*. If I have some time between making it and selling it, I can slowly mourn the loss. But when it's sold really fast, I have a little bit of a melancholy.

DR: Did you have a mentor when you were building your career? Are you mentoring others at this stage in your career?

MB: I had several mentors and people, some gallerists, some curators, some artists, some friends, and I try to do the same. I have a foundation and I work with young people. If young artists reach out to me, I take the time to share what I've learned along the way.

DR: How would you describe your style of art? What is attractive to you about using a grid in your works of art? Do you use Google Maps? Is city culture a major influence?

MB: Grids are what I call my safety net. A grid underpins everything. That's important to me.

DR: What types of materials do you try to use on your works? What influences your decision about the materials?

MB: I like paper because it's very unforgiving and it goes from the high to the low. The Gutenberg Bible is on paper, and then the pad that you're writing on now is on paper. I love this material that's both historical and also social.

DR: I read that you used to go to someplace like Lowe's to buy the paint you use. Is that true?

MB: Home Depot, Lowe's. I still do.

DR: When you walk in there, do they say, "Hey, here's a famous artist coming in," or they don't know who you are?

MB: They think I'm just a painter. A tall painter. Because I wear painting clothes.

DR: When you get identified with a certain style, is it tempting to try something else after a while, or is it enjoyable and stimulating to continue to refine your existing style?

MB: It's continually enjoyable to just refine my style. I look at other artists and I love what they do. But I'm still fascinated by what I do.

DR: How does it feel when you have an exhibition and an art critic might not like some of your works? Is it hard to not take that personally?

MB: You always take it personally. You get your feelings hurt, for a few minutes, and then you put your bootstraps back on and you go back and do what you do.

DR: When people criticize what I do, I take it personally only for about fifty years. After about fifty years I forget.

MB: It's good to let it go.

DR: How difficult is it to prepare for an exhibition of new works of art? Does it take a lot of time to do that?

MB: It's always difficult. It's always anxiety-ridden, but I've done it enough that I know how to work with the nerves.

DR: How did it feel to win a MacArthur "genius grant"? Did that change your life in any way?

MB: I wouldn't say it changed my life, but I definitely feel like it gave me a certain amount of economic security.

DR: Did you tell all your friends you won the MacArthur grant or you didn't have to tell them, they just read about it?

MB: I didn't tell anybody. If they found out, that's fine.

DR: How has it felt to represent the United States abroad, such as at the Venice Biennale?

MB: For me it was a wonderful experience. It's a heavy experience, a heavy burden, but I enjoyed it. I enjoyed it tremendously.

DR: When you were beginning your career, did you feel discrimination because of your race? Do you think you still face racial discrimination?

MB: When you enter into anything, there are always going to be certain biases. Being an abstract painter and not seeing as many African American abstract painters in the field, I thought we should expand it and go back and reclaim some of that history. That's kind of what I was focusing on.

DR: Do you think there are unique opportunities for artists just getting started in the United States today that might not have existed at other times and places? In other words, is it easier to get started today or is it harder to get started today?

MB: Because of the advent of the Internet there are probably more opportunities. Artists have more ability to get their work out and have people have a conversation about their work. So in some ways it has made it easier, and there are more opportunities today. But in some places, the nonprofits have closed down, which means fewer places to show the work because of the pulling of public funds for arts.

DR: What advice do you give young artists about how to jumpstart their careers?

MB: My advice to young artists is to understand that they're a 1099 employee and not a W-2. You have to be responsible for setting up your studio and retirement and everything. It's on you.

DR: Are there artists you have particularly admired or been influenced by?

MB: Jack Whitten, absolutely. I would probably say Charles Gaines. Those are the closest to really influencing me.

DR: What is the pleasure of being a visual artist? Do you ever wish you had chosen a different career? Or is this one extremely satisfying?

MB: It kind of chose me. I never thought of myself as being an artist. It really chose me. So, I don't know, the suit fit.

DR: So you're happy?

MB: Yes, I'm happy.

DR: Can you explain how difficult it was to produce *Pickett's Charge,* which is now on display at the Hirshhorn?

MB: I knew I wanted to make it. I knew I wanted something that felt like paint, but I use paper, so I had to immerse all of this material in water to make it fluid. Then it was just a matter of working with the space, that kind of optics, that cyclorama, that circular space, and then digging into that history. The architecture of the Hirshhorn led me to the making of the work. I don't think that I would have made *Pickett's Charge* if it had not been in this cylinder.

DR: By the way, if there hadn't been a Pickett's Charge and Robert E. Lee had won, the Civil War would have been reversed, probably. That's another matter. Do you own *Pickett's Charge*?

MB: I do.

DR: Is it on long-term display there?

MB: Yes, it is.

DR: If somebody comes to you and says, "I'll pay you $20 million for it," do you say, "Maybe I won't lend it forever"? At some point you might want to sell it?

MB: When I made it, it was just an interesting epic work, but now it has such a resonance. I'd really have to think about where I wanted to see that work live long-term.

DR: How long did it take to paint it?

MB: I worked over two years — maybe three, actually.

DR: But you're working on other projects at the same time?

MB: I set up temporary walls to work on *Pickett's Charge,* and I would jump to other works and then always come back to *Pickett's*

Charge. I love big, epic paintings that you can fall into. I like long, big novels. I like James Michener, those big novels.

DR: Are you working on other epic pieces like that now?

MB: Not at the moment.

DR: What do you ultimately hope, many years down the road, will be your artistic legacy?

MB: A snapshot of the time I lived in.

BILLIE JEAN KING
ON TENNIS AND ACTIVISM

Sports Icon; Champion of Equality

"Our job is to leave our guts on the court, not only for ourselves, but for them. The audience is everything."

In nearly all countries, national sports champions tend to become larger-than-life heroes. And the United States is no different in that respect. But in the U.S., we often expect our national stars not only to become international champions in their sport but also to help solve major social challenges (as Jackie Robinson did in breaking the color barrier in major league baseball).

Over the past half century, one such national/international/social-barrier-breaking sports champion, and role model, was a tennis player who captured the country's and the world's attention in ways unlike most other athletes, male or female: the great tennis star and champion of equality Billie Jean King.

As an athlete, she became one of the world's finest tennis players, the winner of 39 Grand Slam titles (12 singles titles, 16 doubles titles, and 11 mixed-doubles titles), including a record 20 Wimbledon championships and 3 World TeamTennis titles.

In doing this, she also broke the existing mold for champion tennis players. She came from a blue-collar background, without the resources typically available to championship-level players for training, travel, and equipment.

As an athlete who wanted to change her sport, King was, certainly in the tennis world, in a league of her own. She pushed to create the first women's tennis tour — the Virginia Slims Circuit — and later she co-founded World TeamTennis, where men and women play together on teams representing various cities.

But her most meaningful achievement in changing the tennis world may well have been her successful fight for equal prize money for women and men at the Grand Slams. No doubt, though, her most visible effort to advance women's tennis was when she beat, in three straight sets, Bobby Riggs, a former men's number-one-ranked player and Wimbledon champion, in a highly promoted "Battle of the Sexes," winning the then enormous sum of $100,000.

As an athlete who helped change the world,

Billie Jean King disclosed, at great personal and professional risk, that she was a lesbian at a time when that was almost never publicly acknowledged by women in sports. And with her disclosure, she fought hard to allay the discrimination then common against gay and lesbian athletes.

While retired from active playing, she is not retired from her pursuit of gender equality and LGBTQ rights, having become a tireless advocate for those issues. Her mark on the sport might be seen in many ways; one quite visible way occurred in 2006 when the United States Tennis Association renamed the site of the U.S. Open as the USTA Billie Jean King National Tennis Center.

This interview took place on September 25, 2018, as part of the Great Americans series at the Smithsonian.

DAVID M. RUBENSTEIN (DR): You grew up in Long Beach [California], a very nice community. It's part of L.A. in some ways. When you were growing up, most people who played tennis were from upper-income families. They were country-club members. Your family was not. Your father was a blue-collar worker?

BILLIE JEAN KING (BJK): Right. He was a firefighter.

DR: How did you actually afford the lessons to play tennis, and where did you get the chance to play?

BJK: The reason I was able to play was because it was free and it was accessible. The Parks and Rec Department of Long Beach provided free instruction every week. The second time I picked up a racket, at the end of that I knew I wanted to be number one in the world. My poor mother picked me up. I said, "Mom, I want to be number one in the world!" She's going, "That's nice, but you have homework."

DR: When did you realize you were better than the people you were playing with and that you might actually be good enough to be the best in California, the country, the world?

BJK: When I was thirteen, I saw Althea Gibson play at the Los Angeles Tennis Club. That was kind of the hub for Southern California tennis in those days.

If you can see it, you can be it. And I remember seeing Althea. Now I knew what number one looked like, how good you have to be. I thought, "Wow, I've got a lot of work to do!" I just couldn't wait to go work.

The one thing my dad always taught us was that every generation gets better. I'm looking at how well she plays, and yet I'm younger.

"I'm going to have to get better than that to be number one? How am I going to do that?"

It was so inspiring, though. And she's our Jackie Robinson of tennis. Althea was the first African American to ever win a major. African Americans weren't allowed to play in any sanctioned tennis tournament until 1950, which is three years after Jackie Robinson had played for the Brooklyn Dodgers.

Then we know about Arthur Ashe, the wonderful Arthur Ashe, who came later, and who won the first Open in which professionals could compete. That was the first time we got paid money to win a tournament that wasn't under the table. I fought against amateurism. I fought like crazy, got in big trouble for that. But 1968 we finally received a check. At Wimbledon, Rod Laver won men's singles and won £2,000. Then I won £750 as a woman, and I'm like, "Oh God, not another thing to worry about."

DR: You were winning tournaments in California, then you're winning national tournaments. When did you win your first Grand Slam?

BJK: Doubles in 1961. I prefer doubles over singles. I like mixed doubles, then women's doubles, and then women's singles. All three experiences bring something different to the table and it's exciting.

I like collaboration. I grew up in all team sports. Basketball was my first love. I played baseball, but if you're a girl, they make you go and play softball, which isn't right either. That's a whole other discussion. I've talked to the Dodgers about that. All these things drive you crazy. Just reverse it. Men, reverse it. You got £750 and I got £2,000. Do you think that's right? It's not right. It just isn't right.

DR: Today many of the leading tennis players do not play doubles or mixed doubles. You played mixed doubles, doubles, and singles, all in the same tournament.

BJK: Yes. I'd be so bored the way they do it.

DR: Why do you think players today who are great players don't want to play doubles or mixed doubles?

BJK: It's much more demanding physically than it used to be. But it's about money, really. Everyone only cares about players in tennis that are great in singles. In the old days, what I call the A players, we played everything.

DR: As you look at your career, who were the best women tennis players you played against, or that you have ever observed?

BJK: It's all the number ones of each generation. It'd be Chris Evert and Martina Navratilova, who had probably the greatest tennis rivalry of all time. If they had been two men, we would be hearing about it constantly. They had such a contrast of styles. Chris is a baseliner, this one's a serve-and-volleyer, and they're just clashing. The contrast of styles was really what made it so interesting.

DR: And what about men players? Who were the greatest singles players?

BJK: Rod Laver's one of them. Roger Federer, I think, is the all-time great. Rafael Nadal's right there, just side by side. Jimmy Connors was one guy I loved to go watch. He was so intense. He was crazy. But I love the way he's competitive. He just shared everything with the people and got them excited. John McEnroe, great hands, great competitor. Probably didn't take as good care of himself as he could have. He probably could have won a lot more. He stopped winning around twenty-six.

Björn Borg quit at twenty-six. He was a tremendous player. Pete Sampras, unbelievable — best serve ever. Greatest second serve. You're only as good as your second serve. Andre Agassi, the best returner. But Nadal and Federer — I just think each generation gets better. Same with Steffi Graf, Monica

Seles, Martina Hingis, all these great women players.

DR: Let me ask you a few tennis questions as an amateur. I'm not really a great tennis player. Nobody would suspect that I am. So when I watch tennis, I wonder, why do the players bounce the ball? And is there a thing about how many times you're supposed to bounce it before you serve?

BJK: That is totally up to the person. It's an inner rhythm. You have to have your rituals. It's a sense of inner rhythm inside your soul.

I used to bounce it twice. The younger players had to bounce it forever. The women tennis players would sit in the locker room when Jimmy Connors played, and we used to count how many times he bounced the ball. It would be seventeen, eighteen. Now we have a service clock. Aha! Only twenty-five seconds. And the players are having trouble.

It's like everyone has this inner rhythm. It's very ritualistic. And they've proven that when you do have your rituals, it helps. If I was really nervous and recognized it, the most important thing was to take ownership and say, "I am nervous." A lot of players go, "I'm fine. I'm fine." I'd bounce it again twice, and try to really slow down. You really have to understand and be self-aware of what you're doing.

DR: Do you think the game is better when you have the kind of TV camera that can show you whether a ball is out or not out?

BJK: I love it. It reduces anxiety from the players, but it also helps the lines people. In World TeamTennis this year, we had no lines people, we only had an umpire and the triangulation of twelve different cameras. You'd hear an "out" by a female or a male voice. And it worked out unbelievably. The players would start to argue. They'd show it up on the screen, and they call it right every time, so bad luck. The thing I didn't like is we're costing jobs for the lines people. But I prefer this way as far as keeping it absolutely clear in who really won and who didn't.

DR: With or without the cameras, do you think fighting with the umpires makes a difference? Does it help you, hurt you?

BJK: Some people think it depends on your personality. That's self-awareness again. Someone like John McEnroe, it got him all hyped up and he played better.

DR: Is there coaching from the sidelines a lot? What can they really tell you? Work harder? Hit the ball harder?

BJK: No, no. Here's what they do. You can

say, "This could be a lob," or "Go to their forehand," or "Go to net," or whatever.

DR: When you're playing baseball, you can have somebody throwing a ball at one hundred miles an hour and it could hit somebody in the head. People are yelling and screaming. When you're a tennis player, if anybody says anything when you're tossing the ball up, people get upset. Why does there have to be so much silence?

BJK: I think tennis has got it all wrong. They think the fans are there to watch them. I tell the players, "No, we're there to entertain them. Without the fans, we are nothing." We are entertainers. Our job is to leave our guts on the court, not only for ourselves, but for them. The audience is everything.

DR: Talk about money. When you first started playing, as you pointed out, players weren't paid very much.

BJK: Fourteen dollars [for tournaments]. Expense money.

DR: If I have my numbers right, you won 129 career titles.

BJK: I don't know. I don't care about that.

DR: Thirty-nine Grand Slam titles. But the grand total of money that you won, according to the statistics, is about $1.9 million.

BJK: That's correct.

DR: Today you would probably win almost that much for winning one tournament.

BJK: I would win that for sure, because the winner of the Open got $3.8 million [in 2018]. I know there's inflation, but still, it's a lot better.

DR: Did you think this was because women weren't getting paid as much or just that inflation has made prizes much bigger than they were when you were playing?

BJK: No, but we got equal prize money in 1973. Billy Talbert at the U.S. Tennis Association was a great player in the late '40s. I went and talked to him at USTA in 1972, one-on-one, quietly, calmly. That's what you always try — behind the scenes first. When you go to the media, it is a last resort.

Before I went to the meeting, Ceci Martinez [a fellow player] had done a survey she passed to the fans at the U.S. Open in 1972. I said, "I want information. Do they think we should be here? Should we get equal prize money?"

My former husband [attorney and promoter Larry King] and I already owned tournaments by then, so I'm a businesswoman. I understand the sponsor side. I understand the challenges, the risk. I went to Philip Morris, to Bristol Myers, and some others. I said, "If any of you would put up the money to make up the difference between what we're getting now and if we got equal prize money with the men, would you be willing to do that?"

I don't want to just go and ask without bringing something to the table. I had two things. The survey came out much more positive than we thought. That was good. But then I said, "And Billy's a great business guy himself. He married a woman that's very wealthy, and her dad had been great in business." I said [to him], "We have Bristol Myers, willing to make up the difference in the prize money."

Billy got real quiet. He was in shock, because what are you going to say when someone's willing to bring a sponsor to the table for you? And he's the one that announced it. I thought the board of directors of the USTA had passed it. I have been looking into it lately because I was working on a book. So now I'm finding out they never voted on it. He just announced it.

This is why when people are in leadership positions, they can change things overnight.

He changed it from 60 or 50 percent [of the men's prize money], or whatever we were getting, overnight. Everyone's an influencer, and people have to speak up, but people don't like to give up power. They just need to do this.

DR: You've played professional tennis for quite a number of years. Why did you actually decide to retire? Was it your knees or was it just harder to compete?

BJK: I was anxious to go into business and, yes, I wasn't winning. Bill Bradley, who played [basketball] for the [New York] Knicks, was great about this. He talks about full circle in sports. They always tell you, "Get out on top."

I did that. It was a mistake. I could have had one more big year, and I didn't do it because I bought into that. I won Wimbledon in '75. I go, "Okay. I'll retire now."

Should have never done that. I was beating Martina and Chris in practice. Chris says, "Why aren't you still playing?" I said, "Good question." So it was a big mistake. I could have won one more year.

DR: Did your parents live to see your great success in tennis?

BJK: Yes, but they only went to Wimbledon

once. They did go to the King-Riggs match. I begged them both times.

DR: And did they say, "We always knew you were going to be a champion"?

BJK: No. My parents were really good. My parents were unbelievable, my dad particularly, because he was the jock. My mother's a jock, but you never knew it because she's a woman and women of her generation didn't talk about themselves. She told me when she was eighty, "I just wanted to tell you, I beat the boys running." I go, "Why didn't you tell me when you were younger?" She says, "Oh, I like your dad to have all the focus. Let everybody talk about your dad."

He was a really good basketball player. He was asked to join the NBA when it first started in '48. I'm named after him because he was in World War II, and in 1943 I was born. My mom didn't know if he was going to come home.

He was brilliant. He never let me read a press clipping after fifteen years of age because I got upset. The *Long Beach Press-Telegram* put me on the front page for the first time when I lost a match love and love. I went, "I've won tournaments. I finally make the front page —"

He goes, "Stop. What's that match about?" I said, "What do you mean?" He said, "When did it happen?" I said, "Yesterday." He says, "Exactly. It was about yesterday. Forget it. It's what you do with your life today and tomorrow that matters. I don't want you ever, ever to read your clippings. You're not allowed to do any of that anymore."

I stopped that day. He was correct.

Another thing — they never asked Randy [her brother] and me if we won, ever. You know how parents are — your kid walks in, and, "Well, did you win?" Oh my God, it's the worst. Don't go there. They'll tell you how they did.

DR: You've won in your career more than 80 percent of your professional matches, which is pretty good. But the one that gets the most attention is not one of the thirty-nine Grand Slams.

BJK: It's about a guy, baby.

DR: You had a match in 1973 against somebody named Bobby Riggs. Ninety million people watched it. Probably the most-watched tennis match in history, certainly at that time, maybe ever.

BJK: I think it still is probably.

DR: Margaret Court had played him earlier and lost. Why did you agree to play him? Were you ever worried you could lose? And what kind of person was he?

BJK: He kept asking me to play for two years and I turned him down. Then he got Margaret to play. And when I saw her, I went, "Margaret, you have to win."

Now, you have to remember, she's Australian, and she's — well, we're different. I said, "You have to win. This has much more meaning than a tennis match."

I don't think she prepared herself for the circus that was going to happen and the way he is. I knew all about Bobby. He was one of my heroes. I thought he got a bad deal in not getting the attention he deserved, because right in the sweet spot of his career was the Second World War.

I felt bad for him, but I respected him because I love my history. I knew every champion. I'd watched everything. I'd read everything I could on him, but when Margaret lost, I had to play him. I didn't *want* to play him. I *had* to play him.

DR: So you did play him. And was a lot of what he was doing trying to get you riled up?

BJK: Oh, yes. That's good, though. I love him for that.

DR: Did you practice against men when you

were practicing for this, or you practiced against women? How did you practice?

BJK: I just practiced. I had Pete Collins, who was a tennis director at Hilton Head [South Carolina]. I went to Hilton Head for two weeks because we still had the Virginia Slims tour. In fact, during the week that I played Bobby, I had to play in the Virginia Slims of Houston. It's two matches on Monday. We played the match on Thursday.

DR: Did you ever have any doubt you were going to win?

BJK: I didn't know. Two months out or six weeks out, whenever we announced it, I'm very anxious, not happy. Start visualizing, start thinking about it. I think about anything that could go wrong, how I would stay calm and focused.

I have to visualize everything. I just love visualization. I would think about getting a bad line call. I went out to the Astrodome the day before the match. I went up in the stands and looked at it. I looked at how the court was structured. I knew there would be no wall behind the court, so the depth perception was going to be shocking, but I knew whatever it was for me it was going to be for him as well.

We'd never played against each other. So I

knew I'd never hit a ball against him, but neither had he hit a ball against me. So I'm like, "You know what? Okay."

One thing you don't want to do is get lost in an arena, because that can get you crazy. So I wanted to make sure I was very clear on all that. I went and met every security guard. I like to meet everybody, like the administration, people, everybody that runs the arena.

DR: At what point in the match did you realize you were better than him and you were going to win?

BJK: I never think like that when I'm in a match. It's one ball at a time. Anything can happen.

DR: When you won, you got an enormous amount of attention.

BJK: When he jumped over the net, he said, "I underestimated you," and we put our arms around each other.

DR: Did he want a rematch?

BJK: Oh yes, but I told him before the match, I said, "I'm only going to play this once because this is about history. It's about equality." I'm explaining these things to him. "We're going to make lots of money. It's not about the money." And he finally understood that.

DR: That's a good segue into equality and the other part of your life. Many professional athletes are great at their sport, but they say, "I don't want to get involved in social issues."

BJK: They want to sell things.

DR: How did you decide you wanted to make more than an athletic career out of your life?

BJK: When I was twelve.

DR: So you always knew this.

BJK: No, when I had my epiphany about white people only. Where is everybody else? I promised myself that day at the Los Angeles Tennis Club — then I saw Althea a year later — I promised myself if I was number one, if I was ever good enough — and I knew tennis was played all over the world — I thought, "This is an amazing opportunity."

I wouldn't have used the word *platform* then, but that's what I was really thinking as a child. I was thinking, "I can do something greater than just winning tennis matches if I'm fortunate enough, but I've got to become number one," particularly as a woman. As a girl I knew I probably had no chance for people to listen to me because people usually talk about boys.

DR: The U.S. Tennis Association named their stadium after you. You must be very proud of that.

BJK: I think it's amazing. Arthur Ashe and I are really fortunate. It's his stadium — that was 1997. We had the parade of champions out on that court.

DR: In your career as a pioneer for inclusion, equality, and social justice, what would you say you're most proud of having achieved to date, and what is your next objective or goal?

BJK: I don't really think like that at all. I think about, "I'm not done yet." I always think about the people that got me there. Talk about it takes a village. Just think about what that took to get me just to be standing there, winning at Wimbledon. I was really lucky.

DR: The Equal Rights Amendment has never been ratified.

BJK: I think we're one state short, aren't we?

DR: Is that something you're focused on or not?

BJK: I'd like to see the word *woman* in the Constitution someplace. That would be nice.

DR: You have been a fighter for AIDS issues and the prevention of AIDS, and that's been a major push.

BJK: Yes. Ilana [Kloss] and I are founding members of the Elton John AIDS Foundation. I founded the Women's Sports Foundation in '74. We've invested $80 million. We are the one women's sport that does research. There's no research on us, and we are the first ones to start doing that. We're also the guardian angels of Title IX for the sports part.

DR: With your partner, you've started the Leadership Initiative.

BJK: Yes, we did, Ilana and I and probably eight others.

DR: And what is that designed to do?

BJK: That is to help with equality in the workplace — not just by money. It means by culture, by color, by race. It means by just everyone being able to be their authentic self to go to work.

Deloitte did this research with us about being your authentic self when you go to work. So if you grow up poor and you're ashamed

551

of it and you can't talk about it, like this one guy had all these university diplomas up and he's talking about this and that. He never would talk about his beginnings. You've got to be your authentic self.

DR: What do you do to stay in shape now? You don't play tennis as much.

BJK: The doctors are great about this. They always say, "Whatever you can do, just do it. Don't worry about it's the newest thing, greatest thing."

I like to do the bike because I've had eight knee operations. I try to do at least two to three minutes of sprints in intervals, because you want to get that difference of heartbeat. Lifting weights, or weight resistance, is hugely important as you get older, especially for women with osteoporosis. I think yoga is great, but I can't stand to get on my knees.

I think whatever works for you. For me, it's the bike and weights, and I like to stretch after.

DR: So today, when you look back on your life, what are you most proud of? Your tennis career, your career as a social pioneer?

BJK: They go hand in hand, but probably the off-the-court stuff is more important to me. It's always been more important to me. From that time I was twelve, I was pretty clear on that as a kid.

You listen to young people, and they've done research on this too, that anywhere from, like, nine to twelve, kids really do know what they want to do. They have these dreams, and they think anything is possible at that age, and it's true.

One thing my dad and my parents and other people have taught me is never take anything personally. That's one of the greatest things you can teach somebody.

I'm very big on forgiveness, because that allows you to move on. If you take things personally, it just hinders your life.

DR: That perspective is one you should bring to Washington.

BJK: Would you explain to me why we cannot care about the people anymore and why we have these two sports teams trying to win? Are the American people winning? That's all I want to know. What is wrong with us?

DR: Have you thought of ever running for office?

BJK: I thought about it in the '70s. Because of my sexuality challenges, I did not, because you have to tell the truth if you're going to run in politics, and if you don't tell the truth, you're toast.

DR: I bet today that wouldn't be a challenge.

BJK: I didn't know that then. I wouldn't want to be that kind of candidate. I want to be honest with my constituents and the people of America, because having democracy, it's a huge responsibility. I know I probably could have won, but I was going through such turmoil with my sexuality in the '70s, and that's when I should have run if I was going to run.

DR: Well, if you ever change your mind, I know you have a lot of supporters.

CAL RIPKEN JR.
ON BASEBALL

Baseball Hall of Famer

"The real key is to push yourself through. The only time you're a hundred percent for a season is the first day of spring training."

For at least a hundred years, since its emergence in the late 1800s, baseball was widely considered America's pastime — its most popular spectator sport, the subject of endless discussions about team rivalries and player abilities, the game supposedly invented in Cooperstown, New York — later the site of baseball's legendary Hall of Fame — but perfected and loved in all parts of the country.

In recent years, professional football and professional basketball, among other activities, have made their own claims to being the country's favorite spectator sport. But there is no doubt that the country's long history is more intertwined with baseball, or that the stars of the sport have been the idols of youth and much of the country's population for generations. Babe Ruth, Lou Gehrig, Joe DiMaggio, Ted Williams, Hank Aaron, Mickey Mantle, Willie Mays, Sandy Koufax — all names known well beyond those who paid attention to the daily box scores and other essential data of a sport seemingly created for statistics.

Over the past few decades, with baseball attendance and TV audiences declining, and with some of the leading players caught up in performance-enhancing drug scandals, baseball has produced fewer national heroes and idols for the country's youth, as well as for the sports-rabid, ESPN-dependent adult population. Perhaps the most admired, untarnished baseball hero to emerge in recent decades — a person who was known as much for his unrivaled skills as for his humble, team-first approach to the sport — was Cal Ripken Jr., the unquestioned star of the 1980s and 1990s Baltimore Orioles.

Like the very few others who made it to the Hall of Fame with near-unanimous support, Cal Ripken had the credentials of a natural — a player with achievements that seem hard to fathom: more than 3,000 hits, 400 home runs, 1,600 runs batted in, two-time American League Most Valuable Player and nineteen-time All-Star, and a shortstop on the Major League Baseball All-Century Team.

But Cal Ripken had one other credential —

one that has separated him from everyone else. In 1939, Lou Gehrig, the New York Yankees' "Iron Horse," finished his streak of 2,130 consecutive games played over a fourteen-year period. (Gehrig's ability to continue playing at that pace was undermined by the onset of ALS, the disease from which he died two years later at age thirty-seven.) That record, which stood for fifty-six years, was considered by many the least likely baseball record to ever be broken.

But Cal Ripken broke it. He played 2,632 consecutive games over a seventeen-year period, spanning a record 8,243 consecutive innings played, to great national acclaim and adulation.

If any baseball record is likely to endure for the ages, surely it is this one. And if any baseball personality is to be remembered for his steady, low-key, and team-oriented play, it is Cal Ripken.

I interviewed him in 2018 as part of the Great Americans series at the Smithsonian's National Museum of American History. Although I am from Baltimore and had, like so many others, long admired his baseball talents, durability, and self-effacing manner, I had not actually met him before the interview. I quickly realized what a terrible mistake that had been on my part. How could one not have figured out a way much earlier to spend time with one of Baltimore's and baseball's finest? My failure. But Cal Ripken did not hold it against me — to my relief.

DAVID M. RUBENSTEIN (DR): Let me start by asking you about "the Streak," as it's called. Does a day go by in your life now when you're not asked about it?

CAL RIPKEN JR. (CR): No. The special part about the Streak was that everybody has their own idea of what their own streak is in their lives. During that particular year, people would share their streaks with me: "Haven't missed a day of work." "My kid hasn't missed a day of school for twelve years." The important thing was showing up. I found that to be a wonderful sharing moment that went through that year.

DR: If you had not had the Streak, you still would have been one of the greatest baseball players ever by all measurements. When did you realize that you were doing something that was unusual? You didn't start out saying, "I'm going to break the Lou Gehrig record."

CR: I look back and say it was the manager's fault that I started the Streak. Because my first manager was Earl Weaver, and you couldn't imagine me going up and telling Earl Weaver, "I'm going to play every single game." I just kept playing and they put me in the lineup. Everything started off with a bang. I played pretty well.

DR: At the end of five years, six years, ten years, did somebody say, "You know, you're playing a lot of games in a row here"?

CR: I think around eight hundred to a thousand games, and I'm not sure why that was the case. My first year I won Rookie of the Year, and we finished one game out of the playoffs. Second year we won the World Series. I was the MVP of the league that season, and I played every inning of that year. And that just continued on. Once I got close to a thousand games, people started to take notice.

DR: Over sixteen years, major-league baseball plays 162 games a year. Sometimes you have a World Series or playoffs. You're playing all those games, no injuries. I can't go more than two or three days without something going wrong. How did you avoid injuries?

CR: I had a good body where I was resilient. You get hit by pitches, you slide wrong. I have a real funny finger that got caught on first base one time and dislocated. So you have all these small injuries that somehow you figure out how you can play through.

The real key is to push yourself through.

The only time you're a hundred percent for a season is the first day of spring training. After that, you're playing something less, and some players can feel like they can compete and play with a little bit more than others. To me, if you find yourself and you push yourself through and then you do well, then you've answered your question.

DR: So you get to 2,130 games, Lou Gehrig's record. That was thought, in baseball lore, to be one of the unbreakable records, 56 straight games by Joe DiMaggio [the longest hitting streak] maybe being the other. So you get to this point and all you have to do is play one more game, four and a half innings so the game is complete.

You get to the four and a half innings, it's over. What was the emotion going through your head? You have the president of the United States there, the vice president of the United States there. It's been voted perhaps the most memorable moment in baseball history.

CR: They made some plans to celebrate, but nobody could have choreographed how it played out. I never felt any pressure by playing in the games because it wasn't my goal to break Lou Gehrig's record. It was just to continue to play and keep your approach as pure as it was on the first day you walked on the field as the last.

But when I got to game number 2,130 and that game was over and I was going home — I got home at two thirty, three in the morning — I felt a sense of relief that it was a foregone conclusion that tomorrow's game would happen.

DR: So 2,131 games, you break the record. Everybody's happy. Most emotional moment in your life in terms of the baseball part. Why not just say, "Okay, I'm done. I broke the record. I can sit out"? Why did you continue?

CR: I thought it would be disingenuous or dishonest to stop playing, because I never played for that reason — to obtain that record and say, "Okay, now I've accomplished this. Let me just stop."

It was almost as ridiculous to me as when somebody would suggest, "Why don't you stop at 2,130 games and take the next game off and share that record with Lou, because Lou was such a great icon and a great person?" I'm thinking, "He would be mad at me if I did that," because the idea is to play.

All good things I guess have to come to an end, but I remember thinking early in that season [1998, three years after he tied Gehrig's record] that if we fall out of the pennant race, if there's no purpose to play toward the end of the year, I'll end this thing called the

Streak, and we'll start over brand-new. I first thought that I was going to do it the last day of the season, almost just to say I could have played 162 if I wanted, but the last day of the season was in Boston and that was on the road.

Some of the closest advisors to me said, "You should do it at home because everybody really celebrates it. They've been with you the whole time." The last home game was against the Yankees. I went in and told the manager ten minutes before the game started that this was the game that I wasn't going to play in.

And to see the look on his face — it was kind of shocked. He didn't know what to do. I said, "Look, this is how I want it to play out. I don't want to make an announcement saying, 'Cal's not playing tonight,' and then have everyone react. I just want them to react to it as if I'm not there." It was an opportunity to celebrate it as opposed to mourn.

DR: When the Yankees recognized you weren't playing, what did they do?

CR: They looked over and they saw me not taking the field, and they looked in the dugout. I remember Derek Jeter was puzzled. He was looking both ways, thinking, "What are you doing?"

Then they got it. They all stood on the top step of the dugout and started giving me an ovation, which spread around the whole ballpark in Camden Yards. People realized what was happening and it became what I was hoping it would become — a celebration of the accomplishment as opposed to mourning the end.

DR: Let's talk about how you got to be a professional baseball player. I played Little League baseball — as a shortstop, I should point out — but my career peaked at about eleven or twelve. When you were growing up, did you realize that you had athletic skills that were better than the average player like me? When did you realize you were really pretty good?

CR: I knew I was pretty good. I hung around the ballpark and I had a glove in my hand the whole time and I'd play catch and I always played with older kids. I realized I was pretty good. But when you play with older kids, you're measuring yourself a little differently, and so you don't stand out as much.

I was pitching in high school and I started to get a little bit of my size and I started to have really good success. My dad came to me, being a lifer in baseball and evaluating talent and being in the developmental system, and he said, "I usually can tell when a player has a chance at sixteen years old. You're going to get a chance to play pro ball. You got a chance to make it."

DR: In one high school game, you struck out seventeen players.

CR: Seventeen out of twenty-one.

DR: Did you think about being a pitcher?

CR: Yes. I was drafted mostly as a pitcher. All the teams that came to watch me play, except the Orioles, put me down as a pitcher and they were going to draft me pretty high as a pitcher. The Orioles drafted me in the second round. They had four second-round picks that year, so they had a better chance in the early rounds.

When I signed, I think most of the people in the Orioles organization wanted me to pitch. Earl Weaver had a chance to see me hit in Memorial Stadium a couple of times, and he and my dad, who played a very diplomatic role in the decision, couldn't decide where they wanted to place me.

Dad said, "When we've had a player like this, we've had great success starting him out as a regular player. If it doesn't work out, then we can always move him back to a pitcher." Then they all looked at each other and they looked at me and they go, "Cal, what do you want to do?" I said, "Pitchers only get to play one out of every five days. I want to play every day."

DR: Your father didn't think of Babe Ruth. Babe Ruth started out as a pitcher and then he turned out to be a pretty good hitter.

CR: Now, they're starting to consider you can do both in the big leagues, which is pretty exciting.

DR: So you were drafted by the Orioles. You played in minor-league baseball. Now when you play minor-league baseball, you don't stay at Ritz-Carltons and Four Seasons and charter planes, right?

CR: No, we don't. I still don't do that [chartered air travel], by the way.

DR: When do you realize that, yes, you can make it in the majors?

CR: It's the success that you have, or you don't have. I remember coming in at seventeen years old. You were a pretty big fish in your small pond, but now all of a sudden you're a very small fish in a big pond and everybody was a star.

I was intimidated right from the get-go. They had a shortstop by the name of Bobby Bonner who was on that rookie card, star of the future. He came out of Texas A&M. He was twenty-three, I think, and he was great. I was taking ground balls behind him and I got all upset. I'm like, "I'm never going to play. This guy is way better than me."

They sent him from rookie ball up to AA and then to AAA in the same year. And in two years I caught up to him and passed him, which is pretty interesting.

DR: He gave up baseball and became a Christian missionary, right?

CR: He did. Nice going.

DR: He got so depressed seeing how good you were.

CR: I'm trying to think if Earl yelled at him one or two times, and that made him quit too.

DR: You come up to the major leagues, and originally you were a third baseman. How did you become a shortstop? Shortstops were thought to be people who should be five foot nine, five foot ten. You were six foot four. How did they decide to switch you to shortstop?

CR: They had nicknames like Pee Wee and Scooter, those guys, but Earl Weaver had always seen me take ground balls as a fourteen-, fifteen-year-old hanging out at the ballpark. When I developed as a third baseman, probably that's when my career started to take off. My skill set at the time was more suited to third base. My hitting really took off when I went and played third.

Then Earl wasn't satisfied with who he was having for shortstop, and one day he just decided he was going to play me at shortstop. He called me into the office. He said, "Okay, when you go to shortstop, if the ball's hit to you, I want you to catch it. Then I want you to get a good grip on the ball, take your time, and make a good throw to first base. If he's safe, he's only on first."

I said, "That's how I'm supposed to play shortstop?" I think what he was trying to tell me is, "Don't try to reinvent it, just go and play, be yourself."

I came back and I played pretty well. That move was supposed to be a temporary move to bolster the offense and get the team going. But that temporary move lasted fifteen straight years.

Let me speak to the size issue. I graduated high school about six two and about 180. I was roughly putting on about 10 pounds a year, and I grew almost three inches. So when I came to the big leagues, I was just a little under 220. The stereotype was a bigger person couldn't play shortstop, but Earl had the ability to foresee that I had a chance. And he took a chance on putting me at shortstop.

DR: I know what it's like to gain ten pounds a year, but not grow an inch or two. You became the Rookie of the Year. The next year, you were the Most Valuable Player. That, I think, was the first time a Rookie of the Year became the Most Valuable Player the next year.

So tell us about what it's like to be a major-league baseball player. Is there camaraderie among the players on your team? Are you allowed to talk to people on the opposite side?

CR: Fraternization, I think that's called. In the old school, you were supposed to hate the other team, but I found great value in befriending the other team.

I'll use the example of Rick Henderson, one of the best base stealers in the history of the game. When he's running to second base, he's not paying attention when the pitch goes to home to see if the ball is fouled off, or taken, or if the ball is hit on the ground. He'll come into second base with the idea "I'm going to slide no matter what."

So early on, I'm covering second base and I see it. I say, "Hey, Rickey, you don't have to slide." He looks at me like, "Are you trying to trick me or something?" And he stands up and he looks at the umpire and the umpire says, "Yeah, it's a foul ball." So Rickey looks at me and he goes, "Rickey thanks you, you saved Rickey's body."

I found out really early on, and I think I was just being a good sport about playing, that there's no sense in making him slide. If you can help him out at certain times, it doesn't cost you anything, then you can ask him questions. By doing small things in there that would help them out in the game, I got information back that could help me.

DR: In the locker rooms, what's it like in there? You just sit around for a couple of hours, talking about what the game is going to be like?

CR: Things have changed a lot since I left the game. Now players eat four meals a day in the clubhouse. I think it's better that you have a balance of your time away from the ball-park, so you can recharge your batteries. When you come to the ballpark, you're being pulled in many different directions.

DR: You're flying around the country, you're playing, what, eighty-one games outside of your hometown. Fans are coming, they're looking for autographs. How do you get the rest you need?

CR: It's pretty exciting, and it's a lifestyle you get used to. You spend more time with that group of guys than you do with your family during the course of the year. So you make good friendships.

I used to always like the back of the plane and the back of the bus because people would sit around as we were traveling, and they would talk about their childhood. It was a very diverse group of people. You had rich, poor, country, city, any race back there, and you could share different stories. I enjoyed that part of it.

DR: Some players get on your nerves, don't they?

CR: Oh yes. There's a lot of internal fighting, too, that goes on.

DR: When you're playing baseball, the scariest thing, I think, is if you're a batter, somebody throws a ball at you and could hit you in the head. A famous baseball player was once killed that way. Did you ever worry that a baseball would hit you in the head?

CR: Yes, particularly if somebody was intentionally trying to hit me in the head. That's a reality of the sport. There are people that try to intimidate you and intentionally throw the ball up around your head. And the league does it, pretty much when you first come in, to see if you can be intimidated. If you respond in another way, where you start getting hits and it doesn't bother you, they end up leaving you alone.

Do you know how many times I was hit in the head?

DR: Three?

CR: No.

DR: More?

CR: Seven. Seven times hit in the head. And every time I got hit in the head, I was looking for a curve ball, and I was looking for the wrong pitch at the wrong time.

In the big leagues, if you have a weakness, they're going to exploit your weakness. And either you make the adjustment and are able to hit those pitches, or you're not going to stay around too long.

DR: You're up at bat, you're getting ready to hit the ball, and you're talking to the umpire, talking to the catcher. You're saying, "Hey, let's have dinner afterwards"?

CR: The old-school catchers used to try to chatter to get inside your head and make you not concentrate as a hitter. Sometimes you want to tell the catcher, "You better shut up, or I'm going to hit you in the mask with this bat."

DR: When the umpire calls a strike and you think it's not a strike, do you ever have any chance of convincing them otherwise? Do you say, "You're wrong"?

CR: Oh, I was pretty sarcastic. I got thrown out of three games.

The first time I got thrown out of the game, the guy missed the first pitch strike on me. I swung at a pitch over my head and he called me out on the pitch, and I go, "Okay, you're off to a good start. You missed two out of the three, the only one you didn't miss, I swung out over my head." And I started to walk away, and he started following me. I could hear him saying something to me, so I stopped, and I turned around and looked, and he runs into me.

And because there was contact made, all of a sudden he blanked out a little bit and threw me out of the game. I said, "Why'd you throw me out of the game?" And he didn't have an answer for me. So that was kind of an accident.

The next time I got thrown out of the game was in the first inning. The first two hitters got called out on strikes. And I thought, "If this umpire's got a big strike zone, I got to be the one to let him know he does."

I take the first pitch, it's barely on the outside corner and he calls it a strike. I go, "Okay, that's not too bad. If that's what it is, I can't say anything."

The next pitch was like a foot outside, and he calls it a strike. I said, "Hey, the first pitch was pretty good, but the second pitch was way outside." He comes out from behind home plate and starts saying things like, "You guys are always crying." And I said, "I get it. You're the only one that counts." That didn't make him too happy.

He got so close to me that I told him to get out of my face. Then he told me to get out of his face. I said, "You brought your body out from behind home plate up here, and you're telling me to get out of your face? You're not very smart."

DR: That was the end of it.

CR: That was the end of that. I got thrown out in the first inning, and so I'm waiting inside the clubhouse. I decided that I was still too mad, I didn't really want to talk to the media.

The umpires never get interviewed. They never accept any interviews, but he decided he wanted to talk to the media that time. There was a big headline in the paper the next day that says, "It was the worst night of my life throwing Cal Ripken out. I got yelled

573

at. It was like throwing God out of Sunday school."

DR: Presumably he's not going to heaven.

Who was the greatest player you ever played against? During the time you were playing, was there some player you really admired?

CR: The guy I thought was the most talented I played against was Ken Griffey Jr. There was nothing on the baseball field that he couldn't do. He was fast, he could throw, he could hit, he could hit in the clutch. He could make the big play in any part of the game.

DR: Who was the toughest pitcher? Did you ever have any pitchers you thought were throwing spitballs?

CR: Oh yes. I read Gaylord Perry's book when I was a kid — it's called *Me and the Spitter* — where he acknowledged that he was throwing spitballs, and how he did it, and how he practiced it, and how he put Vaseline on different parts of his body.

Then I get to the big leagues and I'm facing him. I asked everybody, "Does he still throw grease balls or spitballs?" Everybody says, "Yeah, he still does it."

But the first two times I faced him, I think I got a hit off him the first time. I went, "Well, that's not that great of a pitch." Then I came up with bases loaded, and he threw three pitches that just dropped out. I struck out and I looked at him in disbelief, and he kind of looked over at me and went like this [*puts hand behind his ear*].

DR: For a while, the [Orioles] manager was your father. Is it awkward to have the manager be your father? What do you call him?

CR: I called him "Forty-Seven," his number at the time. I got to the big leagues about a month before my twenty-first birthday. I was still used to calling him Dad. I felt like I had to call him something else.

DR: You played before the steroid era. Were there steroids being used by players then?

CR: I didn't see any of that. There were some players that all of a sudden they'd be thirty-five pounds heavier and you'd be a little suspicious, but it's not like they wanted you to know they were doing it. It was more of a secret society.

DR: You retired at the age of forty-one. You were voted into the Hall of Fame five years later. Do you think that people who are thought to have used steroids should be allowed to get into the Hall of Fame?

CR: Obviously, the steroids work, and the numbers go up. The hard part, if you're voting for the Hall of Fame, is "What am I voting for?" Is it the player that did it himself, or was he enhanced to do it?

The worst thing you can do is put a blanket over it and say, "Okay, that was the steroid era. We don't know who did what, so we're just going to judge them for their numbers." I think that's unfair to those of us who didn't.

DR: Baseball used to be called the American pastime. But attendance is down and TV viewership is down. The average viewer now is about fifty-three years old, which seems to me young —

CR: That's young to me too.

DR: Right. Do you think that baseball has passed its prime, in that pro basketball, college basketball, pro football are now in the ascendancy?

CR: I don't know. I think it's as popular. I'm in the kids business, and we're trying to get kids to play more baseball, and play longer. Maybe they're not all going to be big-league players, but they're going to become baseball fans.

Baseball does face an older demographic. I think kids, and people in general, have more things to do. More things compete for their time.

If you understand baseball, it's a really cerebral game. The more you understand, the more you don't mind the pace of the game. Sometimes you're focusing too much on the pace. Maybe we need to do a better job of explaining what's happening.

DR: You retired, it's hard to believe, twenty years ago. When you retire from baseball, you can, as some famous baseball players do, just do nothing but sign autographs the rest of your life. You decided to do something more than that. Can you explain what you decided to do after you retired?

CR: I was worried that when you retire at forty-one, you're really young for retirement. I remember sitting in the back of the bus early in my career and people like Jim Palmer, Ken Singleton, and Al Bumbry, they were contemplating retirement at that time. They were thirty-five, thirty-six. I kept thinking, "What are you going to do now?" They didn't really have an answer.

Ken Singleton, in his last couple of years, started to become a broadcaster. He worked at Channel 13 in the off-season because he knew he wanted to do something beyond that. I kept thinking, "While you're in baseball, and you're meeting everybody and you're making contacts, why don't you start to prepare for life after baseball?"

I started to think of what I might want to do. Toward the end of my career, I thought that I wanted to use my influence to help kids. Dad was a teacher. I wanted to help kids learn the game. There was an opportunity to expand his baseball school, build some complexes and do it that way.

I didn't want to sit around doing nothing. You could play golf, you could take golf lessons, you could stay around in your pajamas, but that doesn't do anything for you.

DR: Trust me, golf lessons don't work.

You have created a foundation, the Ripken Foundation. What does that do?

CR: When my dad died, he died of lung cancer. You would think that maybe our cause would be to go help find a cure for cancer, or help people not smoke. We started to think about what Dad's legacy was. My brother Billy and I, we got to witness how he used baseball to get in front of kids that didn't have all the same advantages. He did free clinics in all the areas that he managed in the minor leagues.

I would go along with him sometimes to those free clinics. I never really got it. I kept thinking, "You have a choice where you could spend time with me, or our family, or you're going to go do this," but it was important for him to try to use his position to help other kids that didn't have all the same support structures at home that we did. He lost his dad to a car accident, I think when he was ten, and he had to become the man of the family.

He always had a fatherly sort of feeling toward his team, and also out there. Billy and I started to think, "We'll use baseball the way he did — to capture kids, to be an icebreaker of sorts, and start to talk to them."

We're trying to give them an opportunity and a direction in life. In the very beginning, Dad would say, "You're getting too big for your britches," if we started to do something too fast. We were very content helping one kid at a time.

We started getting some more influence, and now we're a national organization. Last year, I think we affected a million and a half kids.

DR: Are any of them Jewish? There're not that many Jewish major leaguers. Can you get more Jewish major leaguers? Sandy Koufax was the last famous one.

CR: Sandy is probably the most well-respected guy in the Hall of Fame. When he speaks, everybody listens. He handles himself marvelously and with a lot of respect. Whatever he's done, he's done it really right.

DR: I would say the same about you. Everybody listens to you, and I want to congratulate you on what you've done, being a great baseball player, a great role model for youth, and giving back to society as you are now.

CR: Thank you.

■ ■ ■ ■

6
BECOMING AND
BELONGING

■ ■ ■ ■

"It was we, the people; not we, the white male citizens; nor yet we, the male citizens; but we, the whole people, who formed the Union. And we formed it, not to give the blessings of liberty, but to secure them; not to the half of ourselves and the half of our posterity, but to the whole people–women as well as men."
— Susan B. Anthony, "Women's Rights to the Suffrage," 1873

LILLIAN FADERMAN
ON THE STRUGGLE FOR
GAY RIGHTS

Historian; author of *The Gay Revolution: The Story of the Struggle* and other books

"How we went from being pariahs, to being invited to the White House, to being able to serve openly in the military — that's what I asked myself when I was writing the book. What had to happen before we could achieve the successes that we finally achieved?"

For much of American history, there has been tension between those who felt the American Experiment was "their" experiment and those who felt excluded from it. Those who most visibly felt excluded were slaves, and later their freed descendants. But among those who felt shut out for most of American history but whose exclusion was in some ways less visible and less public — until about fifty years ago — were Americans who were not heterosexual.

While the efforts to expand basic rights to

all Americans in the United States started at least a century ago, if not two centuries ago, the effort to ensure that gay people have equal protections and rights is a comparatively recent phenomenon. (*Gay* is used in this context as the historical umbrella term, as Lillian Faderman has done in her book, to refer to the LGBTQ community.)

The effort to seek these rights did not surface publicly until the late 1960s. Prior to that time, because of prejudice and laws against homosexuality, gay people were generally more focused on not being publicly identified. Those so identified were often arrested or fired from their jobs, or both. Often they accepted that fate, recognizing that American society seemed completely against any effort to legalize gay activity.

That changed in a very public way in late June of 1969 in New York City when the police, in an otherwise routine raid of a gay bar — the Stonewall Inn — met physical resistance from bar patrons to the effort to place them under arrest. For several of the following nights, at Stonewall and in the surrounding neighborhood, there were demonstrations against the arrests and physical resistance to further arrests.

The gay revolution in America might be said to have been born from these events. Gay people organized to seek not only protection from arrests, but also rights that they had long been denied. The effort took many forms — legal challenges, legislative efforts, marches and protests, and public education.

Progress was slower than might have been expected. Not until 2003 did the Supreme Court invalidate state sodomy laws, which had often prohibited any form of gay sexual activity; not until 2015 did the Supreme Court legalize same-sex marriage, long seen by many in the gay community as a basic human right denied to them; and not until 2020 did the Supreme Court state that the protections of the 1964 Civil Rights Act applied to gay people. These Supreme Court decisions did not resolve all legal issues affecting the gay community, but the progress seen in this century likely could not have been anticipated in the latter years of the previous century.

The effort to describe the fight for gay rights over the past seventy-plus years was tackled quite well by Lillian Faderman in her epic book *The Gay Revolution: The Story of the Struggle.* As a participant in many of the episodes that were part of this revolution, she has firsthand knowledge of many of the critical events described in the book. I had the opportunity to interview her about her book as part of a virtual New-York Historical Society program on September 25, 2020.

DAVID M. RUBENSTEIN (DR): What prompted you to write this book? This is a fairly definitive history of the gay revolution. We'll talk about that phrase, *gay revolution,* in a moment. You didn't feel there was enough literature on this already?

LILLIAN FADERMAN (LF): All of my books come out of a personal desire to know something. I came out in the 1950s, into the gay-girls, working-class bar culture. Things were absolutely awful. We were victimized by the police, we were crazies to the mental health profession, we were subversives to the government.

I wanted to know how we got from 1956, when I came out as a teenager, to what was happening in the Obama administration, when one of my great heroes, Frank Kameny — who had been fired from his government job in the late 1950s because he was a homosexual — had been invited to the White House no less than eight times. How did that happen?

Just about the time I was ready to write the book, when I was putting together a proposal, "Don't Ask, Don't Tell" was finally repealed. It was such an incredible evolution. How we went from being pariahs, to being invited to the White House, to being able to serve openly in the military — that's what I asked myself when I was writing the book. What had to happen before we could achieve the successes we finally achieved?

DR: You call your book *The Gay Revolution.* Why do you use the word *gay,* not *gay and lesbian?*

LF: My original title was *Our America Too: A Gay and Lesbian History.* I realized I wanted to add *bisexual,* and then I wanted to add *transgender.* But by the time I finished the book, the alphabetism was LGBTQQIAAPP. There wasn't enough room on the cover for all of that to describe our entire community.

When I came out, *gay* was the umbrella term for all of us in the 1950s. The straight world really didn't know that *gay* meant homosexual. It had been an underground term, at least since the beginning of the twentieth century.

DR: Your book mostly is from the 1940s and '50s forward. In the beginning of our country, I assume there were gay and lesbian people, but there was no mention of it. What was going on the 1700s and 1800s?

LF: They wouldn't have called themselves gay or lesbian. *Homosexual* was a term that was coined in the nineteenth century. In the course of my research for other books, I discovered a very interesting case of a woman in 1642, who was sentenced to be "severely whipped and fined" for being caught on a bed with another woman.

Of course there were women who had relationships with other women. There was evidence of men who were whipped and, in one case, even hanged for having committed sodomy, but it was thought that anyone could commit an "immoral act" of that nature.

It wasn't an identity. There was no such thing as "the homosexual" — no such thing as a person who declared, "This is my identity." There were certainly sodomites, there were women who committed "unnatural acts," but identity began to develop in the nineteenth century.

DR: In ancient Greece and Rome, it was fairly common to have homosexual relationships, and it wasn't looked upon with great horror. Why do you think, as civilization advanced for several thousand years, that changed? Was it religion?

LF: It was the Judeo-Christian religion. Same-sex relationships, or sodomy as we came to call it, became a sin. Western culture inherited that notion. It was considered sinful, men who had sex with men and women who had sex with women. The sexologists who emerged in the later nineteenth century also pathologized homosexuality. So it became a sin on the one hand and a pathology on the other hand.

DR: Let's go to the 1940s and 1950s. In the United States, you didn't need to be caught doing something that was a homosexual act. If you were just thought to have engaged in this practice, you could be arrested. Isn't that right?

LF: You could be arrested if you were caught in a gay bar. Gay men were very often entrapped by vice-squad officers. In the 1950s, if you were thought to be homosexual, if you worked for the government, even if you worked in a private business, if you were thought to be homosexual, you could be fired. And many homosexuals were.

There was a real witch hunt of homosexuals, beginning in the State Department, and it filtered down to homosexuals in all government, a witch hunt that fired numerous gay men and lesbians. Businesses emerged such as Fidelifacts that offered private companies a thorough investigation of employees or potential employees to see if they were homosexuals. If you were a known homosexual in the 1950s, it was very hard to be employed.

DR: The gay community organized a bit in the 1950s. Gays had the Mattachine Society, and lesbians organized the Daughters of Bilitis. Those organizations weren't saying, "Let's go lobby for our rights, let's go to the Supreme Court." They were saying, "Let's just talk about our challenges and how we can help each other." Is that more or less right?

LF: The founders of the Daughters of Bilitis, Del Martin and Phyllis Lyon, wanted to be a little more political than the women who joined were interested in being. And so it became primarily an organization, and a fairly small one, that offered an alternative to the very dangerous lesbian bars.

Mattachine wanted to get rid of the sodomy laws. They were a little more political, but they started small. A huge victory for them was a case in Los Angeles with a man by the name of Dale Jennings, who was entrapped by an undercover officer. The Mattachine Society decided that they would fight that. They sponsored Dale Jennings going to court. He said, "Yes, I'm a homosexual, but just because I'm a homosexual does not mean I'm guilty of what I was charged with."

And they won the case. It was that kind of very small victory, usually local victories, in the 1950s.

DR: In the 1950s and 1960s, there was an organization in Congress called the House Un-American Activities Committee. They interested themselves in homosexual activities. Were they trying to get people to admit that they were homosexual and get them out of government?

LF: Beginning in the late 1940s, a man by the name of John Peurifoy, who was the undersecretary of state, decided that would be a good thing to do. It would give him a major role to play in government. He announced that he had identified ninety-one homosexuals who were working in the State Department and fired them.

This was the beginning of a witch hunt of homosexuals at all levels of government, not only the State Department. Homosexuals simply could not work in government. The original idea was that it was so terrible to be a homosexual, if the Soviets found out about it, they could easily blackmail the person into giving away state secrets. But people were fired who had jobs that had nothing to do with the nation's security, and it ballooned from there. Hundreds of people were fired from federal employment and then state employment and private businesses as well.

It wasn't simply that there was a concern that homosexuals were a threat to the nation's security because they could be blackmailed. It was also a moral prejudice against homosexuals that spread like a virus.

DR: Were any members of Congress standing on the floor of the House or Senate saying, "These individuals have certain rights under our Constitution and we shouldn't be doing these things to them"?

LF: No, because it was absolutely not believed that we had rights under the Constitution. It took a long, hard fight to convince politicians that homosexuals, or LGBTQ people as we would say today, had any rights under the Constitution.

The first battle that was won was won by a magazine called *ONE* that came out of the Mattachine Society. It was a homophile magazine. In 1954, it was declared obscene. There was absolutely nothing obscene about it, but the Post Office announced that it would not mail copies of the magazine.

ONE decided, with the help of the ACLU, that they would fight for their rights. They fought first in California courts, went all the way to the Supreme Court. And in 1958, the Supreme Court actually declared that *ONE* had a right to publish. This was the first real legal victory for the lesbian and gay community.

DR: The psychiatric community, what did they say about homosexuality?

LF: In 1952, the first edition of the *Diagnostic and Statistical Manual of Mental Disorders* was published. It was sort of the bible for the psychiatric community. And homosexuality was there as a mental disorder. Frank Kameny, one of the great heroes of the gay rights movement, realized that homosexuals would never get their rights as long as they were considered mentally disordered.

Finally, in 1973, because of his activism and the activism of other gay and lesbian people such as Barbara Gittings and Jack Nichols, the American Psychiatric Association decided that they would declassify homosexuality per se from the *Diagnostic and Statistical Manual of Mental Disorders.*

There was some wonderful research that they had simply ignored. For instance, in the 1950s, a psychologist by the name of Evelyn Hooker did an absolutely crucial study in which she asked thirty gay men and thirty heterosexual men to do a battery of diagnostic tests that psychiatrists used to decide if someone was mentally disordered. These were blind tests.

She then gave the results to specialists, psychiatrists, specialists in the field. She asked them to distinguish between the homosexuals and the heterosexuals in those diagnostic tests, and they could not make that distinction.

This was in the 1950s that Evelyn Hooker did her work. It was totally ignored by the American Psychiatric Association until Frank Kameny and other activists insisted that they look at such research. That was influential in convincing the APA that we were not mentally disordered.

DR: Some people would say that the most important date in the gay revolution was in July of 1969, when the New York Police Department raided a gay bar in Greenwich Village called the Stonewall Inn. What happened that night?

LF: The first response was actually June 28, 1969. The police did what they had done for decades. They decided they would raid the Stonewall Inn. They came in, lights went up, they asked for everyone's ID. To some people they said, "Okay, you can go." Those people went out.

Usually, if the police raided a gay bar and dismissed someone after looking at his ID or her ID, that person would be so delighted that they would just run off. But this time they waited outside, they waited for their friends, and a crowd began to congregate. It was Greenwich Village, after all. The crowd got bigger and bigger.

Finally the police took out a very butch lesbian and put her in the police car. The other door of the police car was open. She got out the other door, they threw her back in, she got out the other door, they threw her in again, and she escaped once more.

She said to the crowd, "Why don't you guys

do something?" And somebody threw a rock. That was the beginning of the riots that lasted four nights.

It happened at the end of the 1960s, in June 1969, after a whole decade of protests by people for their rights, protests against the wrongs that the government had done. This was the decade of the protests against the Vietnam War, for instance. It was the decade of Black Power and protests for Black civil rights. It was the decade when feminists were doing zaps on the American beauty pageant, for instance.

Whether it was conscious on the part of the rioters or if it was subconscious, gay people realized that they had to send a message that they weren't putting up with this abuse anymore. And I think that's why these Stonewall riots happened on that particular night.

DR: After the civil rights protests and the Vietnam War protests of the 1960s, it was recognized by the gay community that if you did some protesting, marches on Washington, you might actually get more attention. Is it fair to say that, subsequent to Stonewall, the gay community began to say, "Let's do more things publicly and actively"?

LF: The first protests were in 1965, when Frank Kameny organized pickets of the White House and the Pentagon and the State Department. At the first protest in April of 1965 at the White House, there were ten picketers, but they were so brave. They were carrying signs saying, "We're homosexuals and we demand our civil rights." They also picketed Independence Hall in Philadelphia on July 4. They did that every year until 1969.

DR: In the late 1970s, I worked in the White House for President Carter, and an aide to President Carter, Midge Costanza, invited a number of gays to come to the White House for a meeting. Why did that cause such a big controversy?

LF: She had the job of being his window to the world, as Midge Costanza liked to call it. She would very often meet with various groups, such as veterans groups or women's groups. She thought it was perfectly plausible to invite those fourteen lesbian and gay leaders to the White House. President Carter conveniently was at Camp David. He was not present.

Nothing much came out of that meeting except that it was a huge morale boost to the gay community. But President Carter suffered a lot of flak from that meeting. He was very uncomfortable when he discovered what had happened.

DR: President Carter lost his effort for reelection and he was succeeded by Ronald Reagan. Reagan, as president, saw that a number of men who were gay were dying of a disease that later became known as AIDS. What was the impact of AIDS in the gay community initially? And why was Ronald Reagan unwilling to utter the word "AIDS," at least for a number of years?

LF: The impact was huge. Ultimately, over three hundred thousand people died before protease inhibitors were distributed to stop the deaths from AIDS. The religious right was delighted that this was happening. Pat Buchanan, for instance, wrote numerous editorials about "this is God's judgment on the homosexual community; before they were spreading their moral disease, and now they're spreading their physical disease to innocent people." He and others on the far right wanted people to be quarantined or homosexuals to be tattooed.

The religious right victimized the gay community, and the government did absolutely nothing. Larry Speakes was Ronald Reagan's press secretary. He made a joke of AIDS. He was asked about it by a reporter, and he said, "I don't have it. Do you? Homosexuals get it."

Reagan never mentioned AIDS for years into his presidency. Even when his good friend Rock Hudson, the movie star, died of

AIDS, he would not acknowledge that's what killed his buddy.

Reagan finally mentioned AIDS in 1987. Because we had no leadership from the White House, people in Congress were permitted to go ahead with their prejudices. People like Jesse Helms said that the only funding should go to abstinence education rather than research to figure out how to get rid of this disease.

Because there was no leadership in the White House in the 1980s, it was a huge tragedy. Reagan was in good part responsible for the fact that AIDS was not stemmed until the 1990s.

DR: Subsequently, President Bill Clinton, at the beginning of his administration, was under some pressure to allow gays to serve in the military, but the military resisted that. What was the compromise that was developed?

LF: Clinton was very much beloved by the lesbian and gay community when he was running for office, and he actually made some promises. One was that if he were elected president, he would make sure that gays and lesbians could serve openly in the military. I think it was a sincere promise. It was one of the first things he tried to do when he took office.

600

He learned very quickly that there was a lot of blowback from the military. "Don't Ask, Don't Tell" was supposed to be a compromise. If you were gay or lesbian, you could serve in the military as long as you didn't talk about it.

There wouldn't be witch hunts as there were in the military before. People wouldn't be dismissed when it was discovered that they were homosexual, but the job would be to keep it a secret. But it didn't work, because eventually people were outed. They suffered almost as much as they had before.

DR: There was also an effort by Congress in those days to pass a bill called the Defense of Marriage Act, which basically said that states couldn't allow homosexuals or lesbians to marry. President Clinton, under a lot of pressure, signed that legislation. What was the impact of that legislation on the country at that time?

LF: What had happened is that in Hawaii, three same-sex couples in 1991 made an issue of it. They wanted to get married, and finally went to the Hawaiian courts in '93. By 1996, it looked as though the State Supreme Court of Hawaii was going to approve same-sex marriage.

Immediately various other states reacted by passing their own state Defense of Marriage

Acts. There was pressure on Clinton in 1996 to sign a federal Defense of Marriage Act. He was up for reelection and he threw us under the bus, as sympathetic as I know he was to the gay community. He appointed many lesbians and gays to various offices in his administration, but he also wanted to get reelected.

DR: Eventually the gay community began to litigate that issue, among others, and a number of important issues went to the United States Supreme Court. And the court, in opinions authored by Justice Anthony Kennedy, basically said it was illegal to deny gays certain rights.

How did that impact the gay community? Were people surprised that somebody appointed by Ronald Reagan would write such important decisions for the future of the gay and lesbian community?

LF: It began in the 1990s with *Romer v. Evans,* involving a Colorado law that came to the Supreme Court that said that gay people could not petition their government for equal rights and cities and counties in Colorado couldn't pass "special laws" [banning discrimination against] homosexuals.

Homosexuals challenged that, and it went all the way to the Supreme Court. Kennedy wrote the majority opinion, saying that you could not make one class of citizens a stranger to the law. He said that [the state's] Amendment 2 was unconstitutional, that Colorado could not say cities and counties could not give gay people equal rights.

Then, in 2003, Justice Kennedy wrote another very surprising majority opinion, in *Lawrence v. Texas.* That repealed all of the sodomy laws. There were only about thirteen states that still had sodomy laws by that time. But because of the Supreme Court, so-called sodomy was no longer illegal. It was one's constitutional right to privacy.

Sodomy, I should say, did not refer to just one specific act. In some states it referred to any act that was outside of the marriage act. Lesbians too were often penalized and punished under the sodomy law.

Then Justice Kennedy wrote the opinion on the Edith Windsor case. At that time there were several states that already permitted same-sex marriage, including New York, but the federal government would not recognize same-sex marriage.

So when her partner died, Edith Windsor was supposed to pay the federal government an inheritance tax that amounted to over one-third of a million dollars. If she had been heterosexual and married, she wouldn't have had to pay that tax. So that went to the Supreme Court. And again, Justice Kennedy wrote the wonderful majority opinion saying that the Defense of Marriage Act in that case was illegal. And Edith Windsor did not have to pay one-third of a million dollars.

Finally he wrote the majority opinion in *Obergefell v. Hodges,* which said that it was unconstitutional to deny same-sex couples the right to marry. That was in 2015.

DR: The gay and lesbian community has obviously received a lot of support from the Supreme Court in recent cases, as you've mentioned. How has the Congress done? Has it been willing to make changes in existing laws like the 1964 Civil Rights Act to accommodate gay issues?

LF: The Congress has not yet been as sympathetic. In 1974 and again in 1975, Bella Abzug and Ed Koch [both representatives from New York City] tried to get Congress to pass an equality act, which would have added lesbians and gays to the 1964 and 1968 Civil Rights Acts. That didn't get much traction at all. It had never gotten traction, but it's again up for discussion in Congress.

But what happened more recently, last June, with the Supreme Court, which was just such a welcome surprise is that the court declared that LGBTQ people really fit under the 1964 Civil Rights Act. The act banned discrimination on the basis of sex, and the court said that should apply to LGBTQ people.

There were three cases before the Supreme Court, two cases of gay men and one of a transgender woman. Astonishingly and wonderfully, John Roberts and Neil Gorsuch sided with the liberal justices, and Gorsuch wrote the majority opinion there. So the Supreme Court in some ways has been truly wonderful.

DR: In recent years, there have been some fights in certain state legislatures about allowing transgender individuals to use certain bathrooms. What has that fight been about, and where does it now stand?

LF: There was a false allegation that straight, cisgendered men would dress as women just to get into the women's bathroom. I don't think there's a single case in which that has happened.

It has caused a huge uproar, particularly from the religious right. In Houston, Texas, for instance, there was a liberal mayor who was usually popular, Annise Parker. The transgender bathroom issue became huge when she was up for reelection. It was presented in such a way by the religious right that it scared voters that there would be all of these straight guys dressing as women, invading women's bathrooms in order to rape women. Parker lost her office, which was a tragedy. That kind of thing has happened in various cities and counties around the country.

DR: Were you surprised that the business community and the sporting community sided with those who cared about civil rights and civil liberties on those issues?

LF: I was so pleased by it. There was one instance where I was particularly delighted, and that was in the state of Indiana. There was a so-called Religious Freedoms Bill that was going to be signed by, at that time, Governor Mike Pence, and the business community stepped up, beginning with Marc Benioff of Salesforce.com and Angie Hicks of Angie's List and a number of other major businesses. They said, "This is discriminatory, and if you sign it, we are not doing business in Indiana." And Governor Pence backed down. It became a bill that was not so patently discriminatory against the LGBTQ community. Then he became vice president.

DR: As you look back on the last seventy years or so, who would you say are the one or two most important people in terms of winning rights for gays and lesbians?

LF: My great hero is Frank Kameny because

he saw it all. He understood what needed to be done. He understood that we had to come out. He understood that the American Psychiatric Association had to stop calling us mentally ill. He began those early battles that finally we won. He had such vision. He's, for me, the grandfather of gay rights.

Another person who was very important in the movement, someone I wrote a biography about, in fact, is Harvey Milk. Now, Harvey Milk had huge charisma. He was a wonderful speaker, had terrific ideas. He wasn't in office very long, but he played a role that was tragic and yet very important for the movement. He became our martyr. He became our instance of "This is what homophobes do to gay people, and this is a huge injustice." I think that the straight world understood our grief because he was martyred.

DR: For those who may not know, Harvey Milk was elected to be a supervisor in San Francisco — I think the first openly gay person to be elected to a major position in the United States.

LF: There were two women who were elected to public office in 1974, two lesbians, but he was the first openly gay man in public office.

DR: He was assassinated while in his offices. Ultimately the killer went to jail.

LF: He was given a wrist slap of something like eight years, and he got three years off for good behavior. He was a fellow supervisor who had made it clear all along that he hated the gay community and hated Harvey Milk. It was certainly a homophobic act on his part.

DR: If you look back on the gay revolution, would you say the most important or seminal event was the Stonewall rioting? What would you say are the one or two most important events?

LF: Stonewall was very important, not because of the event itself, which could easily have gotten lost to history, but because of what happened afterward. Immediately young people realized they had to organize, and they had to organize militantly. There had been these organizations in the 1950s, like Mattachine and Daughters of Bilitis, but they were not militant organizations. Frank Kameny had these very important pickets in front of the White House and the State Department, but they didn't attract many people.

The Gay Liberation Front that emerged out of Stonewall decided that we would do marches, pride parades that attracted, in the beginning, thousands of people, and then eventually hundreds of thousands of people. And then marches on Washington that attracted almost a million people to one of the marches, in 1993. Stonewall was a huge trigger in bringing to young people's attention that there is a cause to fight for here.

DR: What would you like the government of the United States or society to do to make certain that gays and lesbians have the rights they're entitled to?

LF: What the Supreme Court decided in June 2020 was crucial, but there needs to be the equality act that Bella Abzug and Ed Koch introduced in 1974 and in 1975 to assure the rights of the LGBTQ community. Because as has happened in many places, you can get married on a Sunday and still be fired from your job on a Monday. Hopefully because of the Supreme Court decision, that won't happen so often, but the word needs to be spread that the Supreme Court made that decision last June.

DR: Should somebody use the word *gay, lesbian,* or an acronym? What would you say is the right way to identify people?

LF: Our community is so diverse in terms of all demographics, race and class and generation. People of my generation, for instance, will never adjust to the word *queer.* Young people love it. It's a good umbrella term for young people. I prefer *lesbian* or *gay.* A lot of people now, within the community, call themselves *nonbinary*. I think it's important to ask someone what their preferred pronouns are. Maybe the best approach is always to ask, "How should I refer to you?"

JIA LYNN YANG
ON THE HISTORY OF
IMMIGRATION

National Editor, *New York Times;* author of
*One Mighty and Irresistible Tide: The Epic
Struggle over American Immigration,
1924–1965*

"We don't have some kind of inherent right
to be here that was guaranteed by the
founders. These are laws that are fought
over, that have been fought over, that are
being fought over very fiercely right now.
We, as a nation, are always tussling over
who gets to count as an American and what
requirements you have to have."

Far more than any other country in the
world, the United States has been a nation of
immigrants. The country was founded by immigrant settlers from Europe; during much
of the country's history, immigration was
encouraged, in part to provide workers for
the expanding territory and the growing
economy; and as a result, today the country
has by far a higher number of immigrants

(about forty-six million) and children of immigrants (about forty million) than any other country.

But the welcoming image and words on the Statue of Liberty can be misleading, for there have certainly been long periods when the U.S. was clearly not very welcoming to immigrants unless they were from certain western European countries or belonged to certain religions. Indeed, the country whose self-image has long been that of a "melting pot" was anything but that for long periods of time.

For instance, following the events of 9/11, immigration from most Middle Eastern countries saw increased regulation and enforcement. And during the Trump administration, efforts were made to limit immigration from Muslim-majority countries; to restrict visas for students, academics, and highly skilled workers; and to erect a wall between Mexico and the United States in order to restrict illegal immigration, which, in combination with other measures, slowed legal Mexican and Latin American immigration.

But the Trump period was relatively short in the nation's time span. The far greater constraint on immigration began to occur in the late 1800s and early 1900s when members of Congress (presumably reflecting constituent concern) felt that the homogeneity of the country was being threatened by increased immigration from southern and eastern Europe, from Asia, and by Jews.

After many failed efforts in Congress to restrict the influx to the "desired" immigrants, the Johnson-Reed Act was passed in 1924. That act placed tight quotas on immigrants from countries or with backgrounds deemed less desirable. The result was reduced immigration generally, but particularly by those from eastern and southern Europe or who were Asian or Jewish.

While that legislation was seen by many as discriminatory and effectively barring from the country many talented and educated individuals, efforts to amend or repeal the legislation were met with fierce resistance in Congress and the State Department. But in the 1960s, President John Kennedy was interested in seeking a repeal, and President Lyndon Johnson completed that effort, working closely with Congress's most ardent opponent of the existing law, House Judiciary Committee Chair Emanuel Celler.

The result was the Hart-Celler Immigration and Nationality Act of 1965, which removed discriminatory country and ethnic quotas and encouraged immigration of talented individuals or those with family ties to the United States. From that moment forward, largely until the Trump era, the United States was again seen as a welcoming beacon for those seeking a better and more productive life.

The story of this oscillating American welcome mat is told well by Jia Lynn Yang, then a deputy national editor at the *New York Times,* in a September 11, 2020, New-York Historical Society interview based on a book that she wrote on this subject. (She has since been named the *Times*'s national editor.) Her interest in this area, and the resulting book, was spurred by a look at how her forebears from China and Taiwan managed to get into the United States. As Yang researched the subject, she realized that, for a fair bit of American history, the country was not as immigrant-friendly as the Statue of Liberty might suggest.

DAVID M. RUBENSTEIN (DR): We like to say we are a nation of immigrants, but as you point out in the book, we were a nation of immigrants from certain places. If they came from China or Japan or southern Europe or Latin America, they weren't as welcome for a long part of our history. Is that right?

JIA LYNN YANG (JLY): Yes, for the most part. We had pretty much open borders, period, until about a hundred years ago. At that point, we began to restrict immigration by ethnicity. All of us can trace our families to different points, right? At the beginning, you have many people from England. You have Irish immigrants, Germans, and then later you have people from other parts of the world. As those waves of new immigrants come in, there's inevitably something of a backlash.

DR: Let's talk about the beginning of the country. The settlers in the thirteen original colonies were mostly from England?

JLY: That's right.

DR: Did they need a passport or visa to come here?

JLY: No, no documentation. This entire infrastructure we have is very recent.

DR: When the Constitution was ratified in 1788, was there any provision for immigration? Was there anything then about people coming in? Anybody could just show up in those days?

JLY: Pretty much. Benjamin Franklin helped create the earliest passports, which were kind of like letters of reference. When you traveled abroad, you had this piece of paper, but it wasn't about your citizenship or your legal status. There were no visas. Passports didn't become codified the way we think of them now until after World War I, when the League of Nations created a worldwide standard out of Europe.

Again, all this paperwork that we're used to didn't really exist then. The only thing from those early days that we're still very much living the legacy of is that, in 1790, the founders created naturalization requirements. Those requirements said that only free white men of, quote-unquote, good moral character could become citizens, could naturalize. For a long time, only those people could become citizens after immigrating here.

DR: To become a citizen in the early days, did you have to take a test? You had to be here a certain number of years?

JLY: It changed over time. At some point there was a sense that if you came here, we really wanted to encourage you to become a citizen. You would basically file a petition for citizenship so that you were in an interim period of trying out being a citizen. I think in fact you could vote during that time. It's almost like training wheels for citizenship.

It's only now that we have a very different view. We cultivated immigrants as citizens more than we do today.

DR: I should point out that there was one provision in the Constitution that dealt with people coming to the country involuntarily. The slave trade was supposed to be eliminated by 1808. But coming voluntarily wasn't really dealt with at all in the Constitution. When did Congress pass a law that said if you're from a certain country, you cannot come to this country?

JLY: The first instance of this, of singling out a group of people based on their ethnicity, is the 1882 Chinese Exclusion Act. It's a really important historic point, because once you see that law pass, there's a succession of such attempts, peaking in the 1920s.

That is the beginning of a long era of adding restrictions based on people's race and ethnicity. This law is really a backlash to the wave of Chinese migrant laborers, who were showing up in the West, searching for gold and, as we all know, helping to build railroads. They were competition for a lot of white workers on the West Coast. Out of that backlash this law's passed, and it's Chinese laborers in particular who are banned.

This changes immigration forever. There are more Korean and Japanese immigrants who come after, but this is such an important law for people — even those who aren't Asian American — to know, because it's the bedrock law that says, "We're going to start restricting immigration, and the way we're going to do it is singling you out by your ethnicity."

DR: Most of the people coming to the United States were not from China. They weren't from Mexico or Latin America. Most of the people coming in the 1800s to the United States were from western Europe, where the colonists had originally come from. They were coming from England, or they might have been coming from Ireland or Germany or Scandinavia.

But in the early part of the twentieth century, all of a sudden people are coming from southern Europe — Italians, Greeks. And a lot of people are coming who are Jewish.

This began to make people a little uncomfortable in the United States. They were thinking that the wrong type of people were coming. So during the early part of the twentieth century, the first twenty years, was there a big debate? What ultimately happened in 1924?

JLY: This is such an important period of American history. I think of New York, for instance, which overnight had a flood of Italian and Jewish immigrants who left a powerful and permanent imprint on the city that you can see if you spend any time in New York.

There were people who were Catholic, who

were Jewish. They had different religions, they spoke different languages. They seemed really different, in different ways, and this set off a lot of alarm among, in particular, white Protestants.

This is when the idea of the melting pot is in the air. There's a sense that there's some assimilation, but there was also a feeling that these people were too different. They couldn't be assimilated. There needed to be restrictions to protect America's identity and, by that measure, ethnic identity. So they begin to pass ethnic quotas in the '20s to stop this big migration from southern and eastern Europe.

DR: The concern was a little bit that these people were coming in and they were not well educated and they would work for lower wages than existing American citizens. But the main point you're making is that there was a concern that there would be people who were not going to assimilate. They weren't going to be white, Anglo-Saxon, Protestant types, and the culture of the United States would dramatically change. Was that the main concern?

JLY: Yes. It was about the stability of the democracy, in these people's minds, and they had a kind of science backing them. This is also a time when eugenics is completely mainstream — the breaking up of all of the human race down to the smaller groupings of ethnicities and race, and measuring the size of your head, and saying, for example, if you're Jewish, it means that you have these inherent traits.

There was this sort of prejudice, especially from people in the white elite. People on the Upper East Side especially were horrified by these Jewish and Italian immigrants coming, but they also could point to this pseudoscience, which was later discredited, of course. But at the time this was fully accepted among American elites and intellectuals: "I'm uncomfortable personally with these people, but also the science tells me these are inferior people whom we don't want coming into the U.S. and intermarrying and having children and diluting the quality of the typical American."

DR: Before 1924 and the legislation we'll talk about in a moment, if somebody who was Jewish or Italian or Greek came into New York or wherever and said, "Here I am," there was no way to say, "Go back." They just were here and you couldn't kick them out?

JLY: There was a literacy test that had been added in 1917 as an early effort to begin to restrict all these different-seeming people, but it wasn't all that effective. They didn't want people with epilepsy or people who seemed mentally ill. A minuscule percentage of people were turned away.

Again, because there weren't visas, you didn't need to go to a consulate in your home country before you came. You just came on the boat.

If you could make the journey, you show up at Ellis Island and they basically say yes or no. If yes, then you're in and that's it. People weren't deported either. So once you came in and you began to settle, it was unthinkable that you would be forced to leave.

DR: One time the National Archives gave me something that showed my grandfather at the age of eleven coming into the United States. It lists the ship, and it had the manifest, and it said, "Eleven years old Hebrew." They emphasized religion.

In 1924, the Johnson-Reed Act passed. What is that act, and why was it so significant in terms of changing the way we let people into the country?

JLY: This is such an important law to understand in American history. As we've been talking about, it's open borders. You can just show up. There's no paperwork really needed.

In 1924, based on this sort of world-of-eugenics ranking, all these races and ethnicities, Congress passes a series of very strict ethnic quotas that says, "We're going to codify that we want people who are white Anglo-Saxons from northern and western Europe. We don't want people from other parts of the world."

They literally created quotas. They would say, "We want most of the people to come from these countries and only a few hundred from places where there had been no numerical limits before."

And it wasn't just that there were quotas. It was the symbolism of it. It was a very explicit way to say, as a nation, that America is defined by the races of the people who are living in the country. And so to preserve that idea of America, we have to turn away from this idea of a melting pot, turn away from the famous Emma Lazarus poem about being a place for the "huddled masses."

People who supported the law explicitly said this. They said, "We are no longer to be a place for the huddled masses. We are going to keep America America by using these quotas."

Once these quotas were passed, overnight there was a dramatic difference. Ellis Island is suddenly quiet, because you have to have a visa to come, and people don't have them.

The ethnic makeup of the country is frozen in time. The percentage of immigrants really plummets, so that by the time you get to the

1950s, the '60s, even into the '70s, the percentage of foreign-born just keeps dropping. The older immigrants who had come in this wave that we've been discussing were dying, and there weren't new people coming in.

And so by the '50s — it's astonishing to me — people thought about immigration as kind of a past era of American history. That there had been this mass migration before, but we had turned away from that. That was all part of the past, and we were never going to do that again.

DR: Many people thought in the 1920s, '30s, and '40s that this legislation was racist and anti-Semitic, among other things, and was hurting the country, because we weren't getting immigrants coming in and we weren't expanding the population, which we do with immigrants to some extent. Were efforts made to change the legislation?

JLY: Very much. There were people, in particular Jewish Americans, who understood what these laws symbolized right away. It wasn't a mystery that people who supported them were quite openly anti-Semitic and anti-Catholic.

When the laws were passed, they were passed quite easily. There was mainstream support for this. This was a time of enormous isolationism in America generally, but from

623

the moment they were passed, Jewish activists and lawmakers in particular really tried to overturn them.

This became a huge tragedy during World War II, because during the Holocaust, there was of course a huge demand for people to escape Nazi Germany and to escape all the countries that Nazi troops were invading, and there were all these Jewish refugees looking for a place to resettle. But because of these quotas the U.S. had, it was impossible for them to come here.

There are just so many tragic stories of people desperately trying to leave Europe in this time of genocide and war and total upheaval. And they can't come to the U.S. because of these quotas.

And so, motivated by how awful the quotas seemed to be, especially to those who watched what happened during World War II, people like President Truman tried to overturn them. In 1952, there was a huge fight on the Hill over it, but they kept failing. They kept failing because the quotas seemed very much by then common sense to people — like we want to keep America this way ethnically.

DR: During World War II, there were many people who went to President Roosevelt and said, "Jews are being killed in Europe. We have to either let them in on a special refugee exception or change the existing quotas." You write about a very famous ship that came to our shores, the *St. Louis.* Can you describe what happened?

JLY: This ship arrives with all these Jewish refugees who have uncertain paperwork, and they are desperate to get to the U.S. They get so close that there are reports from the time that they can see the lights of Miami. That's how close they are to the U.S., but essentially they don't have the right papers.

They have a scheme that they're going to go through Cuba somehow, but that all falls through. So this ship is sitting there, unable to dock. The State Department — which at the time was also quite anti-Semitic — is going through all the visa applications and saying yes and no and determining the fates of people's entire families.

They see this ship and say, "We get that this is a desperate situation, but you don't have the right visas, so we do have to turn you away." There were people on board who were threatening to commit suicide, they were so desperate. The ship had to go back.

DR: When they went back, several hundred passengers were ultimately killed by the Nazis.

President Truman wanted to change the law, but he couldn't get it done. In fact, the

625

law actually probably got worse in some respects, because there were some constraints imposed that he did not support. Eisenhower didn't do very much.

Then you write about a young man running for Congress named John Kennedy, a man who'd never really worried about immigration before. He's Irish, but an Irish Brahmin, you could say. Why does he care about immigration in his first congressional election? Why does he take this up as an issue?

JLY: We sometimes associate Kennedy with immigration because he wrote this very slim book called *A Nation of Immigrants* that became quite popular in schools. Many people know that, when he runs for Congress, he's faced with a demographic challenge, which is that the district he wants to win in Boston is filled with immigrants.

Massachusetts at this point has probably one of the highest percentages of foreign-born of any state in the country. So if you want to be successful politically in Massachusetts, you've got to be able to speak to immigrants.

When Kennedy's father is ambassador to England, they don't even go to Ireland. They're really not super in touch with their Irish roots. Yet he does find a way to get in touch with his roots, because he's got to

626

relate to these working-class immigrants and children of immigrants he's trying to win over and get their votes.

He begins to invoke the memory of his mother's father, Honey Fitz [Fitzgerald]. He was a very successful Irish politician in Boston who became the mayor of the city, in the vanguard of Irish Catholics and political power in America. Kennedy plays up this part of his heritage and begins to build a body of work politically, when he gets to the Hill, on immigration reform in particular.

DR: When he gets to Congress, he's supportive of changing the existing law but doesn't have the power to get anything done, and nothing really is done. But when he runs for president, he does talk about this a bit. When he's elected, he says, "I'm going to do something about it." What did he try to do in the early years of his presidency?

JLY: By this time, in the late '50s, early '60s, there's a bipartisan feeling that maybe the quotas aren't so great. This is the Cold War, and there's a sense that these quotas are pretty indefensible at this point. They're based on race science, discredited by Nazi Germany. They are discriminatory, and they are making it hard in this war with the Soviet Union over ideology and moral purity. It's hard to defend them.

By the time JFK arrives in the White House, there's a general agreement that they should go. He gets the Department of Justice and the State Department to begin to figure out what kind of legislation they can send to Congress saying, "Here's how to abolish these quotas, and here's what you can replace them with."

DR: He does propose legislation, but it doesn't really go anywhere because many of the key people in Congress are dead-set against it. When Lyndon Johnson succeeds him as president, Johnson took up much of the Kennedy agenda. Why did he care about immigration? There weren't a lot of immigrants in his district in Texas, presumably, when he was a congressman or even a senator.

JLY: There were some who came through the Galveston port. He spoke a lot about teaching these young Mexican American children in schools as a young man, so he'd have had some exposure. When he was an aide to a congressman on the Hill during World War II, he made some efforts to help rescue Jewish refugees. So he had some passing knowledge.

When he's in the Senate, it's not one of his big issues. When he gets to the White House and he's looking at how to try to heal the country and take what JFK left unfinished and make it a reality, we think a lot about the civil rights legislation.

He does that with immigration too. He picks it up, I think, because he sees it as being of a piece with the civil rights fight. Like the fight against Jim Crow, this too is about discriminatory laws that are all about treating people differently just because of their race.

So when his aides say to him, "We should really go for this," it clicks for him that this is an important moral fight. He's not really a technocrat. He's not all about those deep technocratic details and policymaking.

Once he decides that he wants something done and there's a moral sweep to the argument — as we saw, unfortunately, with the Vietnam War — he gets really behind it. Unlike JFK, he is a genius at working the levers of Congress. Once he injects that interest and attention, the legislation really does have a chance, after forty years, to pass.

DR: The legislation goes to the judiciary committees in both the House and the Senate. In the Senate, in those days, the chairman of the Judiciary Committee is Senator James Eastland from Mississippi, not famous for an interest in civil rights or in immigration by people who are Jewish. How did he get persuaded to do this?

JLY: He sees the writing on the wall. He's a practical person. He's deeply prejudiced, one of the hard-core segregationists during this period, and so powerful because he's running the Judiciary Committee. All of this important legislation runs through him, all the judicial appointments.

But he sees that the votes are there. There's momentum for this. It doesn't really make sense to stand in the way of it.

Interestingly, he has taken Ted Kennedy, who's just joined the Senate, under his wing, and he sees that Teddy Kennedy is really interested in this too. So, after standing up against it for many years, he realizes, "I can't keep fighting this." He basically let Teddy Kennedy run the show on the Senate floor to get this legislation passed.

DR: Manny Celler was a congressman who was then, I think, in his fiftieth year as a member of the House. He was chairman of the House Judiciary Committee, from Brooklyn and with a big Jewish constituency. Was he the leading advocate in the House for getting this done?

JLY: He was probably the fifth-longest-serving member of Congress ever in American history. He joins in the '20s and he's there all the way up to when Nixon is president.

So he sees it all. The quotas that we've been

talking about are passed right after he joins Congress, and he really has been at the center of fighting against them for a long time. By the time we get to the '60s, he's a truly liberal congressman who's behind every liberal cause you can imagine.

He's a very powerful figure as chair of the House Judiciary Committee on all the civil rights legislation that's being passed. The Voting Rights Act, the Civil Rights Act, all of it has his fingerprints all over it. But probably nothing was closer to his heart than this immigration law, which bears his name, the Hart-Celler Act, I think because he sees the very beginning of the fight, through World War II and the Holocaust, through the Cold War and Truman, through JFK up to this point in 1965.

It's also personal. He's the grandson of German Jews. His constituents are Jews and Italians. He really takes personally this idea that the U.S. has a bedrock system of immigration that openly discriminates against people like him and his constituents.

DR: So the legislation is called the Hart-Celler Act. Phil Hart is the senator for Michigan who introduced the legislation. What is in the legislation that changes the way our immigration system now operates?

JLY: There was kind of a funny moment when

631

Kennedy is still alive and his aides are trying to figure out what to put in the legislation. Everyone is like, "We get rid of these quotas, but what do we replace them with?" No one really knows. Everyone's been fighting so hard to eliminate them, but then you have this very difficult question: If you're not going to judge people based on their ethnicity, what is your system?

People don't want to go back to open borders at that time. They want some kind of numerical limit, but they're not sure how to begin to establish preferences. The 1965 act is fascinating because they're debating what to put in place of these ethnic quotas. They come down to a couple of criteria that should sound familiar to all of us because they're still with us now.

One is family reunification, meaning if you have immediate family already in the U.S., you get priority over somebody else. This preference is so interesting because the people who wanted it as the number-one thing that would help you get in were trying to keep America stable racially. Their thinking was: "If we get rid of these quotas, we still have to have some kind of mechanism to keep America white, more or less. We can't allow things to get out of control. The people who are here are already white, so if their immediate family members get preference, that shouldn't change things very much." So that was number one, the highest preference, in the '65 act.

Number two is people with special skills — people with technical skills, people with graduate degrees, people who were scientists, people with some special thing that the U.S. government felt like it needed more of. That second preference is actually what my parents, my mom in particular, benefited from to be able to come here.

DR: What about where you came from in the Western Hemisphere? Was there a concern about people coming from, let's say, Latin America, and how was that dealt with?

JLY: This part really surprised me when I was doing my research. When these ethnic quotas were passed, there was a huge carve-out for the Western Hemisphere. This is so different from how it is now, but it was thought for a very long time that it didn't make sense to restrict immigration from places like Mexico, because these countries in Latin America are our neighbors and we have to treat them with some deference.

So even in these '20s quotas, the Western Hemisphere was basically carved out of all of it. There were no quotas, no limits. Now, you get to 1965 and people are saying, "Why do we have this weird system where the Western Hemisphere has no limits and yet the rest of the world does?" And so in '65, oddly enough, the Western Hemisphere loses that kind of limitless immigration system and becomes part of this overall numerical cap.

For some scholars, this is a really pivotal moment, because the U.S.-Mexico border, which, again, had no numerical limits before — there were some guest-worker programs, but it was very much an open-border situation, aside from the literacy test — suddenly there's a numerical limit and many more people could be considered illegal.

This is the root, in a way. The law is trying to loosen the immigration laws a bit, but then it almost inadvertently introduces this other factor, which is that Western Hemisphere immigration has these numerical caps, which transforms how we see immigrants from Latin America.

DR: The Hart-Celler Act passed in 1965 is still the law of the land?

JLY: It's pretty much the bedrock of our immigration system. We have gone back to it and changed things and added things. But when you talk about the modern infrastructure, it's really this law.

DR: Right now, what percentage of the population in the United States is immigrants, and is that much different than it was before the Hart-Celler Act?

JLY: It's in the low teens, somewhere around 12 or 14 percent. More than one in four Americans now is either an immigrant or a child of immigrants. We have not been at this kind of peak of foreign-born since that earlier historic wave of Jews and Italians showing up at the turn of the twentieth century.

Immigration has fallen off pretty dramatically under the Trump administration for lots of different reasons, but when we think about our society and the percentage of foreign-born, we are at a relative historic high — the difference being that now the people who are here are not only from Europe, they're from all over the world.

DR: If you want to be a U.S. resident now, you have to meet one of the quotas. How many people a year are permitted to come into the United States?

JLY: It's a couple of hundred thousand. It changes year to year, that number. The Trump administration was always reducing that number. On net, I think right now we have about two hundred thousand immigrants coming in a year. Again, that number has been dropping. The trend is downward.

And, for those who want to become citizens, there are requirements, as we've been talking about. You have to have been a permanent resident with a green card for at least five years. You have to pass a civics test. You have to pass the basic English proficiency test. About half of the immigrants in the U.S. now are naturalized, the rest are not.

DR: I think it's about eight hundred thousand people a year are now sworn in through naturalization ceremonies in the United States. If you could summarize it in one paragraph, what would you want somebody to take away from your book?

JLY: We don't have some kind of inherent right to be here that was guaranteed by the founders. These are laws that are fought over, that have been fought over, that are being fought over very fiercely right now. We, as a nation, are always tussling over who gets to count as an American and what requirements you have to have.

Sometimes we've said we want immigrants here, sometimes we don't, but these are knobs that we're always turning. These questions of who's allowed here, who's not, they determine the fates of entire families. They can feel completely arbitrary.

You can talk to anyone who's gone through the system. It can feel like a fluke, like this one line in the law lets me in, but this one doesn't. We have to look at it as kind of a legalistic structure that we've built together, and that one day it can change. Just as it's changed before, it can change again.

Madeleine K. Albright on Being an Immigrant

Former U.S. Ambassador to the United
Nations; former U.S. Secretary of State

"My mantra has always been and is that the
U.S. needs to be involved, and that is what
made me grateful to be an American."

There are many reasons why more individuals in the world by far want to immigrate
every year to the United States than to any
other country. Among those reasons is that
immigrants have shown that they can rise to
the highest levels of American companies,
cultural organizations, and society.

The only exception is the U.S. presidency
— that position is reserved, under the Constitution, for natural-born Americans. But two
immigrants have risen to the highest level of
a president's cabinet: secretary of state. The
first was Henry Kissinger, a German refugee
in the 1930s who, following a sterling academic career at Harvard, became secretary of
state under Richard Nixon, and then contin-

ued under Gerald Ford.

The second was Madeleine Albright, a refugee from communist Czechoslovakia in the late 1940s. She became the first woman to serve as secretary of state, during President Bill Clinton's second term, after having acted as his ambassador to the United Nations during his first term.

Secretary Albright's father was a distinguished Czech diplomat and academic who recognized that his country was, following World War II, going to be effectively controlled by the Soviet Union. So he left with his wife and three children, and ultimately became a professor of international affairs at the University of Denver. (His prize student there was a young woman who would also become secretary of state a few decades down the road — Condoleezza Rice.)

After graduating from Wellesley College and getting her master's and PhD in public law and government from Columbia University in New York, Madeleine Albright became a foreign policy advisor to a number of Democratic policymakers and presidential candidates. However, it was a former professor at Columbia, Zbigniew Brzezinski, who first brought Madeleine Albright into the executive branch as a congressional liaison for him during part of his tenure as national security advisor to President Jimmy Carter.

That is when I first met Madeleine, at a

staff lunch table in the White House Mess during the Carter years. I empathized with her — she told me of the constant challenges of keeping the peace between her current boss and her former boss, Senator Edmund Muskie of Maine, who became Carter's second secretary of state.

At the time, I did not imagine that this young staffer would herself one day become secretary of state. I suspect she did not see me as a budding capitalist — in those days, the furthest thing from my mind. I have interviewed Madeleine over the years about her life and views on international affairs. But for this book I asked her to do a special virtual interview in December 2020 about her life as an immigrant — the challenges and the opportunities.

DAVID M. RUBENSTEIN (DR): You were born in what was then Czechoslovakia. Your name was not actually Madeleine?

MADELEINE ALBRIGHT (MA): It was Marie Jana, which is basically Mary Jane in Czech.

DR: Your father, Josef Korbel, was an official with the Czech government. Then, when the Nazis invaded, your father and your family escaped to London?

MA: When I was born, my father was actually

the Czechoslovak press attaché in Belgrade. My mother wanted me born in Prague, where her mother was. So I was born in Czechoslovakia. But my father at the time was a diplomat. Then he was recalled and was in Prague in March 1939 when the Nazis marched in. I was two years old.

DR: Your father was able to get the right to go to London. Was it hard to get passage to London?

MA: They just had to escape. According to something my mother wrote, they managed to bribe some officials, and they got out with me. We went out via Yugoslavia and ended up in London, where my father was with the Czechoslovak government in exile.

DR: Do you remember the bombings of London during that time? That was when the Nazis were bombing London during the Battle of Britain.

MA: I do. We had an apartment in London in Notting Hill Gate. Before it got fancy, there were these big buildings that had a lot of refugees in them. We spent every night in the cellar, and that I remember very well.

My father broadcasted for the BBC at the time into Czechoslovakia. We had an apartment, and he would come down. I remember his saying, "You have to go down, but there are hot water pipes and gas pipes down there, so who knows what will happen?"

When I was writing one of my books, I went back to visit that apartment house. And I, stupidly enough, asked the superintendent there, "Does the cellar still exist?" He said, "Of course." He took me down there, and I remembered the ugly green paint that had been there.

We spent every night down there, and then would come up in the morning and see destroyed buildings.

DR: Did you speak English then?

MA: I learned English. I grew up bilingual. We were in London all through the Blitz, then we moved out to Walton-on-Thames in the country. In London I went to the Kensington School for Girls, and then I went to a school in Walton-on-Thames called Ingomar.

DR: When the war ended, your father returned to Czechoslovakia and became an official in the government?

MA: He went back on one of the first planes and then we came a couple of months later. We lived in Prague during the summer of 1945. There was a beautiful apartment owned by the Czechoslovak Foreign Ministry that we lived in, right up by the castle. I briefly went to a Czech school. Then my father was made the Czechoslovak ambassador to Yugoslavia, and my mother and I moved to Belgrade. By then I had a little sister who had been born in England.

DR: Ultimately the communists took over control of the Czech government. Your father resigned?

MA: By the way, my father did not want me going to school with communists, so I had a governess while we were in Belgrade. And in Europe, you can't go to the next level until you are a certain age, so I was ahead of myself. They sent me to a school in Switzerland for a year when I was ten, and I didn't go home for the whole year. In the spring of 1948, my parents came through Switzerland and said, "We're not going back."

He was a professional diplomat, and he had been in Belgrade for three years. His next assignment was to be the Czechoslovak representative for a new commission to deal with India and Pakistan over Kashmir. He accepted that. He was very pleased to do it. And then in February 1948 there was the communist coup in Czechoslovakia. He went to see his best friends in Belgrade, the British and American ambassadors, and they said, "If you resign, they will name some communist and nothing will happen. Take the job. Don't report to your own government. Report to us."

What happened was my father did that. He went to India and Pakistan, and my mother and sister and by then brother and I lived in London until November 1948, when we came to the United States.

But it's not a terrible story. We didn't crawl through barbed wire or anything. We had diplomatic passports. And then my father came to the United States in December 1948, and he defected and asked for political asylum.

DR: When you came over, you came over on a ship?

MA: The SS *America.*

DR: Do you have any memory of actually seeing the Statue of Liberty going by when you arrived?

MA: Absolutely. It's very vivid in my mind. We did not come in through Ellis Island. We did come on this ship and then into New York Harbor, and I definitely remember seeing the Statue of Liberty.

DR: When you came in, did you think you were not going back ever to Czechoslovakia?

Or did you think you would just be in the U.S. for a couple of years?

MA: The truth is, I don't remember that. My parents didn't talk about it. We didn't talk about going back.

DR: Ultimately, your father gets a position at the University of Denver. He goes out there and takes you with him?

MA: No. When we first came to the U.S., we lived on Long Island, because the United Nations was at Lake Success on Long Island. I started in the sixth grade at the time. At that stage, the Rockefeller Foundation was finding jobs for European intellectuals, and they found my father a job at the University of Denver.

We had no idea where Denver was. My parents bought a car and started driving. And my mother — I remember her saying this, with three kids in the backseat — said, "They say Denver is the Mile High City, but we're not going up, so maybe we're going the wrong direction."

But we all went there together. There was a lot of moving around in faculty housing, or people that lent us their houses.

DR: You grew up and graduated from high school in Denver. Then you applied to a lot of colleges? You went to Wellesley, right?

MA: I applied to a lot of colleges because I knew that I couldn't go to college if I didn't have a scholarship. I applied to five schools. And I'll never forget, the first answer came from Stanford, saying, "You've been accepted but no scholarship." I went screaming out of the house, thinking that was the end — that I wouldn't ever go anywhere. It turned out later that I got the Colorado State Scholarship to Stanford. But I went to Wellesley. The reason I even applied to it was because one summer my father taught at MIT, so I'd seen Wellesley, and then my English teacher and my Latin teacher had gone to Wellesley. I thought it would be great to go there.

DR: Have you ever mentioned this to the people at Stanford?

MA: They know.

DR: Okay. So you go to Wellesley. You graduated in 1959, but in 1957 you became an American citizen. In those days, to become an American citizen, you had to be in the United States for five years and then take some kind of citizenship test?

MA: Yes. And in our case it was somewhat more complicated. We came in 1948, and my father defected. But it took us longer to get our citizenship because technically he had worked for a communist government for a while, even though he didn't report to them. It was during the McCarthy period, so it all took longer.

When I got to Wellesley, there was this whole system where if somebody came to visit, they announced it over the whole loudspeaker. So somebody said, "Madeleine Korbel, there are some ladies here to take you into Boston to show you what the American girl wears," and I come downstairs in my Shetland sweater and Bermuda shorts. They thought I was a foreign student, and the truth is that it was very strange because I was not a citizen.

There was this club called the Cosmos Club that was partially foreign students and partially American students. But when I went to see the dean about how I'd done on my SATs, because they didn't used to tell people directly, she said, "Remarkable, remarkable." I think it's because she thought I was a foreign student and didn't speak English.

I did not become a citizen until between my sophomore and junior years. And you did have to study to take the test. My parents had become citizens a few months earlier, but I became a citizen at the courthouse in Denver, Colorado.

DR: Before you became a citizen, did you feel discrimination in high school or in college because you were not an American?

MA: Yes and no. We lived in Denver and my parents were very ethnic, you know. And people were so kind to us, in terms of lending us things. We were refugees.

I started out going to public school, and then my father heard there was a private school that was giving scholarships. So, he made me go to this private school, and there were only sixteen girls in the class and they were primarily rich.

I felt out of it mainly because we lived under fairly modest circumstances, had these parents that cooked strange food, and we all had to be together every Sunday. I did in some ways feel that I was not part of the group.

DR: After you became a citizen, you went and got your PhD at Columbia and did many other things, worked on Capitol Hill. Did you ever feel that as an immigrant you were not fully accepted in America or that you were any different than somebody who had been born here?

MA: I really did not. When we were in London, people would say, "We're so sorry your country's been taken over by a terrible dictator. You're welcome here. What can we do to help you, and when are you going home?" When we came to the United States, people said, "We're so sorry your country has been taken over by a terrible system. You're welcome here. What can we do to help you, and when will you become a citizen?" My father said, "That is what made America different from every other country."

That is what I grew up with. I was proud that I had become an American. I didn't feel discriminated against when I was working. One of the first things that happened when we were living on Long Island, it was Thanksgiving and we were singing "We Gather Together," and I heard somebody "aahsk"-ing for God's blessing. I was the one "aahsk"-ing. From then on I did everything I could to lose my British accent. I didn't want to stand out. But I felt more that I didn't fit in because we didn't have money.

DR: You became ambassador to the United Nations under Bill Clinton, in his first term. At that point, you'd been an American citizen for quite some time, so you didn't feel that becoming the ambassador to the U.N. was unrealistic for somebody who wasn't born in the United States, I assume.

MA: No. I'd had to get my clearances to be on the NSC staff. The question obviously came up: "Where were you born?" I filled out an awful lot of papers. But you also have to remember, I worked for Zbigniew Brzezinski, who hadn't been born in the United States either, so it didn't seem to be an issue.

DR: When you were appointed by President Clinton to be secretary of state, you must have had a great deal of pride to think that you, a not-born-in-America person, could have become secretary of state. Henry Kissinger did as well, but you were the first woman to be secretary of state. Did you ever feel there was any chance you wouldn't get it because you had been born elsewhere?

MA: That was never a factor. Henry Kissinger was the first person to call me to congratulate me. He said, "Madeleine, you've taken away my one unique characteristic of being an immigrant secretary of state." I said to him, "No, Henry, I don't have an accent."

DR: What makes you most proud to be an American?

MA: I believed when I represented the United States — and I continue to believe — that we are an exceptional country in terms of our capabilities and the kinds of things that we had done. I was very, very proud to represent the United States. The part that I saw at the time was the things we had done in partnership with other countries.

As I was trying to sort out what our policies should be, first at the U.N. and then as secretary of state, I used to make the argument that when the U.S. was absent, as it was during the Munich Conference when the British and French made this agreement with the Germans and Italians over the heads of the Czechoslovaks, the country was sold down the river.

When I was a little girl, I remember the American soldiers coming to London. I remember the parades. I remember the Iron Curtain, when Europe was divided.

My mantra has always been and is that the U.S. needs to be involved, and that is what made me grateful to be an American. Certainly grateful for what happened with my family, but also for what in office I was able to do, with the backing of the government and President Clinton, to make a difference by having the U.S. be a partner with other countries.

I recently was at a dinner and had to describe myself in six words, and I said, "Worried optimist problem solver grateful American." And really I am a grateful American.

SONIA SOTOMAYOR ON CIVICS AND CIVIC EDUCATION

Associate Justice of the U.S. Supreme Court

"When you are asked to serve, there is a moral compulsion to serve your country. To be a federal judge is service as a lawyer, the most service that you can do for your country."

On August 6, 2009, after an appointment by President Barack Obama, Sonia Sotomayor became only the third woman in the country's long history to serve on the Supreme Court of the United States, and the first justice with Latinx heritage. She also embodied the classic American Dream story: the daughter of blue-collar Puerto Rican parents; raised by her mother after her father's premature death; a summa cum laude Princeton graduate (when there were very few Puerto Ricans from the Bronx at Princeton); winner of the Pyne Prize, the highest honor awarded to a Princeton undergraduate; a Yale Law School graduate; a U.S. district court judge at the age of thirty-eight, appointed by George H. W. Bush (a Republican president); and a U.S. court of appeals judge at the age of forty-four, appointed by Bill Clinton (a Democratic president).

Like her two female predecessors on the court, Sandra Day O'Connor and Ruth Bader Ginsburg, Justice Sotomayor has tried to lead a normal life, staying in contact with close friends and avoiding the often isolated life that is possible for a justice. Her outgoing, gregarious personality would probably make an isolated life almost impossible for her.

Justice Sotomayor has also tried to follow one of her predecessors, Justice O'Connor, in another way. After leaving the court, Justice O'Connor helped to start iCivics, a nonprofit designed to help students — through the use of online games — learn more about civics. She felt strongly that civics education had been pushed aside in the American school curriculum, and thought the result increasingly was citizens who are largely uninformed about basic information about government and civic responsibilities. Justice Sotomayor shares that concern, and as a result has joined the board of iCivics.

The need for better civics education was the principal topic of my interview with Justice Sotomayor, whom I have known for a number of years and previously interviewed.

The interview was part of a 2021 leadership series being held virtually between Mount Vernon and the Brookings Institution.

DAVID M. RUBENSTEIN (DR): Was it clear from your early days that you wanted to be a lawyer?

SONIA SOTOMAYOR (SS): It was, but for reasons that weren't self-evident. I grew up in a housing project in the South Bronx, and there were no lawyers or judges in the projects in which I lived.

But when I was seven, I developed diabetes. It's not so true now, but back then, if you had juvenile diabetes, which I did, you were not permitted to become a law enforcement agent. And that's what I wanted to become, a detective, because of Nancy Drew. The first chapter books I began to read, at about seven and a half or eight years old, were Nancy Drew mysteries.

By the time I was ten, Perry Mason appeared on TV. He was the first TV lawyer, and the first lawyer about whom TV ran a weekly series. From him I learned of the work of lawyers. And I began to think about that as a potential alternative to being a detective, because Perry Mason spent the first half of his show investigating the crime his client was charged with, and the second half in court proving his client was innocent. I thought, "Gee, that might marry the two skills that I really admire — playing sleuth to a mystery, and liking to talk a lot."

DR: When you were growing up in the Bronx, in junior high school and high school, did you get very much civic education? Do you feel that you learned a lot about the way our government works at that time?

SS: Nothing. I was an early product of the change in the country. When Sputnik was launched by Russia, the United States had an immediate visceral reaction that it was behind in technology and science and that we needed to catch up. What started to happen after Sputnik in the 1960s is that the country became much more concerned with STEM education, as it should have been. It is an important issue that needed correcting in our country at the time.

But one of the things that began to suffer was civic education. There's only a certain number of hours in a school day, and if you were going to load up more on STEM subjects, you had to reduce other subjects. Most schools began to forgo civic education. And that, I think, was a great detriment to our country.

DR: When you became a member of the United States Supreme Court, Justice Sandra

Day O'Connor was already a member of the court, and you had a chance to get to know her. Did she talk about her interest in civic education? When did you get so interested in this?

SS: When I joined the court, Sandra Day O'Connor had stepped down as an active member. As most people may know, she was the first female justice on the Supreme Court, and she was appointed in 1981. It was a momentous time for me because I had just graduated from law school in 1979, two years earlier, and at the time there were no women on the Supreme Court. There were no women on the highest court of my state, New York, the court of appeals. And women were still a fraction of the judges throughout the country — a tiny, tiny fraction.

When Sandra was appointed, it was such a beacon of hope for me. An idea formed in my head that my future wasn't limited the way I thought at first it might be, that I had the potential to achieve other things in life besides just being a working lawyer, which is not unimportant, but that I could aspire myself to do something like becoming a judge eventually.

Sandra took senior status [a form of retirement], and she had decided that there were two things she wanted to commit to doing. One was educating the public about the dangers of electing judges. She thought that judges participating in elections might be tempted to make promises to voters that they should not keep, because judges are required to keep an open mind in all cases.

But the second, and probably the more important, object of her education of the public was civic education. She had seen that civic education had declined in school. She had also seen that civics was being taught in a really boring way. What are the three branches of government? Who's the president? Who's the vice president? How many senators are there? How many people in the House of Representatives? It was filled with facts, but not with understanding about what our civic process was about.

Sandra believed, having watched the decline of civic discourse in our country, that was directly tied to the time in which civic education had declined in the U.S. She became committed to starting an organization called iCivics.org, which uses game-playing to teach kids about civics in a creative and innovative way. It has reached over 7.5 million students, and over 120,000 teachers are using iCivics to engage kids in learning about our republican form of government and about their role in participating in that government.

Sandra's involvement in civic education dovetailed with my own aim of devoting my time on the Supreme Court to educating students on the importance of civic participation. You cannot participate in something you do not know about.

I tell students all the time, "It is your obligation to learn about your system of government. But more importantly, it's your obligation not to be a bystander in life, but to become an active participant in understanding how you can better your community."

That is what civic participation is about. You do not have to be a politician and you do not have to be involved in politics, but you do have to be involved in improving the world you are in.

DR: Is the biggest problem getting money from governments to fund civic education programs in schools, or is it getting students interested in this subject?

SS: The lack of resources that we put into civic education is a significant problem. We put fifty dollars per student per year into STEM classes. We put five cents per student into civic education. That disparity is way off, given how important civic education is to making better students. There is a tremendous amount of social science research that shows that students who become involved in civic education and civic participation overall become better students.

But the very first problem, and the most

significant, is that neither our government nor our citizens understand the importance of civic education. Ignorance of what our laws mean, ignorance of what our society needs in terms of functioning and being vibrant, is our biggest problem right now. We have to educate students, but in some ways we have to educate ourselves as adults and as citizens. I do not mean citizens with a capital *C,* as in are you a citizen of the United States, but are you what I call a citizen with a small *c*? Are you a citizen of your community? Do you understand that to keep it healthy, to keep it flourishing, we have to work together? What civic involvement means is figuring out ways to work together to make a more perfect union.

DR: It's interesting that one of the only times in the United States where one has to actually know something about civics is if you're a naturalized-citizen candidate. Was your mother a naturalized citizen?

SS: No, because she was born in Puerto Rico, and under a 1917 law called the Jones Act, Puerto Ricans are born U.S. citizens as soon as they move to the mainland. So when she came over in World War II, she was considered and is an American citizen.

DR: For those who are born, let's say, somewhere else, if you want to be a U.S. citizen after roughly five years of residency, you have to take a citizenship test. Out of a hundred potential questions, you're asked, I think, ten of them. And you have to get six correct. Amazingly, 91 percent of the people who take it pass. But when the same test was given to native-born Americans not long ago, as you know, in forty-nine out of fifty states and the District of Columbia, the majority failed. So it's a sad situation.

SS: That is a very sad situation.

DR: Let me ask you about what judges and justices do toward civic education. For hundreds of years, judges have written opinions, which explain why they made their decisions. I assume that's to some extent about civic education — coming up with a reasoning to justify your decision. Is that how you look at that? Or it's different than civic education?

SS: There is a civic education component to judicial writing. We are explaining the reasons why we are coming to our conclusions, so that is always educational. In particular, when you have a majority opinion and you have a dissenting opinion, you get to see two sides of the issue. And you get to see in writing how people can disagree about something

660

but still engage with each other's thinking. So that's an important educational process.

But one of my colleagues, Justice Stephen Breyer, has written a book about making a democracy, in which he argues that our decision-making is there to ensure that people continue to respect the judiciary. Opinion-writing is our way of explaining to the public why the law requires what it does. That is educational, but it also serves another function — ensuring the legitimacy of the courts, that we are not a monarchy, we are not making up rules, we are following the law as we the justices best understand it.

DR: I was surprised to read that when our first president, George Washington, appointed the first chief justice, John Jay, he had so little to do in the first two years. He was practicing law and negotiating treaties on the side. Can you imagine how that possibly could happen today?

SS: I do not think it would. Do you know that Jay did not want to become chief justice? He had to be talked into it. And if I understand the historical lore, he was placed in that position to get him out as competition for running for president in the future. It did not quite work long-term.

But the point is that at the very beginning, we were thirteen colonies who had become thirteen states. The amount of business for the court was very small. It was also difficult to do. To become a justice, you had to travel the circuits, the different states, by horseback, so it was physically demanding as well. Over time, as the country grew, so did the legal problems, and with it, I think, so did the importance of the court.

DR: As you were beginning your career, you graduated from Yale Law School and then you became a prosecutor working for Robert Morgenthau [then the Manhattan district attorney]. How did that come about? Did you always want to be a prosecutor, or did you have an inspiration to want to work for him?

SS: Perry Mason. Going back to the TV show, that was my initial motivation for becoming a lawyer. In one episode, [Hamilton] Burger, the long-suffering prosecutor who always lost to Perry Mason, met him at a restaurant after he had proven his client not guilty. Perry said to Berger something along the lines of "I know how hard you worked on this case. It must feel a little frustrating to have lost to me." And Burger said, "Yes, I worked hard on the case, but as a prosecutor, I am always seeking justice. And justice means for me that the persons who are guilty are proven guilty, and the people who are not guilty are let free. You proved that the defendant was not guilty, so justice was done."

And I remembered those words when I went through law school. I was not planning then to become a prosecutor. I was following the path of most of my law school friends, who were thinking of joining a law firm. But in my third year, after a chance meeting with the then-legendary Robert Morgenthau at Yale Law School, he invited me to come interview with him, which I did. And the rest is history, because I became convinced that maybe my original thought of becoming a prosecutor was not a bad idea.

DR: You wrote in your book about your life story [*My Beloved World*], which was a bestseller a few years ago, that it was complicated for you, because you were often prosecuting people who came from the same type of neighborhood that you did. You kind of knew the families, in effect, and it was difficult to prosecute those people. Is that a fair statement?

SS: That is a fair statement. It was an emotionally difficult choice. Most of my friends who came from backgrounds like my own felt that people accused of crimes were often not treated fairly in the legal system. They considered it inappropriate for me to think about becoming a prosecutor, and that I should consider becoming a defense attorney instead. I did think about their viewpoint, but I realized for myself that Hamilton Burger's statement — that what prosecutors do is seek justice — had to be my guiding light as a prosecutor. Those who were guilty should be prosecuted and treated fairly under the law and in accordance with the rules of law. And that with those who were not guilty, I had to work just as hard to prove them not guilty. I was a prosecutor who had one of the highest records in my office for top-count convictions, meaning the very top count instead of plea-bargaining it down. I would go to trial and prove those people guilty.

But I also had a fairly high number of dismissals of cases, where I thought that the proof was inadequate to prove the defendant guilty beyond a reasonable doubt. I describe some of those situations in my book.

There is a misunderstanding about the role of lawyers in the judicial system. You are not favoring one side or another when you become a prosecutor or a defense attorney. Both prosecutors and defense attorneys are serving justice. We are each doing our job.

The prosecutor represents the people of the state. The defense attorney represents the defendant. Each of us is ensuring that our legal system is properly working. We are really partners in a common pursuit, and too often people see us as enemies. That is an attitude that should be changed.

DR: I practiced law for a few years in New York, and nobody ever called me up and said, "You know, you should be a judge someday." It never happened, and there was a good reason for that. I wasn't that good a lawyer. But when you practiced law, eventually a number of people recommended you to be a judge. How do you get to be recommended for judge? Who picks federal judges?

SS: Let me start by saying that all federal judges are nominated by the president of the United States and confirmed by the Senate. When I say "all federal judges," I mean district, circuit, and Supreme Court justices.

Every president has a slightly different way of picking their judges. For the longest time, the president would take recommendations from the senators of his state for district court judges, the trial-level judges. Senators of each state, particularly if they were of the same party as the president, could nominate people for the president to consider.

DR: When you're a nominee, who actually interviews you?

SS: Each senator has his or her own method of selecting people. Some senators have a committee of lawyers and academics and other community leaders who interview people seeking nomination and ask them questions. They then make recommendations to the senator, who will likely interview those candidates. Other senators have different ways of doing it and may rely on individuals they know or on staff members. Every senator does it slightly differently. I'm not familiar with all hundred senators' practices today, but a lot of them have review committees of one sort or another.

Once the senator recommends you, every president has a different committee that decides who is going to review each nominee. It is generally someone from the Department of Justice, one or more people from the White House counsel's office, or it could just be an advisor the president trusts with respect to nominations. Again, every president picks his or her own method of selecting who they will nominate.

DR: And how does the court of appeals work? Is that slightly different?

SS: That is slightly different, because as a matter of course, historically, presidents will consider the views of senators — but only consider them, meaning their priority is different for the court of appeals. There are only about two hundred court of appeals judges and there are seven hundred or eight hundred district court judges. For the court of appeals, again, every president has a committee of some sort made up of people from the White House counsel's office, the Department of Justice, and advisors of various kinds, and they get together and supply recommendations to the president.

DR: You were appointed by President Clinton to the court of appeals. Is it unusual to have a Republican president appoint you to one position and then a Democratic president appoint you to another position?

SS: Very unusual. Only a handful of judges and justices have had that happen in their careers.

DR: When you were appointed to the federal district court judgeship, I assume you told your mother about it and she said terrific things. Did you tell her how low the compensation is?

SS: Yes. Senator Moynihan gave me permission to tell my parents that he was going to send my name to the president. He asked me to wait before making a public announcement until he first announced it, but he gave me permission to tell my mother and my then-stepfather.

They came to my home in Brooklyn and I

told them, "Senator Moynihan is going to appoint me to the United States District Court for the Southern District of New York." My mother's custom her entire life has been that every time I get excited, she gets excited. She does not know what has happened, but she gets excited. She did not know what was happening then, and she said to me, "That is wonderful. You are going to make a lot more money, aren't you?" I looked at her and I said, "Mommy, no. I am going to make less money. I am going to take a pay cut. Judges don't make as much as practicing lawyers, and I won't get raises for a very long time." And in fact I had to be on the court for more than fifteen years before I got my first raise.

At any rate, she then looks at me and she says, "That is all right, but you are going to travel as much as you do now, right?" My practice had consisted of international commercial litigation, and I had some very famous clients in Europe and around the world. I had traveled extensively in private practice. And my response to her was, "Well, Mommy, no. My office will be in downtown Manhattan in a courtroom. I really will not travel. People come to me for me to hear their cases as a judge."

I can see her wheels turning in her head, and she looks at me and she says, "Okay, but you're going to meet and befriend as many interesting people as you do now, right? All these famous fashion designers, all of these people involved in wonderful industries around the world, they'll become your friends too." And I looked at her and I said, "No, Mommy, the people who come before me want me to be impartial. So I can't become friendly with them. I won't have the same kinds of relationships I had before."

She finally looked at me and said, after pondering this for a few seconds, "So why are you taking this job?" Interestingly enough, her husband, Omar, said, "Celina, you have to know that if Sonia's excited and she wants to do it, it's because it's something important to do and she will help people doing it." My mom looked at him and said, "You're right. I should know that." It is a perfect explanation of my mother being excited for me, but not always fully understanding why.

DR: How do you prepare for an interview with the president of the United States for an associate justice position? Do you stay up all night preparing?

SS: I called a bunch of friends who had been involved in other administrations to ask them the kinds of questions that tended to be asked during this process. This was a different president. It was President Obama, and this was his first nomination, so no one could tell

669

me what questions his people were likely to ask. But I understood that there was a process, and that there was a likelihood that some questions would be the same over different presidential administrations.

I then sent out an e-mail to my family of law clerks — over seventy of them at the time — and asked them to think of questions I might be asked and issues that I should consider, and to provide me with any reading materials they thought might be helpful to prepare me. I called up some professor friends and asked them to make a list for me of the issues they thought were currently most important before the Supreme Court. I knew what I thought was important, but academics are studying it from a different angle, and so I thought, "Let me get the academics to tell me what they think is important."

The preparation is the way it should be for any job you undertake. You should be talking to other people who have gone through the process, understanding what the job entails before you go in for an interview, and thinking about what your position is on issues that might arise.

DR: When you were interviewed by President Obama, a man who had been the president of the *Harvard Law Review,* did you tell him why you decided not to go to Harvard Law

School and went to Yale Law School instead?

SS: He never asked, believe it or not. Although he did say that the one thing he almost held against me was that I was a Yankees fan.

DR: He was a Chicago Cubs fan.

SS: Exactly.

DR: There's a famous picture of you being sworn in. Your mother is there, holding a family Bible. What is it like to have your mother see you being sworn in as a justice of the Supreme Court?

SS: There is nothing more amazing in one's life than to go further than your dreams. As I explained to you, when I was a child, I never dreamt of being a lawyer, never mind being a Supreme Court justice. I didn't know what that was.

To get to a point where I had achieved something so extraordinary, and being given the gift of sharing that with the most important person in my life, my mother, was such a deeply felt moment. Most of us do not have the privilege of having parents alive at the end of our careers, or at points in our career where we achieve the most. I am eternally grateful that my mom was there.

DR: The salary you get as an associate justice of the Supreme Court is not all that much higher than the salary you got many years ago as a federal district judge. Why is there so little corruption in the federal judiciary system when people are paid so little money, and why are so many people still interested in being judges? Is it because they really want to serve their country?

SS: When you are asked to serve, there is a moral compulsion to serve your country. To be a federal judge is service as a lawyer, the most service that you can do for your country.

You ask a very important question that I have asked in many lectures in which I have talked about judicial ethics. In our country, we take for granted that we have the lowest amount of judicial corruption in the world. We don't pay our judges enough. We pay our federal judges very little. We pay most of our state judges even less. Now, one could always point to a few corruption cases that have been prosecuted, but by and large, we are, in the world, the most respected judicial system. That is because, as a nation, we have insisted on that level of commitment to the rule of law.

DR: If people want to do more for civic education, what can they do? What can an average person do?

SS: Educate yourself. In virtually all states today, there are campaigns aimed at increasing civic education in local schools. In 2010, after an impassioned speech by Sandra Day O'Connor, Florida started a civic education program that has been highly successful. You cannot graduate from, I think, either middle school or high school in Florida unless you can pass that immigration test. It is a simple measure, but a very important one, in having institutionalized civics education in Florida.

There are other states, like Massachusetts, Illinois, Washington, and New York, that have campaigns going on to increase civic education in state school systems. Everybody across the United States should learn more about what those programs are in their individual states.

There are also national programs occurring. iCivics is leading one called "Educating for American Democracy." It is a program looking at establishing a national model of civic education.

There are so many different ways to participate. I tell people it is not just simply politics. There are ways of participating in your community that involve service in so many different ways. You do not have to be a political figure. You just have to be a person who cares.

DR: My final question is this. Suppose somebody says, "I want to be Sonia Sotomayor when I grow up. I want to be a leader. I want to be a great justice." What are the one or two attributes that you would recommend to young women and young men that they develop if they really want to become a leader as they get older?

ss: Passion. That is the first quality. To become a leader, you have to show people that you care deeply about things. People only follow those they think are passionate. So you have to possess passion and, second, commitment driven by dedication and hard work. You do not get anywhere unless you work hard.

I tell kids all the time, "Think of every sports athlete that you admire. They did not wake up a star. They had to work at it. Every basketball star you know has been on the court for hours, days, months, and years, practicing that throw shot." You have to work hard to achieve anything in this life. You have to have perseverance and dedication and a sense of commitment to working hard, to doing things right.

ACKNOWLEDGMENTS

There were many people who helped make this book possible, and I would like to acknowledge here their invaluable help.

Of course, the book could not have been written without the support and cooperation of each of the interviewees, for which I am extremely grateful.

The book also required a world-class publisher, and I was fortunate to again have Simon & Schuster's willingness to publish this work. For that, I am quite appreciative of the support and help of Jonathan Karp, Simon & Schuster's CEO, and Dana Canedy, Simon & Schuster's senior vice president and publisher. And I could not have had a better, more helpful editor than Stuart Roberts.

My relationship with Simon & Schuster was initially made possible by my counsel, advisor and law school friend of forty-plus years, Bob Barnett. His support has been indispensable to this book's being published.

Many of the interviews occurred as part of

675

the Congressional Dialogues series that I have cohosted at the Library of Congress since 2013. Both Jim Billington, who served as Librarian of Congress from 1987 to 2015, and Carla Hayden, who became the Librarian of Congress in 2016, could not have been more helpful. Jim launched the Dialogues with great enthusiasm, and Carla has also been a devoted and totally engaged supporter of the Dialogues.

At the Library, a number of individuals have also been actively involved in helping the Dialogues work so well. Marie Arana has done a spectacular job of working to secure the participation of the authors.

I also helped to start a series of interviews with historians at the New-York Historical Society. Several of the interviews from that series are included in this book. Louise Mirrer, the president and CEO of the society, has worked tirelessly to ensure that this series has worked so well, and I am indebted as well to her for her support of this book.

A few of the interviews occurred as part of the Smithsonian Institution's Great Americans Award Program that I helped to start. Anthea Hartig, the director of the Smithsonian's National Museum of American History, made these interviews possible, for which I am grateful.

I want to thank Doug Bradburn, director of Mount Vernon, for his assistance in making one of the interviews possible.

Another of the interviews was part of the "Peer to Peer" show that I host on Bloomberg TV and PBS. I want to thank the show's producer, Kelly Belknap, for helping to arrange the interview.

And, finally, one of the interviews occurred as part of a series at the Kennedy Center. I appreciate the center's president, Deborah Rutter, making this interview possible.

As with my other books, this one could not have been completed without all of the able and tireless editing by Jennifer Howard of the interviews and my introductory summaries. Jennifer is a consummate editor (and writer) whose introduction to me by Marie Arana has been a real godsend.

My longtime personal staff members have also been invaluable in making this book possible. MaryPat Decker, my chief of staff, made the whole process of getting this book put together possible (most especially coordinating my schedule with all of the others involved in doing the interviews and assembling the book). Both Laura Boring and Amanda Mangum helped immeasurably in preparing the texts of my own introductory pieces. And Robert Haben and Trenton Pfister, my research associates, were tireless and indispensable in gathering the information needed to help me prepare for the interviews. I would also like to thank Mandeep Singh

Sandhu for all of his help with the audio and video technical aspects of many of these interviews.

I would also like to thank my partners at Carlyle, particularly my cofounders, Bill Conway and Dan D'Aniello, for their long-time forbearance as I worked on these interviews, this book, and so many other non-Carlyle projects over the past thirty-plus years.

Inevitably, there will be some mistakes in what I have written in this book. The buck stops with the author, and I therefore take responsibility for all of these mistakes.

678

ABOUT THE CONTRIBUTORS

Madeleine K. Albright is a professor, author, diplomat, and businesswoman who served as the sixty-fourth secretary of state of the United States. In 1997, she was named the first female secretary of state and became, at that time, the highest-ranking woman in the history of the U.S. government. From 1993 to 1997, Dr. Albright served as the U.S. permanent representative to the United Nations and was a member of the president's cabinet. She is a professor in the practice of diplomacy at the Georgetown University School of Foreign Service. Dr. Albright is chair of Albright Stonebridge Group, a global strategy firm, and chair of Albright Capital Management LLC, an investment advisory firm focused on emerging markets. She also chairs the National Democratic Institute and is honorary chair of the World Refugee & Migration Council. In 2012, she was chosen by President Obama to receive the nation's highest civilian honor, the Presidential Medal of Freedom, in recognition of her contributions to international peace and democracy. Dr. Albright is a seven-time *New York Times* bestselling author. Her most recent book, *Hell and Other Destinations,* was published in April 2020. Her other books include *Madam Secretary: A Memoir* (2003) and *Fascism: A Warning* (2018).

Danielle S. Allen is James Bryant Conant University Professor at Harvard University. She is a political philosopher and public policy expert who focuses on democracy innovation, public health and health equity, justice reform, education, and political economy. She also directs the Democratic Knowledge Project, a K-16 civic education provider. Her books include *Our Declaration: A Reading of the Declaration of Independence in Defense of Equality, Cuz: An American Tragedy,* and *Talking to Strangers: Anxieties of Citizenship Since* Brown v. Board of Education. She has chaired numerous commission processes and is a lead author on influential policy road maps, including *Pursuing Excellence on a Foundation of Inclusion, Roadmap to Pandemic Resilience, Pandemic Resilience: Getting It Done, Our Common Purpose: Reinventing American Democracy for the 21st Century,* and *Educating for American Democracy: Excellence in History and Civics for All Learn-*

ers K-12. She was for many years a contributing columnist for the *Washington Post* and writes for the *Atlantic.*

Michael Beschloss is an award-winning historian, scholar of leadership, and best-selling author of ten books, most recently the acclaimed *New York Times* and *Wall Street Journal* best-seller *Presidents of War.* Beschloss appears regularly on television as the NBC News presidential historian and as a contributor to the *PBS NewsHour.* He has also been a contributing columnist to the *New York Times.* He has won an Emmy for his television work and received six honorary degrees and numerous other awards. He has the largest Twitter following of any American historian, more than half a million. Born in Chicago, Beschloss is an alumnus of Phillips Academy (Andover) and Williams College, where he studied under James MacGregor Burns, author of what remains the classic book on leadership. At the Harvard Business School, Beschloss studied leadership in both the private and public sectors. He has served as a historian at the Smithsonian, a scholar at the University of Oxford, and a senior fellow of the Annenberg Foundation. Among his earlier books are two volumes on Lyndon Johnson's secret tapes; *The Conquerors,* about Franklin Roosevelt, Nazi Germany, and the

Holocaust; and *Presidential Courage.* He is also coauthor (with Caroline Kennedy) of the number-one global bestseller *Jacqueline Kennedy: Historic Conversations on Life with John F. Kennedy.*

David W. Blight is Sterling Professor of History and director of the Gilder Lehrman Center for the Study of Slavery, Resistance, and Abolition at Yale University. He previously taught at North Central College in Illinois, Harvard University, and Amherst College. He is the author or editor of a dozen books, including *Frederick Douglass: Prophet of Freedom; American Oracle: The Civil War in the Civil Rights Era; Race and Reunion: The Civil War in American Memory;* and annotated editions of Douglass's first two autobiographies. He has worked on Douglass much of his professional life and has been awarded the Pulitzer Prize, the Bancroft Prize, the Abraham Lincoln Prize, and the Frederick Douglass Prize, among others. He writes frequently for the popular press, including the *Atlantic,* the *New York Times,* and many other publications. His lecture course on the Civil War and Reconstruction era at Yale is online at oyc.yale.edu/history/hist-119. Blight has always been a teacher first. At the beginning of his career, he spent seven years as a high school history teacher in his hometown of Flint, Michigan. Blight maintains a website including information about public lectures, books, articles, and interviews at www.davidwblight.com.

Mark Bradford is a contemporary artist known for his large-scale abstract paintings created out of paper. Characterized by its layered formal, material, and conceptual complexity, his work explores social and political structures that objectify marginalized communities and the bodies of vulnerable populations. After accumulating layers of various types of paper onto canvas, Bradford excavates their surfaces using power tools to explore economic and social structures that define contemporary subjects. His practice includes painting, sculpture, video, photography, printmaking, and other media. In addition to his studio practice, Bradford engages in social projects alongside exhibitions of his work that bring contemporary ideas outside the walls of exhibition spaces and into communities with limited exposure to art. Bradford received his BFA from the California Institute of the Arts (CalArts) in 1995 and his MFA from CalArts in 1997. He has since been widely exhibited internationally and received numerous awards. Recent solo exhibitions have taken place at the Modern Art Museum of Fort Worth; Hauser & Wirth, London; the Hirshhorn

Museum and Sculpture Garden, Washington, D.C.; and Long Museum West Bund, Shanghai.

Catherine Brekus is Charles Warren Professor of the History of Religion in America at Harvard Divinity School. Her research focuses on the relationship between religion and American culture, with particular emphasis on the history of women, gender, Christianity, and the evangelical movement. She is the author of many articles and books, including *Strangers and Pilgrims: Female Preaching in America, 1740–1845,* which explores the rise of female preaching during the eighteenth and early nineteenth centuries, and *Sarah Osborn's World: The Rise of Evangelicalism in Early America,* which argues that the evangelical movement emerged in dialogue with the Enlightenment. A companion volume, *Sarah Osborn's Collected Writings,* is a critical edition of some of Osborn's eighteenth-century manuscripts. Brekus is also the editor of *The Religious History of American Women: Reimagining the Past,* a collection of essays that asks how women's history changes our understanding of American religion, and the coeditor (with W. Clark Gilpin) of *American Christianities: A History of Dominance and Diversity,* an introduction to the multiple forms of Christian expression in the United States. Brekus has received several awards, including a John Simon Guggenheim Memorial Foundation Fellowship, a Henry Luce III Faculty Fellowship in Theology, and a Pew Faculty Fellowship in Religion and American History.

Douglas Brinkley is the Katherine Tsanoff Brown Chair in Humanities and professor of history at Rice University, the CNN presidential historian, and a contributing editor at *Vanity Fair*. He works in many capacities in the world of public history, including on boards, museums, colleges, and historical societies. The *Chicago Tribune* dubbed him "America's New Past Master." The New-York Historical Society has chosen Brinkley their official U.S. presidential historian. His book *Cronkite* won the Sperber Prize, while *The Great Deluge: Hurricane Katrina, New Orleans, and the Mississippi Gulf Coast* received the Robert F. Kennedy Book Award. He has received a Grammy Award for *Presidential Suite* and seven honorary doctorates in American studies. His two-volume annotated *The Nixon Tapes* won the Arthur S. Link-Warren F. Kuehl Prize. His most recent book, *American Moonshot: John F. Kennedy and the Great Space Race,* was a *New York Times* best-seller. He is a member of the Century Association, Council of Foreign Relations, and the James Madison Council of the Library of Congress. He lives in Austin, Texas, with his wife and three children.

Ken Burns has been making documentary films for more than forty years. Since the Academy Award–nominated *Brooklyn Bridge* in 1981, Ken has gone on to direct and produce some of the most acclaimed historical documentaries ever made, including *The Civil War, Baseball, Jazz, The War, The National Parks: America's Best Idea, The Roosevelts: An Intimate History, Jackie Robinson, The Vietnam War,* and *Country Music.* Future film projects include *Muhammad Ali, Benjamin Franklin, The Holocaust and the United States, The American Buffalo, Leonardo da Vinci, The American Revolution, Emancipation to Exodus,* and *LBJ & the Great Society,* among others. Ken's films have been honored with dozens of major awards, including sixteen Emmy Awards, two Grammy Awards, and two Oscar nominations; and in September 2008, at the News & Documentary Emmy Awards, Ken was honored by the National Academy of Television Arts & Sciences with a Lifetime Achievement Award.

Francis S. Collins, MD, PhD, was appointed the sixteenth director of the National Institutes of Health (NIH) by President

Barack Obama and confirmed by the Senate. In 2017, President Donald Trump asked Dr. Collins to continue to serve as the NIH director. President Joe Biden did the same in 2021. Dr. Collins is the only presidentially appointed NIH director to serve more than one administration. In this role, Dr. Collins oversees the work of the largest supporter of biomedical research in the world, spanning the spectrum from basic to clinical research. Dr. Collins is a physician-geneticist noted for his landmark discoveries of disease genes and his leadership of the international Human Genome Project, which culminated in April 2003 with the completion of a finished sequence of the human DNA instruction book. He served as director of the National Human Genome Research Institute at NIH from 1993 to 2008. Dr. Collins is an elected member of both the National Academy of Medicine and the National Academy of Sciences, was awarded the Presidential Medal of Freedom in November 2007, and received the National Medal of Science in 2009. In 2020, he was named the fiftieth winner of the Templeton Prize, which celebrates scientific and spiritual curiosity.

Philip J. Deloria is the Leverett Saltonstall Professor of History at Harvard University, where his research and teaching focus on the social, cultural, and political histories of the relations among American Indian peoples and the United States. He is the author of several books, including *Playing Indian* (Yale University Press, 1998), *Indians in Unexpected Places* (University Press of Kansas, 2004), *American Studies: A User's Guide* (University of California Press, 2017) with Alexander Olson, and *Becoming Mary Sully: Toward an American Indian Abstract* (University of Washington Press, 2019), as well as two coedited books and numerous articles and chapters. Deloria received a PhD in American studies from Yale University in 1994, taught at the University of Colorado, and then, from 2001 to 2017, at the University of Michigan before joining the faculty at Harvard in January 2018. Deloria is a trustee of the Smithsonian Institution's National Museum of the American Indian. He is former president of the American Studies Association, an elected member of the American Academy of Arts and Sciences, the recipient of numerous prizes and recognitions, and will serve as president of the Organization of American Historians in 2022.

Lillian Faderman is the author of several award-winning books of lesbian, gay, and LGBTQ history, including *Surpassing the Love of Men: Romantic Friendship and Love Between Women from the Renaissance to the*

Present, Odd Girls and Twilight Lovers: A History of Lesbian Life in Twentieth-Century America, The Gay Revolution: The Story of the Struggle, and *Harvey Milk: His Lives and Death.* Her memoir, *Naked in the Promised Land,* was reissued by Bloomsbury Press in 2020.

Drew Gilpin Faust is the Arthur Kingsley Porter University Professor at Harvard University, where she served as president from 2007 to 2018. Faust was the founding dean of Harvard's Radcliffe Institute for Advanced Study (2001–2007). Before coming to Radcliffe, she was the Annenberg Professor of History at the University of Pennsylvania, where she was a member of the faculty for twenty-five years. She is the author of six books, including most recently *This Republic of Suffering: Death and the American Civil War* (2008), which was awarded the 2009 Bancroft Prize, the New-York Historical Society's 2009 American History Book Prize, and was recognized by the *New York Times* as one of the "Ten Best Books of 2008." Faust is a contributing writer at the *Atlantic.* Her honors include awards for distinguished teaching at the University of Pennsylvania. In 2018, she was awarded the John W. Kluge Prize for Achievement in the Study of Humanity by the Library of Congress. She received her bachelor's degree from Bryn Mawr in 1968, magna cum laude with honors in history, and master's (1971) and doctoral (1975) degrees in American civilization from the University of Pennsylvania.

Henry Louis Gates Jr. is the Alphonse Fletcher University Professor and director of the Hutchins Center for African & African American Research at Harvard University. Emmy and Peabody Award–winning film-maker, literary scholar, journalist, cultural critic, and institution builder, Professor Gates has authored or coauthored more than twenty books and created more than twenty documentary films, including *The African Americans: Many Rivers to Cross; Black in Latin America; Black America Since MLK: And Still I Rise; Africa's Great Civilizations; Reconstruction: America After the Civil War; The Black Church: This Is Our Story, This Is Our Song;* and *Finding Your Roots,* his groundbreaking genealogy series on PBS. Gates was a member of the first class awarded "Genius Grants" by the MacArthur Foundation in 1981, and in 1998 he became the first African American scholar to be awarded the National Humanities Medal. A native of Piedmont, West Virginia, Gates earned his BA in history from Yale University in 1973 and his MA and PhD in English literature from Clare College at the University of Cambridge in 1979. A former chair of the Pulitzer Prize board, he is a member of the American Academy of Arts and Letters and serves on a wide array of boards, including the New York Public Library, the NAACP Legal Defense Fund, the Aspen Institute, and the Brookings Institution.

Donald E. Graham has been the chairman of the board of the Graham Holdings Company (previously the Washington Post Company) since 1993. He was chief executive officer of the company from May 1991 until November 2015. He was publisher of the *Washington Post* newspaper from January 1979 until September 2000. Graham was born on April 22, 1945, in Baltimore, Maryland, a son of Philip L. and Katharine Meyer Graham. After graduating from college in 1966, Graham was drafted and served as an information specialist with the 1st Cavalry Division in Vietnam from 1967 to 1968. He was a patrolman with the Washington Metropolitan Police Department from January 1969 to June 1970. Graham joined the *Washington Post* newspaper in 1971 as a reporter. He is a cofounder of TheDream.US, the largest national scholarship fund for Dreamers. Previously, he served as chairman of the District of Columbia College Access Program. He remains a member of the DC-CAP board. DC-CAP has assisted more than

23,000 D.C. students enroll in college and has provided scholarships totaling more than $33 million. Graham is a trustee of the Federal City Council and Gates Policy Initiative.

Walter Isaacson, a professor of history at Tulane University, has been CEO of the Aspen Institute, chair of CNN, and editor of *Time*. He is the author of *Leonardo da Vinci; The Innovators; Steve Jobs; Einstein: His Life and Universe; Benjamin Franklin: An American Life;* and *Kissinger: A Biography,* and the coauthor of *The Wise Men: Six Friends and the World They Made.*

Jack Jacobs received bachelor's and master's degrees from Rutgers University and served in the U.S. Army for twenty years, retiring as a colonel. For his actions in Vietnam, he was awarded three Bronze Stars, two Silver Stars, and the Medal of Honor, the nation's highest combat decoration. After retiring from the army, he founded a securitization firm, subsequently sold to Key Bank, and he was a managing director of Bankers Trust, where he ran foreign exchange options, and, subsequently, of Lehman Brothers, where he established an institutional hedge fund business. He is an on-air analyst for NBC News and MSNBC and serves on a number of corporate and charity boards. His memoir, *If Not Now, When?,* won a Colby Award, and he was an executive producer of the series *Ten Weeks,* which will appear on Hulu.

Billie Jean King was named one of the "100 Most Important Americans of the 20th Century" by *Life* magazine and is a 2009 recipient of the Presidential Medal of Freedom. She is the founder of the Billie Jean King Leadership Initiative, founder of the Women's Tennis Association and the Women's Sports Foundation, and part of the ownership group of the Los Angeles Dodgers, Los Angeles Sparks, and Angel City FC. In September 2020, King became the first woman to have an annual global team sports event named in her honor when Fed Cup, the women's world cup of tennis, was rebranded as the Billie Jean King Cup. The National Tennis Center, home of the U.S. Open, was renamed the USTA Billie Jean King National Tennis Center in 2006 in honor of her accomplishments on and off the court. King serves on the board of the Women's Sports Foundation, is an Adidas Global Ambassador, and is a past member of the board of the Elton John AIDS Foundation and a past member of the President's Council on Fitness, Sports and Nutrition. Her memoir, *All In: An Autobiography,* was published by Knopf in August 2021.

Jill Lepore is the David Woods Kemper '41 Professor of American History at Harvard University. She is also a staff writer at the *New Yorker,* and the host of the podcast *The Last Archive.* A prize-winning professor, she teaches classes in evidence, historical methods, humanistic inquiry, and American history. Much of her scholarship explores absences and asymmetries in the historical record, with a particular emphasis on the history and technology of evidence. As a wide-ranging and prolific essayist, Lepore writes about American history, law, literature, and politics. She is the author of many award-winning books, including the international best-seller *These Truths: A History of the United States* (2018). Her latest book, *If Then: How the Simulmatics Corporation Invented the Future,* is long-listed for the National Book Award.

Wynton Marsalis, world-renowned trumpeter, bandleader, and composer, is a leading advocate of American culture. Wynton assembled his own band in 1981 and began touring, performing more than 120 concerts annually for fifteen consecutive years. With the power of his musicianship, the infectious sound of his swinging bands, and a far-reaching series of performances and music workshops, Marsalis rekindled interest in jazz worldwide, inspiring a renaissance that attracted a new generation of fine young talent to jazz. Marsalis has recorded more than one hundred jazz and classical recordings, garnering nine Grammy Awards and selling more than seven million copies worldwide. In 1997, Marsalis became the first jazz artist to be awarded the prestigious Pulitzer Prize in Music for his oratorio *Blood on the Fields.* Marsalis is a 2021 inductee into the American Academy of Arts and Letters; he was honored with the National Humanities Medal by Barack Obama and holds honorary degrees from more than thirty colleges and universities across the nation. As an educator, Wynton reaches students through innumerable avenues, from his children's books to his Jazz for Young People concerts and his Harvard lecture series. Marsalis presently serves as managing and artistic director of Jazz at Lincoln Center and director of jazz studies at Juilliard.

David McCullough has been acclaimed as a "master of the art of narrative history." He has written twelve books that have been published in nineteen languages. He is twice winner of the Pulitzer Prize, twice winner of the National Book Award, and has received the Presidential Medal of Freedom, the nation's highest civilian award. As may be said of few writers, none of his books has ever been out of print. In the words of the citation accompanying his honorary degree from Yale, "As an historian, he paints with words, giving us pictures of the American people that live, breathe, and above all, confront the fundamental issues of courage, achievement, and moral character." Born in Pittsburgh in 1933, he was educated there and at Yale. He has enjoyed a lifelong interest in art and architecture and is as well a devoted painter. He and his wife, Rosalee Barnes McCullough, have five children and nineteen grandchildren.

Jon Meacham is a Pulitzer Prize–winning biographer. The author of the *New York Times* best-sellers *Thomas Jefferson: The Art of Power, American Lion: Andrew Jackson in the White House, Franklin and Winston, Destiny and Power: The American Odyssey of George Herbert Walker Bush,* and *The Soul of America: The Battle for Our Better Angels,* he is a distinguished visiting professor at Vanderbilt University, a contributing writer for the *New York Times Book Review,* and a fellow of the Society of American Historians. Meacham lives in Nashville and in Sewanee with his wife and children.

Rita Moreno has won all four of the most

prestigious awards in show business: an Oscar, a Tony, two Emmys, and a Grammy. Moreno has starred on Broadway and London's West End, appeared in more than forty feature films, and has performed in numerous regional theaters, including her one-woman show, *Life Without Makeup,* at the Berkeley Repertory Theatre. Moreno recently costarred in the Latinx reimagining of Norman Lear's classic sitcom *One Day at a Time.* Her critically acclaimed documentary, *Rita Moreno: Just a Girl Who Decided to Go for It,* debuted at the Sundance Film Festival and had its worldwide theatrical release in summer 2021. Moreno also costars in and is an executive producer of the Steven Spielberg remake of *West Side Story,* scheduled for December 2021 release. A recipient of the Peabody Career Achievement Award and the Kennedy Center Honor for her lifetime contributions to American culture, she was also honored by her peers as the fiftieth recipient of the Screen Actors Guild Life Achievement Award. Moreno's all-Spanish-language album, *Una Vez Más,* was produced by her good friend Emilio Estefan, and she is a *New York Times* bestselling author with her first book, *Rita Moreno: A Memoir.* Moreno has received the Presidential Medal of Freedom from President George W. Bush and the National Medal of Arts from President Barack Obama.

Cal Ripken Jr. is baseball's all-time Iron Man. He retired from baseball in October 2021, after twenty-one seasons with his hometown Baltimore Orioles. During his career he was Rookie of the Year, a nineteen-time All-Star, a two-time AL MVP, and is one of only ten players in history to amass over 400 home runs and 3,000 hits. In 2007 he was inducted into the National Baseball Hall of Fame. In 1995, Ripken broke Lou Gehrig's Major League record for consecutive games played (2,130) and voluntarily ended his streak on September 20, 1998, after playing 2,632 consecutive games. Today Ripken is a successful business leader and philanthropist. He owns and operates Ripken Baseball, which runs youth baseball and softball complexes that host thousands of young ballplayers each year. He also owns the Aberdeen IronBirds, a Baltimore Orioles minor league affiliate that plays in his hometown in Maryland. In 2001, Cal and his family established the Cal Ripken Sr. Foundation in memory of the family's patriarch. Since its inception, the foundation has impacted over 10 million kids in underserved communities, providing them with safe places to play and learn. Since 2007 Cal has served as a Special Public Diplomacy Envoy to the U.S. State Department and has traveled internationally on goodwill trips using baseball to bring people together.

Sonia Sotomayor was born in the Bronx, New York, on June 25, 1954. She earned a BA in 1976 from Princeton University, graduating summa cum laude and receiving the university's highest academic honor. In 1979, she earned a JD from Yale Law School, where she served as an editor of the *Yale Law Journal.* She served as assistant district attorney in the New York County District Attorney's Office from 1979 to 1984. She then litigated international commercial matters in New York City at Pavia & Harcourt, where she served as an associate and then partner from 1984 to 1992. In 1991, President George H. W. Bush nominated her to the U.S. District Court, Southern District of New York, and she served in that role from 1992 to 1998. She served as a judge on the United States Court of Appeals for the Second Circuit from 1998 to 2009. President Barack Obama nominated her as an associate justice of the Supreme Court on May 26, 2009, and she assumed this role August 8, 2009.

Bhu Srinivasan is a writer focused on the history of business and capitalism. Starting from the days of the Internet's commercialization in the 1990s, his career has spanned across ventures in digital media, pop culture, technology, and financial data. Srinivasan arrived in the United States with his family at the age of eight, and as a child lived in the

South, the Rust Belt, Southern California, and the Pacific Northwest. He lives in Marin County, California, with his wife and four children.

Elaine Weiss is a journalist and author whose feature writing has been recognized with prizes from the Society of Professional Journalists, and her byline has appeared in many national publications. Her first book, *Fruits of Victory,* explored an organization of women activists during WWI. Her next, *The Woman's Hour: The Great Fight to Win the Vote* (Viking/Penguin), won critical acclaim from the *New York Times, Wall Street Journal,* and the *New Yorker,* and was hailed as a "riveting, nail-biting political thriller" with powerful parallels to today's political environment. *The Woman's Hour* was a Goodreads Choice Award winner, was short-listed for the 2019 Chautauqua Prize, and received the American Bar Association's highest honor, the Silver Gavel Award, also in 2019. Weiss is a popular speaker and media commentator on the themes of women's history and political organization as well as voting rights. She lives in Baltimore.

Jia Lynn Yang is national editor at the *New York Times.* Before joining the *Times* in 2017, she was deputy national security editor at the *Washington Post,* where she was part of a team that won a Pulitzer Prize for coverage of Trump and Russia. Before becoming an editor, Yang wrote about business and economics at the *Post* and at *Fortune* magazine for over a decade. Yang's family immigrated to the United States from Taiwan in the 1970s and was able to stay in the country thanks to the 1965 Immigration and Nationality Act. *One Mighty and Irresistible Tide* is her effort to understand the people who fought to give her family a place in America.

APPENDIX I:
CITIZENSHIP TEST

A major part of the American Experiment has been immigration. More than any other country, the United States was built and largely populated by immigrants and their descendants.

Today, out of a U.S. population of roughly 331 million people, about 46 million are immigrants, and 40 million are second-generation Americans. At the country's outset, there were essentially no constraints on who could enter the country, or even who could become citizens.

But in 1790, as the new U.S. government was getting organized under the Constitution, legislation was passed to permit immigrants who were white, over twenty-one, and residents of the U.S. for two years to petition a federal court for citizenship.

Five years later, the residency requirement was extended to five years, and an affidavit of a U.S. citizen witness vouching that the applicant "possessed a good moral character" was added. From 1795 to 1906, requirements for citizenship changed — an oath to support the Constitution was added; previous citizenship (and any nobility title) had to be renounced; and Blacks were finally permitted to become citizens after the Fourteenth Amendment was ratified in 1868.

In 1906, under new legislation, a Bureau of Immigration and Naturalization was created; an English literacy test was essentially established (later officially required in 1917); and federal judges (who administered the citizenship process) were allowed to ask questions about U.S. history and civics — though no preparatory materials were provided and each judge was the sole arbiter of the answers' accuracy.

In subsequent years, different requirements were imposed before citizenship was granted — literacy; nationality quotas; basic verbal English proficiency; race and ethnicity. From time to time, these requirements were amended, allowed to lapse, or made more precise.

But not until new legislation was enacted in 1990 was the process of judicial admission ended; federal naturalization examiners would now review whether the applicants met the various standards, and judges would be limited to administering the oath of allegiance to the United States.

As part of the citizenship process, a requirement was established in 1952 to ensure that the prospective citizen had a "knowledge and understanding of the fundamentals of the history, and of the principles and form of government, of the United States."

In short, a history and civics requirement was imposed. This was met in a variety of ways, but the current system provides prospective citizens with materials outlining one hundred potential questions in the American history and civics area. The prospective citizens can study these questions and appear for the test when they are ready to do so.

When an applicant is being considered for citizenship, the examiner (now a U.S. Citizenship and Immigration Services officer) orally asks the applicant ten of the potential one hundred questions. Six correct answers are required to pass.*

* On November 13, 2020, U.S. Citizenship and Immigration Services announced a revised version of the civics test. Under the revised version, the list of potential test questions increased from 100 to 128, the number of test questions asked increased from 10 to 20, and the number of correct answers required to pass increased from 6 to 12. The test score required to pass (60 percent correct) did not change. The revised version was viewed by some as an effort by the Trump administration to make the test more difficult. On February 22, 2021, under

Currently, about 91 percent of prospective citizens pass both this test (presumably after some studying of the potential one hundred questions) and the English proficiency test (the other component of the citizenship test).

The questions are basic ones, and it would be presumed that nonnaturalized Americans — who likely had the benefit of civics or history classes in school — would be able to readily pass the same test.

That presumption, it turns out, is wrong. In 2018, the Woodrow Wilson National Fellowship Foundation (now the Institute for Citizens and Scholars) created a process under which mostly natural-born Americans (who volunteered to participate in advance) were given five minutes to complete an online, multiple-choice survey. Twenty questions were chosen, at random, from the standard citizenship one hundred–question list.

The results were largely shocking. Forty-one thousand adults (approximately 90 percent were U.S. citizens at birth) from all

---

the Biden administration, U.S. Citizenship and Immigration Services announced it would revert back to the previous version of the test, which had been in use since October 1, 2008. The version implemented under the Trump administration was phased out on April 19, 2021.

fifty states and the District of Columbia participated. In only one state (Vermont) did a majority (53 percent) of the respondents pass (i.e. getting twelve questions correct out of the twenty that were asked). In forty-nine other states and the District, a majority of those interviewed could not answer correctly twelve questions out of the twenty asked.

How would you do in taking this portion of the U.S. citizenship test?

The actual test involves ten questions out of a potential one hundred. I have included over the next few pages those one hundred questions (available on the U.S. Citizenship and Immigration Services website, uscis.gov/citizenship). I have arranged them in a format of ten questions — and thus there are in effect ten tests. The questions are in nine categories; in each mini test, I have included one question from each of the categories to the extent possible. Take any one of the ten tests — or all of them — to gauge your own ability to pass this basic civics and history test.

U.S. Citizenship — Sample Test One

1. What is the supreme law of the land?
2. Name one branch or part of the government.
3. There are four amendments to the Constitution about who can vote.

Describe one of them.

4. What is one reason colonists came to America?
5. What territory did the United States buy from France in 1803?
6. Name one war fought by the United States in the 1900s.
7. Name one of the two longest rivers in the United States.
8. Why does the flag have 13 stripes?
9. When do we celebrate Independence Day?
10. What stops one branch of government from becoming too powerful?

U.S. Citizenship — Sample Test Two

1. What does the Constitution do?
2. Who is in charge of the executive branch?
3. What is one responsibility that is only for United States citizens?
4. Who lived in America before the Europeans arrived?
5. Name one war fought by the United States in the 1800s.
6. Who was President during World War I?
7. What ocean is on the West Coast of the United States?
8. Why does the flag have 50 stars?
9. Name two national U.S. holidays.

10. Who makes federal laws?

U.S. Citizenship — Sample Test Three

1. What is an amendment?
2. What are the two parts of the U.S. Congress?
3. Name one right only for United States citizens.
4. What group of people was taken to America and sold as slaves?
5. Name the U.S. war between the North and the South.
6. Who was President during the Great Depression and World War II?
7. What ocean is on the East Coast of the United States?
8. What is the name of the national anthem?
9. How many U.S. Senators are there?
10. We elect a U.S. Senator for how many years?

U.S. Citizenship — Sample Test Four

1. What do we call the first ten amendments to the Constitution?
2. Who is one of your state's U.S. Senators now?
3. What are two rights of everyone living in the United States?

4. Why did the colonists fight the British?
5. Name one problem that led to the Civil War.
6. Who did the United States fight in World War II?
7. Name one U.S. territory.
8. The House of Representatives has how many voting members?
9. We elect a U.S. Representative for how many years?
10. Name your U.S. Representative.

U.S. Citizenship — Sample Test Five

1. What is one right or freedom from the First Amendment?
2. Who does a U.S. Senator represent?
3. What do we show loyalty to when we say the Pledge of Allegiance?
4. Who wrote the Declaration of Independence?
5. What was one important thing that Abraham Lincoln did?
6. Before he was President, Eisenhower was a general. What war was he in?
7. Name one state that borders Canada.
8. Why do some states have more Representatives than other states?
9. We elect a President for how many years?

10. In what month do we vote for President?

U.S. Citizenship — Sample Test Six

1. How many amendments does the Constitution have?
2. What is the name of the President of the United States now?
3. What is one promise you make when you become a United States citizen?
4. When was the Declaration of Independence adopted?
5. What did the Emancipation Proclamation do?
6. During the Cold War, what was the main concern of the United States?
7. Name one state that borders Mexico.
8. What is the name of the Vice President of the United States now?
9. If the President can no longer serve, who becomes President?
10. If both the President and the Vice President can no longer serve, who becomes President?

U.S. Citizenship — Sample Test Seven

1. What did the Declaration of Independence do?
2. Who is the Commander in Chief of the military?

3. How old do citizens have to be to vote for President?
4. There were 13 original states. Name three.
5. What did Susan B. Anthony do?
6. What movement tried to end racial discrimination?
7. What is the capital of the United States?
8. Who signs bills to become laws?
9. Who vetoes bills?
10. What does the President's Cabinet do?

U.S. Citizenship — Sample Test Eight

1. What are two rights in the Declaration of Independence?
2. What are two Cabinet-level positions?
3. What are two ways that Americans can participate in their democracy?
4. What happened at the Constitutional Convention?
5. What did Martin Luther King Jr. do?
6. Where is the Statue of Liberty?
7. What does the judicial branch do?
8. What is the highest court in the United States?
9. How many justices are on the Supreme Court?
10. Who is the Chief Justice of the

United States now?

U.S. Citizenship — Sample Test Nine

1. What is freedom of religion?
2. Under our Constitution, some powers belong to the federal government. What is one power of the federal government?
3. When is the last day you can send in federal income tax forms?
4. When was the Constitution written?
5. What major event happened on September 11, 2001, in the United States?
6. What is the economic system in the United States?
7. Under our Constitution, some powers belong to the states. What is one power of the states?
8. Who is the Governor of your state now?
9. What is the capital of your state?
10. The Federalist Papers supported the passage of the U.S. Constitution. Name one of the writers.

U.S. Citizenship — Sample Test Ten

1. What is the "rule of law"?
2. What are the two major political parties in the United States?

3. When must all men register for the Selective Service?

4. What is one thing Benjamin Franklin is famous for?

5. Name one American Indian tribe in the United States.

6. The idea of self-government is in the first three words of the Constitution. What are these words?

7. What is the political party of the President now?

8. What is the name of the Speaker of the House of Representatives now?

9. Who is the "Father of Our Country"?

10. Who was the first President?

SOLUTIONS

U.S. Citizenship — Sample Test One

1. What is the supreme law of the land?
   - the Constitution

2. Name one branch or part of the government.
   - Congress
   - legislative
   - President
   - executive
   - the courts
   - judicial

3. There are four amendments to the Constitution about who can vote. Describe one of them.
   - Citizens eighteen (18) and older (can vote).
   - You don't have to pay (a poll tax) to vote.
   - Any citizen can vote. (Women and men can vote.)
   - A male citizen of any race (can vote).

4. What is one reason colonists came to America?
   - freedom
   - political liberty
   - religious freedom
   - economic opportunity
   - practice their religion
   - escape persecution

5. What territory did the United States buy from France in 1803?
   - the Louisiana Territory
   - Louisiana

6. Name one war fought by the United States in the 1900s.
   - World War I
   - World War II
   - Korean War
   - Vietnam War
   - (Persian) Gulf War

7. Name one of the two longest rivers in the United States.
   - Missouri (River)
   - Mississippi (River)

8. Why does the flag have 13 stripes?
   - because there were 13 original colonies
   - because the stripes represent the original colonies

9. When do we celebrate Independence Day?
   - July 4

10. What stops one branch of government from becoming too powerful?
    - checks and balances
    - separation of powers

U.S. Citizenship — Sample Test Two

1. What does the Constitution do?
   - sets up the government
   - defines the government
   - protects basic rights of Americans

2. Who is in charge of the executive branch?
   - the President

3. What is one responsibility that is

716

only for United States citizens?

- serve on a jury
- vote in a federal election

4. Who lived in America before the Europeans arrived?
   - American Indians
   - Native Americans

5. Name one war fought by the United States in the 1800s.
   - War of 1812
   - Mexican-American War
   - Civil War
   - Spanish-American War

6. Who was President during World War I?
   - (Woodrow) Wilson

7. What ocean is on the West Coast of the United States?
   - Pacific (Ocean)

8. Why does the flag have 50 stars?
   - because there is one star for each state
   - because each star represents a state
   - because there are 50 states

9. Name two national U.S. holidays.
   - New Year's Day

- Martin Luther King Jr. Day
- Presidents' Day
- Memorial Day
- Independence Day
- Labor Day
- Columbus Day
- Veterans Day
- Thanksgiving
- Christmas

10. Who makes federal laws?
    - Congress
    - Senate and House (of Representatives)
    - (U.S. or national) legislature

U.S. Citizenship — Sample Test Three

1. What is an amendment?
    - a change (to the Constitution)
    - an addition (to the Constitution)

2. What are the two parts of the U.S. Congress?
    - the Senate and House (of Representatives)

3. Name one right only for United States citizens.
    - vote in a federal election
    - run for federal office

4. What group of people was taken to America and sold as slaves?
   - Africans
   - people from Africa

5. Name the U.S. war between the North and the South.
   - the Civil War
   - the War between the States

6. Who was President during the Great Depression and World War II?
   - (Franklin) Roosevelt

7. What ocean is on the East Coast of the United States?
   - Atlantic (Ocean)

8. What is the name of the national anthem?
   - The Star-Spangled Banner

9. How many U.S. Senators are there?
   - one hundred (100)

10. We elect a U.S. Senator for how many years?
    - six (6)

U.S. Citizenship — Sample Test Four

1. What do we call the first ten amend-

ments to the Constitution?
- the Bill of Rights

2. Who is one of your state's U.S. Senators now?
   - Answers will vary. [District of Columbia residents and residents of U.S. territories should answer that D.C. (or the territory where the applicant lives) has no U.S. Senators.]

3. What are two rights of everyone living in the United States?
   - freedom of expression
   - freedom of speech
   - freedom of assembly
   - freedom to petition the government
   - freedom of religion
   - the right to bear arms

4. Why did the colonists fight the British?
   - because of high taxes (taxation without representation)
   - because the British army stayed in their houses (boarding, quartering)
   - because they didn't have self-government

5. Name one problem that led to the Civil War.
   - slavery

- economic reasons
- states' rights

6. Who did the United States fight in World War II?
   - Japan, Germany, and Italy

7. Name one U.S. territory.
   - Puerto Rico
   - U.S. Virgin Islands
   - American Samoa
   - Northern Mariana Islands
   - Guam

8. The House of Representatives has how many voting members?
   - four hundred thirty-five (435)

9. We elect a U.S. Representative for how many years?
   - two (2)

10. Name your U.S. Representative.
    - Answers will vary. [Residents of territories with nonvoting Delegates or Resident Commissioners may provide the name of that Delegate or Commissioner. Also acceptable is any statement that the territory has no (voting) Representatives in Congress.]

1. What is one right or freedom from the First Amendment?
   - speech
   - religion
   - assembly
   - press
   - petition the government

2. Who does a U.S. Senator represent?
   - all people of the state

3. What do we show loyalty to when we say the Pledge of Allegiance?
   - the United States
   - the flag

4. Who wrote the Declaration of Independence?
   - (Thomas) Jefferson

5. What was one important thing that Abraham Lincoln did?
   - freed the slaves (Emancipation Proclamation)
   - saved (or preserved) the Union
   - led the United States during the Civil War

6. Before he was President, Eisenhower was a general. What war was he in?

- World War II

7. Name one state that borders Canada.
   - Maine
   - New Hampshire
   - Vermont
   - New York
   - Pennsylvania
   - Ohio
   - Michigan
   - Minnesota
   - North Dakota
   - Montana
   - Idaho
   - Washington
   - Alaska

8. Why do some states have more Representatives than other states?
   - (because of) the state's population
   - (because) they have more people
   - (because) some states have more people

9. We elect a President for how many years?
   - four (4)

10. In what month do we vote for President?
    - November

U.S. Citizenship — Sample Test Six

1. How many amendments does the Constitution have?
   - twenty-seven(27)

2. What is the name of the President of the United States now?
   - Visit uscis.gov/citizenship/testupdates for the name of the President of the United States.

3. What is one promise you make when you become a United States citizen?
   - give up loyalty to other countries
   - defend the Constitution and laws of the United States
   - obey the laws of the United States
   - serve in the U.S. military (if needed)
   - serve (do important work for) the nation (if needed)
   - be loyal to the United States

4. When was the Declaration of Independence adopted?
   - July 4, 1776

5. What did the Emancipation Proclamation do?
   - freed the slaves
   - freed slaves in the Confederacy
   - freed slaves in the Confederate states

- freed slaves in most southern states

6. During the Cold War, what was the main concern of the United States?
   - Communism

7. Name one state that borders Mexico.
   - California
   - Arizona
   - New Mexico
   - Texas

8. What is the name of the Vice President of the United States now?
   - Visit uscis.gov/citizenship/testupdates for the name of the Vice President of the United States.

9. If the President can no longer serve, who becomes President?
   - the Vice President

10. If both the President and the Vice President can no longer serve, who becomes President?
    - the Speaker of the House

U.S. Citizenship — Sample Test Seven

1. What did the Declaration of Independence do?
   - announced our independence (from

725

Great Britain)
- declared our independence (from Great Britain)
- said that the United States is free (from Great Britain)

2. Who is the Commander in Chief of the military?
   - the President

3. How old do citizens have to be to vote for President?
   - eighteen (18) and older

4. There were 13 original states. Name three.
   - New Hampshire
   - Massachusetts
   - Rhode Island
   - Connecticut
   - New York
   - New Jersey
   - Pennsylvania
   - Delaware
   - Maryland
   - Virginia
   - North Carolina
   - South Carolina
   - Georgia

5. What did Susan B. Anthony do?
   - fought for women's rights

- fought for civil rights

6. What movement tried to end racial discrimination?
   - civil rights (movement)

7. What is the capital of the United States?
   - Washington, D.C.

8. Who signs bills to become laws?
   - the President

9. Who vetoes bills?
   - the President

10. What does the President's Cabinet do?
    - advises the President

U.S. Citizenship — Sample Test Eight

1. What are two rights in the Declaration of Independence?
   - life
   - liberty
   - pursuit of happiness

2. What are two Cabinet-level positions?
   - Secretary of Agriculture
   - Secretary of Commerce

- Secretary of Defense
- Secretary of Education
- Secretary of Energy
- Secretary of Health and Human Services
- Secretary of Homeland Security
- Secretary of Housing and Urban Development
- Secretary of the Interior
- Secretary of Labor
- Secretary of State
- Secretary of Transportation
- Secretary of the Treasury
- Secretary of Veterans Affairs
- Attorney General
- Vice President

3. What are two ways that Americans can participate in their democracy?
- vote
- join a political party
- help with a campaign
- join a civic group
- join a community group
- give an elected official your opinion on an issue
- call Senators and Representatives
- publicly support or oppose an issue or policy
- run for office
- write to a newspaper

4. What happened at the Constitutional Convention?
   - The Constitution was written.
   - The Founding Fathers wrote the Constitution.

5. What did Martin Luther King Jr. do?
   - fought for civil rights
   - worked for equality for all Americans

6. Where is the Statue of Liberty?
   - New York (Harbor)
   - Liberty Island [Also acceptable are New Jersey, near New York City, and on the Hudson (River).]

7. What does the judicial branch do?
   - reviews laws
   - explains laws
   - resolves disputes (disagreements)
   - decides if a law goes against the Constitution

8. What is the highest court in the United States?
   - the Supreme Court

9. How many justices are on the Supreme Court?
   - Visit uscis.gov/citizenship/testupdates for the number of justices on the Supreme Court.

10. Who is the Chief Justice of the United States now?
    - Visit uscis.gov/citizenship/testupdates for the name of the Chief Justice of the United States.

U.S. Citizenship — Sample Test Nine

1. What is freedom of religion?
    - You can practice any religion, or not practice a religion.

2. Under our Constitution, some powers belong to the federal government. What is one power of the federal government?
    - to print money
    - to declare war
    - to create an army
    - to make treaties

3. When is the last day you can send in federal income tax forms?
    - April 15

4. When was the Constitution written?
    - 1787

5. What major event happened on September 11, 2001, in the United States?
    - Terrorists attacked the United States.

6. What is the economic system in the United States?
   - capitalist economy
   - market economy

7. Under our Constitution, some powers belong to the states. What is one power of the states?
   - provide schooling and education
   - provide protection (police)
   - provide safety (fire departments)
   - give a driver's license
   - approve zoning and land use

8. Who is the Governor of your state now?
   - Answers will vary. [District of Columbia residents should answer that D.C. does not have a Governor.]

9. What is the capital of your state?
   - Answers will vary. [District of Columbia residents should answer that D.C. is not a state and does not have a capital. Residents of U.S. territories should name the capital of the territory.]

10. The Federalist Papers supported the passage of the U.S. Constitution. Name one of the writers.
    - (James) Madison

- (Alexander) Hamilton
- (John) Jay
- Publius

U.S. Citizenship — Sample Test Ten

1. What is the "rule of law"?
   - Everyone must follow the law.
   - Leaders must obey the law.
   - Government must obey the law.
   - No one is above the law.

2. What are the two major political parties in the United States?
   - Democratic and Republican

3. When must all men register for the Selective Service?
   - at age eighteen (18)
   - between eighteen (18) and twenty-six (26)

4. What is one thing Benjamin Franklin is famous for?
   - U.S. diplomat
   - oldest member of the Constitutional Convention
   - first Postmaster General of the United States
   - writer of "Poor Richard's Almanac"
   - started the first free libraries

5. Name one American Indian tribe in the United States. [USCIS Officers will be supplied with a list of federally recognized American Indian tribes.]
- Cherokee
- Navajo
- Sioux
- Chippewa
- Choctaw
- Pueblo
- Apache
- Iroquois
- Creek
- Blackfeet
- Seminole
- Cheyenne
- Arawak
- Shawnee
- Mohegan
- Huron
- Oneida
- Lakota
- Crow
- Teton
- Hopi
- Inuit

6. The idea of self-government is in the first three words of the Constitution. What are these words?
- We the People

7. What is the political party of the President now?
   - Visit uscis.gov/citizenship/testupdates for the political party of the President.

8. What is the name of the Speaker of the House of Representatives now?
   - Visit uscis.gov/citizenship/testupdates for the name of the Speaker of the House of Representatives.

9. Who is the "Father of Our Country"?
   - (George) Washington

10. Who was the first President?
    - (George) Washington

■ ■ ■ ■

APPENDIX II:
FULL HARRIS POLL
SURVEY RESULTS

■ ■ ■ ■

More than two-thirds of Americans think America is the best country in the world; this majority holds true across almost all demographics.

69%

of Americans think America is the best country in the world

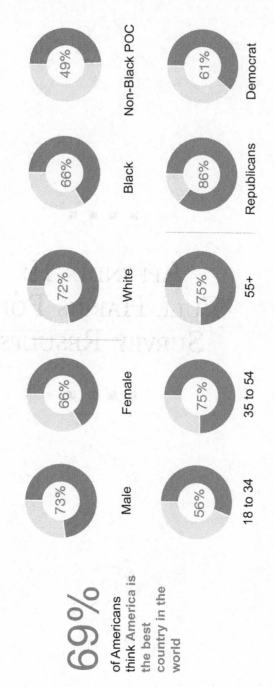

73%	66%	72%
Male	Female	White

66%	49%
Black	Non-Black POC

56%	75%	75%
18 to 34	35 to 54	55+

86%	61%
Republicans	Democrat

Q22 Do you think America is the best country in the world?
Source: Survey conducted with n=2000 gen pop Americans between October 15 and October 20.

Harris Insights & Analytics LLC, A Stagwell Company © 2020

Despite the current situation of 2020, nearly three in five Americans say they are living/expect to achieve the American Dream, and that America's best days are ahead.

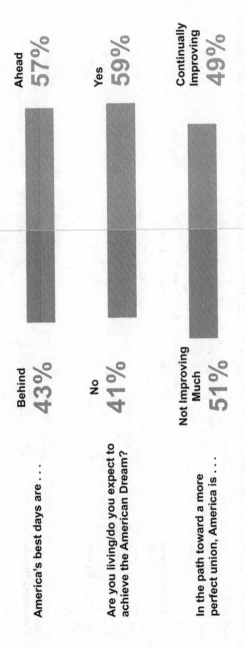

America's best days are . . .

Behind **43%**   Ahead **57%**

Are you living/do you expect to achieve the American Dream?

No **41%**   Yes **59%**

In the path toward a more perfect union, America is . . .

Not Improving Much **51%**   Continually Improving **49%**

Q12: On the whole, do you think America's best days are behind it or ahead of it?
Q15: Would you say you are living the American Dream or expect to achieve the American Dream?
Q20: Thinking about the long term, has America generally been on the path to a more perfect union-continually improving in terms of greater equality and freedom - or has it not been improving much over time?

A majority of Americans across demos expect to achieve the American dream (exceptions: BIPOC Females, especially Black Females; those with less than a HS education, and those with <$35k income).

Are you Living or Do you Expect to Achieve the American Dream?

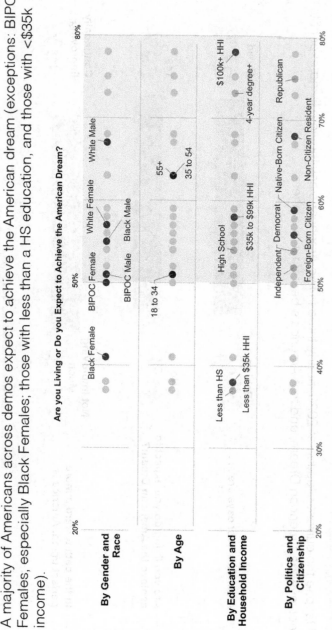

By Gender and Race

Black Female · BIPOC Female · White Female · White Male · BIPOC Male · Black Male

By Age

18 to 34 · 35 to 54 · 55+

By Education and Household Income

Less than HS · Less than $35k HHI · High School · $35k to $99k HHI · $100k+ HHI · 4-year degree+

By Politics and Citizenship

Independent · Democrat · Native-Born Citizen · Foreign-Born Citizen · Non-Citizen Resident · Republican

20%   30%   40%   50%   60%   70%   80%

Q15: Would you say you are living the American Dream or expect to achieve the American Dream?

Harris Insights & Analytics LLC, A Stagwell Company © 2020

Americans highly value living in America, and the vast majority would never consider leaving.

How much do you value living in America?
(On a 10-point scale)

4% 7% 15% 74%

■ 1 to 3   ■ 4 to 5   ■ 6 to 7   ■ 8 to 10

Rating of 8, 9, or 10 for:

- Native-born citizens: 76%
- Citizens born Elsewhere: 59%
- Non-citizen Residents: 60%

Would you ever give up your citizenship and leave the country?

Native-Born Citizens

85%   15%

Citizens born Elsewhere

71%   29%

Would you ever leave the country to permanently live somewhere else?

Non-citizen Residents

58%   42%

Q18: On the whole, how much do you value living in America?

Harris Insights & Analytics LLC, A Stagwell Company © 2020

Q2   Would you ever give up your citizenship and leave the country?
To non-citizens: Would you ever leave the United States to permanently live somewhere else?

Many factors—including freedoms, stability, and opportunity—go into making a country great.

What is a Major Contributor to Making A Country Great?

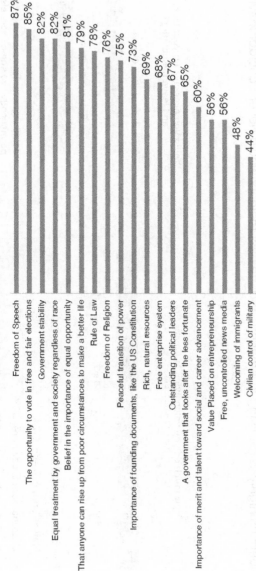

Freedom of Speech	87%
The opportunity to vote in free and fair elections	85%
Government stability	82%
Equal treatment by government and society regardless of race	82%
Belief in the importance of equal opportunity	81%
That anyone can rise up from poor circumstances to make a better life	79%
Rule of Law	78%
Freedom of Religion	76%
Peaceful transition of power	75%
Importance of founding documents, like the US Constitution	73%
Rich, natural resources	69%
Free enterprise system	68%
Outstanding political leaders	67%
A government that looks after the less fortunate	65%
Importance of merit and talent toward social and career advancement	60%
Value Placed on entrepreneurship	56%
Free, uncontrolled news media	56%
Welcoming of immigrants	48%
Civilian control of military	44%

Q4 In your opinion, which of the following contribute to making a country great? For each, please say whether it is a major contributor, a minor contributor, or not factor.

Harris Insights & Analytics LLC, A Stagwell Company © 2020

America's particular greatness is defined by the ideal of the melting pot—including a multi-ethnic society and tolerance of differences—and a willingness to fight for what is right.

What most captures what makes America great?

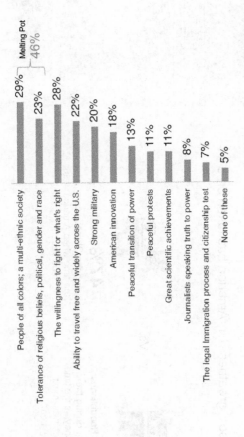

People of all colors; a multi-ethnic society	29%
	Melting Pot **46%**
Tolerance of religious beliefs, political, gender and race	23%
The willingness to fight for what's right	28%
Ability to travel free and widely across the U.S.	22%
Strong military	20%
American innovation	18%
Peaceful transition of power	13%
Peaceful protests	11%
Great scientific achievements	11%
Journalists speaking truth to power	8%
The legal Immigration process and citizenship test	7%
None of these	5%

Q10: What types of activities listed below most capture the essence of what makes America great? Please select two.

WHAT MAKES AMERICA GREAT

Like so much else, "greatness" in America has taken on a political flavor.

47% of Republicans name a year during the Trump presidency as the time when America was 'most recently great'.

Vs.

47% of Democrats cite the Obama years as the time when America was 'most recently great'.

40% of BIPOC* Americans (vs. 30% of white Americans) cite the Obama years as the most recently great ones

30% of White Americans (vs. 16% of BIPOC) cite one of the last four years

*BIPOC includes Black, Indigenous, and People of Color

Q8   When would you say America was most recently great?

Additionally, what counts as greatness is often filtered through the lens of time.

What is now uncomfortable—like social unrest—may in retrospect be seen as something hard-won (e.g., protesting that results in more freedoms).

What about America has happened in your lifetime that has made you most _____ to be an American?

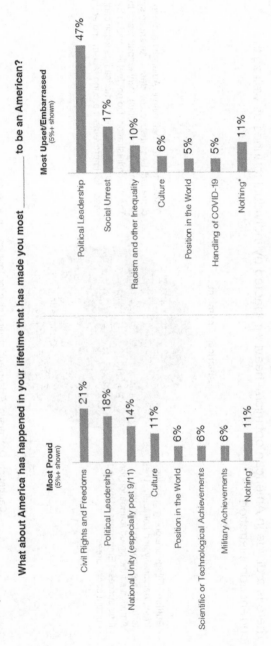

Most Proud
(5%+ shown)

Civil Rights and Freedoms	21%
Political Leadership	18%
National Unity (especially post 9/11)	14%
Culture	11%
Position in the World	6%
Scientific or Technological Achievements	6%
Military Achievements	6%
Nothing*	11%

Most Upset/Embarrassed
(5%+ shown)

Political Leadership	47%
Social Unrest	17%
Racism and other Inequality	10%
Culture	6%
Position in the World	5%
Handling of COVID-19	5%
Nothing*	11%

*Nothing includes people that said 'nothing' and 'don't know'.

Q9. What about America has happened in your lifetime that has made you most PROUD to be an American? *Coded open-end.*
Q11. What about America has happened in your lifetime that has made you most UPSET or EMBARRASSED to be an American? *Coded open-end.*

There is a divide in American optimism, heavily impacted by individual fortunes as well as the current administration.

American Optimism

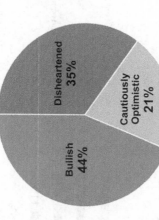

Bullish: Things are going great for them, personally and politically. Their fortunes are good and they view America as the proud foundation for their success. Embarrassed by the current social unrest.

Disheartened: Their faith in America has been damaged. Less inspired by classic American symbols (like founding documents); very embarrassed by the Trump administration. Do not feel listened to by current politicians, think America has significant needs for improvement around racism and equality.

Cautiously Optimistic. A deep and abiding love for America, but unlike the Bullish group, they feel less represented by current power structures: e.g., they're less positive about the last 4 years, more likely to think politicians are getting less empathetic. They are less likely to think America is on the right track *right now*.

Harris Insights & Analytics LLC. A Stagwell Company © 2020

Categories calculated via an optimism index which is a combination of q12, q15 q18 q20 and q22.

A majority of Americans agree on two qualities that are distinctive of America: Freedom of Speech, and Free and Fair Elections.

Which are distinctive qualities of America?

Freedom of speech	64%
The opportunity to vote in free and fair elections	51%
Freedom of religion/separation of church and state	50%
Importance of founding documents, like the US Constitution	46%
That anyone can rise up from poor circumstances to make a better life	44%
Rich, natural resources	42%
Rule of law	41%
Belief in the importance of equal opportunity	41%
Free enterprise system	39%
Government stability	37%
Equal treatment by government and society regardless of race	35%
Peaceful transition of power	35%
Free, uncontrolled news media	33%
Value placed on entrepreneurship	31%
A government that looks after the less fortunate	30%
Welcoming of immigrants	29%
Importance of merit and talent toward social and career advancement	26%
Civilian control of military	23%
Outstanding political leaders	22%
None of these	7%

50% of Americans

Q5. And which of these would you consider distinctive qualities of America, if any?
Please select all that apply.

More than half of Americans would risk their life for Freedom of Speech and/or the Right to Equal Justice.

Which American freedoms would you risk your life to protect?

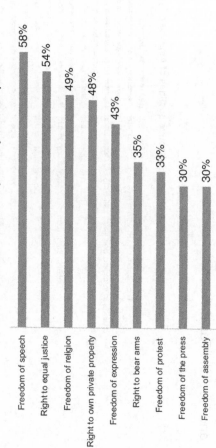

Freedom	Percentage
Freedom of speech	58%
Right to equal justice	54%
Freedom of religion	49%
Right to own private property	48%
Freedom of expression	43%
Right to bear arms	35%
Freedom of protest	33%
Freedom of the press	30%
Freedom of assembly	30%

Right to Equal Justice over-indexes for:
- BIPOC (60% vs. 52% of white Americans)

Right to Own Property over-indexes for:
- White Americans (50% vs. 42% of BIPOC)
- Americans over 55 (55% vs. 38% of 18 to 34)
- Republicans (54% vs. 42% of Dems)

Right to Bear Arms over-indexes for:
- White Americans (38% vs. 28% of BIPOC)
- Republicans (50% vs. 21% of Dems)

Q6 Which of the following American freedoms would you risk your life to protect?

Traditional symbols of America still resonate: Founding documents, the American flag, the Statue of Liberty.

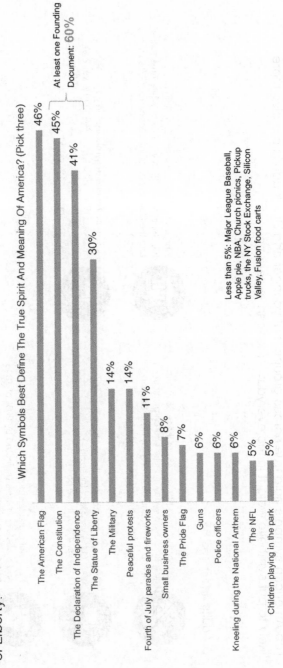

Which Symbols Best Define The True Spirit And Meaning Of America? (Pick three)

The American Flag	46%
The Constitution	45%
The Declaration of Independence	41%
The Statue of Liberty	30%
The Military	14%
Peaceful protests	14%
Fourth of July parades and fireworks	11%
Small business owners	8%
The Pride Flag	7%
Guns	6%
Police officers	6%
Kneeling during the National Anthem	6%
The NFL	5%
Children playing in the park	5%

At least one Founding Document: 60%

Less than 5%: Major League Baseball, Apple pie, NBA, Church picnics, Pickup trucks, the NY Stock Exchange, Silicon Valley, Fusion food carts

Q7: Which of the following symbols best define the true spirit and meaning of America? Please select up to three symbols.

Top American symbols hold true across groups, but younger and Black adults are also more likely to put symbolic weight in the everyday American experience.

Adults under age 35 . . .

 Also cite sports (17% vs. 4% of those 55+) and elements of everyday life. like church picnics, pickup trucks, and children playing in the park (16% vs. 8% of those 55+).

 They also over-index on the symbolic power of guns (11% vs. 3% of those 55+) and the Pride flag (11% vs. 4% of those 55+).

 Peaceful protests index highest for the youngest and oldest Americans (selected by 20% of 18 to 24 YO and 18% of those 65+ vs. ~12% of everyone else).

Black Americans . . .

 Find less symbolism in the Founding documents: the Constitution (25% vs. 50% of White Americans) and the Declaration of Independence (27% vs. 45%).

 Find more American symbolism in peaceful protests (19% vs. 13%), the NBA (11% vs. 2%), kneeling during the national anthem (10% vs. 5%), and guns (11% vs. 5%).

The majority of both white and Black Americans value living in America, despite shared and separately felt embarrassments.

- Both white and Black Americans are proud of Civil Rights and Freedoms; both are embarrassed by current politics and political leadership.
- Some distinctions emerge:
  - Black Americans are most proud of **Political Leadership** (primarily the election and administration of Barack Obama).
  - While White Americans over-index on the **feeling of National Unity** (primarily felt post 9/11).
  - White Americans are more embarrassed by the current **Social Unrest.**
  - Black Americans are more embarrassed about the root cause—racism and other inequality.

Both White and Black Americans value living in America.

	White Americans	Black Americans	All BIPOC
Value Living in America	8.6 (out of 10)	7.7	7.8

Most Proud (5%+ shown)	White Americans	Black Americans
Civil Rights and Freedoms	21%	19%
Political Leadership	16%	27%
National Unity	17%	5%
Culture	11%	12%
Position in the World	6%	2%
Scientific or Technological Achievements	7%	1%
Military Achievements	6%	4%
Nothing	7%	12%

Most Upset/Embarrassed (5%+ shown)	White Americans	Black Americans
Political Leadership	48%	42%
Social Unrest	18%	12%
Racism and other inequality	8%	18%
Culture	6%	4%
Position in the World	5%	4%
Handling of COVID-19	5%	6%
Nothing	11%	9%

Three in five Americans believe that the country is still impacted by the fact that it was founded while sanctioning slavery.

Is America Still Impacted From Being Founded While Sanctioning Slavery?

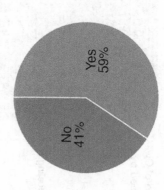

No
41%

Yes
59%

Q16: Do you think America is still impacted by the fact that the country was founded while sanctioning slavery?

Americans believe that our leaders have gotten less empathetic over the last 10 years, and that America is moving further away from the ideals of the Founding Fathers.

Do you think America is getting closer or further away from the ideals of the Founding Fathers?

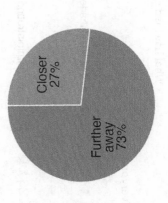

Q13: Do you think America is getting closer to living up to the ideals of the Founding Fathers or moving further away from those ideals?

Compared to ten years ago, how empathetic are America's leaders?

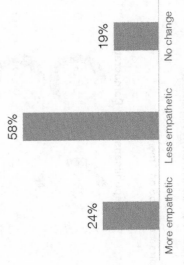

Q14: Do you think America's leaders (whether Republican, Democrat or Independent) are more or less empathetic to the needs of its citizens than ten years ago?

The current political climate—especially the Trump presidency—is dividing America.

What has made you most upset or embarrassed to be an American?

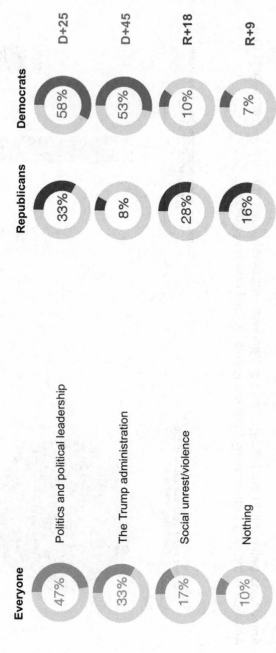

Everyone		Republicans	Democrats	
Politics and political leadership	47%	33%	58%	D+25
The Trump administration	33%	8%	53%	D+45
Social unrest/violence	17%	28%	10%	R+18
Nothing	10%	16%	7%	R+9

Harris Insights & Analytics LLC, A Stagwell Company © 2020

Q11   What about America has happened in your lifetime that has made you most UPSET or EMBARRASSED to be an American?

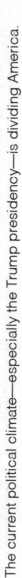

And optimism about the future varies highly by political affiliation.

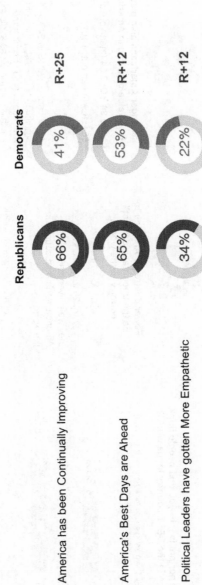

Republicans   **Democrats**

America has been Continually Improving — 66% — 41% — R+25

America's Best Days are Ahead — 65% — 53% — R+12

Political Leaders have gotten More Empathetic — 34% — 22% — R+12

Q12: On the whole, do you think America's best days are behind it or ahead of it?
Q14: Do you think America's leaders (whether Republican, Democrat or Independent) are more or less empathetic to the needs of its citizens than ten years ago?
Q20: Thinking about the long term, has America generally been on the path to a more perfect union-continually improving in terms of greater equality and freedom - or has it not been improving much over time?

Younger American adults are less concerned that everyone think America is the best.

How important is it to you that people think America is the BEST country in the world?

% saying "I want everyone to think America is the BEST country in the world."

18 to 34	38%
35 to 54	58%
55+	60%

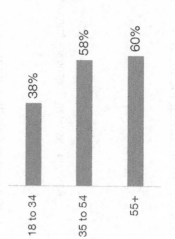

Fewer desire for America to be the uncontested "best" country in the world.

32% of 18 to 24 YO and 41% of 25 to 34 YOs say they want everyone to think America is the best country in the world

19% of adults ages 18 to 24 can't think of ANYTHING that has happened in their lifetime that has made them proud to be American.

Younger Americans also place less value on living in America.

- **18 to 34 YO:** 7.34 (mean out of 10)
- **55+:** 8.9 (mean out of 10)

Americans ages 18 to 34 are significantly less likely than older Americans (45+) to cite almost anything on the list as a 'distinctive' quality of America.

Q21: Regardless of how you feel about America, how important is it to you that people think America is the BEST country in the world?

Those 18 to 34 are less likely to think America is 'distinctive'.

Distinctive Characteristics of America	18-34	35-54	55+
Freedom of Speech	53%	63%	74%
Freedom of religion/separation of church and state	40%	47%	61%
Rule of law (a system of just laws, accountability, open government, and accessible justice)	33%	38%	51%
Civilian control of military	16%	21%	31%
Free enterprise system	25%	36%	51%
Value placed on entrepreneurship	25%	28%	37%
Government stability	27%	38%	45%
That anyone can rise up from poor circumstances to make a better life	29%	42%	58%
Welcoming of immigrants	22%	29%	34%
Importance of merit and talent toward social and career advancement	20%	24%	32%
Equal treatment by government and society regardless of race	23%	37%	43%
Belief in the importance of equal opportunity	27%	39%	53%
The opportunity to vote in free and fair elections	36%	46%	67%
Importance of founding documents, like the US Constitution	31%	43%	61%
Outstanding political leaders	17%	21%	27%
Free, uncontrolled news media	25%	29%	44%
A government that looks after the less fortunate	21%	27%	40%
Rich, natural resources (such as farmland, fresh water, coastlines, shale oil, coal, natural gas)	31%	39%	54%
Peaceful transition of power	27%	34%	43%

Q5. And which of these would you consider distinctive qualities of America, if any? Please select all that apply.

To make America better: end systemic racism, provide accessible and affordable healthcare for everyone, and reducing the politicization and partisanship in society today.

What What Would You Change About America?

End systemic racism	18%
Accessible, affordable healthcare for everyone	14%
Reduce the politicization and partisanship in society today	13%
More income equality	10%
End the electoral college for a national vote instead	9%
End political correctness	8%
Make higher education free for everyone	7%
End all preferences based on race	7%
Reaffirm the values of freedom of religion and speech	4%
Curb the power of tech companies	2%
Something else	4%
I wouldn't change a thing	4%

Q19: If you could change one thing about America, what would it be? Please select one

Should Americans be Required to Complete Some Kind of Public Service?

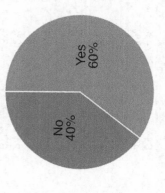

Yes 60%

No 40%

Q17: Do you think all Americans should be required to complete some kind of public service?

American Optimism Index

Metrics evaluated:	All In	Cautiously Optimistic	Disheartened
Definition of Group	'High' on 4 or 5 out of 5 possible metrics	'High' on 3 out of 5 possible metrics	'High' on 0, 1, or 2 of 5 possible metrics
% of Americans in Group	44%	21%	35%
Believe America's Best Days are Ahead	87%	49%	22%
Living/Will Achieve the American Dream	91%	60%	18%
Value living in America (10-point scale)	9.47	8.67	6.83
Believe America is continually improving	84%	32%	14%
Think America is the best country in the world	97%	78%	29%

Optimism index is a combination of q12, q15, q18, q20 and q22
Q12: On the whole, do you think America's best days are behind it or ahead of it? [AHEAD]
Q15: Would you say you are living the American Dream or expect to achieve the American Dream? [YES]
Q18: On the whole, how much do you value living in America? [8, 9, OR 10]
Q20: Thinking about the long term, has America generally been on the path to a more perfect union-continually improving in terms of greater equality and freedom - or has it not been improving much over time? [CONTINUALLY IMPROVING]
Q22: Do you think America is the best country in the world? [YES]

Study conducted by Harris Insights and Analytics. The authors on the study are Mark Penn, John Gerzema, and Amber Broughton.

ABOUT THE AUTHOR

David M. Rubenstein is a cofounder and cochairman of The Carlyle Group, one of the world's largest and most successful private investment firms.

Mr. Rubenstein is chairman of the boards of trustees of the John F. Kennedy Center for the Performing Arts and the Council on Foreign Relations; a fellow of the Harvard Corporation; a trustee of the National Gallery of Art, the University of Chicago, Memorial Sloan Kettering Cancer Center, Johns Hopkins Medicine, the Institute for Advanced Study, the National Constitution Center, the Brookings Institution, and the World Economic Forum; a director of the Lincoln Center for the Performing Arts and the American Academy of Arts and Sciences; and chairman of the Economic Club of Washington, D.C. He has served as chairman of the board of trustees of Duke University and the Smithsonian Institution, and cochairman of the board of the Brookings Institution. Mr.

Rubenstein is an original signer of the Giving Pledge and a recipient of the Carnegie Medal of Philanthropy.

Mr. Rubenstein is the host of *The David Rubenstein Show: Peer to Peer Conversations* on Bloomberg TV and PBS, and the author of *The American Story: Conversations with Master Historians* (Simon & Schuster, 2019) and the *New York Times* bestseller *How to Lead: Wisdom from the World's Greatest CEOs, Founders, and Game Changers* (Simon & Schuster, 2020).

A native of Baltimore, Mr. Rubenstein is a 1970 magna cum laude graduate of Duke University, where he was elected Phi Beta Kappa. Following Duke, he graduated from the University of Chicago Law School in 1973. Prior to cofounding Carlyle in 1987, Mr. Rubenstein practiced law in New York and in Washington, and during the Carter administration he was deputy assistant to the president for domestic policy.

The employees of Thorndike Press hope you have enjoyed this Large Print book. All our Thorndike, Wheeler, and Kennebec Large Print titles are designed for easy reading, and all our books are made to last. Other Thorndike Press Large Print books are available at your library, through selected bookstores, or directly from us.

For information about titles, please call:
(800) 223-1244

or visit our website at:
gale.com/thorndike

To share your comments, please write:
Publisher
Thorndike Press
10 Water St., Suite 310
Waterville, ME 04901